Sovereign Acts

EDITED BY
FRANCES NEGRÓN-MUNTANER

Sovereign Acts

Contesting Colonialism Across Indigenous Nations and Latinx America

THE UNIVERSITY OF
ARIZONA PRESS
TUCSON

The University of Arizona Press
www.uapress.arizona.edu

© 2017 by The Arizona Board of Regents
All rights reserved. Published 2017

Printed in the United States of America

22 21 20 19 18 17   6 5 4 3 2 1

ISBN-13: 978-0-8165-3212-4 (paper)

Cover design by Lisa Force
Cover photo: *Border Door*, 1988. Site Specific Installation/Intervention Performance. Golden wooden door, nails, keys, door knob, blue wooden frame and hinges. Free-standing workable door installed on the Mexico/USA border ¼ mile east of the Rodriguez International Airport. The performance extended to the neighborhood where the artist grew up in Tijuana, where he gave out over 250 keys, inviting the residents of La Colonia Roma and Altamira to use his Border Door. Artist: Richard A. Lou. Photo by James Elliott, 1988.

Publication of this book is made possible in part by the proceeds of a permanent endowment created with the assistance of a Challenge Grant from the National Endowment for the Humanities, a federal agency.

Library of Congress Cataloging-in-Publication Data
Names: Negrón-Muntaner, Frances, editor.
Title: Sovereign acts : contesting colonialism across indigenous nations and Latinx America /
  edited by Frances Negrón-Muntaner.
Description: Tucson : The University of Arizona Press, 2017. | Includes bibliographical
  references and index.
Identifiers: LCCN 2017007889 | ISBN 9780816532124 (pbk. : alk. paper)
Subjects: LCSH: Indians of North America—Government relations. | Indians of North America—
  Politics and government. | Indians of North America—Civil rights. | Hawaiians—Government
  relations. | Hawaiians—Politics and government. | Hawaiians—Civil rights. | Sovereignty.
Classification: LCC GN380 .S7 2017 | DDC 323.1197—dc23 LC record available
  at https://lccn.loc.gov/2017007889

∞ This paper meets the requirements of ANSI/NISO Z39.48-1992 (Permanence of Paper).

Contents

Acknowledgments   vii

Introduction   3
FRANCES NEGRÓN-MUNTANER

I. NAVIGATING SOVEREIGNTY

1. Contested Sovereignties: Puerto Rico and American Samoa   39
   FA'ANOFO LISACLAIRE UPERESA AND ADRIANA MARÍA GARRIGA-LÓPEZ

2. Indigenous Peoples and the Politics of Recognition   82
   GLEN COULTHARD

3. The Decolonial Deadlock in Guam   107
   MICHAEL LUJAN BEVACQUA

4. Recognizing Native Hawaiians: Reality Bites   125
   DAVIANNA PŌMAIKA'I MCGREGOR

II. SOVEREIGN BODIES

5. Chairmen, Presidents, and Princesses: The Navajo Nation, Gender, and the Politics of Tradition   153
   JENNIFER NEZ DENETDALE

6. Same-Sex Marriage in the Cherokee Nation: Toward Decolonial Queer Indigeneities 175
   JESSICA A. F. HARKINS

7. Bloodline Is All I Need?: Sovereignty and Hawaiian Hip-Hop 199
   STEPHANIE NOHELANI TEVES

8. Of Shadows and Doubts: White Supremacy, Decolonization, and Black-Indian Relations 230
   BRIAN KLOPOTEK

9. The Look of Sovereignty: Style and Politics in the Young Lords 254
   FRANCES NEGRÓN-MUNTANER

III. LIFE WITHOUT SOVEREIGNTY

10. Sovereignty Still? 285
    MADELINE ROMÁN

11. Indigenizing Agamben: Rethinking Sovereignty in Light of the "Peculiar" Status of Native Peoples 296
    MARK RIFKIN

12. King of the Line: The Sovereign Acts of Jean-Michel Basquiat 336
    FRANCES NEGRÓN-MUNTANER WITH YASMIN RAMIREZ

    Contributors *373*
    Index *379*

Acknowledgments

This book is based on a conference titled "Sovereignty Matters" that I organized at Columbia University in 2005. The conference's main goal was to explore the praxis of sovereignty for various groups that are often viewed as partially or totally "sovereignless," including Native Americans, First Nations, Pacific Islanders, and Puerto Ricans. Since the volume would not have come into being without the lively conference debates, I would like to begin by thanking all the participants, including Amílcar Antonio Barreto, Michael Lujan Bevacqua, Ahimsa Timoteo Bodhrán, Maivân Clech Lâm, Christine DeLisle, Vicente M. Diaz, Adriana María Garriga-López, Guillermo Irizarry, Arnaldo Cruz-Malavé, Dan Taulapapa McMullin, Angelia Means, Davianna Pōmaikaʻi McGregor, Jon Osorio, Elizabeth Povinelli, Bruce Robbins, Audra Simpson, Andrea Smith, Robert Underwood, Faʻanofo Lisaclaire Uperesa, Charles Venator-Santiago, and L. Lehuanani Lono Yim. Many thanks also to the Center for the Study of Ethnicity and Race's past and current staff—Teresa Aguayo, Josephine Caputo, Arleny Guerrero, and Johnny Roldán-Chacón—for their invaluable support in organizing the conference and assisting in the completion of this volume.

As the collection took shape, it came to comprise the work of scholars from different fields and countries who were not present at the event. Several colleagues played important roles in identifying and connecting me with new contributors. The first was historian Roxanne Dunbar-Ortiz. Simply put, without her, this book would not exist. When the conference ended, I had not yet decided whether I would embark on the editing of what is now my third volume when she had already contacted a possible publisher on my behalf. Scholar and activist Andrea Smith similarly led me to the research of key contributors, and I am deeply grateful for her generosity. I would also like to express my appreciation to scholars Mishuana Goeman and Gary Okihiro, who kindly shared their thoughts about the most daring recent work on sovereignty in indigenous, Hawaiian, and Pacific Islander studies.

In addition, the collection is fortunate to include writings that have become essential reading in crucial debates. Many thanks to Claire Smith (Palgrave Macmillan), Jeff Moen (University of Minnesota Press), Miriam Juarez (University of California, Los Angeles), and Xavier Totti (*CENTRO: Journal of the Center for Puerto Rican Studies*) for permission to include versions of the following texts: Mark Rifkin's "Indigenizing Agamben: Rethinking Sovereignty in Light of the 'Peculiar' Status of Native Peoples" from *Cultural Critique* (73 [Fall 2009]); Glen Coulthard's "Subjects of Empire: Indigenous Peoples and the 'Politics of Recognition' in Canada" gathered in *Contemporary Political Theory* (6 [November 2007]), presently titled "Indigenous Peoples and the Politics of Recognition"; Jennifer Nez Denetdale's "Chairmen, Presidents, and Princesses: The Navajo Nation, Gender, and the Politics of Tradition," originally printed in *Wicazo Sa Review* (21, no. 1 [Spring 2006]); Stephanie Nohelani Teves's "Bloodline Is All I Need?," published in *American Indian Culture and Research Journal* (35, no. 4 [2011]); and my essay "The Look of Sovereignty: Style and Politics in the Young Lords," which first appeared in *Centro Journal* (27, no. 1 [2015]). Portions of Brian Klopotek's "Of Shadows and Doubts: White Supremacy, Decolonization, and Black-Indian Relations" appeared in *IndiVisible: African-Native American Lives in the Americas*, edited by Gabrielle Tayac (Washington, DC: Smithsonian Institution, 2009), and "Dangerous Decolonizing: Indians and Blacks and the Legacy of Jim Crow" in *Decolonizing Native Histories: Collaboration, Knowledge, and Language in the Americas*, edited by

Florencia E. Mallon (Durham, NC: Duke University Press, 2012). Similarly, I thank Janet Hicks, Todd Leibowitz, and the Artists Rights Society for allowing us to reproduce three images by artist Jean-Michel Basquiat.

I am also very thankful to the University of Arizona Press peer reviewers for their detailed and insightful comments on the entire manuscript and to Audra Simpson, who was a constant source of support throughout the entire process in multiple ways, from participating in the conference to lifting my spirits and reading the introduction: *muy agradecida*. My immense gratitude likewise goes to Deborah Cullen-Morales, Celeste Fraser Delgado, Sandy Grande, Elizabeth West Hutchinson, Yolanda Martínez-San Miguel, Myra Mendible, Iris Morales, Matthew Sandler, Franklin Sirmans, and Neferti Xina M. Tadiar for their generous and sharp comments on my chapters. Moreover, I am grateful for the indispensable and critical support of editor Michael Koch, fact-checker Kim Leiken, and indexer Leonard S. Rosenbaum during the writing and preparation of the manuscript.

In closing, there are no words to express my gratitude to editorial, design, and production manager Amanda Krause for her generosity of spirit, intelligence, and professionalism. We would not have made it without her. I also thank Kristen Buckles, the best editor anyone could ever wish for. I am deeply appreciative for her smart editorial suggestions, saintly patience, and great faith in both the volume and me. It has been a long journey. *Mil gracias* to all.

Sovereign Acts

Introduction

FRANCES NEGRÓN-MUNTANER

From Brexit voters' call of "Take back control" to Donald J. Trump's chant "Build the wall" to guard against Mexican "bad hombres," the question of sovereignty is back—with a vengeance. After migrating to the margins of European and U.S. discourse in part because of twentieth-century decolonization movements and the presumably neat spheres of influence that characterized the Cold War, the concept and praxis of sovereignty are increasingly the object of heated discussions for scholars, political figures, and activists. Whether to say that nation-state sovereignty must be affirmed or that it is over, attention to the "sovereign" problems of regions such as Europe, the Middle East, Asia, and the United States has mushroomed over the last decades.

Among the most visible political debates are the limits of Israeli state sovereignty and Palestinian nation-building, the Two-Chinas policy, and the carrying out of torture at the U.S. Guantánamo Bay Naval Station in Cuba. A growing number are also concerned by what they perceive as the eroding effect of globalization on national sovereignties either via supranational regulating entities—such as the International Monetary Fund (IMF), the World Trade Organization (WTO), and the International Criminal Court (ICC)—or through immigrants equipped with digital technology and diverse cultural and religious practices. The idea that sovereignty "remains a systemic property" of the global order yet border crossers of many stripes have "chipped away at that exclusivity,"[1] in sociologist Saskia Sassen's words, is at the center of much contemporary politics and scholarship in Europe and North America.

Generally absent from these discussions, however, are the over ten million members of presumably "nonsovereign" polities that live "under" the U.S. and Canadian flags who continue to either affirm their own sovereignty within settler nation-states (what anthropologist Audra Simpson refers to as "nested sovereignty") or otherwise assert their desire for a noncolonial present in their own epistemological and political terms.[2] Also largely missing are the perspectives from Pacific Islander, indigenous, Caribbean, and Latinx studies whose neglect makes it difficult if not impossible to engage with and think about the contours of contemporary politics across the Americas and beyond. Ultimately, the near exclusive theorization of sovereignty from the vantage point of powerful nation-states and practiced in fields such as international and area studies often obscures that various forms of sovereign claims have been—and continue to be—sites of tension within presumably "settled" nation-states.[3]

A dramatic recent example is the nearly year-long protests begun in 2016 of the Standing Rock Sioux and Cheyenne River Sioux tribes to stop a Texas-based oil company from building the Dakota Access Pipeline, a means to transport oil from North Dakota to southern Illinois, crossing under part of Lake Oahe close to the Standing Rock Indian Reservation. While President Trump eventually signed an executive order to authorize the pipeline's construction, activists continue to organize against the project.[4] Under the slogan of "indigenous sovereignty protects the land and water," they insist that the pipeline should not be permitted because it will destroy culturally valuable Native sites, pollute soil, and endanger drinking water, as it has done in other indigenous communities, including in Canada. A second striking instance is taking place in Puerto Rico, an unincorporated territory of the United States burdened with more than $120 billion in public debt and pension obligations. Declaring "no more promises," mass protests erupted in opposition to the Puerto Rico Oversight, Management, and Economic Stability Act (PROMESA) of 2016, a law approved by the U.S. Congress that established the Financial Oversight and Management Board ("la Junta de Control Fiscal"). Returning Puerto Rico to the early days of U.S. colonial governance, when Washington-appointed officials directly ruled the territory, *la junta* is composed of seven members with broad powers over locally elected representatives and government agencies who support vast cuts to education and other fundamental human services to resolve the debt crisis.[5]

Yet as this volume makes clear, these tensions are not new. Read from the colonial present, Guantanamo's Camp X-Ray, Puerto Rico's unincorporated territorial status, and the continuous intrusion on indigenous land are but part of a longer history of U.S. and Canadian nation-building and capitalist expansion that has relied on the denial, curtailing, and reconstitution of Native American, First Nation, Pacific Islander, and Latinx political spaces. Given this juncture, *Sovereign Acts* offers a critique to the politics of sovereignty by examining and theorizing from and in relation to specific indigenous and modern colonial contexts in the United States and Canada.[6] In doing so, the collection builds on a growing scholarship about sovereignty produced in multiple fields, including history, international relations, legal theory, and philosophy.[7] The book is also in close dialogue with recent and classic works in indigenous and Caribbean studies by Joanne Barker (*Critically Sovereign: Indigenous Gender, Sexuality, and Feminist Studies*), Frantz Fanon (*The Wretched of the Earth* and *Black Skin, White Masks*), Mark Rifkin (*The Erotics of Sovereignty: Queer Native Writing in the Era of Self-Determination*), and Audra Simpson (*Mohawk Interruptus: Political Life Across the Borders of Settler States*), among many others.

At one level, the volume considers a series of questions regarding the reproduction of U.S. and Canadian nation-state sovereignty. For example, what are the political, symbolic, and economic forms of power that rationalize U.S. and Canadian state sovereignty over indigenous nations and/or the unincorporated territories? What are the alternatives not only to colonial and settler-state sovereignty but also to the Western idea of sovereignty? How and to what effects have the United States and Canada produced "divided" sovereignty arrangements to constrain indigenous and Caribbean polities? How do indigenous and modern colonial groups contest and transform the state's imposed sovereign policies and discourses into new political terrains?

At another level, the volume reflects on seemingly more basic if no less complex questions with substantial repercussions for a broad range of intellectual and political practices. What (or when) is sovereignty? Is it a matter of legal right, symbolic iteration, or self-fashioning; a state attribute, a capacity to act, or a zone of "nothingness"? Is it possible to engage in sovereign acts without "having" (or being indifferent to, or even rejecting) state sovereignty? Can sovereignty be thought of as less of a thing that one "has" and more as a tension between control and resistance, an argument over power? If so, under what conditions and through which practices do people and peoples affirm themselves as sovereign above other possibilities?

Finding tremendous benefits in reading across fields, the book brings together influential texts and new work to promote crucial conversations through contrast and comparison. This counterpoint method is particularly productive in bringing attention to how parallel discourses of sovereign power are differently engaged by indigenous and modern colonial groups; it equally foregrounds the productivity of transdisciplinary theorization. For instance, both Glen Coulthard and Michael Lujan Bevacqua's chapters examine questions of recognition and sovereignty in indigenous Canada and Guam, respectively, through engaging with Martinican theorist Frantz Fanon's critique of colonial sovereignty.[8] Similarly, Adriana María Garriga-López and Fa'anofo Lisaclaire Uperesa's work compares American Samoan and Puerto Rican conceptual taxonomies to consider what they describe as the "zones of attenuated sovereignty produced by the doctrine of territorial unincorporation and its myriad political, economic, and social effects" (chap. 1).

Sovereign Acts likewise includes scholars whose work theorizes sovereignty at odds with one another. This was a key decision because it accentuates the polysemy, instability, and various genealogies of the term and the extent to which the concept's ability to signify, mobilize, and analyze greatly depends on historical context and relation to other discourses.[9] Even further, advancing this method, the book proposes not only that sovereignty designates a diversity of practices and sites but also that this diversity has epistemic and political significance. Ultimately, the volume suggests that to think about sovereignty in the contemporary juncture requires an awareness of what can be called *geographies of sovereignty*, the diverse geopolitical and discursive locations in (and through) which the concept of sovereignty is called on to imagine, enact, or limit certain political possibilities.

Placing It: Geographies of Sovereignty in Indigenous Polities

As will become evident in the following chapters, the multiple meanings of sovereignty underscore the concept's shifting and at times incommensurable deployments and histories. In addition to the wide range of indigenous precontact political epistemologies, there are the diverse elaborations of the European concept of sovereignty itself with which all colonial and indigenous people have had to contend since the sixteenth century. On the one hand, as political theorist Wendy Brown has observed, the concept is (at least) Janus-faced.[10] In modern Western thought and political discourse, sovereignty may simultaneously refer to the nation-state's absolute and indivisible power to control all matters within its boundaries (following philosopher Thomas Hobbes) and for the nation-state—often understood since the late eighteenth century as "the people"—to be free from external interference while also recognizing the sovereignty of other states. On the other hand, in twentieth-century European political theory, the sovereign can similarly be conceived in political theorist Carl Schmitt's influential sense of he "who decides on the exception" outside of the rule of law to preserve a political community, including through the use of violence and taking of life.[11] That *sovereignty* could refer to the state's right to internal control as well as noninterference and to acts that guarantee the political order allows scholars and others to selectively engage with some but not all of the conceptual implications of the term at any given juncture.

Moreover, whereas most Western theorizations of sovereignty, particularly through the first half of the twentieth century, accept the idealized version of European history that emphasizes its achievement of an orderly interstate system following the Peace of Westphalia in 1648,[12] this is an ideological illusion. Although the state emerged as the core site of political authority in Europe by the late seventeenth century, the inter-European treaties did not succeed in establishing that sovereignty is something that a given state inherently "has" and cannot be violated, whether in Europe or in its expanding possessions "overseas."[13] Likewise, the classical notion of sovereignty understood as absolute control of a territory has never been so. For example, as the constitutionalist Christina Duffy Ponsa has remarked, the nineteenth century—a pivotal moment for the reconstitution of modern colonial and indigenous politics—was an extraordinarily creative time of experimentation on sovereignty arrangements, a moment "during which international lawyers devised increasingly unorthodox ways of manipulating the concept as they grappled with the problems posed by imperialist expansion and colonial rule."[14]

These trends could not be more evident than in the contorted language of U.S. Indian law and the unincorporated territories (chap. 1) as well as the 1901 Platt Amendment in Cuba, which detailed under what conditions the United States could intervene at will in the island's affairs, and the various protectorates in Africa, including the East Africa Protectorate (1895–1920). Additionally, in the post–World War II period, the rise of human rights discourse and political instability in several parts of the world did not so much eliminate *sovereignty* from the political vocabulary as make the idea of "divisible" or "delegated" sovereignty increasingly acceptable to both national and transnational political actors as ways to retain a degree of control, affirm national legitimacy, or mask the state's constitutive violence. Sovereignty's flexibility is partly due to the fact that, as literary theorist Mark Rifkin writes (chap. 11), the concept of state sovereignty is a discursive placeholder that has no determinate content yet enacts "a process of compulsory relation, one predicated on the supposedly unquestionable fact of national territorial boundaries."[15]

Furthermore, the fluidity of sovereignty or the idea that it can be "managed" by multiple parties is historically linked to globalization—but from the start. Contrary to much current political and academic discourse, it is not economic globalization, as a recent occurrence or subsequent phenomenon to the rise of the interstate system, that "weakens" sovereignty. Rather, it could be argued that, as historians Douglas Howland and Luise White suggest, the "Westphalian peace, as an incipient international system, served to coordinate the rise of the global economy and, in particular, its legal and colonial institutions."[16] These constitutive tensions between globalization and sovereign claims continue throughout the twentieth and twenty-first centuries. For instance, starting in the early twentieth century, corporations such as United

Fruit Company in Guatemala took on state functions such as building railroads and delivering mail. More recently, Southeast Asian "tiger" nation-states have responded to globalization by "becoming more flexible in their management of sovereignty,"[17] in anthropologist Aihwa Ong's words. In this case, Ong refers to the process through which "even as the state maintains control over its territory, it is also willing in some cases to let corporate entities set the terms for constituting and regulating some domains."[18]

At the same time—and rarely acknowledged in most European and American scholarship—who can be sovereign and how is sovereignty defined and exercised has changed to a large extent because of political and epistemological resistance to colonialism in various parts of the world. As Uperesa and Garriga-López note, the process is an ongoing one and includes the "political claims made by postcolonial states and societies, historically stateless nations, and indigenous peoples" in the Americas and beyond (chap. 1). In this process, political communities subject to settler- and/or colonial state authority have often drawn from alternative epistemologies and infused the notion of sovereignty with different meanings and practices, as they pose a challenge to the very legitimacy, logic, and foundations of settler-state sovereign power. Through this critical engagement, state sovereignty is exposed as based not only on brute force but also on the ability to "make literal," as Rifkin adds, the "process of enacting a particular kind of figuration of territory and political authority as if it were simply empirical truth."[19] Importantly, the practice of resignification has varied in scope, content, and effect across indigenous and modern colonial political spaces, underscoring that less than a fixed object or concept aligned with European or settler-state temporality, sovereignty is "constituted in a vast array of places and things that mediate practices of authorization and subjection,"[20] in the words of archaeologist Adam T. Smith.

For Native Americans in what became the contiguous United States, the grammar of sovereignty emerged in the nineteenth century as a powerful notion, full of promise and potential to protect Native polities.[21] "Our claims to sovereignty," writes scholar Scott Richard Lyons, "are nothing less than our attempt to survive and flourish as a people. Sovereignty is the guiding story in our pursuit of self-determination, the general strategy by which we aim to best recover our losses from the ravages of colonization: our lands, our languages, our cultures, our self-respect."[22] This conception is linked to how their independent governance structures and ways of political deliberation became constrained first by European monarchies claiming "divine right" over indigenous land and later American nation-state building projects that aimed to curtail or eliminate Native polities. It is also intimately connected to a series of nineteenth-century legal decisions that progressively sought to reconfigure Native political and cultural identities while rationalizing ongoing land dispossession and subjection. As literary scholar Eric Cheyfitz summarized, "Indians are the only ethnic/racial group in the United States governed by a separate body of law, the primary action of which is not on the *individual*, as is the case in mainstream US constitutional law, but on the *tribe* or *nation*; the primary agenda of which is not individual rights but sovereignty or, to be precise (from the federal perspective), its limitation."[23]

In contrast to the late eighteenth century, when the U.S. Congress passed the Commerce Clause, Article I, which gave the federal government plenary power "to recognize tribes as sovereign entities,"[24] by the nineteenth century, a series of Supreme Court decisions began to undo this understanding with major consequences. Broadly fueled by assumptions of the Indians' alleged lack of civilization, subsistence way of life, and racial inferiority to whites,[25] the Nonintercourse Act and its subsequent amendments (1790–1834) affirmed that "the right to acquire Indian land was reserved exclusively for the U.S. government; Indian tribes and states were prohibited from engaging in tribal land transactions without federal approval."[26] This power became further naturalized through three Supreme Court cases that came to be known as the Marshall Trilogy, after Chief Justice John Marshall—*Johnson v. M'Intosh* (1823), *Cherokee Nation v. Georgia* (1831), and *Worcester v. Georgia* (1832).[27]

Overall, the Marshall Trilogy recognized Native polities as (somewhat) sovereign but simultaneously declared that "as indigenous nations conquered by 'force of arms,' their inherent sovereign rights were subordinate to the United States and its lawmaking authority."[28] Even further, whereas in *Cherokee Nation v. Georgia*—the first case to be filed by a Native polity—the court admitted that Indians constituted a "distinct political society," this knowledge was ultimately discarded. In his majority opinion, Chief Justice Marshall went on to unilaterally redefine Native polities as "domestic dependent nations" that required the protection of the state at a federal level, as "of a ward to his guardian."[29] Later Congressional actions and legal cases continued to reiterate the supremacy of U.S. sovereignty in the context of Indian removal and accelerating land dispossession.[30] While the 1871 Indian Appropriations Act affirmed that "No Indian nation or tribe within the territory of the United States shall be acknowledged or recognized as an independent nation, tribe, or power with whom the United States may contract by treaty,"[31] *United States v. Kagama* (1886) asserted that only the federal government had authority to recognize the sovereign status of Indian tribes because they "were, and always have been, regarded . . . not as States, not as nations, not as possessed of the full attributes of sovereignty, but as a separate people."[32]

The progressive denial of Native sovereignty as a means to bound and contain Native polities continued well into the twentieth century through policies and legislation such as the Dawes (or General Allotment) Act (1887–1934), adopted by Congress to individualize Indian land tenure, transform land into property, and sell off "surplus" land to non-Natives; the Indian Reorganization Act (1934), which consolidated the notion of "nonrecognized" tribe;[33] and the Indian Termination Act (1953–69), a policy that sought to relocate Native Americans to urban areas, allowed states to assert jurisdiction over indigenous polities and ended government-to-government relations between Native polities and the federal government. Since the late 1960s, however, Native Americans have renewed their demands for sovereignty and respect for treaties. As a result of greater organization and support from indigenous and transnational institutions, Native Americans have secured legal wins and federal legislation that have begun to overturn centuries of curtailed fishing, hunting, land, and water rights, declining populations and life expectancy, limited access to indigenous education, and barely livable conditions on reservations.

In Canada, sovereignty is also a key concept for indigenous peoples for similar reasons as in the United States. European settlers initially viewed indigenous polities as part of their own survival and treated them accordingly. This is evident in the 1763 Royal Proclamation that recognized indigenous people as self-governing polities and by the fact that political relationships were negotiated "nation-to-nation" through informal agreements and accords, not excluding the eleven treaties that were signed between First Nations and the reigning Monarch of Canada starting in 1871.[34] Yet the process by which settlers agreed to not usurp aboriginal sovereignty but pursued policies and legislation that resulted in land dispossession, political subordination, and attempts at forced assimilation, including residential schools and other means in the name of the "Crown," ingrained the language of sovereignty in indigenous politics. A critical moment was the Indian Act of 1876, an effort to systematize existing Indian law, which insisted that title to aboriginal land belonged to the Crown and attempted to confine indigenous peoples to "reserves," defined as "a tract of land, the legal title to which is vested in Her Majesty, that has been set apart by Her Majesty for the use and benefit of a band."[35] Ultimately, although First Nations never relinquished most of their rights, including how "to determine their own citizenship, forms of government, administration of justice, law enforcement, taxation, domestic relations of citizens, property use and education," Canadian law discursively transformed indigenous peoples into "wards of the Crown."[36]

In the second half of the twentieth century, the relevance of sovereignty as a political signifier intensified for a number of reasons. In addition to persistent plans to terminate aboriginal rights and promote assimilation contained in documents such as the 1969 White Paper on Indian Policy, Canada's Constitution Act, 1982, included section 35(1), which declared that "The existing aboriginal and treaty rights of the aboriginal peoples of Canada are hereby recognized and affirmed."[37] This development opened up new opportunities for contesting the state in paradoxical ways: while some indigenous communities understood the section to mean a broader recognition of political equality, Canada's Supreme Court has consistently interpreted the section as recognizing Crown but not aboriginal sovereignty. An example is *R. v. Van der Peet* (1996), a case involving the right of indigenous people to fish and sell the catch, where the majority opinion argued that Section 35(1) "provides the constitutional framework through which the fact that aboriginals lived on the land in distinctive societies, with their own practices, customs and traditions, is acknowledged and reconciled with the sovereignty of the Crown."[38] Moreover, in a series of cases such as *Gladstone* (1996), *Marshall II* (1999) and *Mitchell v. MNR* (2001),[39] the courts have repeatedly defined the rights at stake in terms of cultural authenticity rather than political practice and have generally favored the "public purpose" or "public interest" of "All Canadians" against First Nation claims.

The aboriginal investment in sovereignty was also bolstered by the Quebecois nationalist movement, which came to be viewed by some as threatening to Canada's national integrity. As scholar Harry S. LaForme has noted, it was not until indigenous peoples in Canada consistently shifted their rhetorical strategies from demands for "self-government" to "sovereignty" in the early 1990s that most Canadians became aware of indigenous political distinctiveness and long-standing political traditions, given the more publicized discussions regarding Quebec's claim to separate national sovereignty.[40] A turning point was the 1990 Oka Crisis in Mohawk territory north of Montreal. On July 11, 1990, Mohawks armed themselves to deter a plan proposed by the town of Oka to expropriate Mohawk land with the goal of building nine new holes in a golf course and expanding a residential development. Although the state dropped the immediate issue and Prime Minister Brian Mulroney "refused to discuss sovereignty," Mohawks insisted on it: "We have a written agreement with Great Britain (from Colonial times)," Mohawk journalist Brian Maracle stated, "which recognizes our sovereignty and our separateness, which we feel Canada is obligated to honor."[41] More recently, in 2014, the seven-thousand-member Atikamekw First Nation based in La Tuque "declared sovereignty over the 31,000 square miles of boreal forest in north-central Quebec" that was being exploited by forestry companies without any benefits to the community. Through affirming their sovereignty, the tribe sought "to have more control and better environmental protections and ensure the Atikamekw Nation benefits financially" as well as "be heard," in the words of grand chief Christian Awashish.[42]

In the case of Hawai'i, the importance of sovereignty has a different genealogy and temporality than in Native North America, yet it is equally significant for contemporary politics. A recognized constitutional monarchy at the close of the nineteenth century, the Kingdom of Hawai'i suffered a coup on January 17, 1893. Triggered by fears that Queen Lili'uokalani aimed to restore powers lost to the Hawaiian monarch as a result of the 1887 constitution and further enfranchise Hawaiian voters, white settlers Lorrin A. Thurston and Sanford B. Dole led the overthrow with the support of the U.S. Navy. The coup's core objectives were to end the monarchy, annex the Hawaiian archipelago to the United States, and promote the interests of white sugar planters and other business sectors. Initially, U.S. president Grover Cleveland did not accept the new government as legitimate and in fact called the coup "an act of war."[43] But by 1898, a new Congress under President McKinley recognized the recently created Republic of Hawai'i and accepted its government's "cession" of Hawaiian sovereignty. In 1959, despite protest from many Native Hawaiians, the Hawaiian archipelago was admitted as the fiftieth state of the union.

The fact that a constitutional sovereign ruled the Kingdom of Hawai'i produced a context for sovereignty—which is locally understood in a variety of ways, including self-determination, nation-state status, and *ea*, a Hawaiian term that can be translated in the sense of life, breath, air, spirit, and sovereignty—to persist as a core signifier in the coup's long aftermath.[44] Moreover, the 1993 apology of the U.S. government signed by President Bill Clinton conceding that "the native Hawaiian people never directly relinquished to the United States their claims to their inherent sovereignty"[45] also strengthened the concept's political value and boosted demands for sovereign rights over land and other resources. As Davianna Pōmaika'i McGregor argues (chap. 4), the ongoing significance of sovereignty in Hawai'i over the last two decades is related to how various forms of political action—from civilian pressure to court litigation and state political representation—have largely failed to improve the lives of Native Hawaiians who became a demographic minority and continue to have higher rates of infant mortality, suicide, school dropouts, incarceration, and homelessness than whites. The centrality of sovereign claims is similarly linked to the rejection of U.S. policy regarding militarization, environmental hazards such as nuclear testing, and the imposition of blood quantum as the main criteria for political belonging among Native Hawaiians.[46]

In sum, as the legal rationale for the taking of land and for the transformation of indigenous polities into "domestic dependent nations," "wards of the Crown," or "minorities" was often proclaimed in the name of European, Canadian, or American nation-state sovereignty and codified as such in law, most political claims were, and to a large extent, continue to be couched in the idiom of sovereignty through both affirming their own sovereignty in the imposed Western terms and inflecting the concept with different needs, histories and aspirations. In this sense, while clearly shaped by the courts, sovereignty cannot be simply understood as a legal matter. It is also often an epistemological and ontological concept; an affirmation of indigenous political traditions and governance systems and a critique of power that has converted (legal) acts of indigenous dispossession into acts of resistance, creativity, and/or refusal.[47]

Islands Apart: Critical Sovereignties in Unincorporated "America"

The question of sovereignty is also omnipresent, if not always raised as such, in the termed U.S. territories, including Puerto Rico, Guam, and American Samoa. Not unlike indigenous North America, the alleged racial, cultural, economic, or class inferiority of its inhabitants came to justify the production of a new body of law that would distinguish the islands from both states and prior incorporated territories on the path to statehood like Hawai'i. In contrast, the new acquisitions came to be imagined and legally construed as "unincorporated territories," defined by the Supreme Court through the Insular Cases (1901–22) as territories that "belong to but are not part of, the United States."[48] Concretely, this came to mean that not all constitutional or citizenship rights apply (if extended) and that ultimate sovereignty over the territories would reside in the "plenary power" of Congress.[49]

Yet it is not until relatively recently that sovereignty-specific discourse has become salient in some contexts. This is largely because in contrast to Native polities and Hawai'i, Puerto Rico and Guam were not sovereign nations, states, and/or seeking independence at the time of U.S. intervention. Both remained Spanish colonies during the Spanish-American War (1898) and were later ceded to the United States. In the case of Samoa, a Samoan envoy had requested U.S. protection or annexation in 1877, but the islands remained a part of the German empire until the 1899 Tripartite Convention, which partitioned the archipelago into a German colony (present-day Samoa) and a U.S. territory, "American Samoa."[50] Given that many in the territories regarded, and to an extent continue to view, relations with the United States ambivalently, anticolonial politics have historically been framed more as a desire for "autonomy" or "self-government," and to a lesser extent "independence," than for "sovereignty."

In Guam, anticolonial political discourse has been anchored around obtaining equal rights through U.S. citizenship. As early as 1901, the native Chamorro leadership resisted the imposition of military governance by petitioning the U.S. naval governor and Congress for citizenship rights that were, predictably and repeatedly denied or ignored. Yet the correlation of forces shifted after World War II as Chamorros endured a brutal Japanese occupation but remained loyal to the United States. At this point, and with the support of the American Civil Liberties Union, among other allies the citizenship movement was revived but this time as a form of protest against mass land takings for military purposes after the United States turned the island into a massive Allied military base housing more than 200,000 soldiers and other military personnel.[51] The movement culminated in the 1950 Organic Act of Guam extending U.S. citizenship to the people of Guam, but it produced a new insight: territorial citizenship did little to curb military power and did not guarantee land rights. Instead, it camouflaged and assured a continued process of dispossession as the Organic Act explicitly stated that "nothing contained herein shall be construed as limiting the authority of the President to designate parts of Guam as naval or military reservations."

Consequently, since the 1970s, as land devolution failed to materialize, attempts to reform the current status to include "'mutual consent' in the changing of laws and treaties" were ignored or rejected by Congress,[52] and as the U.S. military started to draw plans to build up the island again to post–World War II levels, arguments for decolonization became more commonplace. Over the last decade, mobilizations by land devolution and anti-military-buildup activists have succeeded in slowing down and scaling back the military's expansion plans, while discontent has continued to grow. Fittingly, in 2016, Guam's Republican governor Eddie Baza Calvo appointed a new decolonization commission and argued for the holding of a plebiscite claiming that "anything is better than being an unincorporated territory."[53]

The Puerto Rican case shares some commonalities with Guam: throughout the twentieth century, the majority of Puerto Ricans have supported close relations with the United States instead of separate nation-state status or formal independence. This is due in part to the fact that by the middle of the twentieth century, the United States had extended most individual democratic rights to Puerto Rico, accelerated the island's economic modernization, and provided access to higher standards of living. Moreover, the question of sovereignty was largely avoided through three major congressional and diplomatic acts. One was the extension of a limited form of U.S. citizenship through the 1917 Jones-Shafroth Act, which allowed for free movement between the island and the mainland but was not accompanied by fundamental rights such as voting for the U.S. president or electing a voting delegation to Congress. The second was the establishment of the Estado Libre Asociado (ELA, mistranslated as "commonwealth") in 1952, which provided for the crafting of a constitution that offered a greater degree of self-rule even if it had to be ultimately approved by Congress. Finally, in a gesture that at the time favored both the Puerto Rican pro-Commonwealth leaders and the U.S. government, the latter successfully pushed through the 1953 Resolution 748 (VII) at the United Nations declaring that through the ELA, the "Puerto Rican people had exercised their self-determination" and had "achieved attributes of political sovereignty."[54]

However, to the extent that during the second half of the twentieth century Puerto Ricans continued to have limited citizenship rights, and because the island remained poor and subordinated to the U.S. Constitution's territorial clause, the question of sovereignty shadowed most political discourse. As anthropologist Yarimar Bonilla summarized, "Coming of age politically in the Puerto Rico of the 1990s . . . we often heard from politicians that the issues that concerned us most—depressed incomes, high prices, unemployment, crime, violence, and government corruption—all hinged on resolving our sovereignty problem."[55] In the last ten years, the term has become more visible in mainstream politics. This was evident in the November 6, 2012, plebiscite results, which for the first time registered majority discontent with the territorial status quo not only with greater support for statehood (61 percent) but also with an unprecedented 33 percent of voters choosing the option of Estado Libre Asociado Soberano (Sovereign Free Associated State),[56] defined on the ballot as "a status outside of the Territory Clause of the Constitution of the United States that recognizes the sovereignty of the People of Puerto Rico."[57]

Recent events have similarly made sovereignty a more central political category. In contrast to how the United States maintained an ambiguous position regarding the actual sovereign powers of the ELA depending on the political forum to avoid international rebuke, a 2016 Supreme Court decision in *Puerto Rico v. Sanchez Valle*, a double jeopardy case, unambiguously rejected the Puerto Rican government's position that it has authority "to prosecute someone for the same crime that has been charged in federal court."[58] Instead, in a six-to-two decision, the court asserted that "the Commonwealth and the United States are not separate sovereigns"[59] since, unlike any of the fifty American states or an independent nation-state, ultimate sovereign authority over the unincorporated territories resides in Congress. In other words, the imposition of PROMESA, the economic collapse of the ELA, the massive displacement of the population to the continental United States, and enduringly colonial forms of governance have produced the conditions for a specifically *soberanista* (sovereigntist) discourse to emerge. A position largely shared by proindependence organizations and former supporters of the ELA, some groups define sovereignty as "a necessary condition to reorganize our collective life and our full insertion in the affairs of our region and the world."[60] Not surprisingly, while a boycott ultimately prevailed, in early 2017, a coalition of groups organized under the banner of *Ahora sí . . . Ganamos con la soberanía* (Now we will win with sovereignty) in support of free association and independence in Puerto Rico's June 11, 2017, status plebiscite.[61]

For different reasons, overtly sovereign discourse is even less central in American Samoa than in Guam and Puerto Rico—if for a paradoxically sovereign reason. As Garriga-López and Uperesa discuss in this volume (chap. 1), Samoan political discourse understands the arguably colonial relationship between American Samoa and the United States as one of cogovernment in which Samoans already enjoy sovereignty through political practices based on the extended family (*aiga*) and communal structures. The context of possibility for this understanding is rooted in key differences between U.S. governance there and in Guam and Puerto Rico. At one level, capitalist relations are weaker in American Samoa than in any other U.S. "territory": a striking 90 percent of American Samoan land is communally owned. At another, American Samoa is not only an "unincorporated territory" but also an "unorganized one," which means that the islands are theoretically ruled by a 1967 locally approved constitution rather than a congressional organic act. (Although solely Congress, as in Puerto Rico, has the power to amend American Samoa's constitution, and the Department of the Interior administers the territory.)

Equally relevant, American Samoans are nationals rather than citizens on Samoa and on the mainland. American Samoan politics are similarly bound by a representative democratic system headed by an elected governor akin to that of other U.S. territories since 1976 and a traditional politics based on the *fa'amatai* (the chiefly system) and the *fa'asāmoa* (Samoan way), the domain of language, culture, and customs. To the extent that both operate at all levels of the Samoan body politic, a majority of Samoans tend to view further U.S. incorporation as potentially undermining their sovereignty (see chap. 1). In 2016, for instance, when it seemed plausible that *Tuaua v. United States*, a case involving a group of American Samoans suing the U.S. government for birthright citizenship, could be heard by the U.S. Supreme Court, the government of American Samoa expressed opposition to the extension of U.S. citizenship "on the ground that it would threaten their cultural practices."[62]

In sum, as it is evident throughout indigenous and "territorial" junctures, there is tremendous variety in what political actors and scholars seek when invoking the concept of sovereignty, how it is defined, and when the notion becomes salient. Moreover, given that in some cases overt claims to sovereignty have consolidated in recent times, it is important to note that the articulation of these does not align or wane in direct correlation with the proliferation of global political actors or institutions. Puerto Rico's case, for example, demonstrates specific shifts related to globalization, including the rising hegemony of financial capital and the increase of migratory flows, may shape and even produce such demands. As anthropologist Stefano Varese has observed, it was not until global capital began to further encroach on Native land during the second half of the twentieth century that indigenous movements in Latin America envisioned their political goals through the affirmation of sovereignty.[63] At the end, the significance of sovereignty as a conceptual and political resource depends on a range of factors, including the importance of legal discourses in producing state authority and political subjects, the centrality of land to political conflict, and how relationships of power are understood locally. This recalls scholars Hent Kalmo and Quentin Skinner's conclusion that "if we prefer . . . to conceive of sovereignty as an argument, as a claim to authority, than there is no sense at all in which it can be 'reduced.'"[64]

Imagining Things: Other Sovereignties and Creative States

Another way of considering the intricate ways in which sovereignty is a mobile and unsettled sign is the explosion of sovereign discourse onto areas other than the law and the state in indigenous, Caribbean, and Latinx studies. Whereas up until the 1990s, sovereignty was almost exclusively thought of in relation to the legal realm, this is no longer the case. If one were to take even a small sample of key indigenous scholarship during the last twenty years, it would be possible to encounter a plurality of conceptual sovereignties, including cultural, intellectual, hermeneutical, visual, gender, and sexual, to name a few. In his influential essay, "Rhetorical Sovereignty," for instance, Lyons defines this form of sovereignty as "the inherent right and ability of *peoples* to determine their own communicative needs and desires in this pursuit, to decide for themselves the goals, modes, styles, and languages of public discourse."[65]

Similarly, in Caribbean, Latinx, and Native visual studies, various notions of sovereignty have facilitated a number of critiques. Scholar Michelle H. Raheja defined "visual sovereignty" as "a creative act of self-representation that has the potential to both undermine stereotypes of indigenous peoples and to strengthen . . . the 'intellectual health' of communities in the wake of genocide and colonialism."[66] Bonilla and Max Hantel also observe that when thinking from the Caribbean, "visualizing sovereignty is a first step in retheorizing the meaning of sovereignty itself beyond the regulatory limits of insular, nation-state autonomy."[67] In succinct language, art historian Dylan Miner affirms that, "the process of affirming Xicano sovereignty, is itself a creative work."[68] Overall, these interventions engage with how representation, narrative, and form are a "complex instantiation of jurisdiction and authority," in Simpson's words, that shape cultural production, economic organization and governance.[69]

The (over)productivity of sovereignty in its richest site, indigenous studies, however, has not been unanimously accepted. Influential scholar Vine Deloria Jr., for instance, once decried the extension of the concept into nonlegal political matters: "Today the definition of sovereignty covers a multitude of sins, having lost its political moorings, and now is adrift on the currents of individual fancy."[70] Coming from a different place yet converging on the centrality of state conceptions of sovereignty in Hawaiian discourse, nationalist writer Haunani-Kay Trask has dismissed the idea that other forms of politics such as feminism may constitute an important part of sovereignty movements. For Trask, "Sovereignty for our people is a larger goal than legal or educational or political equality with our men. As we struggle for sovereignty, our women come to the fore anyway."[71] On the other end of the spectrum, activist and scholar Taiaiake Alfred has called for the abandonment of state sovereigntist discourse in First Nations politics because of its implication in hierarchical power structures and origin in European colonialism: "The next phase of scholarship and activism, then, will need to transcend the mentality that supports the colonization of indigenous nations, beginning with the rejection of the term and notion of indigenous 'sovereignty.'"[72]

Yet regardless of whether one concurs politically or conceptually with Deloria, Trask, or Alfred, the proliferation of textual sovereignties has had various effects on knowledge production and the location of intellectual authority. It has, for instance, enabled some scholars, often women, to redefine what can be considered political beyond the confines of state legal and institutional discourse. Likewise, it has served to demonstrate how notions of sovereignty are complicated by and implicated in other hierarchical forms of difference, including gender, race, and sexuality, among others. These trends are clearly evident throughout the volume, especially in Jennifer Nez Denetdale's chapter on how Navajo male leaders challenge women in politics through reproducing Western-based gender discourses even as they claim to promote traditional Navajo philosophy and sovereignty (chap. 5); in Jessica A. F. Harkins's essay about the way that debates regarding same-sex marriage in Cherokee Nation can be a central part of "sovereignty making" by challenging settler-colonial definitions of acceptable gender and sexual identities (chap. 6); and in Stephanie Nohelani Teves's contribution on how Hawaiian hip-hop performer Krystilez brings forth assertions of sovereignty that simultaneously defy racism and affirm dominant gender discourses (chap. 7). Critically, in moving sovereignty into the "private" sphere and across feminist and queer spaces, these writings have made hierarchical gender and sexual regimes within and between Native contexts an integral part of what is today considered Native politics.

Equally significant, this discursive terrain, which Deloria also criticized because it moved the debate from sovereignty to "fancy," that is, to what people want it to be, founds an open space for transformative thought. As Raheja has argued in relation to the notion of visual sovereignty, the shifting to cultural practices incorporates "play" into Native thinking: "Because visual sovereignty . . . is not always directly involved in political debates that determine Native American survival and livelihood . . . there is more room for narrative play. . . . Under visual sovereignty, filmmakers can . . . frame more imaginative renderings of Native American intellectual and cultural paradigms . . . than are often possible in official political contexts."[73] Along similar lines, historian Robert Allen Warrior acknowledges that while the term *sovereignty* may be compromised, he argues for the practice of "intellectual sovereignty" as a "long critical reflection on the meaning of freedom."[74] These interventions imply that in some circumstances, the citation of sovereignty can constitute an expansive politics of "the right now" away from the prerogative of privileged political actors such as the state and Eurocentric epistemologies. In others, referencing sovereignty constitutes—in however a contingent, contradictory way—a space of intellectual play and political desire *for itself*. This underscores that it is perhaps in the realm of so-called fantasy—which is neither tied to what is perceived to be "real" or "useful"—where Native thought more radically challenges how the contemporary order produces Native people as fixed identities with limited potentialities.

Given the centrality of cultural production to the affirmation of freer political imaginings, this collection similarly seeks to further understand the importance of aesthetics to sovereign claims and claims to sovereignty. As historian Michel Foucault, one of a few theorists to consider the relation between aesthetics and sovereignty, noted, "if I want people to accept me as king, I must have the kind of glory which will survive me, and this glory cannot be disassociated from aesthetic value."[75] These questions are at the center of my essay with Yasmin Ramirez, "King of the Line: The Sovereign Acts of Jean-Michel Basquiat" (chap. 12). Here, we examine why, how, and to what effects Basquiat deployed crowns and other sovereignty symbols and words to critique racism in and out of the art world, detail how colonial discourses gain authority and power, and disrupt Eurocentric knowledge and institutions that have sought to delegitimize African, Afro-diasporic, and indigenous lives and epistemologies. While Basquiat eventually came to doubt the viability of sovereign acts to free black subjectivity from coloniality, that today a simple drawing of a crown is enough to connote his decolonial method and texts remains a testament to the complexity of sovereignty as a mode of cultural and political critique.

In addition, the book explores how aesthetic acts are not only present in the arts, as is the case of Basquiat and the rapper Krystilez, but also in a wide range of symbolic actions, including rituals, narratives, and forms of dress. In my second essay "The Look of Sovereignty: Style and Politics in the Young Lords" (chap. 9), I focus on the New York branch of the radical youth group the Young Lords, publicly launched in 1969. Specifically, I consider how the Lords successfully challenged the idea of Puerto Ricans as inherently subject peoples to U.S. sovereignty and law via what I describe as the "look of sovereignty"—a way to display and mobilize the body to signal that Puerto Ricans were sovereign actors within city politics and on the island. The centrality of style to the Young Lords' politics and effectiveness in reconfiguring institutional power suggests that nonstate sovereign acts may be related to the process of refashioning the public self to produce what philosopher Georges Bataille once called a "miraculous" disruption of the symbolic order.[76] This may be accomplished via a *dramatic persona* that simultaneously performs the self as a sovereign, refuses its subordinate place, and calls into question the legitimacy of the social and political order.

The transformative potential of sovereign performance is also crucially at play in Michael Lujan Bevacqua's reflection on Nasion Chamoru leader Angel Leon Guerrero Santos (chap. 3). A veteran of the U.S. Air Force, in 1993,

Santos jumped over a U.S. military fence in Guam to protest land dispossession. Although Chamorros had a variety of responses to Santos and many viewed his jump as a "mad" act, Bevacqua theorizes it as a sovereign act that exemplifies a broader definition of sovereignty as "not invested in particular political status categories or notions of local and everyday sovereignty. Rather, it is sovereignty as contained in an act that has the potential to break the decolonial deadlock" (chap. 3). By defying what is normal and expected, Santos simultaneously disrupted the idea that the U.S. military is all-powerful and that Chamorro subjection to the United States is the "natural" social order. Even further, as the Young Lords, Santos's act unsettled the temporal expectation that the relationship between the United States and the territories would proceed as it "always" has. In this sense, to act sovereign (rather than "be" sovereign), might at times constitute a way to preclude "the well-functioning of routine," as Mete Ulaş Aksoy proposes via Bataille,[77] or "interrupt what otherwise would have proceeded automatically and therefore predictably," as Hannah Arendt observes in *On Violence*.[78] It can also, to follow Jacques Rancière, be an exercise in "dissensus," that is, a path to "put into contention the objective status of what is 'given' and impose an examination and discussion of those things that were not 'visible,' that were not accounted for."[79]

The volume thus argues that although influential political theorists such as Wendy Brown imply that state "theatrics," such as wall building to contain immigration, are the symptoms of waning state sovereignty,[80] and this may indeed be the case in multiple instances, performativity is constitutive of sovereign acts under most definitions and not only in times of crisis for the state. In cultural theorist Friedrich Balke's terms (via Foucault), "there are two operations with which the sovereign wins the hearts: *binding* (law) and *dazzling* (magic)."[81] Or as Derrida put it, "the essence of political force and power, where that power makes the law, where it gives itself right, where it appropriates legitimate violence and legitimates its own arbitrary violence—this unchaining and enchaining of power passes via the fable, i.e., speech that is both fictional and performative."[82] "Theatrics" are then part and parcel of all sovereign acts even if to different ends and effects. While for the state, spectacular actions of violence and acts of negation are often required because state power is "always far more fragile than it appears,"[83] for other political actors, sovereign acts, understood as freedom to act and imagine in excess of an imposed law, order, or norm, may be capable of opening up other ways of being in the world. Their fundamental importance is that in some instances, if never entirely, these acts allow subjects to realize that "we are much freer than we feel," in Foucault's words.[84]

Hard to Follow: Sovereignty's Third Act

As suggested in the previous sections, the notion of absolute control or the ability to decide on the exception central to Western classical and contemporary conceptions of sovereignty is often less central and even antithetical to the praxis of sovereignty in some Native, anticolonial, and decolonial contexts. When thought in relation to the self and political communities, sovereignty can likewise be understood as the capacity to act and to be otherwise: the "I can" that serves as a prerequisite for freedom and politics.[85] Not coincidentally, as Jacques Derrida stated, "All the fundamental axiomatics of responsibility or decision (ethical, juridical, political) are grounded on the sovereignty of the subject, that is, the intentional auto-determination of the conscious self (which is free, autonomous, active, etc.)."[86]

At the same time, several chapters in this volume converge in pointing out that even if sovereignty can be thought of in alternative registers, several entanglements with the Western concept remain. To begin, there is the founding tension of any sovereign authority or act as inherently extrajudicial. As Balke has observed, the "king" is always a usurper: "The legitimacy that he claims owes to an act of erasure of that disruption that his emergence presents."[87] Though indigenous or decolonial movements tend to affirm sovereignty in opposition to imperial authority and often in support for "'non-dominating and non-exploitative' political forms,"[88] the enduring association between sovereignty and the notions of "exclusive possession," "noninterference,"[89] and "jurisdictions"[90] persists in many formulations. That is, whereas there is frequent debate concerning the locus of power—settler or colonial state versus indigenous polity or liberated nation—the idea of "control" (of community and self) or "legitimate order" remains largely unexamined.

Another difficulty relates to the very notion of "act." On the one hand, as Bataille would have it, sovereign acts cannot be "useful" for building an order (or anything else) because they are consumed and exhausted in their transgression and are not transferable for political purposes:[91] "if sovereignty is to be attained," considered Bataille, "one must step out the relations which condition him or her for being useful."[92] In other words, for Bataille, sovereignty is an unknowing that frees the subject from all symbolic and political orders. On the other hand, even if sovereignty could be thought of as "useful," the process would likely not culminate in the intended political outcome. This is the case not only because globalization complicates territoriality, and power is not simply a property of the state and is therefore present "everywhere" in Foucault's terms, but also because the subject is multiple, divided, and produced through incommensurable social discourses and structures. Consequently, there can be no absolute coherency between act, thought, and objective, political or otherwise. As sociologist Madeline Román argues: "all the choices that appear to be made by 'individual people' are mediated by social discourses and technologies such as advertising, the two-party system, or the subjection of people to capital as labor" (chap. 10). This predicament reminds us of psychoanalyst Jacques Lacan's observation in relation to the May 1968 events that "an act always misunderstands itself."[93]

The above ways of complicating the idea of an "act" partly explain why sovereign acts never fully deliver on what they promise yet are part of social mobilizations in many contexts. The discussion further illuminates that sovereignty's complexity is not only about the paradox of signifying freedom from a controlling power and freedom to exercise power but also relates to how the concept is an "act" in the triple sense of action (agential capacity), performance (staging), and law (order). Sovereign acts can thus be deployed to demonstrate an ability to act, to stage legitimacy, and/or to constitute a social order. Yet, following Román, to the extent that sovereignty's last act necessarily imposes identities, enforces rationales (including economic ones), and therefore limits political possibilities, it can make it more difficult to imagine and live nonhierarchical relationships that bypass forms of rule based on subjection to a sovereign or social order.

Linked to this last critique, the volume raises another set of important questions regarding the connection between sovereignty and recognition. A fundamental expectation of numerous Native and decolonial movements, recognition appears in several chapters as a particularly fraught space for a politics of freedom from capitalism, racism, and colonialism in at least two distinct ways. First, as Glen Coulthard argues, state recognition of indigenous and colonized groups preserves colonial dynamics as it is the colonizing and/or settler state that recognizes a groups' sovereignty and what the criteria of recognition are (chap. 2). The appeal to be recognized thus already implies that these polities accept that the settler state can, in fact, recognize them, which compels them to identify with the state's power. Not coincidentally, the unit that recognizes tribes in the United States is called the Office of Federal Acknowledgment. This office claims the unilateral power to recognize (or not) Indians based on racial ("blood count"), cultural, and historical criteria of what constitutes an Indian rather than genealogy, belonging, and other indigenous forms of defining political membership.[94]

A second conundrum of recognition is central in Brian Klopotek's essay on the relationship between race and indigenous sovereignty among the Clifton-Choctaws of Louisiana (chap. 8). In investigating "how racial formations and indigeneity are *tied together*," Klopotek considers how the actions of some U.S. tribes to gain or maintain federally recognized sovereign status can lead indigenous groups to accept colonial racial hierarchies, exclude members that may appear "black," and reject contact with African Americans. In this case, the affirmation of legal sovereignty is in conflict with the process of political constitution itself as tribal sovereignty begins to be constrained "before a tribe even enters the acknowledgment process by powerfully limiting their vision of what an Indian or a tribe can be." The notion of tribal sovereignty is then clearly a racialized practice from the start with multiple manifestations, from the incorporation of racism into U.S. and Canadian law as rationales for colonial subjection to attempts by indigenous polities and groups to affiliate or disaffiliate racially to gain recognition by settler colonial and modern states. In this sense, the desire for political recognition may inevitably be quite different from the process of decolonization, which requires a distance from the very framework of settler thought and law. Or as Brown asked in another context, "When does legal recognition become an instrument of regulation, and political recognition become an instrument of subordination?"[95]

Although not centrally present in the volume's chapters, this last question is also at the heart of another set of complexities involving the concept of sovereignty, namely, the jurisdiction over territory and the movement of people through it. One difficulty is that for some groups, sovereign action may be imagined as controlling movement in or out of a territory and setting criteria for incorporation or rejection, while for others, what is pursued is the freedom of movement across various national territories without legal barriers but with legal rights not tied to a specific state or territory. This last observation is convergent with Román's critique of sovereignty as politically restrictive to the extent that notions based on control of populations constitute one of the biggest obstacles to addressing the loss of rights experienced by millions of people worldwide as a result of mass migration and forced displacement. An associated problem is that because contemporary states often have little control in relation to global economic forces, governments turn to the control of their physical borders to show that they are still sovereign in their national territory, resulting in human rights abuses. The result is that refugees and the undocumented bear the burden of the sovereign's lack of control, whereas anti-immigrant policies do next to nothing in stopping the flow of immigrants or easing the suffering of affected communities.

In other words, even the idea of a radical or decolonial sovereign act may advertently or inadvertently be indebted to a problematic desire for absolute boundaries and control, seamless identification between self and group, and/or complete self-possession. Moreover, while a range of sovereign discourse often presumes an equivalence between word and act as well as acts and power, the sustained analysis of language, performance, and politics found in most of the chapters here indicates that disjuncture rather than sovereignty characterizes many human acts, including in the current era of what philosopher Gilles Deleuze has called "society of control."[96] Equally significant for a different politics, if intent completely matched meaning and effect, it would be impossible to create new meanings, prompting philosopher Judith Butler's truism that "agency begins where sovereignty wanes."[97]

Fully assuming these tensions, this volume thus offers several points of entry and exit into thinking about the concept of sovereignty. By dividing the book into three sections titled "Navigating Sovereignty" (chaps. 1–4), "Sovereign Bodies" (chaps. 5–9), and "Life Without Sovereignty" (chaps. 10–12), it is our hope that it will foster at least three broad conversations. The first, largely concentrated in the first and last sections, examines the theoretical and political effects of deploying the term *sovereignty* in settler-state and modern colonial contexts. Another is centered on the importance and limits of aesthetic and imaginative acts to the production of sovereign selves particularly for nonstate political actors and to practices other than the law (chaps. 6–9). Finally, the third revolves around the contradictions of nation-state sovereignty as a political goal and epistemological reference in decolonization projects.

At the end, this book is largely about "life with/out sovereignty" but understood in very different ways: as a polity devoid of sovereign powers as defined by colonial/settler states and capital; in the literal sense, as a way to imagine the end of political communities based on the idea of absolute and supreme control; and as a form of defiance to Western imperial sovereignty that seeks to constrain its hold and envision alternative forms of nonhierarchical, autonomous, interdependent, and associative ways of life. In this regard, the present book does not (and cannot) resolve the question of what is sovereignty, much less what is life with/out it. But all contributors suggest that many a place—and life itself—may depend upon how sovereignty is thought and acted out (or not).

Notes

1. Saskia Sassen, "Bordering Capabilities Versus Borders: Implications for National Borders," in *Borderities and the Politics of Contemporary Borders*, ed. Julie Evans, Ann Genovese, Alexander Reilly, and Patrick Wolfe (Honolulu: University of Hawai'i Press, 2013), 23.
2. Audra Simpson, *Mohawk Interruptus: Political Life Across the Borders of Settler States* (Durham, NC: Duke University Press, 2014), 11.
3. Simpson, *Mohawk Interruptus*, 11.
4. Rebecca Hersher, "Dakota Access Pipeline Court Challenge Denied, Oil Could Flow As Soon as Next Week," *NPR Now*, March 7, 2017, http://www.npr.org

/sections/thetwo-way/2017/03/07/519040535/dak…=social&utm_campaign=npr&utm_term=nprnews&utm_content=20170307; Stephanie Woodard, "Building on Standing Rock, Native Americans Lead the Way at the People's Climate March in D.C.," *In These Times*, May 1, 2017, http://inthesetimes.com/rural-america/entry/20098/peoples-climate-march-noa-indigenous-environmental-network-energy-policy.

5. "Puerto Rico National Strike Protests 'Colonial' Debt Crisis," *Telesur*, May 1, 2017, http://www.telesurtv.net/english/news/Puerto-Rico-National-Strike-Protests-Colonial-Debt-Crisis-20170501-0014.html.

6. Throughout the introduction, I use the term *indigenous* as encompassing but will also refer to other terms such as *Native*, *aboriginal*, and *First Nations* according to context.

7. Key texts and interlocutors include Antony Anghie (*Imperialism, Sovereignty and the Making of International Law*), Georges Bataille (*The History of Eroticism and Sovereignty*), Jacques Derrida (*The Beast and the Sovereign*), Douglas Howland and Luise White (*The State of Sovereignty: Territories, Laws, Populations*), and Michel Foucault (multiple works).

8. Alexander Hirsch, "Sovereignty Surreal: Bataille and Fanon Beyond the State of Exception," *Contemporary Political Theory* 13, no. 3 (August 2014): 287–306.

9. For further discussion on the articulation of discourse and its effect on signification, see Joanne Barker, "Introductions," in *Native Acts: Law, Recognition, and Cultural Authenticity* (Durham, NC: Duke University Press, 2011), 1–24, 8–9.

10. Wendy Brown, *Walled States, Waning Sovereignty* (New York: Zone Books, 2010), 47, 65.

11. Carl Schmitt, *Political Theology: Four Chapters on the Concept of Sovereignty* (Chicago: University of Chicago Press, 2005), 5.

12. Douglas Howland and Luise White, *State of Sovereignty* (Bloomington: Indiana University Press, 2008), 284.

13. For further discussion, including on how sovereignty was aimed at resolving tensions between monarchs and the papacy in the European context, see Howland and White, *State of Sovereignty*, 3.

14. Christina Duffy Ponsa, "Contingent Constitutions: Empire and Law in the Americas" (PhD diss., Princeton University, 2010).

15. Mark Rifkin, "Indigenizing Agamben: Rethinking Sovereignty in Light of the 'Peculiar' Status of Native Peoples," *Cultural Critique*, no. 73 (2009): 88–24, 105.

16. Howland and White, *State of Sovereignty*, 3.
17. Aihwa Ong, *Flexible Citizenship: The Cultural Logics of Transnationality* (Durham, NC: Duke University Press, 1999), 214.
18. Ibid., 217.
19. Mark Rifkin, *The Erotics of Sovereignty: Queer Native Writing in the Era of Self-Determination* (Minneapolis: University of Minnesota Press, 2012), 14.
20. Adam T. Smith, "Archaeologies of Sovereignty," *Annual Review of Anthropology* 40 (2011): 415–32, 416.
21. The experience of Alaska Natives is different in multiple ways from all other contexts examined in this volume. Yet sovereignty has similarly emerged as a core signifier in political discourse, particularly since the 1980s.
22. Scott Richard Lyons, "Rhetorical Sovereignty: What Do American Indians Want from Writing?," *College Composition and Communication* 51, no. 3 (2000): 447–68, 449.
23. Eric Cheyfitz, "The (Post)Colonial Construction of Indian Country: U.S. American Indian Literatures and Federal Indian Law," in *The Columbia Guide to American Indian Literatures of the United States Since 1945*, ed. Eric Cheyfitz (New York: Columbia University Press, 2006), 1–124; "The (Post)colonial Predicament of Native American Studies," *International Journal of Postcolonial Studies* 4, no. 3 (2002): 405–27, 409.
24. K. Alexa Koenig and Jonathan Stein, "State Recognition of American Indian Tribes: A Survey of State-Recognized Tribes and State Recognition Processes," in *Recognition, Sovereignty Struggles, and Indigenous Rights in the United States: A Sourcebook*, ed. Amy E. Den Ouden and Jean M. O'Brien (Chapel Hill: University of North Carolina Press, 2013), 123.
25. Joanne Barker, "For Whom Sovereignty Matters," in *Sovereignty Matters: Locations of Contestation and Possibility in Indigenous Struggles for Self-Determination*, ed. Joanne Barker (Lincoln: University of Nebraska Press, 2005), 8.
26. Koenig and Stein, "State Recognition of American Indian Tribes," 124.
27. Angela Gonzalez and Timothy Evans, "The Imposition of Law: The Federal Acknowledgment Process and the Legal De/Construction of Tribal Identity," in Den Ouden and O'Brien, *Recognition, Sovereignty Struggles, and Indigenous Rights*, 40.
28. Koenig and Stein, "State Recognition of American Indian Tribes," 124.
29. Quoted in Gonzalez and Evans, "Imposition of Law," 41.

30. Eric Cheyfitz, "The Colonial Double Bind: Sovereignty and Civil Rights in Indian Country," *Journal of Constitutional Law* 5, no. 2 (January 2003): 224.
31. "1871 Indian Appropriations Acts," U.S. Code Title 25: Indian Tribes, http://www.ucs.louisiana.edu/~ras2777/indianlaw/appropriations.htm. For further analysis on the importance of this period to U.S.-Indian relations, see Kevin Bruyneel, *The Third Space of Sovereignty: The Postcolonial Politics of U.S.-Indigenous Relations* (Minneapolis: University of Minnesota Press, 2007), xxiii–xxiv.
32. United States v. Kagama, 118 US 375, 6 S. Ct. 1109.
33. Gonzalez and Evans, "Imposition of Law," 155–56.
34. Eric Johnston and Diane Longboat, "Sovereignty, Jurisdiction and Guiding Principles in Aboriginal Education in Canada," *Canadian Journal of Native Studies* VI (1986): 175.
35. "Indian Act (R.S.C., 1985, c. I-5)," Justice Laws Website, http://laws-lois.justice.gc.ca/eng/acts/i-5/page-1.html#h-1.
36. Johnston and Longboat, "Sovereignty Jurisdiction," 175.
37. "Rights of the Aboriginal Peoples of Canada," Justice Laws Website, http://laws-lois.justice.gc.ca/eng/Const/page-16.html.
38. R. v. Van der Peet, [1996] 2 S.C.R. 507, https://scc-csc.lexum.com/scc-csc/scc-csc/en/item/1407/index.do.
39. Kiera L. Ladner, "Take 35: Reconciling Constitutional Orders," in *First Nations, First Thoughts: The Impact of Indigenous Thought in Canada*, ed. Annis May Timpson (Vancouver: UBC Press, 2009), 279–300.
40. Harry S. LaForme, "Indian Sovereignty: What Does It Mean?" *Canadian Journal of Native Studies* XI, no. 2 (1991): 253–66.
41. Mary Williams Walsh, "Canada/Indian Sovereignty: Mohawk Unrest Tied to Self Rule: But tribal factionalism hinders quest," *Los Angeles Times*, September 8, 1990, http://articles.latimes.com/1990-09-08/news/mn-530_1_indian-sovereignty.
42. Benjamin Shingler, "The Growing Push by Canada's First Nations for Sovereignty," *Al Jazeera*, September 25, 2014, http://america.aljazeera.com/articles/2014/9/25/first-nations-sovereigntycanada.html.
43. Joint Resolution, "100th Anniversary of the Overthrow of the Hawaiian Kingdom Public Law 103-150, S.J. Res. 19," January 5, 1993, https://www.mauimapp.com/moolelo/apology.htm.
44. J. Kehaulani Kauanui, *Hawaiian Blood: Colonialism and the Politics of Sovereignty and Indigeneity* (Durham, NC: Duke University Press, 2008), 25.

45. The Learning Network, "Jan. 17, 1893: Hawaiian Monarchy Overthrown by America-Backed Businessmen," *New York Times*, January 17, 2012. United States Public Law 103–150, 103d Congress Joint Resolution 19, Nov. 23, 1993, https://www.hawaii-nation.org/publawall.html.

46. Alfred makes the same cultural but the opposite sovereignty claim. For him, "the seriousness of the social ills that do continue" suggests that an externally focused assertion of sovereign power vis-à-vis the state is neither complete nor in itself a solution. The answer lies in "retraditionalization . . . rejection of the legitimacy of the state and recovery of the traditional bases of indigenous political society." See Taiaiake Alfred, "Sovereignty," in Barker, *Sovereignty Matters*, 39–40. See also Davianna Pōmaikaʻi McGregor, "Sovereignty: Hawaiians and Locals," paper presented at the Association of Asian American Studies Conference, University of Michigan, 1994, 12–13.

47. For further elaboration of the concept of refusal, see Simpson, *Mohawk Interruptus*, 2014.

48. Efrén Rivera Ramos, "Deconstructing Colonialism: The 'Unincorporated Territory' as a Category of Domination," in *Foreign in a Domestic Sense*, ed. Christina Duffy Burnett and Burke Marshall (Durham, NC: Duke University Press, 2001), 6, 105, 389.

49. Natsu Taylor Saito, "Asserting Plenary Power over the 'Other': Indians, Immigrants, Colonial Subjects, and Why U.S. Jurisprudence Needs to Incorporate International Law," *Yale Law and Policy Review* 20, no. 2 (2002): 429.

50. Stuart Anderson, "'Pacific Destiny' and American Policy in Samoa, 1872–1899," *Hawaiian Journal of History* 12 (1978): 56.

51. For further context, see Anne Perez Hattori, "Righting Civil Wrongs: The Guam Congress Walkout of 1949," *ISLA: A Journal of Micronesian Studies* 3, no. 1 (1995): 1–27, and *War for Guam* (2015), directed by Frances Negrón-Muntaner, Independent Television Service.

52. İlker Gökhan Şen, *Sovereignty Referendums in International and Constitutional Law* (Cham: Springer, 2014): 127–208, 202.

53. Anna Fifield, "Some in Guam Push for Independence from U.S. as Marines Prepare for Buildup," *Washington Post*, June 17, 2016.

54. Ana M. López and Gabriela Reardon, "Puerto Rico at the United Nations," *NACLA*, https://nacla.org/article/puerto-rico-united-nations.

55. Yarimar Bonilla, *Non-Sovereign Futures: French Caribbean Politics in the Wake of Disenchantment* (Chicago: University of Chicago Press, 2015), 1.

56. Charles Venator-Santiago, "The Results of the 2012 Plebiscite on Puerto Rico's Political Status," *Latino Decisions*, December 28, 2012, http://www.latinodecisions.com/blog/2012/12/28/the-results-of-the-2012-plebiscite-on-puerto-ricos-political-status/.
57. Official ballot, Comisión Estatal de Elecciones, November 6, 2012, http://ww2.ceepur.org/es-pr/Documents/PapeletaModeloPlebiscito12.pdf. The original Spanish reads "un estatus fuera de la Cláusula Territorial de la Constitución de Estados Unidos, que reconozca la soberanía del Pueblo de Puerto Rico."
58. Lyle Denniston, "Opinion Analysis: Setback for Puerto Rico's Independent Powers," *SCOTUSBlog*, June 9, 2016, http://www.scotusblog.com/2016/06/opinion-analysis-setback-for-puerto-ricos-independent-powers/.
59. Lydia Wheeler, "Supreme Court Rules Against Puerto Rico in Double Jeopardy Case," *The Hill*, June 9, 2016, http://thehill.com/regulation/court-battles/282854-supreme-court-rules-against-puerto-rico-in-double-jeopardy-case.
60. Instituto Soberanista Puertorriqueño, "Soberanía Frente al Colonialismo," October 1, 2012 (http://www.soberanista.com/?cat=22). Original Spanish: "Una condición necesaria para la reorganización de nuestra vida colectiva y para nuestra inserción plena en los asuntos de la región y del mundo."
61. "Sectores soberanistas de Puerto Rico preparan campaña para plebiscito de junio," *ElPaís.cr*, March 15, 2017, http://www.elpais.cr/2017/03/15/sectores-soberanistas-de-puerto-rico-preparan-campana-para-plebiscito-de-junio/.
62. Christina Duffy Ponsa, "Are American Samoans American?," *New York Times*, June 8, 2016, https://www.nytimes.com/2016/06/08/opinion/are-american-samoans-american.html.
63. Stefano Varese, "Indigenous Epistemologies in the Age of Globalization," in *Critical Latin American and Latino Studies*, ed. Juan Poblete (Minneapolis: University of Minnesota Press, 2003), 138–53.
64. Hent Kalmo and Quentin Skinner, "Introduction: A Concept in Fragments," in *Sovereignty in Fragments: The Past, Present and Future of a Contested Concept*, ed. Hent Kalmo and Quentin Skinner (Cambridge: Cambridge University Press, 2010), 7.
65. Scott Richard Lyons, "Rhetorical Sovereignty: What Do American Indians Want from Writing?," *College Composition and Communication* 51, no. 3 (2000): 447–68, 449.
66. Michelle H. Raheja, "Reading Nanook's Smile: Visual Sovereignty, Indigenous Revisions of Ethnography, and 'Atanarjuat (The Fast Runner),'" *American Quar-*

terly 59, no. 4 (2007): 1161. Raheja is also building on the term as developed by Jolene Rickard in her seminal essay on Native photography, "Sovereignty: A Line in the Sand," *Aperture* 139 (1995): 50–59. Also, see Robert Allen Warrior, *Tribal Secrets: Recovering American Indian Intellectual Traditions* (Minneapolis: University of Minnesota Press, 1994).

67. Bonilla and Hantel, "Visualizing Sovereignty," 1.
68. Dylan A. T. Miner, *Creating Aztlán: Chicano Art, Indigenous Sovereignty, and Lowriding Across Turtle Island* (Tucson: University of Arizona Press, 2014), 4.
69. Simpson, *Mohawk Interruptus*, 105.
70. Vine Deloria Jr., "Intellectual Self-Determination and Sovereignty: Looking at the Windmills in Our Minds," *Wicazo Sa Review* 13, no. 1 (1998): 26–27.
71. Haunani-Kay Trask, "Feminism and Indigenous Hawaiian Nationalism," in *Feminist Nationalism*, ed. Lois A. West (London: Routledge, 1997, 2013), 196.
72. Alfred, "Sovereignty," 41.
73. Raheja, "Reading Nanook's Smile," 1165.
74. Warrior, *Tribal Secrets*, 101. See also David Martínez, "Neither Chief Nor Medicine Man: The Historical Role of the 'Intellectual' in the American Indian Community," *Studies in American Indian Literature* 26, no. 1 (Spring 2014): 50.
75. Michel Foucault, interviewed by Paul Rabinow and Hubert Dreyfus, "On the Genealogy of Ethics: An Overview of Work in Progress," in *The Foucault Reader*, ed. Paul Rabinow (New York: Pantheon Books, 1984), 334.
76. Georges Bataille, *The Accursed Share*, vols. 2 and 3, *The History of Eroticism* and *Sovereignty* (New York: Zone Books, 1993), 102.
77. Mete Ulaş Aksoy, "Hegel and Georges Bataille's Conceptualization of Sovereignty," *Ege Academic Review* 11, no. 2 (April 2011): 220.
78. Hannah Arendt, *On Violence* (New York: Harcourt, Brace and World, 1970), 30–31.
79. Davide Panagia and Jacques Rancière, "Dissenting Words: A Conversation with Jacques Rancière," *Diacritics* 30, no. 2 (2000): 125.
80. Wendy Brown, *Walled States, Waning Sovereignty* (Cambridge, MA: MIT Press, 2010), 93.
81. Friedrich Balke, "Derrida and Foucault on Sovereignty," *German Law Journal* 6, no. 1 (2005): 83.
82. Jacques Derrida, *The Beast and the Sovereign*, vol. 1, ed. Michel Lisse, Marie-Louise Mallet, and Ginette Michaud, trans. Geoffrey Bennington (Chicago: University of Chicago Press, 2009), 291.

83. Sergei Prozorov, *Foucault, Freedom and Sovereignty* (Aldershot, UK: Ashgate, 2007), 92.
84. Ibid.
85. Derrida, *Beast and the Sovereign*.
86. Jacques Derrida, *Without Alibi*, trans. and ed. Peggy Kamuf (Stanford, CA: Stanford University Press, 2002), xix.
87. Balke, "Derrida and Foucault," 81.
88. Glen Coulthard, "Place Against Empire: Marx, Indigenous Peoples, and the Politics of Dispossession in Northern Canada" (unpublished manuscript, 2010).
89. Stephen John Ford, "Sovereignty: Do First Nations Need It?," IdleNoMore (website), December 23, 2013, 1–2, http://www.idlenomore.ca/sovereignty_do_first nations_need_it.
90. Ladner, "Take 35," 287.
91. Bataille, *Accursed Share*, 23–24.
92. Aksoy, "Hegel and Georges Bataille's Conceptualization," 219.
93. Elisabeth Roudinesco, "Revolution: Jean-Paul Sartre and Jacques Lacan, Alternate Contemporaries," in *Jacques Lacan* (New York: Columbia University Press, 1997), 341.
94. Les W. Field, with Alan Leventhal and Rosemary Cambra, "Mapping Erasure: The Power of Nominative Cartography in the Past and Present of the Muwekma Ohlones of the San Francisco Bay Area," in Den Ouden and O'Brien, *Recognition, Sovereignty Struggles and Indigenous Rights*, 287–309.
95. Wendy Brown, "Rights and Identity in Late Modernity: Revisiting the 'Jewish Question,'" in *Identities, Politics, and Rights*, ed. Austin Sarat and Thomas R. Kearns (Ann Arbor: University of Michigan Press, 1997), 85–103, 89.
96. Anne-Laure Amilhat Szary and Frédéric Giraut, "Borderities: The Politics of Contemporary Mobile Borders," in *Borderities and the Politics of Contemporary Mobile Border*, ed. Anne-Laure Amilhat Szary and Frédéric Giraut (New York: Palgrave Macmillan, 2005), 7.
97. Judith Butler, *Excitable Speech: A Politics of the Performative* (New York: Routledge, 1997), 15–16.

I

Navigating Sovereignty

1

Contested Sovereignties

Puerto Rico and American Samoa

FA'ANOFO LISACLAIRE UPERESA AND
ADRIANA MARÍA GARRIGA-LÓPEZ

The United States is often presented as an exception to the colonial model of state power, at worst an accidental imperialist or master of an "informal empire."[1] Discussions of U.S. involvement in the Philippines, for example, cite the burden of a "reluctant colonialist,"[2] while analysts of U.S. foreign policy have concluded that "empire has remained a mere episode in American foreign policy."[3] Yet a growing body of scholarship argues persuasively that empire is a key feature of U.S. American policy.[4] Scholars have also explored the ways in which zones of political ambiguity engender some possibilities for autonomous action and social production even while recognizing such autonomies as contingent, dependent on, or derivative of hegemonic power structures.[5]

The history of legislation in the United States addressing the territorial and civil rights of Native Americans demonstrates one such set of modalities whereby federal powers attempt to circumscribe the scope and practice of competing sovereignties constituted by specific and organized yet marginalized groups.[6] The terms of such exclusions and contingent inclusions are sites of contestation where the question of what or who makes up a nation or sovereign body is posed through and against the specific consequences of federal legislation, as well as through and against indigenous and/or local terms and conceptual taxonomies. Although debates over autochthony are part of the political landscape in both American Samoa and Puerto Rico, the terms of such debates present different kinds of problems for the enactment of an indigenous or decolonial politics in the twenty-first century and are the manifestations of different (though not unconnected) historical trajectories.[7]

Our collaborative work develops a new line of inquiry within anthropology by putting Samoan and Puerto Rican conceptual taxonomies into conversation with each other within a decolonial analytical framework. Even while emphasizing the comparison between these autochthonous political imaginaries, in this paper we trace some of the zones of attenuated sovereignty produced by the doctrine of territorial unincorporation and its myriad political, economic, and social effects.[8] The doctrine of unincorporation groups a number of different national, geopolitical, and social formations in a "third space" of relationality to the United States.[9] Puerto Rico, Guam, the U.S. Virgin Islands, American Samoa, and the Northern Mariana Islands are all unincorporated territories of the United States; American Sāmoa alone remains unorganized. Interpellated by this logic of disembodied sovereignty and largely ignorant of each other's trajectories within it, the territories are not equalized by such relations but exist instead along an axis of political subjugation even while their inhabitants construct strategies for autonomous expression and action.

The epistemological bases of "sovereignty" as a concept with direct political implications have changed over the twentieth and early twenty-first centuries in large part because of the consequences of political claims made by postcolonial states and societies, historically stateless nations, and indigenous peoples. This transformation of the conventional grounds of sovereignty is increasingly noticeable through the blurred figure of a global body politic whose arbiters are international organizations such as the United Nations, the World Bank, and the World Health Organization, and whose tongue draws its vocabulary from the global discourse of human rights. This shift is therefore representative of a politics of sovereignty that is moving away from concerns with exclusive governmental powers over lands and peoples and toward a pluralist ethic based on a discourse of inalienable ("human") rights that can be mobilized within various possible political manifestations.

Nevertheless, these shifts have not interrupted the term's intimacy with statist ideologies in the sense that sovereignty is still generally understood to be an attribute of states. Increasingly, however, there has been a proliferation of interpretations of the meaning of sovereignty that are not fully determined by the nation-state as an organizing principle or linked to preoccupations with exclusive control over territories and peoples. While the long debate over the legitimate source of sovereign power (God, the crown, the nation, or the people) has never been fully resolved, renewed analyses manifest a concerted interest in the plausible legitimacy of interpretations that posit multiple sovereignties existing in the same place and at the same time, albeit in different forms, some of which may even be at odds with each other or with hegemonic state power structures.

We analyze sovereignty as a discursive and political practice in Puerto Rico and American Samoa through a focus on specific forms of "attenuated sovereignty" enacted in these contexts. In particular, we argue that tropes of coercion and consent are foundational to contemporary interpretations of their status as unincorporated territories of the United States. And yet despite the centrality of notions of consent and coercion to political discourse in both Puerto Rican and American Samoan contexts, the local implications of such terms are distinct and historically specific for each. In our analysis, sovereignty emerges as something less than tangible; rather, it seems a complicated terrain of negotiation shaped by distinct but interrelated historico-political alignments.

Our analysis begins with Puerto Rico, since the early twentieth-century legal challenges to the terms of its colonial attachment to the continental United States shaped the doctrine of (un)incorporation, crafted through the series of Supreme Court cases known as the *Insular Cases*. In this extended historical moment, the United States animated a new national body for itself by insisting on the integrity of the states and preventing the full inclusion of the new territories of empire. We then examine the case of American Samoa and the ways in which the territorial legal framework provided by the *Insular Cases* and other case law has been constructed to both bring the islands under U.S. dominion and provide a space for indigenous social organization and cultural practice. We argue that while the limited application of the U.S.

Constitution in the Puerto Rican context is understood as undermining liberal-democratic processes that would include self-determination as a basic right, in American Samoa this limit is understood as enabling spaces of self-determination and sovereign action according to principles that are external to Western liberal-democratic paradigms (i.e., indigenous sociopolitical organization and practice). This understanding of the meanings and implications of the limited application of the U.S. constitution to its territories constitutes one of the most salient differences between Samoa and Puerto Rico. Imperialist discourses have been and continue to be both accommodated and resisted in order to carve out spaces for self-determination in Samoa and Puerto Rico, reminding us that while the legal arena is one important site of contestation, there are multiple sites for enactments of sovereignty. This is one of the most important commonalities between Samoa and Puerto Rico: ongoing negotiation with U.S. political and economic power represents both a conceptual and literal space of coexistence for the island nations, whose nonvoting representatives share meeting rooms and strategies in Washington. While the doctrine of unincorporation contends with a variegated field of political power, it does not fully circumscribe or exhaust the possibilities for the enactment of sovereignty in the territories.

Bodies for New Organs

Puerto Rico became an unincorporated territory of the United States after the Spanish-American War ended in 1898 and through the twenty-three decisions that make up the legal basis of the doctrine of territorial incorporation (known as the *Insular Cases*). The Treaty of Paris accorded the United States Congress plenary powers over Puerto Rico, Cuba, Guam, and the Philippines, including the right to determine the "civil rights and political status of the native inhabitants of the territories."[10] In the same year, the Treaty of Berlin partitioned the Samoan archipelago into German and American colonies. With this agreement,[11] the United States gained dominion over the islands that would become "American Samoa." Along with Hawai'i (annexed in 1898), these archipelagos are among the first noncontiguous and extracontinental territorial possessions of the United States.

The *Insular Cases* established the doctrine of unincorporation as an instrument of colonial governance that reflected important changes in the United States' global political positioning. By the turn of the twentieth century, all of the continental states were federated, and the United States turned its attention toward the international stage, where it sought to consolidate its position as a global superpower. Cuba and the Philippines attained national independence in 1902 and 1946, respectively, and Hawai'i became a state in 1959. Puerto Rico, Guam, and American Samoa, along with the U.S. Virgin Islands and the Mariana Islands, continue to exist as insular territories governed under the plenary powers of the U.S. Congress. Sovereignty over these territories is normatively understood to reside legally with the U.S. Congress and not with the territories' inhabitants.

In 1900 Congress passed the Foraker Act, which effectively extended all federal laws to Puerto Rico. The Foraker Act also provided for the organization of some local governmental structures, including a popularly elected House of Representatives, a judicial system with an appointed Supreme Court, and a nonvoting Resident Commissioner in Congress. The subsequent adoption of the Jones-Shafroth Act of 1917 conferred U.S. citizenship by birth on all Puerto Ricans at the same time as it formed a popularly elected Senate (aligning the local system to the bicameral legislative assembly system). Yet, residents of Puerto Rico are not eligible to vote in presidential elections. Puerto Rico's governors were appointed by the president of the United States until 1948, when Luis Muñoz Marín became the first democratically elected governor of Puerto Rico.

After the passage of the Puerto Rico Federal Relations Act of 1950, Puerto Ricans held a constitutional convention. In 1952 Puerto Ricans adopted a local constitution and established what is known as the Estado Libre Asociado de Puerto Rico (Associated Free State of Puerto Rico), often mistranslated as "Commonwealth of Puerto Rico." The locus of sovereign power over Puerto Rico, however, was not altered by the adoption of this constitution, which itself had to be ratified (and then only after the excision of some provisions and the significant alteration of others) by the U.S. Congress. The drafting of the Puerto Rican Constitution and the establishment of a democratically elected local government were the direct result of Puerto Rican demands for full political participation, representation, and self-determination. Yet, the adoption and application of that constitution in itself does not constitute a sovereign country or a sovereign people.

At the same time, forms of attenuated sovereignty established by the doctrine of unincorporation and entrenched during the early twentieth century were legitimized by the appearance of consensus created by the great modernist metanarratives mobilized during the Muñocista period on the island. Nationalist sentiment and political unrest were partially defused through the adoption of the Puerto Rican Constitution, and Puerto Rico was removed from the United Nations' list of non-self-governing territories at the request of the United States in 1953.[12]

It is possible to interpret the adoption of the Puerto Rican Constitution as ultimately diminishing the possibilities for insular self-determination insofar as it produces the appearance of self-governance while in reality the Puerto Rican legislature is subject to congressional veto and federal oversight in all aspects of government is unrestricted. Nothing in the Puerto Rican Constitution challenges congressional plenary powers over the island and the constitution may itself be revoked (along with U.S. citizenship) at the discretion of the U.S. Congress.

The establishment of the Estado Libre Asociado created local spheres of political contestation and action, thus responding to and reformulating the discursive arena of political resistance to U.S. colonial rule. But the state formation that emerges from the application of the doctrine of unincorporation is not an emanation of the collective political will of the inhabitants of Puerto Rico; it flows, instead, from the plenary powers held over the island by the U.S. Congress. This is most clearly evidenced by the deletion of articles ratified by the Puerto Rican Constitutional Assembly and removed by the U.S. Congress, which provided for the right to health, housing, and work. Consequently, public health in Puerto Rico has suffered greatly under unfair federal limits, U.S. corporate interests have subjugated the housing and labor markets to the point of crisis, and the political will of Puerto Ricans as expressed during the mid-twentieth-century constitutional assembly has been overridden and ignored. In sum, the Puerto Rican Constitution of 1952 did not alter this (im)balance of power between the United States and Puerto Rico, nor did it shift the locus of state sovereignty, although it provided for more local control over insular affairs.[13]

It was also congressional plenary powers that authorized the passage of the Puerto Rico Oversight, Management, and Economic Stability Act of 2016, otherwise known as PROMESA, which established the Financial Oversight and Management Board ("la Junta de Control Fiscal"). This seven-member board has broad powers over all locally elected representatives and government agencies in Puerto Rico and is tasked with exacting austerity measures to generate payment for bondholders and investors. It is widely expected that these austerity measures will cause great strain on the island population, creating large reductions in the labor pool through increased labor migration and unemployment, and escalating soaring poverty levels, infrastructure decay, and the slashing of public education and health care budgets. Even the U.S. federal health department expressed concern over the possible repercussions of these austerity measures, warning that 900,000 people (or a fourth of the current population) could potentially be left without health insurance coverage by the end of 2017.[14] Beginning around 2009, emigration from Puerto Rico increased to (and has remained at) levels higher than those of the mid-twentieth-century period formerly known as the "great migration."[15] The imposition of PROMESA on the island by the U.S. Congress is the latest expression of this long-standing imbalance of power between Puerto Rico and the United States.

Disembodied

Jurisprudence on Puerto Rican sovereignty continues to be dominated by the territorial logic elaborated in the *Insular Cases*.[16] This view was upheld by the 2007 President's Task Force on Puerto Rico's Status, which found that the Puerto Rican Constitution does *not* provide for an arrangement that would require "mutual consent" in order to alter Puerto Rico's status, political organization, or relationship with the United States.[17] The President's Task Force and the Supreme Court have continued to uphold Congressional plenary powers in force over Puerto Rico (and all territories of the United States). They also point out that the vernacular phrase used to designate the political relation with the United States (the "Associated Free State") is not a nonterritorial status option; it is rather a rhetorical strategy with few implications for the free exercise of political power over Puerto Rican territories. Nevertheless, the existence of a constitution and locally elected government in Puerto Rico are often cited as proof of the fulfillment of the promise of access to the procedures of political self-determination. This serves as a welcome reminder that the juridical view is not the entire story and that the relations of economic and social production that jurisprudence facilitates, protects, and orchestrates must always be read against the limits of its reach.[18]

At the same time, the ambivalences embodied by this legal instrument—unincorporation as congressional doctrine—resulted in an opening of the semiotic field with respect to the imperial powers of the United States wherein new offshore zones of gradated rights were demarcated and put under its "tutelage," supposedly en route to a deferred democracy. This produced a wide and multidirectional debate over the proper categorization of Puerto Rico and American Samoa in their relations with the United States and of the possible short- and long-term futures of these relationships.

According to Judge José A. Cabranes, the doctrine adopted in the *Insular Cases* by the Supreme Court, known as the Territorial Incorporation Doctrine, is "in substance, the set of principles articulated in 1899 by Abbott Lawrence Lowell [then a professor of government and later president of Harvard University] in the pages of the *Harvard Law Review*—an interpretation of provisions of the Constitution."[19] Through this interpretation of the Constitution, Lowell was able to synthesize two seemingly antithetical responses to a question that became paradigmatic in U.S. academic and popular media after the Spanish-American War[20]—"Does the Constitution follow the flag?"[21]

This question was at the center of a full public debate about the management of the new colonies. As Cabranes has pointed out, the issue was the question of

> whether colonialism was consistent with the nation's historical values and constitutional traditions. Would it be possible to administer these colonies without according their peoples the full panoply of rights guaranteed in the Constitution? Were the new colonies part of the "United States," as that term is used in the Constitution, implying that their peoples could claim rights such as the right to trial by jury? . . . In other words, were the people of these new

colonies in any sense "Americans," entitled to the rights of citizens and of others who resided in the "United States"?[22]

Some scholars who sought to answer these questions argued that the newly acquired territories did not come under the jurisdiction of the U.S. Constitution, which in their view only applied to formally "incorporated states" and their residents. This view posited U.S. political control over foreign territories as unencumbered by the political rights of the territories' inhabitants until such time as those territories became incorporated into the federal union.[23]

At the other end of the spectrum, prominent commentators argued that provisions of the U.S. Constitution *did* "follow the flag." Adherents of this view argued that sovereignty over these territories should not reside with the United States, lest it find itself forced to guarantee the protections of the Constitution for subjects considered to be unworthy of such liberties. This latter view is often described as "anti-imperialist," although the objections to a U.S. imperial project from this camp were generally not based on the need to respect any autonomous or sovereign Puerto Rican political community. In other words, though arguments were made in favor of the applicability of the Constitution to the unincorporated territories, this did not in itself constitute recognition of any sovereign Puerto Rican political body. Instead, this view rested on the contemptuous belief that "the necessary application of the Constitution to such peoples" would render the colonies ungovernable, because it would mean the application of the laws of "civilized and educated people" to the "half-civilized" natives and to the miscegenational "lawless brigands that infest Puerto Rico."[24] The full legal and political enfranchisement of Puerto Ricans and other inhabitants of the unincorporated territories under the U.S. flag was to these scholars simply a frightening and unwelcome prospect. Statehood for Puerto Rico is still unpalatable to many in Washington, though the Supreme Court of the United States found in 2016 that Puerto Rico did not constitute an independent legal authority in *Puerto Rico v. Sanchez Valle*.

To return to the *Insular Cases*, which lay at the heart of these matters, Lowell's "third view" produced a political theory that synthesized the debate in a way that he claimed was consistent with "the objectives of a policy of territorial expansion and faithful to past constitutional practice," that is, the notion of territorial unincorporation. It was "a theory asserting that the new colonial territories were indeed different from those acquired earlier in American history and that they could be governed differently."²⁵ Lowell's interpretation made it possible to understand the new territories as sites where the U.S. Constitution did apply but only in an attenuated fashion.

This doctrine of incorporation facilitated the Supreme Court's decision in *Downes v. Bidwell* of 1901 that the people of Puerto Rico would be thenceforth designated as "foreign, in a domestic sense" to the political and social body of the United States. Eventually, this view became official congressional doctrine through a series of precedents set in the *Insular Cases* that are still upheld today, though this consensus is beginning to disintegrate.

However, not everyone agreed with the legal soundness of this solution at the time. In his dissenting opinion with respect to *Downes v. Bidwell* (1901), Justice Melville Fuller wrote,

> The contention seems to be that, if an organized and settled province of another sovereignty is acquired by the United States, Congress has the power to keep it, like a disembodied shade, in an intermediate state of ambiguous existence for an indefinite period; and more than that, that after it has been called from that limbo, commerce with it is absolutely subject to the will of Congress, irrespective of constitutional provisions.²⁶

Fuller's description here of the condition of the unincorporated territories as a "disembodiment" provocatively indexes the obverse process of *in*corporation simultaneously carried out through these decisions. It begins to reveal what the category of the unincorporated conceals—that the development of the category of the unincorporated territory necessitated a preceding step, that is, the consolidation of the forty-eight states as an *in*corporated territory, a process that began with British settler colonialism, included genocide and subordination of indigenous communities in North America, relied for its expansion on transatlantic chattel slavery, and continued through the Monroe Doctrine and Manifest Destiny until the continental expansion of the United States reached approximately its current geopolitical limits.²⁷ If the territories were disembodied, it was not only because they were islands some hundreds or even thousands of miles away from the continental United States. They were so because their inhabitants were very clearly understood not to be part of the U.S. American body politic at the turn of the twentieth century.[28]

The congressional doctrine of incorporation also "constituted a new legal and political subject body: the inhabitant of the unincorporated territory."[29] It reflects the taking on of a new national (U.S.) body, one that included its acquired tropical organs, while denying full political participation in the union to their inhabitants. This new *in*corporation was accomplished through the excision of certain parts and the tenuous suturing on of others. The process of national reconstruction was dependent on the designation of the inhabitants of those territories as "backward races,"[30] listless savages,[31] "incapable of legality and thus essentially criminal";[32] lazy Catholics; "needy children and women in distress";[33] mongrels, mutts; or cannibals. Puerto Ricans and others were discursively animalized and represented as antithetical to the "American way of life." These were subjects seen as undeserving of full democratic participation and self-determination; they were not ready for democracy, at the very least not right away.

Moreover, the *Insular Cases* brought forth what Rivera Ramos has called a "transmutation of the meaning of citizenship in the American political system" whereby "being a citizen was not of itself a sufficient condition to be considered a full member of the political community."[34] Citizenship in the United States had always been constituted through its very negation, that is, through the denial of the full extension of the Constitution of the United States to particular bodies and persons (namely black, brown, indigenous, and nonwhite others). This negation takes a variety of forms, ranging from the absence of all civil rights to selective applications of the U.S. Constitution.

If Puerto Rico and the other island "dependencies" and territories entered a highly differentiated array of political states of being through the doctrine of unincorporation in the early twentieth century, in this process the United States also animated a new national body for itself. This new national body was established and is maintained as an effect of its ties to island organs in the Caribbean Sea and the Pacific Ocean. The sociopolitical spheres of these insular territories are largely disconnected from each other, although they share more than their juridical entrapments, their vulnerability to transnational extractive economies, and the presence of U.S. military installations. These territories are also deeply interconnected through shared histories of travel and labor migration and through their insertion into transnationally affective, symbolic, and material economies.

Authentically Ambivalent

Like Puerto Rico, American Samoa is an unincorporated territory whose legal designation can be traced to the *Insular Cases* and earlier rulings on Native American nations within the continental United States. As American Samoa's former delegate to the U.S. Congress Faleomavaega Eni Hunkin notes, the territory is "unorganized" for lack of an organic act by Congress and "unincorporated" because Congress has never intended nor desired Samoa's membership in the state of the union, as demonstrated historically by U.S. Supreme Court decisions regarding insular territories.[35] As a result of these and subsequent rulings, as well as foundational political arrangements with the United States, not all of the provisions of the U.S. constitution apply: as noncitizen U.S. nationals, American Samoans are not eligible to vote in U.S. general elections but may enter, work, and reside in any of the fifty states.[36] Like Puerto Ricans, American Samoa residents pay local income taxes (not federal income tax) as well as Social Security and employment taxes. American Samoans can also become naturalized citizens of the United States.[37]

The partial application of the U.S. Constitution to unincorporated territories along with the incomplete extension of civil rights to their residents has been read in Puerto Rico as evidence of colonial subjugation. But in American Samoa this is increasingly seen as an important limit to the power of the American legal system and the encroachment of fundamental tenets of American political life that conflict with customary Samoan sociopolitical frameworks and practices.

At different points in the 1900s Samoan leaders explored and then opposed the adoption of organic acts, eventually arguing that incorporation into the U.S. national body in this fashion would endanger both the *fa'asāmoa* and the *fa'amatai*.[38] *Fa'asāmoa* is often translated as "Samoan culture" or "the Samoan way" and refers to Samoan customs and traditions that encompass the *fa'amatai* and other aspects of social organization. The *fa'amatai* (also referred to as the "chiefly system") is the organization of customary authority, a structure of family and village titles linked to control and distribution of land and resources. It is recognized as an indigenous system of governance in which each '*āigapotopoto*, or extended family, invests a member with the responsibility of representing the dignity and honor of the family as well as managing and distributing family resources. Within this chiefly system, individual actions ideally adhere to basic principles of the *fa'asāmoa* and reflect a strong communal and family focus, with *matai* invested with *pule* (authority) over family land and resources and other members of the family providing *tautua* (service) to the *matai* and *āiga* (family) as required.[39]

Historically, local leaders have argued that the absence of U.S. citizenship and selective application of the U.S. constitution prevents radical fragmentation of the *fa'asāmoa* and the customary system of governance known as the *fa'amatai*, both of which are formations of deep symbolic and material significance to the Samoan people. Opposition to further incorporation or codification of the political relationship with the United States can therefore be understood as protecting a form of political organization and social practice seen as central to sustaining Samoan culture and society.[40] In the final report of the American Samoa Future Political Status Study Commission (ASFPSSC) released in 2007, the first component of the main recommendation pointed out the need for a special act by Congress "to reaffirm the special protective provisions for lands and titles in the Constitution of American Samoa."[41] Indicative of the sentiment of many Samoans, the report states, "The Samoan communal way of life is built around the *matai*. For our way of live [sic] to continue, it is absolutely necessary to protect and preserve the integrity of the *matai* system."[42]

Since the entry of the first naval governor, there have been clear conceptions of the legitimacy of *fa'asāmoa* and the *matai* system *and* of American liberal-democratic institutions in American Samoa. As different systems linked to distinct social structures and cultural values, however, their interpenetration was deemed potentially dangerous and seen as needing careful management by both local leaders and colonial agents. Shortly after taking office, Governor Tilley (the first American naval governor to serve in the territory) articulated native policy, declaring "the customs of the Samoans not in conflict with the laws of the United States concerning the naval station shall be preserved unless otherwise requested by the representatives of the people."[43]

This effectively recognized the right of village, county, and district councils to meet and manage affairs according to their customary terms even as it firmly stated the legitimacy of U.S. naval rule.[44] The ensuing dominant narrative of the political history of the territory "entering the modern world" that dominates public affairs is thus one of gradual education in Western political bureaucracy and transition to successful self-government under an American democratic system. Local leaders resisted a rapid transition to American-style institutions; worried about loss of land and cultural practice, they favored a more conservative approach. Meanwhile, in the effort to shore up American authority, colonial agents resisted local leaders' early demands for greater self-governance. Ostensibly, they voiced concern with the corruption of the ideal impersonal liberal bureaucracy by wards who were incapable of administering it,[45] but securing the authority of the naval administration was also a primary concern.

Early recognition of local custom thus served both purposes, allowing the continued (albeit limited) practice of self-governance in the form of customary politics even as it mitigated resistance to an expanding American authority exercised by naval governors.[46] This initial policy was later enshrined in the legal code governing the area. Under naval administration, which ended with the transfer of governmental oversight to the Department of the Interior in 1951, *matai* were integrated at various levels of the administration in a form of indirect rule inspired by British colonial administration in Fiji.[47] The preservation of the majority of Samoan customs as well as the maintenance of local village and district political structures allowed a succession of governors (naval officers, civilians appointed by the Department of the Interior and later locally elected) to draw on indigenous political frameworks in official administration of the territory.[48]

In this process of integration, indigenous political formations have been both actively preserved and significantly transformed as they have been harnessed to the Western-style institutions of governance put in place under American "tutelage." The recognition of local custom as legitimate and worthy of preservation has been reiterated and reformulated through Department of Interior policy and judicial rulings over time. Although it has limits, the very existence of this recognition of the legitimacy of the *fa'asāmoa* and *fa'amatai* is connected to American Samoa's unorganized status and (in the absence of a detailed political compact) sets American Samoa apart from other unincorporated U.S. territories.

Unlike Puerto Rico, whose sovereignty was not recognized by the United States since the island passed from Spanish to U.S. colonial control, Samoan sovereignty and indigenous political structure were recognized by the first commercial agreement between High Chief Mauga and Commander Meade of the United States in 1872 and in the treaty of friendship and protection signed by Chief Le Mamea Maaka and U.S. representatives in Washington in 1878. If in Puerto Rico the Americanization project was underway from early on in the twentieth century, with rapid transformation to a "modern colonial welfare state" through ideological, economic, and coercive means,[49] in American Samoa under naval governance, development efforts were limited to copra production and modest social welfare improvements (e.g., training village nurses and opening a limited number of village schools), and most of these changes were often, though certainly not exclusively, initiated at the request of the local residents.

This slow pace of change bolstered the view that the position of the U.S. government and its naval administration toward American Samoa was "benign neglect" and led at least one journalist to declare Samoa to be America's "shame in the South Seas," alleging that the United States had shirked its responsibilities to the territory.[50] In the context of decolonization movements and independence activism in Western Samoa, this declaration that the United States had abrogated its duty to provide a path of development and modernization for Samoans put pressure on the federal administration and inspired modernization efforts in the form of expanded infrastructure, health, and educational programs under Governor Rex Lee in the 1960s.[51] Since then, federal grant-in-aid has increased steadily while commercial development and investment by U.S. companies (aside from the tuna canneries) has been more measured. More recently, local entrepreneurs have invested in major U.S. franchises and consumer items for retail sale.

This overall ebb and flow of "development" in the islands, the absence of clearly coercive and widespread colonial control, and the recognition and continuation of local custom has reinforced the interpretation of the naval administration's policy as that of benign neglect or banal colonialism that continues as a structuring trope of how the historical relationship with the

United States is understood.[52] Taking into account the massive transformation of other American territories, such as Puerto Rico and Guam, which were powered by military and commercial interests coupled with the history of land expropriation, subjugation, and disenfranchisement of Native Americans and Native Hawaiians, it would be naïve in the extreme to take the recognition of Samoan custom for granted. Indeed, it becomes clear that this recognition of indigenous political structure and practices is never guaranteed; rather, it is an effect of continuous local efforts toward greater sovereignty and of the absence of an overwhelming and compelling American interest in the islands.

The narrative of the beneficial alliance is intimately tied to what are understood to be local practices of self-determination. Precisely because of the anomalous protection of Samoan culture and political practice in U.S. law, many Samoans hold a sedimented conception of the relationship with the United States as fundamentally beneficial and sustained by mutual good will. This is often elaborated in political speeches, elaborate Flag Day celebrations that commemorate the raising of the U.S. flag, and in public discourse about military service and sacrifice.[53] One of the registers in which local assumptions of sovereignty occurs is the land tenure system, in which a majority of land remains communally owned.[54] This is in stark contrast to Puerto Rico and other territories, where land appropriation was one of the first strategies of colonial control.

Land, Political Status, and the Law

Debates over land tenure continue to be one of the most important and visible sites of legal evaluations of political status and the vitality of Samoan sociopolitical organization. Communally held land in American Samoa is an active site of political contestation, with the long-standing threat of individualization of land holdings and trends in that direction recently emergent.[55] Provisions of the United States and American Samoa constitutions conflict in their fundamentally different conceptions of private property, an important consideration in American policy in the territory from the time of the Treaty of Berlin as reflected in the wording of the instruments of cession for Tutuila and Aunu'u[56] and the Manu'a group[57] as well as in explicit naval policy. The 1922 act of Congress that ratified the deeds of cession stated that "The existing laws of the United States relative to public lands shall not apply to such lands in the said islands of eastern Samoa," a nod to the *fa'amatai* and customary practices of land tenure.[58] Furthermore, local views reflect an understanding of the continued existence of the communal land system as largely a result of the application of the American Samoa Constitution rather than the U.S. Constitution. The former states in article I, §3,

> It shall be the policy of the Government of American Samoa to protect persons of Samoan ancestry against the alienation of their lands and the destruction of the Samoan way of life and language, contrary to their best interests. Such legislation as may be necessary may be enacted to protect the lands, customs, culture, and traditional Samoan family organization of persons of Samoan ancestry, and to encourage business enterprises by such persons.

Since land ownership is also tied to blood quantum as a measure of American Samoan ancestry,[59] one concern with the application of the U.S. Constitution is that strict application of the Equal Protection clause of the Fourteenth Amendment would remove such restrictions on land ownership and hasten alienation of land from the indigenous population.[60]

In discussions about the applicability of the U.S. Constitution to unincorporated territories, the Supreme Court has not held a clear position, thus enabling divergent interpretations by the lower courts. The D.C. Circuit court, which has jurisdiction over American Samoa, has adopted the "impractical and anomalous" standard in *King v. Morton* (1975), thereby holding that all constitutional protections of individual rights apply except those deemed to be "impractical and anomalous." In contrast, the Ninth Circuit court, which hears appeals from the Northern Mariana Islands and Guam, adopted the "fundamental" constitutional right application in *Commonwealth of the Northern Mariana Islands v. Atalig* (1984), which reinforces the application of "fundamental" rights only.[61] According to legal scholar Robert A. Katz, the disparate decisions by the two circuits reflect a larger moral debate about the legitimacy of U.S. rule over its territories and the question of "how to justify compelling territorial inhabitants to obey the government of the United States."[62]

The absence of clear Supreme Court rulings on the constitutional question "has enabled lower federal courts to maximize the legitimacy of the United States' authority in each particular territory."[63]

In two landmark cases, *Presiding Bishop v. Hodel* (1987) and *Craddick v. Territorial Registrar* (1980), the court recognized the legal imperative of considering Samoan culture in adjudication as well as the intention to respect local tradition and local land control.[64] The *Bishop* ruling voided a sale of land in Malaeimi to the Mormon Church, upholding the restriction on ownership of native land to those of Samoan ancestry and ruling that the restriction did not violate equal protection doctrine. The *Craddick* ruling also upheld "racial classification" (under "the strictest judicial scrutiny") for purposes of land ownership, noting that "the Territory of American Samoa has demonstrated a compelling state interest in preserving the lands of American Samoa for Samoans and in preserving the Fa'a Samoa, or Samoan culture."[65] Thus, the American policy of "Samoa for Samoans" has been key to the legal protection and preservation of the system of communal land tenure sustaining the *matai* system and inextricable from the *fa'asāmoa* even while American institutions have reshaped sociopolitical life on the island.

Recently, the controversial *Tuaua v. United States* case challenged the relationship between citizenship and political status.[66] The stances taken on the case illustrate the conflicting interpretations of the meaning of U.S. citizenship and the extension of constitutional provisions that have implications for the protection of the customary land and titles system in American Samoa. In 2012 the plaintiffs brought a legal challenge to the U.S. national status of American Samoans, arguing that the Fourteenth Amendment, which extends birthright citizenship across the states, also includes the territory of American Sāmoa and therefore those born in the territory should be U.S. citizens.[67] The United States as defendants, in turn, relied on the legal precedent of the *Insular Cases* to argue that the Fourteenth Amendment did not apply to the territory. Ultimately, "The defendants argued, and the District Court agreed, that the *Insular Cases* absolutely bar constitutional citizenship for those born in the territories."[68] The 2015 judgment did not engage a full analysis of the constitutional question and instead "relied on past practices to avoid the question of citizenship."[69]

In the public realm it was alleged that U.S. national status is second-class citizenship based on racist case law. The case was picked up in mainstream U.S. media, which caricatured the racism that shaped judgments and opinions in the *Insular Cases* while asking how American Samoans were not worthy of citizenship in light of their high rate of military service and integration into countless communities across the United States.[70] While the "second-class citizenship" language deliberately evokes the civil rights voting struggles of the twentieth century, the contexts are not the same. From a local perspective, as sovereign signatories to a treaty with the United States that guaranteed protection of lands and culture and with the spirit of self-determination in international law, the position of the American Samoa Government has been that it is not for the courts to decide such an important issue with potentially wide ramifications but rather that the choice rests with the people of American Samoa and should be pursued through referendums on political status. In line with his long-standing position on the issues, Hon. Faleomavaega Eni Hunkin filed an amicus brief for the defendants, arguing against blanket extension of U.S. citizenship to the territory.[71] His successor, Hon. Aumua Amata Radewagen, was pleased with the judgment, proposing instead to amend the federal Immigration and Nationality Act to streamline the process for U.S. nationals who choose to become citizens.[72] The opposition to extending U.S. citizenship to those born in the territory again rested on the fear that it would invoke the full application of the Constitution, and specifically, the Equal Protection Amendment.[73]

Operating with the political fiction that the governed do in fact consent to a social compact with their government, the choice should reside with the people of American Samoa, but if one adheres to the territorial status subject to U.S. plenary power, it is unclear that it actually does. Faleomavaega had long asserted the need to clarify the legal relationship between the United States and American Samoa, stressing that "in the overall context of the substance of both deeds [of cession], it is clear that both documents clearly reaffirmed United States sovereignty over the two island groups."[74] He argued that the current arrangement that permits largely local governance exists because the United States has not chosen to fully exercise its congressional plenary powers. This leaves the sovereignty of the people of American

Samoa in an ambiguous and unstable position. After closing arguments on the *Tuaua* case, the U.S. Assistant Attorney Wynne P. Kelly filed a letter with the court stating that while Congress has the power to extend citizenship via statute, the will of the American Samoa people does not impinge on the federal government's position on the application of the Citizenship Clause to the territories, thereby marking the preeminent power of the Constitution as the law of the land irrespective of the will of those whom it might encompass.

Some scholars have argued that the island chain could be characterized as an "executive fiefdom" lacking formal democratic sanction because it is governed by the Secretary of the Interior by presidential order and federal statute. Robert A. Katz writes, "From a legal perspective . . . the Secretary [of the Interior] is the sole source of lawful authority on the islands. The people of American Samoa . . . have no acknowledged legal right to govern themselves."[75] Yet many local leaders support maintaining the current ambiguous arrangement precisely because it has allowed for both local self-government through the establishment of executive, judiciary, and legislative branches that promulgate laws and address local affairs and the ongoing governance of the *fa'amatai*. There remains a vibrant and powerful social and political realm outside the letter of the law; for this reason other legal scholars argue that American Samoa is in reality self-governed.[76] Both views are correct: the legal framework conveys authority to the United States and subordinate status to the islands are at the same time that American Samoa is in practice self-governed. Although the ASFPSSC "found the political status to be basically sound,"[77] its main recommendation to maintain the status quo and initiate negotiations for a permanent political status suggests some anxiety about legal standing. As a historical view of American imperial policy clearly demonstrates, if this self-governance is subject to the whims of American courts and the Department of the Interior, its foundation is exceedingly precarious.

These debates are important as sites for deliberation over sovereignty, self-governance, and authority. We have set out the legal debates because they dominate discussions of the locus of sovereignty in American Samoa and serve as focal points for the enforcement of state power, but they remain one aspect of sociopolitical life. It is not our intention to definitively determine whether the archipelago is ultimately a sovereign state or not. In what remains, we explore the different registers in which claims to sovereignty are made or enacted and how Puerto Rico and American Samoa have negotiated the unincorporated category.

Coerced Consensus and Symbolic Memory

In American Samoa, the discursive construction of the relationship with the United States as fundamentally fair and beneficial relies on a selective memory process and a will to forget.[78] In some cases, one can detect what appears to be a willful misrecognition of the current state of affairs. For example, the deeds of cession are often cited as proof of the foundation of the association with the United States being one of voluntary choice. Yet the deeds themselves were a response to the threat of colonial powers in the islands, the partition of the archipelago and imposition of U.S. dominion through the Treaty of Berlin, and the ensuing establishment of the authority of the naval governor, constituting, therefore, what could be called a coerced consensus. This elision of U.S. imperial control has been reproduced in the discursive construction of the political association for more than a hundred years, and it allows the contemporary rejection of the adscription of colonial status to American Sāmoa as irrelevant.

The national narrative of harmonious integration of American and Samoan institutions effectively obscures conflicts stimulated by cultural and economic flows between the United States and the Samoan Islands. These conflicts surface in the continuous analysis, discussion, and mobilization of the *fa'asāmoa* as an ideal and as a set of practices even as its continued existence and relatively successful interface with Western-style institutions has been presented as evidence of a resilient, sovereign practice. And within the *fa'asamoa*, the *matai* system comes to represent an alternative to the Western juridical system at the same time that the combination of the two is interpreted as indigenization of Western institutions. In this sense it is not as Morrison suggests, just "a conflict between culture and political status,"[79] but a conflict over the framework of sociopolitical life, a colonial cleavage that may never be resolved.

If, as some scholars have argued, sovereignty relies on the modern nation-state form, then the *fa'amatai* can be read as exceeding the modern American

Samoan national form. Customary Samoan practices of sovereignty as rooted in the *fa'amatai* are not a state-based phenomenon. Although the *matai* system has evolved while tied to the idea of nationhood for over one hundred years,[80] it remains a symbol and practice of Samoan sovereignty—one that precedes the era of colonization and continues throughout the Samoan Islands, reaching into diasporic communities in the United States, New Zealand, Australia, and beyond. While some contend that practices of self-determination and self-government are being misconstrued as "having sovereignty," within the *fa'amatai* the three are arguably inextricable; the act of exercising *pule* relies on the legitimacy to do so.

Negotiating the Unincorporated Category

While we concur with the assertion that the United States enacts political and economic domination through the creation and flexible maintenance of zones of sovereign ambiguity and gradated rights,[81] relying solely on this analysis obscures how zones of ambiguity and gradated rights are strategically engaged and challenged by inhabitants of such "unincorporated" zones.

In the case of American Samoa, the space provided by the ambiguity present around the question of sovereignty has been filled by a continuous yet evolving indigenous political practice and selective engagement with Western-style institutions. In this context, the unincorporated category enables selective application of American political instruments;[82] thus, the space of ambiguity allows the possibility for cultural considerations to be weighed in legal reasoning. Legal scholar Stanley Laughlin writes,

> Ironically, the incorporation doctrine which originally legitimated popular desire to fulfill America's manifest destiny now provides the theoretical basis for assuring a large measure of territorial self-determination.[83]

Though the category of unincorporation currently functions to provide some measure of autonomy in local self-governance and juridical interpretations of congressional doctrine, the outcome of that flexibility and interpretation are *never guaranteed*. The ambiguity inherent in the category of unincorporation can also function to effectively limit spaces of autonomy and circumscribe expressions of indigenous sovereignty.

That American Samoa is in large part self-governing and its leadership exercises a good measure of self-determination owes a considerable debt to its peculiar strategic location.[84] The islands were originally of interest to the United States because Pago Pago's deepwater harbor could facilitate trade and military objectives. Currently, it is of less interest than other islands such as Guam (where the U.S. military controls 39 percent of the land[85] and is embarking on a multibillion dollar redevelopment that includes moving five thousand Okinawa-based Marines and their families to Guam[86]) or the Marshall Islands (where the United States leases islands for missile testing), and thus there is less impetus for direct, present, and active U.S. control. Still, as one of the top recruiting stations per capita in the nation, it remains of value to the U.S. military.

While Puerto Rico's geographic location in the northeastern Caribbean is still strategically advantageous for the United States (due to its proximity to Florida and the southern states), it is not as militarily significant as it was during the period of European colonialism, when the United States was primarily concerned with European interventions in or invasions of its territories. During the Second World War, Puerto Rico became the showcase of American beneficence and modernization efforts, and its rapid industrialization was intended to dissuade other Latin American and Caribbean countries from communist or revolutionary aspirations. This model of economic development in Puerto Rico has been a disastrous failure, with relative increases in quality of life standards, until recently, masking the ongoing expropriation and pollution of land and other natural resources as well as the consolidation of an unsustainable credit and consumer goods market. Alongside these, high unemployment rates and dependence on precarious public assistance programs (themselves again subject to unequal application in the territories) continually plague the island.

Glenn Petersen has argued that "small countries in especially strategic positions cannot operate entirely independently of those who define their position as strategic, so they must finesse the possibilities they do have for autonomy."[87] In his analysis, he notes that "sovereignty, as an abstract or purely legalistic category is, as many Micronesians recognize, irrelevant." Instead, "the insistence on and pursuit of" sovereignty is central for inhabitants of these countries because "it is in the careful exploitation of their equivocal political status that these peoples can work to establish as many of the terms of their own destiny as possible."[88] While we agree with this conclusion, we diverge from his view that sovereignty, even as a formal or purely legalistic category, is irrelevant. We think it is quite relevant; however, it remains only one aspect of a robust political sphere.

It is unlikely that a majority of the island population in American Samoa would favor aligning the local system completely with the American one, and this undoubtedly includes the full imposition of a rights discourse rooted in an individualist Western enlightenment tradition. Yet not all elements of this tradition are rejected as foreign and inappropriate. Rather, American Samoans have historically been concerned with how the relationship with the United States affects local culture and social systems while selectively agitating for greater participation in Western-style institutions.

At the Caribbean Decolonization seminar held in Havana, Cuba, in May of 2001, Samoan governor Tauese P. F. Sunia and congressional delegate Eni F. H. Faleomavaega protested the "mischaracterization of American Samoa as a colony" and noted the existence of a locally elected legislature, governor, and lieutenant governor as well as a local constitution and the fact that "the people of American Samoa had never had their rights suppressed." The governor's assertions may not be completely accurate,[89] but they reflect a particular characterization of the relative balance of power between the islands and the United States that has been discursively reproduced and solidified over time. While some form of indigenous social structure has been maintained, other aspects of U.S. social and political life have been integrated. This integration has been facilitated by American policy, but local participation casts it as both inevitable and positive, because a return to subsistence economies on a wide scale is neither likely nor seen as desirable.

Like many former colonies across the Pacific, American Samoa has limited opportunities for economic prosperity (as defined by contemporary development paradigms). Its position in the American (and global) economy is that of a weak partner whose main exports are canned fish and a transnational migrant labor force. The higher standard of living that people enjoy relative to their counterparts in independent Samoa is supported by continuous migration to the United States, remittances from family members in the United States, and monetary aid from the federal government.[90] However, the wealth generated through labor migration is not understood as dependency but as recompense.

The "benign neglect" of the United States, and the existence of a large state bureaucracy sustaining approximately a third of the working population,[91] has led some to suggest that American Samoans should be grateful for their "free lunch." Yet this obscures what the U.S. receives in return: a foothold in the South Pacific, access to the best deepwater harbor in the area for military and commercial purposes, a high rate of military enlistment,[92] almost unlimited access to cheap local and migrant labor, exclusive economic zones for fishing purposes, and control over the territory. For many American Samoans, the "largesse" received through the relationship with the United States—in the form of higher standards of living, employment and migration opportunities, infrastructure investment, and access to consumer goods—can be understood as appropriate reciprocal contributions rather than welfare.

The dominant local narrative of strategic integration supports the view that residents *chose and continue to consent* to this relationship. Samoans thus rely (largely, though not exclusively) on a discourse of continuously evolving indigenous political practice that encompasses the choice to become an unincorporated territory of the United States. As a native Samoan political gnosis,[93] however, the *fa'amatai* is not derived from, reducible to, nor fully circumscribed by U.S. constitutional frameworks. While the majority of Puerto Ricans see the withholding of full constitutional rights to Puerto Rico as positive proof of the island's colonial status, many Samoans point to this limit as proof that Samoa is *not* a U.S. colony.

In American Samoa, the effort to build consensus among *matai* has framed the association with the United States as voluntary and the product of a sovereign choice. In Puerto Rico, framing the island's association with the United States as a "choice" elides the fact that it was a spoil of war, and thus the operative political logic in annexation was conquest, not consent. Puerto Ricans have not held formal state sovereignty over their nation at any point in history. A discourse of voluntary association with the United States was solidified through the Free Associated State (Estado Libre Asociado) model in the 1950s after the signing of the Puerto Rican Constitution and to some degree still operates today, but as Cabranes notes, "it bears emphasizing that a remarkably broad consensus for change and constitutional reform exists in Puerto Rico."[94] The reality of this anticolonial consensus has only become more solidified in recent years through the deepening of a political economic crisis on the island. Cabranes argues that

> Puerto Ricans do share a common goal of seeing Puerto Rico evolve, by mutual consent, toward a greater measure of control over its own destiny. For a great many, this means statehood or some form of political autonomy. For others, far fewer in number, independence. . . . In short, it is fair to say that *all* of Puerto Rico's political movements seek to chart a path toward a postcolonial future, whatever form it may take. The central political problem of Puerto Rico remains, as ever, decolonization and how it is to be fully achieved.[95]

The Puerto Rican political sphere contains antagonistic and even contradictory claims as to the meaning of decolonization and self-determination, but there is a consensus on the need for decolonization. And across these paradoxical domains of political discourse, Puerto Ricans claim spaces of autonomous practice (or stage particular enactments of counternormative consensus) that cut across or multiply refract the political divides of "status options."

On Sovereignty, Indigeneity, and Political Imaginaries

We understand that "choice" is not a transcendental capacity and that continuity of practice does not represent a seamless trajectory of subjectivity. Instead, the subject of choice that emerges in these relationships is deeply ideological. Deconstructing choice and consent requires that we look at the conditions that enable or deny particular choices or interpretations to emerge within specific historical and imperial contexts.

The consent of American Samoans was produced through processes of decision making that made up the constrained collective agency of Samoans and are understood to express their sovereign will as a people.[96] Throughout those processes, Samoans also endeavored to retain zones of autonomy and self-determination within the limits legally imposed by unincorporation. Meanwhile, the limits themselves were conditioned in part by U.S. governance of Native peoples and overseas territories that relied on what Simpson and Smith call "forms of ethnographic entrapment" to substantiate certain kinds of recognition: conforming to paradigms of authenticity in order to be eligible for legal recognition.[97] Thus, a crucial difference between the political imaginaries of American Samoa and Puerto Rico is the *fa'asāmoa*. For American Samoans, this *fa'a*, *way*, or *gnosis*[98] represents an indigenous sociopolitical tradition to draw from that both organizes social life and serves as a bulwark against U.S. colonial law.

In contrast, we can say that there is no *fa'aboricua*, no historically continuous and specifically political tradition rooted in Taíno culture for Puerto Ricans to enact legally as a limit to U.S. colonial domination. We may find recourse in the surviving fragments of indigenous traditions for Puerto Rican claims to sovereignty over lands and resources, but there is very little politically speaking that survives from the time of Borikén, when no Puerto Ricans existed. As anthropologist Jorge Klor de Alva states, "many places in the world, such as Bali or the Caribbean after the sixteenth century, do not have a way to articulate a category that could have any force to it of 'indigenous.'"[99] This has been true about indigeneity in Puerto Rico until recently, when some cultural organizations have sought to revive the sociopolitical relevance of Taíno indigenous identity. This cultural resurgence is a labor of reconstruction, as Taíno cultural materials are loose and complex fragments from which to derive a social order.[100] As scholars have shown, identity politics in Puerto Rico are deeply shaped by notions of race and identity based in hegemonic U.S. ethnic relations, and this is no less true with regards to indigeneity.[101]

Klor de Alva represents a dominant mode of thought in Puerto Rico and elsewhere: that modern indigeneity is a category of identification accessible in the absence of large-scale genocide (the kind that unravels the fabric of society) and tenable only when the communities in question have been able to sustain at least some coherent social structures. One problem with Klor de Alva's argument is that indigeneity has been and continues to be extremely important as an organizing medium for political contestation in Latin American and Caribbean societies, even where its applicability does not seem immediately evident or transparent.

While some Puerto Ricans may claim indigenous Taíno identity, their claims are only tangentially relevant to the larger Puerto Rican political sphere, because it is widely believed that claiming indigeneity presupposes longstanding genealogical claims to land and community that are mostly at odds with the violent creolization process at the heart of most Caribbean social history. With the exception of some areas in the mountainous interior of the big island and perhaps in smaller keys offshore, it is generally accepted that the scope and extent of the genocide carried out by Spanish conquistadors changed irrevocably the political and social structures of Taíno life to the point of elimination. Arguably, Taíno cultural elements remain very important as acknowledged and celebrated parts of contemporary Puerto Rican social life, including language, diet, emplacement, and identity. However, many view the largely diasporic Puerto Ricans organizing themselves on the basis of their self-identification strictly as indigenous Taínos with derision or outright disbelief, as their claims are seen as largely incongruous with island social realities, and the colonial interruption of Taíno life is understood as evidence of the falsity of these claims. Here the indigenization of local politics that responds to the successful mobilization of indigeneity in the international political arena remains caught in a colonial contradiction and paradox of recognition in the present moment.

Yet some of these groups include people who have been part of return migrations to the islands. In that sense, Taíno revivalism goes beyond the merely symbolic appropriation of Taíno elements within Puerto Rican nationalism. Déborah Berman Santana states:

> [T]he "Taíno revival" went public in 1992 during "500 years of resistance," the anticolonial response to the quincentennial celebration of Columbus' first voyage to the Western Hemisphere. These organizations are dedicated to refuting the dominant view that Taínos ceased to exist centuries ago[,] asserting their continuous existence up to the present—albeit in disjointed and isolated fragments, and until recently only in private. They seek to establish bases for legitimate claims to Taíno ethnic identity; in addition, they work to obtain official recognition by municipal, state, tribal, and federal governments as well as from international bodies.[102]

Where contemporary symbolic and sociopolitical appropriations (and perhaps not only nationalist ones) continue to imbue Taíno historical and cultural fragments, identities, and materials with power, they are reinvigorated with political life and possibility.[103] Therefore, we resist the move toward ethnographic entrapment and wish to recognize the potential validity and usefulness of the terms of indigeneity for some Puerto Ricans. At the same time, we reject the demand for a blood-quanta-driven, racialist "authenticity" that federal legislation and oversight of tribal and indigenous affairs would mandate and to which many groups seeking recognition as Native Americans have been compelled to conform.[104] It remains evidently quite possible for political claims made on the basis of a *resurgent* or what we might call a *fugitive indigeneity* to have political "force" in Puerto Rico, the Caribbean, and beyond.

This force is due in part to a network of activists and movements for indigenous rights and resistance to social, linguistic, and landed dispossession around the world. These global movements have also driven the recognition of indigeneity as a political category with claims to rights on an international scale (especially after the 2007 adoption of the United Nations' Declaration of the Rights of Indigenous Peoples). As discourses of indigeneity expand and diversify, we see a proliferation of engagements with indigeneity as a political modality through which claims to sovereignty may gain traction in Puerto Rico.

This raises some issues that deserve further attention. For example, Berman Santana notes, "some express concern about DNA testing in Puerto Rico to attempt to distinguish indigenous from African ancestry as well as about the emphasis placed by some Taíno activists on 'Taíno physical appearance' (i.e., not Black); accordingly, they question whether Taíno revival is yet another attempt to de-Africanize Puerto Ricans."[105] Like the grand nationalist narrative of creolization as unification represented by the notion of the "great Puerto Rican family" (*la gran familia puertorriqueña*), claims to indigeneity also subsume African heritage or the perceived blackness of Puerto Ricans. The use of DNA testing to substantiate indigenous identities has stimulated vigorous debate,[106] and enactments of indigeneity driven by antiblack politics are deeply troubling. While we recognize the labor of love and humanity entailed in creating autonomous and anti-imperialist social worlds and potential indigenous futures, they cannot be built on other kinds of inequalities.

In his influential and hotly debated 2002 book, *Nación postmortem*, historian Carlos Pabón argued forcefully that the elaboration of political possibilities with regard to Puerto Rico's future has been overdetermined by the status issue.[107] He states, "if it doesn't have to do with *status*—with independence, statehood, or autonomy—it's not political." His argument points to the ways in which statist discourses privileging the terms of citizenship and civil rights in Puerto Rico exist mostly as discourses about Puerto Rico's relationship to the United States. However, there is very little elaborated in the formal political sphere in terms of an autochthonous sociopolitical future for the island, and decolonization exists, but only as a quotidian practice. We concur with Pabón that focusing on the "status question" as the only analytical frame for Puerto Rico (and American Samoa) limits the possibilities for political imagination and action. But, we also recognize the ways in which the political status of the unincorporated territories is a major determining factor in the landscape of our political action.

We argue that a radical, or at least radically fragmentary,[108] position and disposition articulated on the basis of an opposition to the role of the United States in contemporary structures of global capitalism and military might, and to the racist subjugation of peoples in its internal and external imperial peripheries, may enable simultaneous spheres of political action and sovereignty across geopolitical divides. Our hope is that local struggles can be analytically articulated with global forces and formations in such a way as to sustain autonomous political expressions that address but are not entirely circumscribed by the conventional terms of the status debate.

Conclusion

In their contemporary relationships to the United States, Puerto Rico and American Samoa are in similarly liminal positions. It is crucial to understand their simultaneous histories of colonization and of U.S. expansionism as constitutive of each other discursively and materially. Yet, U.S. policy toward

American Samoa and Puerto Rico is shaped by different ethnographic imaginaries about their inhabitants.[109] Samoans were understood as authentic, noble savages with developed, "ancient," and respectably elaborate political systems and social protocols; Puerto Ricans were seen as degenerate and miscegenational "mongrels" existing in a state of colonial backwardness and stagnation.[110] Despite these differences in American ethnographic imaginaries of Samoans and Puerto Ricans, the conclusion drawn was the same—local inhabitants could fulfill possibilities for political subjectivity only under conditions of American tutelage and through concerted processes of modernization. Thus, American Samoa and Puerto Rico were both "unmodern"; the former through perceived noble savagery and alterity and the latter through an assumed miscegenation and racial infirmity. Modernization, as Ann Stoler and Carol McGranahan suggest, exists in a continuous state of deferral.

"Consent" as a historical event in American Samoa was produced by the elision of U.S. dominion and the force of plenary doctrine. We argue that the narrative of consent is related to apprehending the extension of U.S. control to the Samoan Islands in a way that allows for empowerment rather than subjugation and reflects efforts to shape the terms of engagement with an imperial modernity. While efforts to shape the terms of engagement with U.S. imperialism are also evident in the history of Puerto Rican politics, constitutionalism as a foundational state practice reinforced plenary doctrine while also generating a broad social consensus. Accusations of political opportunism hurled at Puerto Ricans play on racialized imaginaries and obscure how Puerto Rican political self-determination has been concertedly foreclosed.

We have explored how imperialist discourses were and continue to be both accommodated and contested in order to carve out spaces for self-determination in American Samoa and Puerto Rico. This collaborative project explores the possibilities offered by translocal analysis, including the nurturing of solidarities across cultural, historical, and analytic divides.[112] Puerto Rico and American Samoa's political histories and destinies are bound together by the U.S. congressional doctrine of unincorporation, making such translocal analyses of U.S. imperial formations and the building of solidarities across differentiated zones of attenuated sovereignty urgently necessary. Moving away from the hegemonic narrative of state-based sovereignty, we have explored some multiply emergent and often contradictory expressions of sovereignty in Puerto Rico and American Samoa, highlighting the ways in which political practice is not fully circumscribed by legal doctrine. This analysis contradicts the view of sovereignty as a settled structure of legal right and authority; rather, contested sovereignties are entangled, unstable, and contingent on the power dynamics at play as well as the specific imaginaries of community and belonging mobilized within any given set of sovereign acts.

Notes

An abbreviated version of this paper was presented at the "Sovereignty Matters" conference sponsored by Columbia University on April 15, 2005. The authors thank Glenn Petersen for his careful reading and generous comments on an earlier draft; Hokulani Aikau, Nicholas DeGenova, Partha Chatterjee, Neni Panourgiá, Antonio Lauria-Perricelli, and J. Kehaulani Kauanui for their feedback and encouragement; Frances Negrón-Muntaner for organizing this volume; and all the conference participants for their thoughtful engagement.

1. Howard Zinn, *A People's History of the United States: 1942–Present* (New York: HarperCollins, 2003), 294, and Soma Hewa, *Colonialism, Tropical Disease, and Imperial Medicine: Rockefeller Philanthropy in Sri Lanka* (Lanham, MD: University Press of America, 1995), 13.
2. Jean Heffer, *The United States and the Pacific: History of a Frontier* (Notre Dame, IN: University of Notre Dame Press, 2002).
3. Klaus Schwabe, "The Global Role of the United States and Its Imperial Consequences, 1898–1973," in *Imperialism and After: Continuities and Discontinuities*, ed. W. J. Mommsen and J. Osterhammel (Boston: Allen and Unwin, 1986), 29.
4. Amy Kaplan and Donald E. Pease, eds., *Cultures of United States Imperialism* (Durham, NC: Duke University Press, 1993); Alyosha Goldstein, ed., *Formations of United States Colonialism* (Durham, NC: Duke University Press, 2014).
5. See, e.g., Arlene Dávila, *Sponsored Identities: Cultural Politics in Puerto Rico* (Philadelphia: Temple University Press, 1997).

6. For analyses of federal jurisprudence with regard to Native Americans, see, e.g., Vine Deloria Jr. and David E. Wilkins, *Tribes, Treaties, and Constitutional Tribulations* (Austin: University of Texas Press, 1999); Petra T. Shattuck and Jill Norgren, *Partial Justice: Federal Indian Law in a Liberal Constitutional System* (Providence, RI: Berg, 1993); David E. Wilkins, *American Indian Sovereignty and the U.S. Supreme Court: The Masking of Justice* (Austin: University of Texas Press, 1997).
7. On "decolonial ethics" see Nelson Maldonado Torres, *Against War: Views from the Underside of Modernity (Latin America Otherwise)* (Durham, NC: Duke University Press, 2008).
8. Ann Laura Stoler, "On Degrees of Imperial Sovereignty," *Public Culture* 18 (2006): 125–46, argues that the United States enacts political and economic domination through the creation and flexible maintenance of zones of ambiguity and gradated rights. Stoler describes the constellation of sovereign ambiguities produced by the doctrine of unincorporation as a set of "imperial formations" that create zones of "attenuated sovereignty."
9. See Kevin Bruyneel *The Third Space of Sovereignty: The Postcolonial Politics of U.S.-Indigenous Relations* (Minneapolis: University of Minnesota Press, 2007), for an elaboration of indigenous resistance in the third space on the borders of colonial rule.
10. Treaty of Paris cited in Matthew Frye Jacobson, *Barbarian Virtues: The United States Encounters Foreign Peoples at Home and Abroad, 1876–1917* (New York: Hill and Wang, 2000), 239.
11. Subsequent cession/treaty documents were signed by local leaders of Tutuila and Aunu'u on April 17, 1900, and the Manu'a Islands on July 14, 1904.
12. It is important to note that the United Nations did not apply its full list of criteria to determine whether Puerto Rico should be considered self-governing when it removed Puerto Rico from the list of non-self-governing territories in 1953. Every year since then Puerto Ricans have petitioned the UN to put Puerto Rico back on the list of non-self-governing territories.
13. The overarching preponderance in legal doctrine of established interpretations of the Territorial Clause of the U.S. Constitution was reiterated in 1997 when the House Committee on Resources stated that "Puerto Rico's current status does not meet the criteria for any of the options for full self-government" because

Congress holds power over it under the Territorial Clause. "Puerto Rico Status Field Hearing," Committee on Resources, U.S. House of Representatives, 105th Cong. (April 19, 1997).

14. José A. Delgado, "Salud federal emite informe sobre los retos en Puerto Rico," *El Nuevo Día* (San Juan), January 12, 2017.

15. Jens Manuel Krogstad, "Historic Population Losses Continue Across Puerto Rico," Pew Research Center, *Fact Tank*, March 24, 2016, http://www.pewresearch.org/fact-tank/2016/03/24/historic-population-losses-continue-across-puerto-rico/.

16. On the Insular Cases and the doctrine of incorporation, see Christina Duffy-Burnett and Burke Marshall, eds., *Foreign in a Domestic Sense: Puerto Rico, American Expansion, and the Constitution* (Durham, NC: Duke University Press, 2001).

17. Report by the President's Task Force on Puerto Rico's Status (December 2007).

18. A recent decision by Judge Gustavo A. Gelpí provides one example of how juridical spaces are zones of contestation against established interpretations. In his controversial opinion, Judge Gelpí states, "Supreme Court jurisprudence treating Puerto Rico disparately from the States premised on the Insular Cases doctrine is anachronistic and, thus, no longer applicable." United States District Court of Puerto Rico, Consejo de Salud Playa de Ponce v. Johnny Rullán, Civil Case nos. 06–1260 and 06–1524 (GAG), October 10, 2008, p. 1. Because the Insular Cases continue to be used as precedent for many cases, including those pertaining to Guantánamo Bay, it seems unlikely that the doctrine of incorporation will be abandoned anytime soon.

19. See Abbott Lawrence Lowell, "The Status of Our New Possessions: A Third View," *Harvard Law Review* 13 (1899): 155–76.

20. See Lanny Thompson, "The Imperial Republic: A Comparison of the Insular Territories Under U.S. Dominion after 1898," *Pacific Historical Review* 71 (2002): 535–74.

21. William H. Rehnquist, "The Supreme Court in the Nineteenth Century," *Journal of Supreme Court History* 27 (2002): 12.

22. José A. Cabranes, "Puerto Rico: Colonialism as Constitutional Doctrine," *Harvard Law Review* 100 (December 1986): 454.

23. These logics were also foundational for the Guantánamo Bay Detention Camp in Guantánamo, Cuba.

24. Simeon Baldwin, quoted in Cabranes, "Puerto Rico," 455.
25. Ibid., 457.
26. Fuller quoted in Natsu Taylor Saito, "'Like a Disembodied Shade': Colonization and Internment as the American Way of Life," *Bad Subjects*, no. 71 (December 2004): 1.
27. In this regard, see especially Brook Thomas, "A Constitution Led by the Flag: The Insular Cases and the Metaphor of Incorporation," in *Foreign in a Domestic Sense*, ed. Christina Duffy-Burnett and Burke Marshall (Durham, NC: Duke University Press, 2001), 82–103.
28. On Alaskan sovereignty debates, see David S. Case and Anne D. Shinkwin, *Alaska Natives and American Laws* (Fairbanks: University of Alaska Press, 2002). On Hawai'i, see Haunani-Kay Trask, *From a Native Daughter: Colonialism and Sovereignty in Hawai'i* (Honolulu: University of Hawaii Press, 1999); J. Kehaulani Kauanui, "Colonialism in Equality: Hawaiian Sovereignty and the Question of U.S. Civil Rights," *South Atlantic Quarterly* 107, no. 4 (Fall 2008): 635–50; Rob Wilson, *Reimagining the American Pacific: From South Pacific to Bamboo Ridge and Beyond* (Durham, NC: Duke University Press, 2000), chap. 2; Jodi A. Byrd, *The Transit of Empire: Indigenous Critiques of Colonialism* (Minneapolis: University of Minnesota Press, 2011), chap. 5; and David Keanu Sai, "Slippery Path Towards Hawaiian Indigeneity: An Analysis and Comparison between Hawaiian State Sovereignty and Hawaiian Indigencity and Its Use and Practice in Hawai'i Today," *Journal of Law and Social Challenges* 10 (2008): 68.
29. E. Rivera Ramos, "Deconstructing Colonialism: The 'Unincorporated Territory' As a Category of Domination," in Duffy-Burnett and Marshall, *Foreign in a Domestic Sense*, 107.
30. Matthew Frye Jacobson, *Barbarian Virtues: The United States Encounters Foreign Peoples at Home and Abroad, 1876–1917* (New York: Hill and Wang, 2000), 222.
31. Juan F. Perea, "Fulfilling Manifest Destiny: Conquest, Race, and the Insular Cases," in Duffy-Burnett and Marshall, *Foreign in a Domestic Sense*, 157.
32. Mark S. Weiner, "Teutonic Constitutionalism: The Role of Ethno-Juridical Discourse in the Spanish-American War," in Duffy-Burnett and Marshall, *Foreign in a Domestic Sense*, 49.
33. Kelvin A. Santiago-Valles, *"Subject People" and Colonial Discourses: Economic Transformation and Social Disorder in Puerto Rico, 1898–1947* (Albany: State University of New York Press, 1994), 63.

34. Rivera Ramos, "Deconstructing Colonialism," 107.
35. Eni F. H. Faleomavaega, *Navigating the Future: A Samoan Perspective on U.S.-Pacific Relations* (Carson, CA: KIN Publications, 1995), 36.
36. United Nations, Special Committee on the Situation with regard to the Implementation of the Declaration on the Granting of Independence to Colonial Countries and Peoples, A/AC.109/2004/6, General Assembly, Distr.: General, March 16, 2004, para. 6.
37. Faleomavaega, *Navigating the Future*, 12.
38. American Samoa Legislature, *A 40-Year History of the Legislature of American Samoa* (Pago Pago: Fono of American Samoa Press, 1998); Sean Morrison, "Foreign in a Domestic Sense: American Samoa and the Last US Nationals," *Hastings Constitutional Law Quarterly* 41 (Fall 2013): 87.
39. For further discussion of the *fa'asamoa* and *fa'amatai*, see Elise Huffer and Asofou So'o, eds., *Governance in Samoa* (Canberra, ACT: Asia Pacific Press, Australian National University; Suva, Fiji: Institute of Pacific Studies, University of the South Pacific, 2000).
40. We are aware that a more cynical analysis might also suggest that the effort to limit federal authority and oversight while investing more authority in local *matai* is a move to shore up a threatened hierarchy. However, we are more interested in the widespread and deep connection to the *fa'amatai* and *fa'asamoa* as twin pillars of Samoan cultural practice and identity. See Stephanie Lawson, *Tradition Versus Democracy in the South Pacific: Fiji, Tonga, and Western Samoa* (New York: Cambridge University Press, 1996) for a consideration of the strategic use of tradition to bolster elite power.
41. American Samoa Future Political Status Study Commission (ASFPSSC), *The Future Political Status Study Commission of American Samoa: Final Report* (Pago Pago: American Samoa Government, 2007). The report's main recommendation is that "American Samoa shall continue as an unorganized and unincorporated territory and that a process of negotiation with the U.S. Congress for permanent political status be initiated" (43).
42. Ibid., 48.
43. American Samoa Legislature, *A 40-Year History*, 14.
44. Felix Maxwell Keesing, *Modern Samoa: Its Government and Changing Life* (London: Allen and Unwin, 1934), 201.

45. This view is clearly stated in communication between naval governors and local leaders as well as communication between naval governors and Department of the Interior staff, excerpts of which appear in American Samoa Legislature, *A 40-Year History*. In *Modern Samoa*, Keesing echoes this sentiment.
46. Keesing, *Modern Samoa*, 200. See also Karen Armstrong, "American Exceptionalism in American Samoa," *Suomen Antropologi: Journal of the Finnish Anthropological Society* 33 (Summer 2008): 49–69, on imperialist activities and militarization in American Samoa. Customs that clearly conflicted with naval ordinance or American sensibilities were prohibited under the authority of the governor.
47. Julian Go, "The Provinciality of American Empire: 'Liberal Exceptionalism' and U.S. Colonial Rule, 1898–1912," *Comparative Studies in Society and History* 49, no. 1 (2007): 84, 89.
48. Dan Taulapapa McMullin, "The Passive Resistance of Samoans to U.S. and Other Colonialisms," in *Sovereignty Matters: Locations of Contestation and Possibility in Indigenous Struggles for Self-Determination*, ed. Joanne Barker (Lincoln: University of Nebraska Press, 2005), 109–22.
49. See Pedro A. Cabán, *Constructing a Colonial People: Puerto Rico and the United States, 1898–1932* (Boulder, CO: Westview Press, 1999) on Americanization, and Rivera Ramos, "Deconstructing Colonialism," 109, on the "modern colonial welfare state."
50. See J. A. C. Gray, *Amerika Samoa: A History of American Samoa and Its United States Naval Administration* (Annapolis, MD: United States Naval Institute, 1960), and Clarence Hall, "Samoa: America's Shame in the South Seas," *Reader's Digest*, July 1961.
51. See Fa'anofo Lisaclaire Uperesa, "Seeking New Fields of Labor: Football and Colonial Political Economies in American Samoa," in *Formations of United States Colonialism*, ed. Alyosha Goldstein (Durham, NC: Duke University Press, 2014), 207–32, for more detail on this period of transformation for Tutuila Island.
52. Go, "Provinciality of American Empire," 90.
53. E.g., see the reprinted text of Governor Tauese Sunia's speech at the centennial Flag Day celebration of American Sāmoa as a United States territory in J. Robert Shaffer, *American Samoa: 100 Years Under the United States Flag* (Honolulu: Island Heritage, 2000), 204.

54. "American Samoa," U.S. Department of the Interior, https://www.doi.gov/oia/islands/american-samoa, states that 90 percent of the land remains communally owned. However, the American Samoa, Department of Commerce, Statistics Division, *American Samoa Statistical Yearbook* (Pago Pago: American Samoa Government, 2012), 78, notes the following: freehold (13.6 percent), government owned (21 percent), church owned (13.1 percent), individually owned (25.7 percent), and communally owned (26.6 percent), http://www.doc.as/wp-content/uploads/2011/06/2012-Statistical-Yearbook-1.pdf. These reflect new categories of land tracked by the Office of the Territorial Registrar.
55. For trends of individualization of land in American Samoa, see Merrily Stover, "Individual Land Tenure in American Samoa," *Contemporary Pacific* 11 (Spring 1999): 69–104. The ASFPSSC, *Future Political Status Study*, 47, acknowledges the threat of individualization of land to prevailing communal land tenure and states, "To preserve the core of the Samoan system, individualization of lands must cease."
56. Faleomavaega, *Navigating the Future*, 24. See also the American Samoa Bar Association website for the wording of the Tutuila and Aunuʻu cession documents, http://www.asbar.org/index.php?option=com_content&view=article&id=1950:cession-of-tutuila-and-aunuu&catid=112&Itemid=184.
57. Faleomavaega, *Navigating the Future*, 12. See also the American Samoa Bar Association website for the wording of the Manuʻa cession documents, http://www.asbar.org/index.php?option=com_content&view=article&id=1951:cession-of-manua-islands&catid=112&Itemid=185.
58. Title 48, U.S.C. §§ 1661.
59. Am. Samoa Code Ann. § 37.0204 (b) and (c) (2004), cited in Stover, "Individual Land Tenure," 76. Stover marks three categories of land by statute and jurisprudence: freehold, which can be freely bought and sold; native land—communal, held in trust by larger family units and subject to the authority of *matai*; and native land—individual, which can be individually owned and deeded to descendants who meet a 50% blood-quantum criterion. Section (d) of the Am. Samoa Code Ann. § 37.0204 exempts from this regulation land transferred to the government as well as to churches (provided it is deeded to native Samoans). See also Rose Cuison Villazor, "Blood Quantum Land Laws and the Race Versus Political Identity Dilemma," *California Law Review* 96 (June 2008): 825.

60. See J. Kehaulani Kauanui, *Hawaiian Blood: Colonialism and the Politics of Sovereignty and Indigeneity* (Durham, NC: Duke University Press, 2008), for an analysis of blood-quantum politics and Hawaiian land.
61. Robert A. Katz, "The Jurisprudence of Legitimacy: Applying the U.S. Constitution to U.S. Territories," *University of Chicago Law Review* 59 (Spring 1992): 779.
62. Ibid., 780.
63. Ibid.
64. Daniel E. Hall, "Curfews, Culture, and Custom in American Samoa: An Analytical Map for Applying the U.S. Constitution to U.S. Territories," *Asian-Pacific Law and Policy Journal* 2 (Winter 2001): 69–107, and Stanley K. Laughlin, "The Application of the Constitution in United States Territories: American Samoa, A Case Study," *University of Hawaii Law Review* 2 (1980–1981): 337–88.
65. Laughlin, "Application of the Constitution," 384.
66. Part of the controversy over the case is tied to the split within Samoan communities, specifically, those resident in American Sāmoa versus the continental United States and Hawaiʻi. In Samoa, the absence of U.S. citizenship has not imposed tangible hardship, and extending citizenship would not substantially benefit island residents. For those in the U.S. military and in the continental United States and Hawaiʻi, being noncitizens does present some obstacles; see Morrison, "Foreign in a Domestic Sense," 85–86. The backlash against the plaintiffs is motivated by what local residents see as potentially serious consequences for the territory without much benefit; there is also resentment of nonresidents attempting to make changes for the islands.
67. Morrison, "Foreign in a Domestic Sense," 72. The complaint relied on the "doctrine of jus soli, which is the common law proposition that individuals born in the territory of a nation are automatically citizens of that nation."
68. Ibid., 73.
69. Ibid.
70. John Oliver, *Last Week Tonight with John Oliver*, U.S. Territories (HBO broadcast), March 8, 2015, https://www.youtube.com/watch?v=CesHr99ezWE.
71. Brief of the Honorable Eni F. H. Faleomavaega, Tuaua v. United States, No. 12-1143-RJL (D.D.C. Nov. 15, 2012).
72. Fili Sagapolutele, "Amata Reiterates: Citizenship Is Political Status Question for Territory," *Samoa News*, March 16, 2015.

73. One contrary interpretation is offered in Morrison, "Foreign in a Domestic Sense." Based on existing case law on the application of the constitution and the compelling state interest in protecting Samoan culture, Morrison argues that citizenship can be granted without mobilizing other constitutional provisions and without changing the territory's political status (145). He writes, "the assumption that Equal Protection does not already apply to the territories is incorrect. So is the second assumption that the faʻasamoa could not survive Equal Protection" (144). Assuming that provisions of existing case law hold, Morrison argues that citizenship could be extended without threatening the land and titles system of Tutuila and Manuʻa because constitutional challenges would be evaluated using the "impractical and anomalous test." Yet he concedes that "no analysis can foresee the potential consequences to a culture" (138); moreover, there is no guarantee of what reasoning will be used in future legal decisions.
74. Faleomavaega, *Navigating the Future*, 35.
75. Katz, "The Jurisprudence of Legitimacy," 799. This has given rise to challenges to the Secretary of the Interior's power to override a governor's veto. The voters have twice defeated a constitutional referendum to transfer the authority to the legislature, or the Fono.
76. Hall, "Curfews, Culture, and Custom."
77. ASFPSSC, *Future Political Status Study*, 43.
78. Leela Gandhi, *Postcolonial Theory: A Critical Introduction* (New York: Columbia University Press, 1998), 4.
79. Morrison, "Foreign in a Domestic Sense," 88.
80. On secularization of the *matai* system, see Malama Meleisea, "'To Whom Gods and Men Crowded': Chieftainship and Hierarchy in Ancient Samoa," in *Tonga and Samoa: Images of Gender and Polity*, ed. Judith Huntsman (Christchurch, New Zealand: Macmillan Brown Centre for Pacific Studies, 1995), 19–34; for a brief historicization of the *matai* system in Samoa, see Serge Tchérkezoff, "Are the Matai 'Out of Time'? Tradition and Democracy: Contemporary Ambiguities and Historical Transformations of the Concept of Chief," in Huffer and Soʻo, *Governance in Samoa*.
81. Stoler, "On Degrees of Imperial Sovereignty."
82. Laughlin, "Application of the Constitution"; Morrison, "Foreign in a Domestic Sense."
83. Laughlin, "Application of the Constitution," 388.

84. Glenn Petersen, "Strategic Location and Sovereignty: Modern Micronesia in the Historical Context of American Expansionism," *Space and Polity* 2 (1998): 179–205.
85. Catherine Lutz, "American Military Bases on Guam: The US Global Military Basing System," *Asia-Pacific Journal: Japan Focus*, July 26, 2010, http://www.globalresearch.ca/american-military-bases-on-guam-the-us-global-military-basing-system/20405.
86. The proposal has been scaled back but if implemented will have enormous environmental and social effect. See http://guambuildupeis.us/.
87. Petersen, "Strategic Location and Sovereignty," 200.
88. Ibid.
89. Local leaders agitated for many years under naval governance before the establishment of a legislature was approved. Toeutu Fa'aleava, "Fitafita: Samoan Landsmen in the United States Navy, 1900–1951" (PhD diss., University of California, Berkeley, 2003) discusses how racist military policies under naval rule segregated and limited promotion and training opportunities for native enlisted personnel. See also Armstrong, "American Exceptionalism in American Samoa," on the skipjack affair and McMullin, "Passive Resistance of Samoans," on the forceful undermining of the power of the Tui Manu'a title.
90. G. Bertram and R. Watters, "The MIRAB Economy in South Pacific Island Microstates," *Pacific Viewpoint* 26 (1985): 497 519.
91. United Nations, A/Ac.109/2004/6, para. 12.
92. Kristen Scharnberg, "Where the U.S. Military Is the Family Business," *Chicago Tribune*, March 7, 2007. One online site places American Sāmoa sixth in military recruitment (Army, Navy, Air Force) per capita among the states and territories based on military data. See http://www.statemaster.com/graph/mil_tot_mil_rec_arm_nav_air_for_percap-navy-air-force-per-capita#source.
93. V. Y. Mudimbe, *The Invention of Africa: Gnosis, Philosophy, and the Order of Knowledge* (Bloomington: Indiana University Press, 1988).
94. José A. Cabranes, "Some Common Ground," in Duffy-Burnett and Marshall, *Foreign in a Domestic Sense*, 41.
95. Ibid.
96. We owe the term *constrained agency* to Iris Lopez's discussion of New York Puerto Rican women's agency in reproductive decision-making processes. Iris López, "Agency and Constraint: Sterilization and Reproductive Freedom Among

Puerto Rican Women in New York City," in *Situated Lives: Gender and Culture in Everyday Life*, ed. Louise Lamphere and Helena Ragoné (New York: Routledge, 1997). For a discussion of the "ideology of choice" and a deconstructive critique of the forced versus voluntary dichotomy, see Kamala Kempadoo and Jo Doezema, eds., *Global Sex Workers: Rights, Resistance, and Redefinition* (New York: Routledge, 1998).

97. Audra Simpson and Andrea Smith, eds., *Theorizing Native Studies* (Duke University Press 2014), 5.
98. Mudimbe, *The Invention of Africa*.
99. J. Jorge Klor de Alva, "The Postcolonization of the (Latin) American Experience: A Reconsideration of 'Colonialism,' 'Postcolonialism,' and 'Mestizaje,'" in *After Colonialism: Imperial Histories and Postcolonial Displacements*, ed. G. Prakash (Princeton, NJ: Princeton University Press, 1995), 249.
100. We owe the term *cultural resurgence* to Taiaike Alfred and Jeff Corntassel, "Being Indigenous: Resurgences Against Contemporary Colonialism," *Government and Opposition* 40 (2005): 597–614.
101. Isar Godreau, *Scripts of Blackness: Race, Cultural Nationalism, and U.S. Colonialism in Puerto Rico* (University of Illinois Press, 2016).
102. Déborah Berman Santana, "Indigenous Identity and the Struggle for Independence in Puerto Rico," in Barker, *Sovereignty Matters*, 212.
103. See Gabriel Haslip-Viera, *Taíno Revival: Critical Perspectives on Puerto Rican Identity and Cultural Politics* (Princeton, NJ: Markus Wiener, 2001).
104. The legacy of blood-quantum laws have had serious consequences for Native Hawaiian communities; see Kauanui, *Hawaiian Blood*, and Brandon C. Ledward, "On Being Hawaiian Enough: Contesting American Racialization with Native Hybridity," *Hulili: Multidisciplinary Research on Hawaiian Well-Being* 4 (2007): 107–43. The shadow of legal blood quantum for land ownership remains lurking in Samoa, but having escaped a settler colonial history, it does not shape discourses of identity, belonging, and legal right in the same way.
105. Santana, "Indigenous Identity," 211.
106. See Kim TallBear, *Native American DNA: Tribal Belonging and the False Promise of Genetic Science* (Minneapolis: University of Minnesota Press, 2013).
107. Carlos Pabón, *Nación Postmortem: Ensayos sobre los tiempos de insoportable ambigüedad* (San Juan: Ediciones Callejon, 2002), 403 (our translation).

108. In the sense of the fragment as Partha Chatterjee articulates it, "To make a claim on behalf of the fragment is also, not surprisingly, to produce a discourse that is itself fragmentary": *The Nation and Its Fragments: Colonial and Postcolonial Histories* (Princeton, NJ: Princeton University Press), 13.
109. See also Lanny Thompson, *Imperial Archipelago: Representation and Rule in the Insular Territories Under U.S. Dominion After 1898* (Honolulu: University of Hawai'i Press, 2010).
110. See also Go, "Provinciality of American Empire," on the importance of U.S. perceptions of the people they were attempting to rule in the territories in shaping colonial policy.
111. Ann Stoler and Carol McGranahan, "Introduction: Refiguring Imperial Terrains," in *Imperial Formations* (Albuquerque, NM: School for Advanced Research Press, 2007), 3–42.
112. In this process of collaboration, we not only identified some of the shared sociohistorical conditions and discourses that produce us as subjects of U.S. imperialism but also contended with several analytic disagreements central to our individual perspectives. In particular, we struggled over the precise meanings and consequences of using the terms *colonialism* versus *imperialism*. Our debate reflects both a lack of consensus among scholars about the accuracy of such terms in any given situation and our own particular attachments to the political economy of such terms, which are rooted in our interpellations as differentially situated subjects of U.S. empire and in our own political convictions. These different positionalities with regard to our analyses of U.S. imperial formations and local political enactments also informed our disagreement about the usefulness of spaces of attenuated sovereignty and gradated rights. Specifically, we continually challenged each other over different interpretations of zones of flexibility as either spaces of freedom or intensified subjection. We came to appreciate the benefits of engaging both perspectives, allowing thereby a more nuanced understanding of unincorporation as a political condition.

2

Indigenous Peoples and the Politics of Recognition

GLEN COULTHARD

Over the last forty years, the self-determination efforts and objectives of Indigenous and other colonized peoples in the Americas have increasingly been cast in the language of not only sovereignty but also "recognition," a presumably essential middle step (see also chap. 3, 12).[1] Consider, for example, the formative declaration issued by my community, the Dene Nation, in 1975:

> We the Dene of the NWT [Northwest Territories] insist on the right to be regarded by ourselves and the world as a nation. Our struggle is for the *recognition* of the Dene Nation by the Government and people of Canada and the peoples and governments of the world.[2]

Now fast-forward to the 2005 policy position on sovereign self-determination issued by Canada's largest Indigenous organization, the Assembly of First Nations (AFN). According to the AFN, "a consensus has emerged ... around a vision of the relationship between First Nations and Canada which would lead to strengthening recognition and implementation of First Nations' governments."[3] This "vision," the AFN goes on to state, expands on the core principles outlined in the 1996 *Report of the Royal Commission on Aboriginal*

Peoples, that is, recognition of the nation-to-nation relationship between First Nations and the Crown, recognition of the equal right of First Nations to self-determination, recognition of the Crown's fiduciary obligation to protect Aboriginal treaty rights, recognition of First Nations' inherent right to self-government, and recognition of the right of First Nations to economically benefit from the use of their lands and resources.[4] When considered from the vantage point of these perspectives, it would appear that recognition has emerged as the hegemonic expression of self-determination within the Indigenous rights movement in Canada.

The increase in recognition demands made by Indigenous and other marginalized minorities over the last decades has prompted a surge of intellectual production seeking to unpack the ethical, political, and legal significance of these types of claims. Influenced by Charles Taylor's catalytic 1992 essay "The Politics of Recognition," much of this literature has tended to focus on the relationship between the affirmative recognition of societal cultural differences on the one hand and the freedom and well-being of marginalized individuals and groups living in ethnically diverse states on the other. In Canada, it has been argued that this synthesis of theory and practice has forced the state to reconceptualize the tenets of its relationship with Aboriginal peoples;[5] whereas before 1969 federal Indian policy was unapologetically assimilationist, now it is couched in the vernacular of "mutual recognition."[6]

In this essay I challenge the idea that the colonial relationship between Indigenous peoples and the state can be significantly transformed via a politics of recognition.[7] Following philosopher Richard Day,[8] I take *politics of recognition* to refer to the now expansive range of recognition-based models of liberal pluralism that seek to reconcile Indigenous claims to nationhood with national sovereignty via the accommodation of Indigenous identities in some form of renewed relationship with the state. Although these models tend to vary in both theory and practice, most involve the delegation of land, capital, and political power from the state to Indigenous communities through land claims, economic development initiatives, and self-government processes. Against this position, I argue that instead of ushering in an era of peaceful coexistence grounded on the ideal of reciprocity, the politics of recognition in its contemporary form promises to reproduce the very configurations of colonial power that Indigenous peoples' demands for recognition have historically sought to transcend.

More specifically, through a sustained engagement with the work of anticolonial theorist and psychiatrist Frantz Fanon,[9] I hope to show that the reproduction of a colonial structure of dominance like that of Canada and the United States rests on its ability to entice Indigenous peoples to identify, either implicitly or explicitly, with the profoundly *asymmetrical* and *nonreciprocal* forms of recognition either imposed on or granted to them by the colonial state and society. Fanon first developed this insight in his 1952 text *Black Skin, White Masks*, where he persuasively challenged the applicability of philosopher G. W. H. Hegel's dialectic of recognition to colonial and racialized settings.

Against Hegel's abstraction, Fanon argued that, in actual contexts of domination (such as colonialism) not only are the terms of recognition usually determined by and in the interests of the master (the colonizer) but also over time slave populations (the colonized) tend to develop what he called "psycho-affective"[10] attachments to these master-sanctioned forms of recognition and that this attachment is essential in maintaining the economic and political structure of master-slave (colonizer-colonized) relations themselves. By the end of this essay I hope to make clear that the contemporary politics of recognition is ill equipped to deal with the interrelated structural and psycho-affective dimensions of imperial power that remain central to the preservation of colonial hierarchies.

From Hegel's Master-Slave Narrative to Taylor's "Politics of Recognition"

Fundamentally, Hegel's master-slave narrative can be read in at least two ways that continue to inform contemporary recognition-based theories of liberal pluralism. In the first reading, Hegel's dialectic outlines a theory of identity formation in which relations of recognition are deemed "constitutive of subjectivity: one becomes an individual subject only in virtue of recognizing, and being recognized by another subject."[11] This insight into the intersubjective nature of identity formation underlies Hegel's often quoted assertion that "self-consciousness exists in and for itself when, and by the fact that, it so exists for another; that is, it exists only in being acknowledged."[12]

In the second reading, Hegel moves beyond highlighting the relational nature of human subjectivity to the intersubjective conditions required for the realization of human freedom. From this perspective, the master-slave narrative can be read as a normative story in that it suggests that the realization of oneself as an essential, self-determining agent requires that one not only be recognized as self-determining but that one be recognized by another self-consciousness that is also recognized as self-determining. It is through these reciprocal processes and exchanges of recognition that the condition of possibility for freedom emerges.[13] This is why Hegel repeatedly insisted that relations of recognition must be mutual.

Political theorist Patchen Markell has suggested that one of the most significant differences between recognition in Hegel's master-slave narrative and the "politics of recognition" today is that state institutions tend to play a fundamental role in mediating relations of recognition in the latter but not the former. For example, regarding policies aimed at preserving cultural diversity, Markell writes, "far from being simple face-to-face encounters between subjects, *à la* Hegel's stylized story in the *Phenomenology*," multiculturalism tends to "involve large-scale exchanges of recognition in which states typically play a crucial role."[14] Charles Taylor's "The Politics of Recognition" provides a case in point.[15]

Taylor mounts a sustained critique of what he claims to be the increasingly "impracticable"[16] nature of "difference-blind"[17] liberalism when applied to culturally diverse polities such as the United States and Canada. Alternatively, Taylor defends a variant of liberal thought that posits that under certain circumstances diverse states can indeed recognize and accommodate a range of group-specific claims without having to abandon their commitment to a core set of fundamental rights.[18] Furthermore, these types of claims can be defended on liberal grounds because it is within and against the horizon of one's cultural community that individuals come to develop their identities and thus the capacity to make sense of their lives and life choices.[19] In short, our identities provide the "background against which our tastes and desires and opinions and aspirations make sense."[20] Without this orienting framework we would be unable to derive meaning from our lives—we would not know "who we are" or "where [we are] coming from."[21] We would be "at sea," as Taylor puts it elsewhere.[22]

Thus, much like Hegel before him, Taylor argues that human actors do not develop their identities in "isolation"; rather, they are "formed" through "dialogue with others, in agreement or struggle with their recognition of us."[23] However, given that our identities are formed through these relations, it follows that they can also be significantly *de*formed when these processes run awry. This is what Taylor means when he asserts that identities are shaped not only by recognition but also by the *mis*recognition of others. A person or a group of people can suffer real damage, real distortion, if the people or society around them mirror back to them a confining or demeaning or contemptible picture of themselves. Nonrecognition or misrecognition can inflict harm, can be a form of oppression, imprisoning one in a false, distorted, and reduced mode of being.[24]

This idea that asymmetrical relations of recognition can impede human freedom by "imprisoning" someone in a distorted relation to self is asserted repeatedly in Taylor's essay. For instance, we are frequently told that disparaging forms of recognition can inflict "wounds" on their "victims," "saddling [them] with a crippling self-hatred,"[25] or that withholding recognition can "inflict damage" on "those who are denied it."[26] And given that misrecognition has the capacity to "harm" others in this manner, it follows, according to Taylor, that it be considered "a form of oppression"[27] on par with "injustices" such as "inequality" and "exploitation."[28] In Taylor, recognition is elevated to the status of a "vital human need."[29]

At this point the practical implications of Taylor's theory begin to reveal themselves. In his more prescriptive moments, Taylor suggests that in Canada, both the Quebecois and Indigenous peoples exemplify the types of threatened minorities that ought to be considered eligible for some form of recognition capable of accommodating their cultural distinctiveness. For Indigenous peoples specifically, this might require the delegation of political and cultural "autonomy" to Native groups through the institutions of "self-government."[30] Elsewhere, Taylor suggests that this could mean "in practice allowing for a new form of jurisdiction in Canada, perhaps weaker than the provinces, but, unlike municipalities."[31] Accommodating the claims of First Nations in this way would ideally allow Native communities to "preserve their cultural integrity" and thus help stave off the psychological disorientation and resultant unfreedom associated with exposure to structured patterns of mis- or nonrecognition.[32] In this way, the institutionalization of a liberal regime of reciprocal recognition would better enable Indigenous peoples' to realize their status as distinct and self-determining actors.

While it is true that the normative dimension of Taylor's project represents a marked improvement over Canada's "past tactics of exclusion, genocide, and assimilation,"[33] in the following section I argue that the logic undergirding this approach—where "recognition" is conceived as something that is ultimately "granted"[34] or "accorded"[35] to a subaltern group or entity by a dominant group or entity—prefigures its failure to significantly modify, let alone transcend, the breadth of power at play in colonial relationships. I also hope to show that Fanon, on whose work Taylor relies to delineate the relationship between misrecognition and the forms of unfreedom and subjection discussed above, anticipated this failure over fifty years ago.

Frantz Fanon and the Problem of Recognition in Colonial Contexts

In the second half of "The Politics of Recognition," Taylor identifies Fanon's classic 1961 treatise on decolonization, *The Wretched of the Earth*, as one of the first texts to identify the role that misrecognition plays in propping up relations of domination.[36] Fanon's analysis is also used to support one of the central political arguments undergirding Taylor's analysis, namely, his call for the cultural recognition of substate groups that have suffered at the hands of a hegemonic political power. Here, I want to challenge Taylor's use of Fanon by contesting his assumption that a more accommodating, liberal regime of mutual recognition might address relations typical of those between Indigenous peoples and settler states.

Fanon's concern with the relationship between human freedom and equality in relations of recognition represents a central and reoccurring theme in an earlier work, *Black Skin, White Masks (BSWM)*.[37] As mentioned before, Fanon convincingly argued that the long-term stability of colonial governance relies as much on "internalization" of racist recognition imposed on the Indigenous or colonized population by the colonial state as it does on brute force. Thus, the longevity of a colonial social formation depends on its capacity to transform the colonized population into subjects of imperial rule. For Fanon, colonialism operates in a dual-structured manner: it includes "not only the interrelations of *objective* historical conditions but also human *attitudes* to these conditions."[38] Fanon argued that it was the interplay between the structural-objective and recognitive-subjective realms of colonialism that ensured its hegemony over time.

On the subjective front, *BSWM* painstakingly outlines the myriad ways that "attitudes" conducive to colonial rule are cultivated among the colonized through the unequal exchange of institutionalized and interpersonal patterns of recognition between the colonial society and the Indigenous population. In effect, Fanon revealed how, over time, colonized populations tend to internalize the derogatory images imposed on them by their colonial "masters" and how as a result of this process, these images, along with the structural relations with which they are entwined, come to be recognized (or at least endured) as more or less natural.

This last point is made agonizingly clear in arguably the most famous passage from *BSWM*, where Fanon shares an alienating encounter on the streets of Paris with a little white child. "Look, a Negro!," Fanon recalled the kid saying. "Momma, see the Negro! I'm frightened! frightened!"[39] At that moment the imposition of the child's racist gaze "sealed" Fanon into a "crushing objecthood," fixing him like "a chemical solution is fixed by a dye."[40] He found himself temporarily accepting that he was indeed the subject of the child's call: "It was true, it amused me,"[41] Fanon thought. But then "I subjected myself to an objective examination, I discovered my blackness, my ethnic characteristics; and I was battered down by tom-toms, cannibalism, intellectual deficiency, fetishism, racial defects."[42] Far from assuring Fanon's humanity, the other's recognition imprisoned him in an externally determined and devalued conception of himself. Instead of being acknowledged as a "man among men," he was reduced to "an object [among] other objects."[43]

Left as is, Fanon's insights into the ultimately subjectifying nature of colonial recognition appear to square nicely with Taylor's work. For example, although Fanon never uses the term himself, he seems to be mapping the debilitating effects associated with *mis*recognition in the same way that Taylor uses the term. In fact, *BSWM* is littered with passages illustrating the innumerable ways that imposition of the settler's gaze can inflict damage on a colonized society at individual collective levels. Yet I believe a close reading of *BSWM* renders Taylor's approach problematic in several ways.

Fanon insisted, for example, that a colonial configuration of power could be transformed only if attacked at the objective and the subjective levels of operation.[44] This point is made at the outset of *BSWM* and reverberates throughout all of Fanon's work. Indeed, Fanon claimed that there "will be an authentic disalienation" of the colonized subject "only to the degree to which things, in the most materialistic meaning of the word, [are] restored to their proper places."[45] Hence the term *sociodiagnostic* for Fanon's project: "if there is an inferiority complex, it is the outcome of a double process . . . primarily economic; [and] subsequently the internalization . . . of his [or her] inferiority."[46] Fanon correctly situated colonial-capitalist exploitation and domination alongside misrecognition and alienation as foundational sources of colonial injustice. "The Negro problem," Fanon wrote, "does not resolve itself into the problem of Negroes living among white men but rather of Negroes being exploited, enslaved, despised by a colonialist, capitalist society that is only accidentally white."[47]

Fanon was enough of a Marxist to understand the role that the capitalist economy plays in overdetermining hierarchical relations of recognition. However, he was also much more perceptive than many Marxists in his insistence that the subjective realm of colonialism be the target of strategic transformation along with the socioeconomic structure. The colonized person "must wage war on both levels," Fanon insisted. "Since historically they influence each other, any unilateral liberation is incomplete, and the gravest mistake would be to believe in their automatic interdependence."[48] For Fanon, attacking colonial power on one front, in other words, would not guarantee the subversion of its effects on the other. In Fanon's theorization, not only is the relationship between base and superstructure posited as both interdependent and semiautonomous, but more significantly, those axes of domination historically relegated in Marxism to the superstructural realm—such as racism and its effects—are attributed a substantive capacity to structure social relations.

Fanon's work, which anticipates the recognition-redistribution debate by half a century, highlights several key shortcomings in Taylor's work. Taylor's approach is insufficient insofar as it tends to, at best, address the political economy of colonialism in a strictly "affirmative" manner through reformist state redistribution schemes such as granting specific cultural rights and concessions to Aboriginal communities via self-government and land claims processes. Although this approach may alter the intensity of some of the effects of colonial-capitalist exploitation and domination, it does little to address their generative structures: a racially stratified capitalist economy and the colonial state. Philosopher Richard Day has succinctly framed the problem this way: "Although Taylor's recognition model allows for diversity of culture within a particular state by admitting the possibility of multiple national identifications," it is less "permissive with regard to polity and economy . . . in assuming that any subaltern group that is granted [recognition] will thereby acquire a *subordinate* articulation with a *capitalist state*."[49] Seen from this angle, Taylor's theory leaves one of the two operative levels of colonial power identified by Fanon untouched.

Moreover, Taylor's variant of liberalism *as liberalism* does not confront the structural-economic aspects of colonialism at its generative roots. And this shortcoming in Taylor's approach is particularly surprising given the fact that although many Indigenous leaders and communities today tend to couch their claims in reformist terms, this has not always been the case. Indeed, historically, Indigenous demands for cultural recognition have often explicitly questioned the dominating nature of capitalist social relations and the state form.[50] A growing number of today's most prominent Indigenous scholars and activists share this approach.[51]

Mohawk political scientist Taiaiake Alfred, for example, has repeatedly argued that any traditionally rooted self-determination struggle should protect the "heart and soul of indigenous nations: a set of values that challenge the homogenizing force of Western liberalism and free-market capitalism; that honor the autonomy of individual conscience, non-coercive authority, and the deep interconnection between human beings and other elements of creation."[52] For Alfred, this vision is embodied in the practical philosophies and ethical systems of many of North America's Indigenous societies and flows from a "realization that capitalist economics and liberal delusions of progress" have historically served as the "engines of colonial aggression and injustice" itself.[53]

If Taylor's account pays insufficient attention to the clearly structural-economic realm of domination, the work of political theorist Nancy Fraser does so from the opposite angle. In order to avoid pitfalls associated with the politics of recognition's latent essentialism and displacement of questions of distributive justice, Fraser proposes a means of integrating struggles for recognition and those of redistribution without subordinating one to the other. To this end, Fraser suggests that instead of understanding recognition to be the revaluation of cultural or group-specific identity and misrecognition to be the disparagement of such identity and its consequent effects, recognition and misrecognition should be conceived of in terms of the "institutionalized patterns of value" that affect one's ability to participate as a peer in social life.[54] "To view recognition" in this manner, writes Fraser, "is to treat it as an issue of *social status*."[55]

Although Fraser's status model curtails some of the problems she attributes to identity politics, it does so at the expense of addressing one of the most pertinent features of injustices related to mis- or nonrecognition: the subjective-psychological dimensions of today's most volatile political conflicts. By avoiding this "psychologizing" tendency within the politics of recognition, Fraser claims to have located what is wrong with misrecognition in "social relations" and not "individual or interpersonal psychology."[56] We are told that this is preferable because when misrecognition "is identified with internal distortions in the structure of the consciousness of the oppressed, it is but a short step to blaming the victim."[57] However, if I understand Fanon correctly, this does not have to be the case.

Fanon unambiguously located the cause of the "inferiority complex" of colonized subjects in the colonial social structure.[58] The problem, however, is that any psychological problems that ensue, although socially constituted, can take on a life of their own and thus need to be dealt with independently and in accordance with their own specific logics. Stated simply, if Fanon's insight into the interdependent yet semiautonomous nature of the two facets of colonial power is correct, then dumping all our efforts into alleviating the institutional-structural impediments to participatory parity (whether redistributive or recognitive) may not do anything to subvert the debilitating forms of unfreedom related to misrecognition in the traditional sense.

The second key weakness of Taylor's theory of recognition is the assumption that the flourishing of Indigenous peoples as distinct and self-determining entities is dependent on cultural recognition and institutional accommodation by the surrounding state. This approach is both intriguing and problematic; Fanon argued against a similar presumption in the penultimate chapter of *BSWM*. Fanon asserted that the dialectical progression to reciprocity in recognition relations is frequently undermined in the colonial setting by the fact that many colonized societies no longer have to struggle for their independence, unlike the subjugated slave in Hegel's *Phenomenology*. Political independence is often negotiated, achieved through constitutional amendment, or simply "declared" by the settler state and bestowed on the Indigenous population in the form of political rights. Whatever the method, in these circumstances the colonized, "steeped in the inessentiality of servitude," are "*set free by [the] master*."[59] "One day the White Master, *without conflict*, recognize[s] the Negro slave."[60] As such, they do not have to lay down their life to prove their "certainty of being" in the way that Hegel insisted.[61]

The "upheaval" of formal freedom and independence thus reaches the colonized "from without": "The black man [is] acted upon. Values that [are] not ... created by his actions, values that [are] not ... born of the systolic tide of his blood, [dance] in a hued whirl around him. The upheaval [does] not make a difference in the Negro. He [goes] from one way of life to another, but not from one life to another."[62]

For Fanon it is through struggle and conflict (and for the later Fanon, *violent* struggle and conflict) that imperial subjects come to be rid of the "arsenal of complexes" driven into the core of their being through the colonial process.[63] I will have more to say about this aspect of Fanon's thought below, but for now I simply want to flag the fact that struggle—or, as I will argue later, *transformative praxis*—serves as the mediating force that allows the colonized to shed their colonial identities and be restored to their "proper place."[64] In contexts where recognition is conferred without struggle or conflict, this fundamental self-transformation—or as Lou Turner has put it, this "inner differentiation"[65] at the level of the colonized's being—cannot occur, thus foreclosing the realization of authentic freedom. Hence, Fanon's claim that the colonized simply go from "one way of life to another, but not from one life to another"; the structure of domination changes, but the subjectivity of the colonized remains the same—they become "emancipated slaves."[66]

Additionally, when Fanon speaks of the absence of struggle in the decolonization movements of his day, he does not imply that all of the colonized in these contexts were passive recipients of colonial practices. He readily admits, for example, that "from time to time" the colonized may indeed fight "for Liberty and Justice."[67] However, when this fight does not pose a foundational challenge to the structures of colonial power as such—which, for Fanon, will always invoke struggle and conflict—then the best the colonized can hope for is "white liberty and white justice; that is, values secreted by [their] masters."[68]

My final challenge to Taylor's politics of recognition stems from the misguided sociological assumption that informs his appropriation of Hegel's notion of mutual recognition. At the heart of Hegel's master-slave dialectic is the idea that both parties engaged in the struggle for recognition are dependent on the other's acknowledgment for their freedom and self-worth. Moreover, Hegel asserts that this dependency is even more crucial for the master, because he or she cannot achieve independence and objective self-certainty through the object of his or her own labor, unlike the slave. Thus, mutual dependency appears to be the background condition that ensures the dialectic progress toward reciprocity. This is why Taylor claims, with reference to Hegel, that "the struggle for recognition can only find *one satisfactory solution, and that is a regime of reciprocal recognition among equals*."[69]

As Fanon's work reminds us, however, the problem with this formulation is that the mutual character of dependency rarely exists when applied to actual struggles for recognition between hegemonic and subaltern communities. This observation is made in a lengthy footnote on page 220 of *BSWM*. There, Fanon claims to have shown how the colonial master "basically differs" from the master depicted in Hegel's *Phenomenology*: "For Hegel there is reciprocity," but in the colonies "the master laughs at the consciousness of the slave." What he wants from the slave is "not recognition but work."⁷⁰ Because it outlines in precise terms the limitations of Hegel's recognition paradigm when applied to the colonial environment, this is one of the most crucial passages in *BSWM*. In these contexts, the "master"—that is, the colonial state and state society—does not require recognition from the previously self-determining communities on which its territorial, economic, and social infrastructure is constituted. What it needs is land, labor, and resources.⁷¹ Thus, rather than leading to a condition of reciprocity, the dialectic either breaks down with the explicit *non*recongnition of the equal status of the colonized population or with the strategic "domestication" of the terms of recognition without disturbing the foundation of the colonial relationship.⁷²

Anyone familiar with the power dynamics that structure the Indigenous rights movement in North America should see the applicability of Fanon's insights immediately here. The liberal discourse of recognition has been limited and constrained in countless ways by the state, the courts, corporate interests, and policy makers to help preserve the colonial status quo. With respect to the law, for example, over the last forty years the Supreme Court of Canada has consistently refused to recognize native peoples' equal and self-determining status. The court has based these refusals on legal precedents founded on the white supremacist myth that Indigenous societies were too primitive to have political rights when they first encountered European powers.⁷³ Thus, even though the court has secured an unprecedented degree of protection for certain "cultural" practices within the state, it has repeatedly declined to challenge the racist origin of Canada's assumed sovereign authority over Indigenous peoples and their territories.

The political and economic ramifications of the court's actions have been clear-cut. The 1997 *Delgamuukw v. British Columbia* decision cleared the way for any residual Aboriginal rights that survived the unilateral assertion of Crown sovereignty to be infringed by the federal and provincial governments as long as this action furthers "a compelling and substantial legislative objective . . . consistent with the special fiduciary relationship between the Crown and the aboriginal peoples."⁷⁴

What "substantial objectives" might justify infringement? According to the court, virtually any exploitative economic venture, including "the development of agriculture, forestry, mining, and hydroelectric power, the general economic development of the interior of British Columbia, protection of the environment or endangered species and the building of infrastructure and the settlement of foreign populations to support those aims."[75] So today it appears, much as it did in Fanon's day, that colonial powers will recognize the collective rights and identities of Indigenous peoples only if this recognition does not call into question the legal, political, and economic framework of the colonial relationship itself.[76]

But these examples confirm only one aspect of Fanon's insight into the problem of recognition in colonial contexts, namely, the limitations of this framework when pitted against these overtly structural expressions of domination. Is this also the case with the subjective or psycho-affective features of colonial power? With respect to the forms of racist recognition driven into the psyches of Indigenous peoples through the institutions of the state, church, schools, media, and intolerant individuals within the dominant society, the answer is clearly yes. Countless studies, novels, and autobiographical narratives have outlined, in painful detail, how these expressions have saddled individuals with low self-esteem, depression, alcohol and drug abuse, and violent behaviors directed both inward against the self and outward toward others.[77]

However, similarly convincing arguments have been made concerning the limited forms of recognition and accommodation offered to Indigenous communities through the law, self-government packages, land claims, and economic development initiatives. The work of political scientists and theorists Isabel Altamirano-Jimenez, Taiaiake Alfred, and Paul Nadasdy,[78] for example, has demonstrated how state institutional and discursive fields (within and against which Indigenous demands for recognition are made) can subtly shape the subjectivities and worldviews of the Indigenous claimants. The problem here, of course, is that these arenas are not neutral: they are profoundly hierarchical and power laden and have the ability to asymmetrically mold and govern how Indigenous subjects think and act in relation to the topic at hand (the recognition claim) *and* to themselves and to others. This is what I take Alfred to mean when he suggests, echoing Fanon, that the dominance of the legal approach to self-determination has, over time, helped produce a class of Aboriginal and Native "citizens" whose rights and identities have become defined solely in relation to the colonial state and its legal apparatus.[79]

Similarly, strategies that have sought self-determination via mainstream economic development have facilitated the creation of a new elite of Native capitalists whose desire for profit now outweighs their ancestral obligations to the land and to others. Land claims processes, for instance, which are couched almost exclusively in the language of property,[80] now threaten to produce Aboriginal property owners whose territories and identities risk expropriation and alienation. Whatever the method, for Alfred, all of these approaches, even when carried out by sincere and well-intentioned individuals, may erode the most traditionally egalitarian aspects of Indigenous ethical systems, ways of life, and forms of social organization. In short, the embodied reciprocity and practical relationality of Indigenous forms of sovereignty are written over in the image of our master: the colonial sovereignty of the nation-state and its attendant capitalist mode of production.

Self-Recognition and Anticolonial Empowerment

The argument that I have sketched is bleak in its implications. Indeed, it would appear that recognition inevitably leads to subjection. One could argue that Indigenous peoples' struggles to secure their freedom has, in fact, cunningly assured their continued subjugation. The assumption of this view is that Indigenous subjects are *always* being interpellated by recognition, constructed by colonial discourse, or assimilated by imperial power structures.[81] Fanon has been implicated in espousing such a totalizing view of colonial power, and some suggest that he was unable to escape the Manichean logic so essential in propping up relations of colonial domination.[82]

Fanon did not attribute a great deal of emancipatory potential to Hegel's politics of recognition when applied to the colonial arena. But he did not reject the recognition paradigm entirely. As we have seen, Fanon, like Hegel and Taylor, maintained that relations of recognition are constitutive of subjectivity and—when unequal—can foreclose the realization of human freedom. However, he was deeply skeptical of the mutuality envisioned by Hegel;

he did not seem to think that it was achievable in conditions indicative of contemporary colonialism. But if Fanon did not see freedom as naturally emanating from the slave being granted recognition from his or her master, where, if at all, did it originate?

In effect, Fanon claimed that self-determination lay in a quasi-Nietzschean form of personal and collective self-affirmation.[83] Rather than remaining dependent on their oppressors, Fanon argued that the colonized must critically reclaim and revaluate the worth of their own histories, traditions, and cultures. This self-initiated process is what "triggers a change of fundamental importance in the colonized's psycho-affective equilibrium."[84] For Fanon, the colonized must initiate the process of decolonization by recognizing themselves as free, dignified, and distinct contributors to humanity.[85]

Significantly, Fanon equated this self-affirmative process with the praxis of the slave in Hegel's *Phenomenology*, which illustrated the necessity of the oppressed to "turn away" from their master dependency and struggle for freedom on their own terms and in accordance with their own values.[86] Although he was critical of the latent essentialism undergirding the work of the negritude poets, Fanon saw their project as necessary;[87] he understood that the individual and collective revaluation of black identity that informed projects such as the negritude movement served as sources of pride and empowerment. These efforts helped to jolt the colonized into an "actional" existence as opposed to a "reactional" one characterized by *ressentiment*.[88] As postcolonial theorist Robert Young has argued, in many cases, these processes of critical self-affirmation led to the development of a "distinctive postcolonial epistemology and ontology" and enabled the colonized to construct radical alternatives to the colonial project itself.[89]

I would argue that Fanon's call in *BSWM* for a simultaneous turn inward and away from the master reflects a profound understanding of the complexity involved in contests over recognition in colonial and racialized environments. Fanon did not support a rigidly binary, Manichean view of power relations. Unlike Hegel's life-and-death struggle between two opposing forces, Fanon added a multidimensional racial-cultural aspect to the dialectic, thereby underscoring the multifarious web of recognition relations that construct identities and establish (or undermine) the conditions necessary for human freedom and flourishing. Fanon showed that the power dynamics that shape and form (and deform) identities are nothing like Hegel's simplistic hegemon-subaltern binary. His innovation was to reveal how recognitive processes worked to "call forth" and empower individuals within communities of resistance.[90]

This is not to say, of course, that Fanon was able to completely escape the "Manicheism delirium" that he himself was so astute at diagnosing.[91] Those familiar with Fanon's later work, for example, know that the "actional" existence he initiated by self-recognition in *BSWM* would take the form of a direct and violent engagement with the colonial society and its institutional structure in *The Wretched of the Earth*. "At the very moment [the colonized come to] discover their humanity," wrote Fanon, they must "begin to sharpen their weapons *to secure its victory*."[92] In Fanon's later work, violence would come to serve as a "kind of psychotherapy of the oppressed," offering "a primary form of agency through which the subject moves from non-being to being, from object to subject."[93] In this sense, acts of revolutionary violence offered the most effective means to transform the subjectivities of the colonized while toppling the social structure that produced colonized subjects to begin with. Violence provided "the means and the end" of decolonization.[94]

Conclusion

In the end, Fanon overstated the "cleansing"[95] value he attributed to anticolonial violence. Indeed, one could argue that many Algerians have not fully recovered from the eight years of carnage and brutality that constituted Algeria's war of independence with France. Nor was the Front de Libération Nationale's revolutionary seizure of the Algerian state apparatus enough to stave off what Fanon would call "the curse of [national] independence,"[96] namely, the subjection of the newly "liberated" people and territories to the tyranny of the market and a postindependence class of bourgeois national elites. But if Fanon mistakenly regarded violence as the "perfect mediation" permitting the colonized to liberate themselves from the structural and psychoaffective features of colonial domination,[97] then what is the relevance of his work here and now? To quote Homi Bhabha, is Fanon's contribution to anticolonial thought and practice "lost in a time warp?"[98]

I don't think so. Throughout this essay I have argued that Fanon's insights into the subjectifying nature of colonial recognition are as applicable today, to contemporary "politics of recognition," as they were when he formulated his critique of Hegel's master-slave relation. I also hope to have shown that Fanon's dual-structured conception of colonial power still captures the subtle (and not so subtle) ways in which a system of imperial domination, not sustained exclusively by force, is reproduced over time. As philosopher Taiaiake Alfred has recently argued, under these "post-modern" imperial conditions, "oppression has become increasingly invisible; [it is] no longer constituted in conventional terms of military occupation, onerous taxation burdens, blatant land thefts, etc.," but rather through a "fluid confluence of politics, economics, psychology and culture."[99] But if the dispersal and effects of colonial and state power are now so diffuse, how is one to transform or resist them?

In this context, Fanon's earlier work is key. In *BSWM*, Fanon claimed to show how the slave in *Phenomenology* differed from those in the colonies and suggested that Hegel provided a partial answer: those struggling against colonialism must "turn away" from the colonial state and society and find in their own transformative praxis the source of their liberation.[100] I think that today this process will and must continue to involve critical individual and collective self-recognition on the part of Indigenous societies, not only in an instrumental sense but with the understanding that our cultures offer many examples of profoundly nonimperialist relationships within and between peoples and the natural world.

Moreover, the empowerment derived from this critically self-affirmative and self-transformative process of desubjectification must be cautiously directed away from the assimilative lure of the statist politics of recognition and instead fashioned toward our own on-the-ground practices of freedom. As the feminist, antiracist theorist bell hooks explains, such a project would minimally require that we stop being so preoccupied with looking "to that Other for recognition"; instead, we should "recogniz[e] ourselves and make contact with all who would engage us in a constructive manner."[101] In Canada, the strategies and tactics adopted by a growing number of Indigenous activists—in reserve settings such as Grassy Narrows and Six Nations, or in the urban centers of Vancouver, Winnipeg, and Toronto—explore the emancipatory potential that this type of politics offers. This politics is less oriented toward attaining an affirmative form of recognition from the settler state and society and more about critically revaluating, reconstructing, and redeploying culture and tradition in ways that seek to prefigure a radical alternative to the structural and psycho-affective facets of colonial domination.[102]

Notes

1. In the Canadian context, I use the terms *Indigenous*, *Aboriginal*, and *Native* interchangeably to refer to the descendants of those who traditionally occupied the territory now known as Canada before the arrival of European settlers. I also occasionally use these terms in an international context to refer to those peoples that have suffered under the weight of European colonialism more generally. I use the terms *Indian* and *First Nation* to refer to those legally recognized as Indians under the Canadian federal government's Indian Act of 1876.
2. Dene Nation, "The Dene Declaration," in *Dene Nation: The Colony Within*, ed. Mel Watkins (Toronto: University of Toronto Press, 1977), 3–4 (emphasis added).
3. Assembly of First Nations, *Our Nations, Our Governments: Choosing Our Own Paths* (Ottawa: Assembly of First Nations, 2005), 18.
4. Ibid., 18–19.
5. See Alan Cairns, *Citizens Plus: Aboriginal Peoples and the Canadian State* (Vancouver: University of British Columbia Press, 2000); *First Nations and the Canadian State: In Search of Coexistence* (Kingston, ON: Institute of Intergovernmental Relations, 2005).
6. See Royal Commission on Aboriginal Peoples, *Report of the Royal Commission on Aboriginal Peoples*, 5 vols. (Ottawa: Minister of Supply and Services, 1996); Department of Indian Affairs and Northern Development, *Gathering Strength: Canada's Aboriginal Action Plan* (Ottawa: Minister of Indian Affairs and Northern Development, 1997); Department of Indian Affairs and Northern Development, *A First Nations-Crown Political Accord on the Recognition and Implementation of First Nation's Governments* (Ottawa: Minister of Indian Affairs and Northern Development, 2005); James Tully, *Strange Multiplicity: Constitutionalism in an Age of Diversity* (Cambridge: Cambridge University Press,

1995); James Tully, "Aboriginal Peoples: Negotiating Reconciliation," in *Canadian Politics*, 3rd ed., ed. James Bickerton and Alain Gagnon (Peterborough: Broadview Press, 2000).

7. I use the terms *colonial* and *imperial* interchangeably to avoid repetitiveness. However, I do so acknowledging the important distinction that Edward Said, Robert Young, James Tully, and others have drawn between these two interrelated concepts. In their work, a colonial relationship is characterized as a more *direct* form of imperial rule. Imperialism is thus a broader concept, which may include colonialism but could also be carried out indirectly through noncolonial means. Following this logic, a significant amount of the world's population can now be said to live in a post*colonial* condition despite the persistent operation of *imperialism* as a form of "political and economic" dominance. See Robert Young, *Postcolonialism: An Historical Introduction* (Oxford: Blackwell, 2001), 27. Canada, of course, remains a settler colony in which indirect imperialism has never typified the relationship between Indigenous peoples and the settler state and society. See Edward Said, *Culture and Imperialism* (New York: Vintage, 1994), and James Tully, "The Persistence of Empire: A Legacy of Colonialism and Decolonization" (paper presented at the international conference "Colonialism and Its Legacies," University of Chicago, April 22–25, 2004).

8. Richard Day, *Multiculturalism and the History of Canadian Diversity* (Toronto: University of Toronto Press, 2000); "Who Is This We That Gives the Gift? Native American Political Theory and the Western Tradition," *Critical Horizons* 2, no. 2 (2001): 173–201.

9. I use the term *anticolonial* in the sense that Fanon and many of his contemporaries did, namely, as embodying not only a *reaction* against the forces of colonization but also an *active* articulation of self-affirmation akin to what theorists of the more recent "decolonial turn" have in mind. As Franz Fanon in *Black Skin, White Masks* (Boston: Grove Press, 1967, 197) states in his creative engagement with Nietzsche toward the end of the book, yes, of course, "Man is an *affirmation* . . . and that we shall not stop repeating it. Yes to life. Yes to love. Yes to generosity"; "But man," he continues on to insist, "is also a *negation*. No to man's contempt. No to the indignity of man. To the exploitation of man. To the massacre of what is most human in man: freedom." In short, for Fanon, the oppositional subject of *anti*colonialism is both a negation and an affirmation:

a negation that prefigures an affirmative enactment of another modality of being, another system of life-affirming cultural values in the face of a systematic mode of colonial valuation that denigrates and seeks to eliminate Native cultural forms and practices. I explore this concept of *affirmative negation* more thoroughly in my book *Red Skin, White Masks: Rejecting the Colonial Politics of Recognition* (Minneapolis: University of Minnesota Press, 2014).

10. Frantz Fanon, *The Wretched of the Earth* (1961; repr. with commentary by Jean-Paul Sartre and Homi K. Babha, Boston: Grove Press, 2005), 148. Citations refers to the 2005 edition.
11. Nancy Fraser and Axel Honneth, *Redistribution or Recognition? A Political-Philosophical Exchange* (London: Verso, 2003), 11.
12. Georg Wilhelm Friedrich Hegel, *The Phenomenology of Spirit* (Oxford: Oxford University Press, 1997), 178.
13. Robert B. Pippin, "What Is the Question for Which Hegel's Theory of Recognition Is the Answer?" *European Journal of Philosophy* 8, no. 2 (2000): 156.
14. Patchen Markell, *Bound by Recognition* (Princeton, NJ: Princeton University Press, 2003), 25.
15. Charles Taylor, "The Politics of Recognition," in *Re-examining the Politics of Recognition*, ed. Amy Guttman (Princeton, NJ: Princeton University Press, 1994), 25–73.
16. Ibid., 61.
17. Ibid., 40.
18. Ibid., 61.
19. Ibid., 32–33.
20. Ibid., 33–34.
21. Ibid., 33.
22. Charles Taylor, *Sources of the Self* (Cambridge: Cambridge University Press, 1989), 27.
23. Charles Taylor, *The Malaise of Modernity* (Toronto: Anansi Press, 1991), 45–46.
24. Taylor, "Politics of Recognition," 25.
25. Ibid., 26.
26. Ibid., 36.
27. Ibid.
28. Ibid., 64.

29. Ibid., 26.
30. Ibid., 40; Charles Taylor, *Reconciling the Solitudes: Essays on Canadian Federalism and Nationalism* (Montreal: McGill-Queen's University Press, 1993), 148, 180.
31. Taylor, *Reconciling the Solitudes*, 180.
32. Taylor, "Politics of Recognition," 40.
33. Richard Day and Tonio Sadik, "The BC Land Question, Liberal Multiculturalism, and the Spectre of Aboriginal Nationhood," *BC Studies* 134 (2002): 6.
34. Taylor, *Reconciling the Solitudes*, 148.
35. Taylor, "Politics of Recognition," 41.
36. Ibid., 65–66.
37. A number of studies have mapped the similarities and differences between the dialectic of recognition as conceived by Fanon and Hegel, but relatively few have applied Fanon's insights to critique the appropriation of Hegel's theory of recognition to address contemporary questions surrounding the recognition of cultural diversity. Even fewer have used Fanon's writings to problematize the utility of a politics of recognition for restructuring hierarchical relations between disparate identities in colonial contexts. For a survey of the available literature, see Irene Gendzier, *Fanon: A Critical Study* (New York: Grove Press, 1974); Hussein Abdilahi Bulhan, *Frantz Fanon and the Psychology of Oppression* (New York: Plenum Press, 1985); Lou Turner, "On the Difference Between the Hegelian and Fanonian Dialectic of Lordship and Bondage," in *Fanon: A Critical Reader*, ed. Lewis Gordon, T. Denean Sharpley-Whiting, and Renee T. White (Oxford: Blackwell, 1996), 134–51; Beatrice Hanssen, "Ethics of the Other," in *The Turn To Ethics*, ed. Marjorie Garber, Beatrice Hanssen, and Rebecca L. Walkowitz (New York: Routledge, 2000), 127–29; Sonia Kruks, *Retrieving Experience: Subjectivity and Recognition in Feminist Politics* (Ithaca, NY: Cornell University Press, 2001); Kelly Oliver, *Witnessing: Beyond Recognition* (Minneapolis: University of Minnesota Press, 2001); Nigel Gibson, "Dialectical Impasse: Turning the Table on Hegel and the Black," *Parallax* 23 (2002): 30–45; *Fanon: The Postcolonial Imagination* (Cambridge: Polity Press, 2003); Anita Chari, "Exceeding Recognition," *Sartre Studies International* 10, no. 2 (2004): 110–22; Andrew Schaap, "Political Reconciliation Through a Struggle for Recognition?," *Social and Legal Studies* 13, no. 4 (2004): 523–40.
38. Fanon, *Black Skin, White Masks*, 84 (emphasis added).

39. Ibid., 111–12.
40. Ibid., 109.
41. Ibid., 111.
42. Ibid., 112.
43. Ibid., 109.
44. Ibid., 11–12.
45. Ibid.
46. Ibid., 11.
47. Ibid., 202.
48. Ibid., 11.
49. Day, "Who Is This We That Gives the Gift?," 189.
50. See Howard Adams, *Prison of Grass: Canada from a Native Point of View* (Saskatoon: Fifth House, 1975); *A Tortured People: The Politics of Colonization* (Penticton, BC: Theytus Books, 1999); Mel Watkins, ed., *Dene Nation: The Colony Within* (Toronto: University of Toronto Press, 1977); Marie Smallface Marule, "Traditional Indian Government: Of the People, For the People, and By the People," in *Pathways to Self-Determination: Canadian Indians and the Canadian State*, ed. Menno Boldt, Leroy Little Bear Long, and J. Anthony Long (Toronto: University of Toronto Press, 1984), 36–45.
51. See Lee Maracle, *I Am Woman: A Native Perspective on Sociology and Feminism* (Vancouver: Press Gang, 1996); Taiaiake Alfred, *Peace, Power, Righteousness: An Indigenous Manifesto* (Don Mills, ON: Oxford University Press, 1999); *Wasase: Indigenous Pathways of Action and Freedom* (Peterborough, ON: Broadview Press, 2005); Andrea Smith, *Conquest: Sexual Violence and the American Indian Genocide* (Boston: South End Press, 2005).
52. Alfred, *Peace, Power, Righteousness*, 60.
53. Alfred, *Wasase*, 133.
54. Fraser and Honneth, *Redistribution or Recognition*, 29.
55. Ibid.
56. Ibid., 31.
57. Ibid.
58. Fanon, *Black Skin, White Masks*, 11.
59. Ibid., 219 (emphasis added).
60. Ibid., 217.
61. Hegel, *Phenomenology of Spirit*, 113–14.

62. Ibid., 220.
63. Ibid., 18.
64. Ibid., 12.
65. Turner, "Difference Between the Hegelian and Fanonian Dialectic," 146.
66. Ibid.
67. Fanon, *Black Skin, White Masks*, 221.
68. Ibid.
69. Taylor, "Politics of Recognition," 50 (emphasis added).
70. Fanon, *Black Skin, White Masks*, 220.
71. Todd Gordon, "Canada, Empire, and Indigenous Peoples in the Americas," *Socialist Studies* 2, no. 1 (2006): 47–75.
72. Isabelle Schulte-Tenckhoff, "Reassessing the Paradigm of Domestication: The Problematic of Indigenous Treaties," *Review of Constitutional Studies* 4, no. 2 (1998): 239–89.
73. Michael Asch, "From 'Calder' to 'Van der Peet': Aboriginal Rights and Canadian Law," in *Indigenous Peoples' Rights in Australia, Canada, and New Zealand*, ed. Paul Havemann (Auckland: Oxford University Press, 1999), 428–46; Patrick Macklem, *Indigenous Difference and the Constitution of Canada* (Toronto: University of Toronto Press, 2001); James Tully, "The Struggles of Indigenous Peoples for and of Freedom," in *Political Theory and the Rights of Indigenous Peoples*, ed. Duncan Ivison, Paul Patton, and Will Saunders (Cambridge: Cambridge University Press, 2001), 36–59.
74. Tully, "Aboriginal Peoples," 413.
75. Ibid.
76. See Elizabeth A. Povinelli, *The Cunning of Recognition: Indigenous Alterities and the Making of Australian Multiculturalism* (Durham, NC: Duke University Press, 2002).
77. See Eduardo Duran and Bonnie Duran, *Native American Postcolonial Psychology* (Albany: State University of New York Press, 1995).
78. Isabel Altamirano-Jimenez, "North American First Peoples: Slipping into Market Citizenship?," *Citizenship Studies* 8, no. 4 (2004): 349–65; Alfred, *Wasase*; Paul Nadasdy, *Hunters and Bureaucrats: Power, Knowledge, and Aboriginal-State Relations in the Southwest Yukon* (Vancouver: University of British Columbia Press, 2005).
79. Alfred, *Wasase*.

80. Nadasdy, *Hunters and Bureaucrats*.
81. Bill Ashcroft, *Post-Colonial Transformations* (Routledge: New York, 2001), 35.
82. Ashcroft, *Post-Colonial Transformations*; David Scott, *Refashioning Futures: Criticism After Postcoloniality* (Princeton, NJ: Princeton University Press, 1999); David Scott, *Conscripts of Modernity: The Tragedy of Colonial Enlightenment* (Durham, NC: Duke University Press, 2004).
83. Fanon, *Black Skin, White Masks*, 222.
84. Fanon, *Wretched of the Earth*, 148.
85. Fanon, *Black Skin, White Masks*, 222.
86. Ibid., 221.
87. Kruks, *Retrieving Experience*, 101.
88. Fanon, *Black Skin, White Masks*, 222.
89. Young, *Postcolonialism*, 275.
90. Jorge Larrain, "Stuart Hall and the Marxist Concept of Ideology," in *Stuart Hall: Critical Dialogues in Cultural Studies*, ed. Kuan-Hsing Chen and David Morley (New York: Routledge, 1996), 49.
91. Fanon, *Black Skin, White Masks*, 183.
92. Fanon, *Wretched of the Earth*, 8.
93. Young, *Postcolonialism*, 295.
94. Fanon, *Wretched of the Earth*, 44.
95. Ibid., 51.
96. Ibid., 54.
97. Ibid., 44.
98. Homi K. Bhabha, "Forward: Framing Fanon," in Fanon, *Wretched of the Earth*, ix.
99. Alfred, *Wasase*, 58, 30.
100. Fanon, *Black Skin, White Masks*, 221.
101. bell hooks, *Yearning: Race, Gender, and Cultural Politics* (Boston: South End Press, 1990), 22.
102. See Taiaiake Alfred, Glen Coulthard, and Deborah Simmons, "Indigenous Resurgence." Special issue, *New Socialist* 58 (September/October 2006).

3

The Decolonial Deadlock in Guam

MICHAEL LUJAN BEVACQUA

A s an indigenous Chamorro from Guam, one of the world's last "official" colonies, the theory and praxis of decolonization is something that constantly preoccupies my mind.[1] In a world that has purportedly "gotten over" colonialism but where the perceived failures of decolonization have created epidemics of imperialistic nostalgia among both the former colonizers and the formerly colonized, the ambiguous political status of the U.S. territory of Guam is posited as a comfortable colonialism even as the island floats atop a sea of banal political inclusions and exclusions.[2]

For instance, legal residents of Guam are eligible for some federal programs such as welfare and food stamps, but they are disallowed from voting for president. They can join the United States military and may travel freely with an American passport, but they are U.S. citizens whose political protections and rights are derived not from the U.S. Constitution, but rather through an act of Congress. They do not pay federal income tax, and instead of full senators or representatives, they receive a single nonvoting delegate to the U.S. Congress. As one of those former nonvoting delegates, Robert Underwood has noted the primary job of the delegate is not to participate in American democracy but rather to suffer its amnesia. That is, the function of the delegate is to simply remind presidents, senators, and congresspeople that Guam exists and that the United States controls its fate.[3]

This political ambiguity readily extends into the cultural realm. While the majority of Americans still seem to have no idea about what or where Guam is, American popular culture produces an impressive barrage of diverse representations about its colony in the Western Pacific. In movies, television shows, and comic books, Guam is portrayed (in no particular order) as a picture-perfect tropical paradise, an overseas military base, an island full of cannibals, an island of exiled homosexuals, a place where military careers go to die, and a foreign country, most notably Guatemala.[4] Interestingly, the only two major American motion pictures that take Guam seriously either mask Guam as a fictional Pacific Island Cold War battleground (*Noon Sunday*) or keep Guam as a signifier but shoot the movie in the Philippines, with Filipino actors playing Chamorros and replacing the Chamorro language with Tagalog (*No Man Is an Island*).

In print media representations, Guam undergoes a similar diffusion of meaning, as if the existence of Guam is up to the writer to determine. Since 2002, newspapers such as the *Washington Post* and the *Los Angeles Times* have given the island a host of demeaning nicknames, such as: "Trailer Park of the Pacific," "Sleepy Hollow [of the Pacific]," "backwater colony," or "dot on the map." By far one of the most intriguing newspaper articles on Guam was printed in the *New York Times*. Its title—"Looking for Friendly Overseas Base, Pentagon Finds It Already Has One"—captures the colonial banality of Guam as an invisible yet crucial military colony.[5] Similarly, in May 2008, when the protracted Democratic primary battle between senators Hillary Clinton and Barack Obama led to the actualization of the democratic mantra "every vote counts," Guam received a brief onslaught of media attention. Newspapers, blogs, and cable news shows created a great deal of coverage displaying incredulity that Guam "suddenly mattered" that was rife with inaccuracies.[6] For example, CNN produced a two-minute story about Guam while showing footage of another Micronesian Island.

Guam's ambiguity in political, cultural, and social terms is not duplicated, however, in military terms. Listed in 2006 by *Foreign Policy* magazine as one of the six most important U.S. bases in the world,[7] military commanders often refer to Guam as the "tip of America's spear" and "an unsinkable aircraft carrier." Ferdinand Magellan stumbled on the island during his 1521 attempt to circumnavigate the globe. In 1668 it became a colony of the Spanish empire and a frequent stop for missionaries, explorers, and merchants crossing the Pacific. During the Spanish-American War the island was captured by the United States in 1898 in a bloodless takeover. Since that time, save for a brief but bloody occupation by the Japanese during World War II, the island has been essential is helping the United States secure its strategic and economic interests in the Asia-Pacific region. From World War II to conflicts in Korea, Vietnam, Iraq, and Afghanistan, Guam has played an important role in staging attacks and transporting troops into Asia and also providing a transit site for refugees from Vietnam, Iraq, and Burma heading toward the United States.

Most recently, this importance of Guam to the United States has been underscored by recent defense compact renegotiations in Asia. As part of an overall realignment of American overseas troops, it was first announced in 2005 that Guam would become the "home" of troops that will be transferred out of Japan.[8] Since this time, massive military and civilian population increases are always looming on the horizon. A 2009 proposal to transfer eight thousand U.S. Marines and their nine thousand dependents to Guam from Okinawa would have built five firing ranges near important cultural sites, dredged seventy acres of coral reef to create a berth for aircraft carriers, and increased the population of Guam (currently 168,000) by as much as fifty thousand. These plans have been delayed and downsized because of local protest, lawsuits, and also funding problems at the U.S. federal level. Without these increases Guam remains a heavily militarized island that already hosts weaponry—bombers, unmanned surveillance vehicles, and nuclear submarines on two bases that occupy approximately one-third of the island's 212 square miles.[9]

The Decolonial Deadlock

Given Guam's status as a politically powerless militarized territory, one would expect that discussions and efforts aimed at changing Guam's colonial status might be common among the island's people. Yet such is not the case. For most Chamorros, decolonization is not an act or a process meant to rectify the island's long colonial history but is instead understood as suicidal, something to be feared and loathed, something to, in fact, be fought against. For many, "decolonization isn't just suicide," as one Chamorro informed me, "It's also stupid."[10]

I have referred to this resistance to any substantive form of decolonization as "the decolonial deadlock," a discursive formation that circles around the idea that the best possible political and social configuration in Guam has already been reached through its colonial relationship to the United States and that hence, nothing more need be done. The discursive mantra that props up this miasma is the idea that the Chamorro people can only exist as a loyal and dependent appendage of the United States, and thus both the Chamorro and any other political arrangement are impossible.[11]

For those who accept the premises of this deadlock as the foundation for their lives, decolonization offers nothing but emptiness, a void where life turns into ugly chaos. Consequently, there is nothing to be more forcefully resisted than any challenges to that position. Decolonization from this perspective is akin to jumping off a cliff knowing full well that you will die or that the future that will catch and claim you could hardly be called a future but rather a nightmare. Decolonization is, then, a kind of suicide.

For most Chamorros, the suicidal nature of decolonization produces a variety of harrowing delusions that haunt and constrict attempts to articulate a project of decolonization. These include fantasies of immediate societal breakdown and disorder following any act that decreases the influence of the United States in Guam. Other fears revolve around a desire to know what the day after decolonization would look like. These fears often seem to take a very simple, inquisitive form, such as "how will this (blank) look or function after Guam is decolonized?" For example, as one elderly Chamorro asked me, "You think you can run a government without the United States?"[12] These questions take up economy, social order, leisure, happiness, provision of services, and so forth, and can be summarized as "How will the schools run?"[13] "Where will we get the money to run our economy?"[14] "What about the power and the water. The Utilities! Do you people ever think about these things? They barely work now, what will happen then?"[15] "Will we still own property?"[16]

The above questions are naturally not neutral and are far from harmless. They come equipped with the sharp edge of "the end of history," poised to shred whatever weak defense of the possibility of something beyond the United States and its gifts may be offered. "The United States has built the strongest greatest economy in the world, what have Chamorros done in the same history? We made canoes and built latte stones . . . I think it's obvious where our future lies."[17] Questions of this nature are asked in a manner so as to prevent a questioning of the content of enunciation—that is, that Guam is, indeed should be, always attached to the United States as it is now. They are asked so that they need not be asked again. In fact, they are meant to elicit a silent understanding that survival is dependent on not asking these questions, that the suicide and chaos of decolonization awaits us if we were ever to find out the answers to these questions.

As both a scholar and an activist, I do not reject these questions as irrelevant or ridiculous; in truth, these questions are what decolonization is all about. But in their current form, the intent of these questions is not to ask in a rational way "how can we do this?" but rather "how can we do this without the United States?" As such these implicit denials of decolonization are meant to defer its possibility and do so in defense of a particular self—that is, a Chamorro not just entangled in the decolonial deadlock but one which is constituted through a forceful colonizing desire.

In the case of Guam, the possibility of enacting decolonization lies in the ability to traverse the fearful form these questions take at present (how will we survive!?) and move into the moment when they are asked in nervous yet creative earnestness, that is, when they are asked in a way such that they do not already have an answer (how will we survive?). The point of decolonization, then, is not to seek a day after tomorrow for which all questions have been answered ahead of time. Rather, it is the process that gets us to that moment where we can reach the actual content of these questions that are vital to the future of any people. In other words, it is only through decolonization that these questions can truly be asked.[18]

Killing Desire

Producing this transformation, however, requires more than simple changes in engagement or inflection. It requires contending with what we may call the "colonial desire" that helps sustain the decolonial deadlock.[19] The colonial desire is a force within the colonized that despite any expressed loathing or hatred they may feel for the figure of the colonizer nonetheless compels them to maintain his power. It insists that the place of the colonizer always be conserved in some form, whether as something that must be possessed or simply must be, in order for the world to function. It is that which is evident, for instance, in the assertion from an elderly Chamorro man living in San Diego:

> Let's pretend for a little while that I do agree with you and support this nonsense.... We get rid of the United States military. We all go down to Anderson [an Air Force Base on Guam] and wave signs that say "Haole Go Home!," and they take the hint and leave.... You will miss them. When China invades or North Korea attacks, or even when the economy falls apart, you'll wish they were still here.... You'll want them back![20]

What is interesting about this statement is how this Chamorro argues that even if the United States left, Chamorros would not only need the United States but also *crave* them. And this desire would persist long after the colonizers were "physically" gone. The persistence of this desire leads to the question of what to do with this desire that makes decolonization unthinkable. In addressing the issue of what to do with this desire, I would submit that we not reject the idea that decolonization is suicide but rather accept it. The work of theorist Frantz Fanon offers some possibilities as to why.

In *The Wretched of the Earth*, Fanon argues that the decolonial battle is never as simple or direct as vanquishing the colonizer. This is the case because the colonized is always consumed with simultaneous hatreds and longings. As Fanon notes, "the native never ceases to dream of putting himself in the place of the settler—not of becoming the settler, but of substituting himself for the settler."[21] In other words, the colonized may detest the colonizer's power as it is the source of his oppression, but he also desires it and craves the objects he associates with it; the colonized constantly dreams of the colonizer's house, of razing it and possessing it.

Decolonization in its least effective form is about physical expulsion or violence, but to be effective it must always be about violence at the symbolic level. For Fanon, decolonization is fundamentally about "freedom"; the freedom sought by the colonized is from the colonial world's restrictions and daily violence.[22] But within this there is a more intense and more difficult dreaming at stake in Fanon's decolonization, namely, a freedom from the desire for the colonizer—for his goods, his gaze. A freedom, perhaps, from the very forms the colonized's dreaming is forced to take. A resistance to the fact that the colonized must always dream in relation to the colonizer, that that colonizer and his example must be followed in order to progress and prosper, and that even if the colonizer is physically evicted from the colonial world, he will still occupy the dreams of its former subjects. Decolonization is about reaching this point of freedom, making it possible for the colonized to break away from that desire and chart their own course.

Reaching this point, however, requires two distinct acts of violence, the first a confrontation with the colonizer. The second is a much more precarious act, as it is an attack on the colonized themselves, in essence a suicide. Both, the colonized and the colonizer are born out of their shared violent world; the eviction or death of one must be accompanied by the other. As the colonized always craves and loathes the castles of the colonizer, unless an act is taken to free himself from that desire, to radically alter the landscape of his world, he will continually demolish and rebuild, in absentia now, the colonizer's castle. Without this suicide of the colonized, his newborn sovereignty will be attested to through "fancy dress parade[s] and the blare of trumpets . . . a few reforms at the top, a flag waving," but nothing more.[23]

In the case of Guam, this double violence, and the ensuing double death, creates a moment where the path forward is far from obvious and secure; one where the notion, proposed by one elderly Chamorro, that "America is the only way we can move forward" is far from assured, far from given.[24] The death of the colonized, then, creates a moment wherein what was once decided now becomes temporarily undecidable.[25] That is, Guam or Chamorros experience a moment of freedom where they are not condemned to follow the path of progress set forth by the United States but are instead able to imagine a future that is open, where another possibility can be sought.

As such, the Chamorro, subjectivity where it must be a defender of America and Americanness, dissipates so that the Chamorro now does not merely look on objects—whether education, military service, diaspora, or the future itself—as if they were new but encounters them in a world that is potentially new.²⁶ Returning to Fanon, this is the moment at which the colonized "finds that the settler's skin is not of any more value than a native's skin; and it must be said that this discovery shakes the world in a very necessary manner."²⁷ Without a dual death, however, the colonized will be compelled to wear the colonizer's skin, to consume it, to continue to desire it.²⁸

The idea that this moment can "shake the world," according to Fanon, is no hyperbole. The suicide, this gesture of negativity, recreates common sense, requilts the notions of (im)possibility, and changes the rules that govern the movement of material and ideas within a society. It is, in sum, a radical reconstitution of the symbolic order. The decolonial act, thus, as philosopher Slavoj Žižek adds, "does not occur *within* the given horizon of what appears to be 'possible'" but instead, "redefines the very contours of what is possible."²⁹ Consequently, my definition of *sovereignty* is not invested in particular political status categories or notions of local and everyday sovereignty. Rather, it is sovereignty as contained in an act that has the potential to break the decolonial deadlock.

Acts of Decolonization

Decolonization is then not a sustained, consistent momentum but rather a series of acts. And these acts of decolonization have the potential to rework or redirect the desire of the colonized and colonizers, thus transforming the world around them. Yet what might such an act look like in practice? How does this sort of radical societal change take place? A relatively recent incident in Guam—a protest against the American military presence—provides important insight.

For most Chamorros, the seizing of nearly two thirds of their land in the years following World War II has been the most painful episode in the attempted Americanization of Guam.³⁰ After World War II, the United States was determined to transform the Pacific Ocean into an "American Lake," and Guam, seated as it is on the edge of Asia, was critical in making that transformation possible.³¹ When the U.S. military invaded Guam in July 1944 and expelled the Japanese, Chamorros enthusiastically welcomed them. The U.S.

military had not returned to save the people per se but had returned to Guam because it would provide an ideal staging point for direct assaults on Japan.

The U.S. military took advantage of the gratitude of Chamorros and began to seize their land. Chamorros were initially willing to give up their lands, as they were promised the lands would be returned once the war was over. However, by 1948, three years after Japan's surrender, the land taking continued. The intent of this landgrab was to turn the whole of Guam into a massive, modern military base. The legality of this land seizure, exercised under the right of "eminent domain," was certainly questionable; one Marine Corps colonel, questioned by Congress in 1946, stated, "I wouldn't say legally, but everything is legal in a time of war."[32] According to Guam scholar Robert Underwood, the issue of land, its theft and its demanded return, was the one issue that could turn any Chamorro—a nurse, a teacher, a serviceman, anyone—into an activist, and perhaps a radical one.[33]

Despite the fact that the land issue on Guam remains unresolved, this has not affected the patriotic veneer of the island or necessarily soured its relationship to the U.S. military. Each year on July 21, Guam's largest celebration, "Liberation Day," takes place to commemorate the American reoccupation of Guam with weeks of beauty pageants, carnivals, parades, and parties.[34] Chamorros as a group not only consider themselves to be "superpatriotic" but attest to this patriotism through overwhelming enlistment statistics in the United States armed forces.[35] The United States military is not simply an abstract institution; because of its heavy presence in Guam and the large number of Chamorros that serve in the military, it is treated as a respected member of Guam's family. Serving in the military is not just a means of improving one's life but also a chance to also repay the debt of liberation that Chamorros have incurred.[36] The trauma of the land takings, however, and the lack of resolution for many families means that it continues to be an object of protest and critique for Chamorros today.

In 1975, the Guam legislature passed the Chamorro Land Trust Act. Modeled after the Hawaiian Homes Commission Act, this legislation was designed to provide land to landless Chamorros.[37] While on the books, the law was not enforced for decades, as questions over who legally qualified as Chamorro were debated. In 1992, however, the group Nasion Chamoru—made up of indigenous rights activists, families seeking the return of their ancestral lands, and a surprisingly large number of disillusioned former American military servicemen—successfully sued the government of Guam for its failure to implement the Chamorro Land Trust Act, forcing the governor of Guam to create the Chamorro Land Trust Commission.[38] During the same year, the United States Navy returned land in the island's central area to the government of Guam, although it is unclear whether the struggles launched by the Nasion Chamoru had any effect on this decision.[39] These contests over land involved a number of different organizations, personalities, and protests in arenas ranging from the legislature of Guam, the Congress of the United States, and the United Nations General Assembly. One figure, however, the late Angel Leon Guerrero Santos, former Maga'låhi, or male leader, of the Nasion Chamoru, emerged as the most prominent, best exemplifying the radical character of these battles.[40]

In 1993 Santos and other members of Nasion Chamoru were protesting outside of Naval Air Station Guam because of the danger of low-altitude training flights that were disrupting the life of people living around the base. Frustrated with the U.S. military's disregard for the safety of the community, Santos and several of his compatriots jumped a military fence—not in the darkness of night but in the stark light of day, before other gathered Chamorros, the media, and the U.S. military. This spectacle was heightened when Santos, while being apprehended by the United States military police, spat in the face of his captor, shocking the sensibilities of nearly every Chamorro present and of those who heard about it.[41]

In deciding to jump the military fence, Angel Santos and members of the Nasion Chamoru assumed an uncertain and perilous fate and accepted the possible social death that would accompany it, thereby, in a sense, committing an act of suicide. Indeed, they demonstrated an acceptance of the fact that they could expect sanctuary from neither side of the fence. Among civilians, they were unprotected, decried in the media as "maladjusted," and whispered about by nearly all on Guam as radicals, lunatics, and troublemakers.[42] These challenges to the military's power placed them outside of the social intelligibility of Chamorro, and thus they were, in the minds of most Chamorros, not Chamorro at all. In their actions they were openly biting the hand that feeds, or in the case of Guam, the hand that liberates. The military was a member of Guam's family, something that was considered sacred and supposed to be beyond reproach in public discourse. On the other side of the fence, where the U.S. military and the police served as markers of universality and the law and the United States was arbiter of both local and global order, they could expect a similar, albeit more viscerally violent fate.

Although the Nasion Chamaru did not spark a revolution in the streets after this incident, what this decolonial act accomplished was a reconfiguration of the island beneath them. They had achieved, in some sense, what Slavoj Žižek refers to as a "symbolic separation."[43] That is, as they leapt into the air above Guam, above the military fence, their radical act allowed them to step out of the symbolic network and in a way "cleanse the plate," or force the symbolic order to reform itself around their act.[44] The drive, the force, and the power of this act comes from the agent's acceptance of a terrifying lack that is always present/absent in the symbolic network.

With this particular act as well as with all ethical acts, what the agent embodies and performs is the fact that the symbolic order does not exist. In other words, such acts demonstrate that the social rules, norms, and meanings that seem to create an aura of social certainty—for example, the norms whereby Santos's act was recognized and labeled as stupid, dangerous, and that of a mindless radical—are in fact contingent, labile, fluid. Ultimately, every order of meaning is always already circling cautiously around a fundamental lack, the dangerous and impossible filling of which has the potential to radically alter the very structure of a sociopolitical space.

Acts that once appeared impossible on Guam could now become regular, even routine. This act helped build a space, small at first perhaps but nonetheless present, where the Chamorro could now critique the U.S. military openly and publicly. It now became possible, against the dubious wisdom of the proverb "You should not bite the hand that feeds you," to bite that very hand, to question whether or not there was life beyond its "generosity." It created the space from within in which Chamorros could, against their hegemonic dependency on the United States, be now articulated against the United States, outside of the United States. Current protests and critiques against U.S. military increases in Guam have their roots first in the land takings that incited Nasion Chamoru to action but also the social possibility created by their act in challenging that military fence. The fences that mark the boundaries are reminders not just of the strategic importance of the island but of the colonial notion that Guam belongs to the United States and is theirs to do with as they please.[45]

Beyond this, however, the act forced the language of sovereignty and decolonization into political discourse and into everyday discussions. Decolonization, as in the recognition of the Chamorro right to self-determination or the changing of Guam's political status from that of an unincorporated territory, was often a difficult concept to discuss because of the perception that the idea itself was anti-American, unpatriotic, or antimilitary. Other than a handful of political leaders and activists, it was something few Chamorros considered seriously. The activities of Nasion Chamoru helped to change this by not only helping to remind people of historical American mistreatment of Chamorros but also by opening up the future to the point where Chamorros and the island deserved more than being a mere American possession. As anthropologist Roland Stade notes in *Pacific Passages: World Culture and Local Politics in Guam*,

> the direct actions of the Nasion Chamoru have changed the public debate about the issue of Guam's sovereignty. As of the late 1990's, not a single politician on the island will abstain from promoting either a higher level ("commonwealth") or the highest level ("independence") of political sovereignty for Guam. What was once an outrageous form of radical activism and anti-Americanism has become more or less mainstream.[46]

However, a question remains: what becomes of colonial desire? It cannot disappear; desire itself does not dissipate, but it can be restructured alongside the reconfigured symbolic network. That is, as already mentioned, while the world becomes recolored through a disruption, desire breaks free of its particular dependencies. We find this recoloring of desire in Chamorro poet Cecilia T. Perez's article "Inside Out," where she ruminates on the act of Angel Santos and how it changes what the fences and the land those fences keep away mean to her.

> Where the fence once made me feel wanting for the treasure I thought it contained, it now makes me feel anger for the stolen treasure it contains. I flash back on the man who scaled that fence in protest of the land being taken. He

was apprehended and shackled by the military police. While others criticized his action, I could only see him as brave. Restrained as he was by human force and metal handcuffs, he was free. He had freed himself in that moment from the mental bondage of our colonial existence. In retaliation, he spat on his captor.

At first I shuddered in disgust. "What low had this cultural hero sunken to" I thought. After much reflexion, my judgement changed. He showed bravery. What else could he do? What makes us believe spitting is so disgusting anyway?[47]

Conclusion

In sum, the act of Angel Santos and Nasion Chamoru and their radical assertion of Chamorro possibility and sovereignty revealed the colonizing structure of Guam in that moment and threatened to collapse the colonizer's order. The actors offered themselves up through their act, and their symbolic suicide offers their potential corpse as the force through which the old order can lose its authority and the foundation on which a new order might be built. All acts, of decolonization or otherwise, involve this same indeterminacy, the same risk of overexposure, and because of this, the language of death and suicide will necessarily always be found nearby.

Importantly, this discussion of societal transformation and action is not limited to Guam or even just to a colonial context but rather has relevance to any situation where a community finds itself chained in a similar way for life and existence, supposedly impossible without following the path laid out by their former colonizer or current global powers, and haunted by the specter of their international suicide if they refuse to comply.

One finds situations similar to that of Guam by merely scanning across the world as different peoples confront imperialism, colonialism, militarism, and differing New World orders. The prognosis is the same regardless of region or history—a path has already been carved out, you can only groan and sputter, clinging to a previous point far behind the apex of this path, and the viability of your existence depends on retracing what has already been decided about the nature of time, reality, and history.

In the work of decolonization, there are numerous points whereby commonsense and strategy must necessarily fall short or fail, where discussions of reform—the debates designed to cling to life, to a particular desire—must end. Here the limits of the obvious and the natural are reached, and the only thing that appears to stretch before you is a bleak, bleeding expanse of impossibility. When confronted with this impasse—where commonsense provides no further bridge, where the collective wisdom of modernity seems to compel a return to the categorical comforts of the native, the local, the national, the pathological, the dependency of desire—one must not turn back. Instead, one must jump.

Notes

1. As of 2015 the United Nations lists seventeen entities that are still non-self-governing territories. These are the world's sixteen remaining "official" colonies: Western Sahara, Anguilla, Bermuda, British Virgin Islands, Cayman Islands, Falkland Islands (Malvinas), Montserrat, St. Helena, Turks and Caicos Islands, United States Virgin Islands, Gibraltar, American Samoa, French Polynesia, New Caledonia, Pitcarin, Tokelau, and Guam. *United Nations and Decolonization: Non-Self-Governing Territories*, http://www.un.org/en/decolonization/nonselfgovterritories.shtml.
2. Robert Cooper, "The Post-modern State," *Observer*, April 7, 2002. Daniel Vernet, "Postmodern Imperialism," *Le Monde*, April 24, 2003; Robert Underwood, "The Status of Having No Status" (speech, College of Arts and Sciences Research Conference, University of Guam, Mangilao, Guam, April 26, 1999). For more information on how this status has been developed over the years from the perspective of Chamorros, see Penelope Bordallo Hofschneider, *Campaign for Political Rights on the Island of Guam, 1898–1950* (Commonwealth of the Northern Marianas Islands, Saipan: CNMI Division of Historic Preservation, 2001). For a legal perspective, see Arnold Leibowitz, *Defining Status: A Comprehensive Analysis of United States–Territorial Relations* (Dordrecht, The Netherlands: Martinus Nijhoff, 1989).
3. Robert Underwood, interview by Michael Lujan Bevacqua, Office of Robert Underwood, Hagatna, Guam, December 5, 2002.

4. The references here come from the films *Dudley Do-Right, Wedding Crashers, Good Morning Vietnam, Yours, Mine and Ours*; the television shows *Family Guy* and *Kim Possible*; and the comic book *G.I. Joe Sigma Six*.
5. Seth Kantor, "Guam: US Showcase? Not with Present Policies," *Guam Tribune*, August 31, 1984, p. 44; Orville F. Desjarlais Jr., "Sleepy Hollow No More," *Airman*, April 4, 2006; Tom Perry, "Dot on the Map Retains Large Strategic Stature," *Los Angeles Times*, January 28, 2002; Patrick Goodenough, "US Has Big Military Plans for Small Pacific Island," *CNSNews.com*, June 11, 2004; James Brooke, "Looking for Friendly Overseas Base, Pentagon Finds It Already Has One," *New York Times*, April 7, 2004.
6. Michael Lujan Bevacqua, "Covering Guam in the 2008 Democratic Primaries," *Fresh View* (online column), Asian American Journalists Association, June 2008 (no longer posted), http://www.aaja.org/news/mediawatch/freshview/2008_06_20_01/.
7. Daniel Widome, "The List: The Six Most Important U.S. Military Bases," *Foreign Policy*, May 13, 2006, http://www.foreignpolicy.com/articles/2006/05/12/the_list_the_six_most_important_us_military_bases.
8. Gene Park, "7,000 Marines, Pentagon Announces Shift to Guam," *Pacific Daily News*, October 30, 2005.
9. Department of Defense, Department of the Navy, "Record of Decision for the Guam and Commonwealth of Northern Mariana Islands Military Relocation: Relocating Marines from Okinawa, Visiting Aircraft Carrier Berthing, Air and Missile Defense Task Force," Fed. Reg. 60438 (September 30, 2010).
10. Anonymous, e-mail message to author, November 24, 2003.
11. *Sinthome* is a term that comes from the work of Jacques Lacan, and it refers to the image through which an ideological system or economy is run. Slavoj Žižek offers as an example of a sinthome "single unwed mother": "It is a point where all the lines of predominant ideological argumentation (the return to family values, the rejection of the welfare state and its 'uncontrolled' spending, etc.) meet." Slavoj Žižek, *The Ticklish Subject: The Absent Centre of Political Ontology* (London: Verso, 1999), 176.
12. Mike Cruz, personal communication, Sons and Daughters of Guam Club, San Diego, California, April 25, 2006.
13. Tom Quinata, interview by Michael Lujan Bevacqua, Isla Center for the Arts, Mangilao, Guam, August 17, 2004.

14. Dan Guerrero, interview by Michael Lujan Bevacqua, home of Dan Guerrero, Mangilao, Guam, December 16, 2005.
15. Fulanu, interview by Michael Lujan Bevacqua, Bank of Guam Building, Hagåtña, Guam, May 7, 2004.
16. Naomi Sablan, personal communication, Isla Center for the Arts, Mangilao, Guam, August 17, 2004.
17. John Salas, e-mail message to author, April 27, 2005. Latte stones are huge basalt megaliths that Chamorros built before Spanish colonization to mark territory and burial grounds. Houses were also built on them.
18. Slavoj Žižek, "Jews, Christians and other Monsters," *Lacanian Ink* 23 (Spring 2004): 97.
19. The song "Guam U.S.A." by Chamorro singer K. C. Leon Guerrero provides an interesting example of the complexity of this desire, which I am, sadly, because of limits of time for this thesis, forced to gloss over: "I'm from Guam USA / And I'm proud that it is true / When I was born in a land and lived in the world of the Chamorro / Guam is good / Guam is hot / Guam is just such a little spot / It's a beautiful island that you've never seen / Where America's day begins." The mechanics of desire are never a clear desire for recognition, as the lack of recognition tends to proliferate its own forms of enjoyment. Throughout this song, Leon Guerrero, while traveling in the states, continually meets people who have no idea where he is from and what Guam is. He asks each of them "Kao guaha un keketungo'?" (Have you ever tried knowing about it?) While the song's clearest desire is the unification of the "Guam" and the "USA," the singer, upon feeling the revocation of this desire, nonetheless takes great enjoyment in being from an America that no one has ever seen. We find a similar dynamic with the lover who speaks endlessly of the pain of his lost love, lost happiness, but when confronted with attempts to reconcile the loss, to stop the soul wrenching, rejects them because of the happiness he now gleans from the mere discussion of his loss.
20. Ray Sablan, interview by Michael Lujan Bevacqua, Sons and Daughters of Guam Club, San Diego, California, February 8, 2006.
21. Ibid., 52.
22. Ibid.
23. Ibid., 147.
24. Frederico Garcia, interview by Michael Lujan Bevacqua, Guam Communications Network, Long Beach, California, November 12, 2003.

25. Rex Butler, *Slavoj Žižek: Live Theory* (London: Continuum, 2005), 68.
26. Slavoj Žižek, *Organs Without Bodies: On Deleuze and Consequences* (New York: Routledge, 2004), 1.
27. Frantz Fanon, *The Wretched of the Earth* (1961; repr. with commentary by Jean-Paul Sartre and Homi K. Babha, Boston: Grove Press, 2005), 45. Citation refers to the 2005 edition.
28. Huey P. Newton, *Revolutionary Suicide* (1973; repr., New York: Penguin Books, 2009).
29. Judith Butler, Ernesto Laclau, and Slavoj Žižek, *Hegemony, Contingency, Universality* (Verso: London, 2000), 121.
30. Mike Phillips, "Land," in , *Kinalamten Pulitikåt: Siñenten I Chamorro: Issues in Guam's Political Development: The Chamorro Perspective*, Political Status Education Coordinating Commission (Guam), Hale'-Ta series (Hagatna, Guam: Political Status Education Coordinating Commission, 1996).
31. Hal M. Friedman, *Creating an American Lake: United States Imperialism and Strategic Security in the Pacific Basin 1945–1947* (Westport, CT: Greenwood Press, 2001).
32. Phillips, "Land," 17.
33. Robert Underwood, "Afterword," in Bordallo Hofschneider, *Campaign for Political Rights*, 211.
34. Vicente M. Diaz, "Deliberating 'Liberation Day': Identity, History, Memory and War in Guam," in *Perilous Memories: The Asia Pacific War(s)*, ed. T. Fujitani, Geoffrey M. White, and Lisa Yoneyama (Durham, NC: Duke University Press, 2001), 155–80.
35. James Brooke, "On Farthest U.S. Shores, Iraq is a way to a Dream," *New York Times*, July 31, 2005.
36. Michael Lujan Bevacqua, "The Exceptional Life and Death of a Chamorro Soldier: Tracing the Militarization of Desire in Guam, USA," in *Militarized Currents: Toward a Decolonized Future in Asia and the Pacific*, ed. Setsu Shigematsu and Keith Lujan Camacho (Minneapolis: University of Minnesota Press, 2010), 33–62.
37. Robert Rogers, *Destiny's Landfall* (Honolulu: University of Hawai'i Press, 1995), 246.
38. Ronald Stade, *Pacific Passages, World Culture and Local Politics in Guam*, Stockholm Studies in Social Anthropology 42 (Stockholm: Department of Social Anthropology, Stockholm University, 1998), 196.

39. Michael Lujan Bevacqua, "'The Illusions of Partnership and the Fear of Sovereignty," *No Rest for the Awake* (blog), September 19, 2007, http://minagahet.blogspot.com/2007/09/illusions-of-partnership-and-fear-of.html.
40. Jayne Flores, "Senot Maga'lahi," *Guahan Magazine* 1, no. 1 (July 2003): 16–17.
41. *Storytellers of the Pacific: Part 1: Identity*, aired December 19, 1996, ITVS, Corporation for Public Broadcasting (Big Island, HI: Visionmaker Video, 1995).
42. Robert Underwood, "Consciousness and the Maladjusted People of Guam," *Chamorro Self-Determination*, ed. Laura Souder and Robert Underwood (Hagatna, Guam, Chamorro Studies Association, 1991).
43. Žižek, "Jews, Christians and other Monsters," 137.
44. Ibid., 140.
45. Stade, *Pacific Passages*, 192–94.
46. Ibid., 196.
47. Cecilia T. Perez, "Inside Out," in *Indigenous Women: The Right to a Voice*, ed. Diana Vinding (Copenhagen: IWGIA, 1998), 86–88.

4

Recognizing Native Hawaiians

Reality Bites

DAVIANNA PŌMAIKA'I MCGREGOR

He aloha la, he aloha
No kuʻu lāhui ʻōiwi
I hoʻokahi puʻuwai
Kūpaʻa me ka lōkāhi
O my love and adoration
For my native people,
Be of one heart
And stand firm with unity
VERSE 2, "KE ALOHA 'ĀINA" (LOVE FOR THE LAND), BY HER
MAJESTY QUEEN LILI'UOKALANI[1]

The quest of Lāhui ʻŌiwi (Native Hawaiians) to reestablish sovereignty and self-determination began on January 16, 1893, when U.S. naval forces invaded Hawaiʻi in support of the illegal overthrow of the Hawaiian monarchy.[2] It is inspired by the thoughts Queen Liliʻuokalani expressed in her writings and songs (such as the one above), which continue to be read and performed from one generation to the next.[3] It is reinforced by the historical and contemporary injustices reflected in the low incomes, high unemployment rates, disparate incarceration rates, the disproportionate reliance on public assistance, and the poor health conditions of Lāhui ʻŌiwi in Hawaiʻi. It is provoked by legal suits seeking to dismantle

Hawaiian land trusts established by Lāhui ʻŌiwi aliʻi (chiefly rulers) and the U.S. Congress and suits seeking to extinguish other Lāhui ʻŌiwi entitlements.[4] It is has been nurtured by the renaissance of Lāhui ʻŌiwi language, music, hula, navigation, and spiritual practices.

The right of sovereignty has been instilled in the hearts and minds of Lāhui ʻŌiwi for generations. It is rooted in the traditional and customary exercise of an indigenous sovereignty that evolved over more than eleven centuries preceding contact and commerce with European, American, and Asian nation-states. The ʻŌiwi word for sovereignty is *Ea*, which also means "life" and "breath," signifying that sovereignty is essential to the survival of a people. Lāhui ʻŌiwi have an inherent right of *Ea*—sovereignty.

Sovereignty and Governance

Sovereignty can be exercised and demonstrated in a number of forms—politically, culturally, and spiritually—and on different levels—individually and collectively as a community and formally as a nation. Individually and as a community, Lāhui ʻŌiwi have continued to exercise political, cultural, and spiritual sovereignty into the twenty-first century.

As a nation, sovereignty is most effectively exercised through a governing entity. For over eleven centuries before European and American contact and through 1810, Lāhui ʻŌiwi exercised sovereignty through the governance of Hawaiʻi aliʻi, or chiefs, who ruled the Hawaiian archipelago. In 1810, one ruling chief, King Kamehameha I, established a monarchial form of government that ruled Hawaiʻi through January 1893, when the Hawaiian monarchy was overthrown. At that point, the governance of the Hawaiʻi nation-state began to be distinct from that of the self-governance of Lāhui ʻŌiwi or the Native Hawaiian indigenous nation.

From 1900 through 1959, the United States governed the multiethnic Hawaiʻi nation-state as an incorporated territory, but it also established a special political and trust relationship with the Lāhui ʻŌiwi community through federal legislation. On November 23, 1993, the U.S. Congress and the president of the United States issued a Joint Resolution of Apology to the Hawaiian people that included the following statements:

The indigenous Hawaiian people never directly relinquished their claims to sovereignty as a people or over their national lands to the United States, either through their monarchy or through a plebiscite or referendum. . . .

The Native Hawaiian people are determined to preserve, develop and transmit to future generations their ancestral territory, and their cultural identity in accordance with their own spiritual and traditional beliefs, customs, practices, language, and social institutions. . . .

[The U.S. Congress] . . . apologizes to Native Hawaiians on behalf of the people of the United States for the overthrow of the Kingdom of Hawaii on January 17, 1893 with the participation of agents and citizens of the United States and the deprivation of the rights of Native Hawaiians to self-determination.[5]

While the Kingdom of Hawai'i was made up of a multiethnic citizenry, the apology was only offered to Lāhui 'Ōiwi. This reflected the dual policy of the United States to govern the multiethnic Hawai'i nation-state as a part of the United States while at the same time acknowledging the sovereignty of the Lāhui 'Ōiwi as an indigenous people within the framework of U.S. laws and policies that apply to Native Americans, Native Alaskans, Eskimos, and Aleuts.

Two Entities, Two Kinds of Status, Two Movements

The overthrow of the Hawaiian Kingdom in 1893 together with the dual governance policy of the United States and demographic changes that reduced Lāhui 'Ōiwi to 20 percent of Hawai'i's resident population by the twenty-first century has resulted in the existence of two sovereign entities. One entity is Lāhui 'Ōiwi, the Native Hawaiian indigenous nation, and the other is Aupuni Hawai'i, the multiethnic Hawai'i state. This political condition has given rise to two distinct movements for sovereignty and self-determination in Hawai'i.

One movement seeks to reestablish the government of Lāhui 'Ōiwi (Native Hawaiian indigenous nation) and define a government-to-government relationship with the U.S. government similar to that of other indigenous peoples. The second movement seeks to reestablish the government of Aupuni Hawai'i the (multiethnic Hawai'i nation-state) separate from the U.S. nation-state. Both movements are rooted in the unique cultural and political history of Hawai'i. Both lay claim to the national lands of the Hawaiian Kingdom currently held by the governments of the United States and the State of Hawai'i. Both have met challenges and obstacles. And both are pursuing distinct political strategies.

In this article I explore the evolution of these two distinct sovereign entities—Lāhui 'Ōiwi (Native Hawaiian indigenous nation) and 'Aupuni Hawai'i (multiethnic Hawai'i state). At present, the dominant narrative about the Lāhui 'Ōiwi movements for sovereignty and independence has represented these two entities as one Hawaiian nation that has two choices for governance—to become a domestic dependent nation within the United States similar to Native Americans or to seek total independence from the U.S. nation-state. A subnarrative for this conflated Hawaiian nation model proposes a two-stage process to achieve sovereignty and independence—first become a domestic dependent nation and then work toward total independence.

In this article, I outline how the governance of Lāhui 'Ōiwi and 'Aupuni Hawai'i were one and the same for centuries. I then describe how the composition and interests of these two entities began to grow apart once foreign settler interests gained influence within 'Aupuni Hawai'i. I identify the point at which the two entities became distinct and describe the social and political processes that reinforced their distinctiveness.[6] Finally, I discuss the distinct strategies being considered for each entity to achieve sovereignty and the obstacles, challenges and anticipated developments. As I present a new perspective on a politically contentious subject, I hope that this chapter will stimulate discussion and debate that can yield new insights regarding Lāhui 'Ōiwi sovereignty.

Common Roots

Lāhui 'Ōiwi are the indigenous people of Hawai'i who developed the unique culture, language, economy, and system of political organization of Ka Pae

'Āina Hawai'i (Hawaiian Archipelago). Linguistic, genealogical, and archaeological evidence places the development of this society in Hawai'i and as being distinct from other Polynesian islands by AD 600. By approximately AD 1000, *ali'i*, or chiefs, emerged as the rulers in every district on each island. They undertook the responsibility of organizing the '*ohana*, or extended families, of the *maka'āinana* (common people) to develop an infrastructure of irrigation networks, roads, and fishponds. This enabled the intensification of the production of food and basic necessities to support a rapidly expanding population.

By AD 1200 the district chiefs formed '*aha ali'i*, or a council of chiefs on each island, and by 1500, the '*aha ali'i* councils on each island selected an *ali'i nui*, or high chief, to rule. While there are eight major inhabited Hawaiian islands, from 1500 through the establishment of a central government in 1810, the islands were divided into and ruled as four major chiefdoms—Hawai'i Island, Maui Nui (islands of Maui, Lāna'i, Moloka'i and Kaho'olawe), O'ahu, and Kaua'i (Kaua'i and Ni'ihau).

By 1795, Kamehameha I, the *ali'i nui* of Hawai'i Island, defeated the chiefs of Maui Nui and O'ahu and controlled all of the islands except Kaua'i and Ni'ihau. In 1810, Kaumuali'i, the *ali'i nui* of Kaua'i, peacefully agreed to accept the governance of Kamehameha I, and Aupuni Hawai'i became a monarchy that ruled a central government for all of the islands. In 1840 King Kamehameha III transformed Aupuni Hawai'i into a constitutional monarchy.[7] The Hawaiian Kingdom and constitutional monarchy was formally recognized as an independent government and entered into treaties and received formal recognition as a sovereign, independent nation from nearly every major world power following the lead of the United States, Great Britain, and France.[8] This constitutional monarchy was the government of both the Lāhui 'Ōiwi and Aupuni Hawai'i through January 17, 1893.

Branching Out in Different Directions

Discernible strands in the evolution of Lāhui 'Ōiwi as a *lāhui* (nation formation) distinct from the Hawai'i state began to form in the 1840s. During this era, King Kamehameha III and the council of chiefs began to focus on protecting the integrity of the government of Aupuni Hawai'i from increasing demands of foreign residents and threats to its independence from foreign governments. Concessions were granted, for example, to French residents to prevent the takeover of Hawai'i by French captain La Place in 1839.[9] The adoption of a constitution in 1840 laid the groundwork for Hawai'i to gain diplomatic recognition from other nations, but it also provided the opening for foreign settlers to gain political influence within Aupuni Hawai'i. Foreign settlers were allowed to become naturalized citizens, to vote, and to hold positions in the government. Settlers began to assume key appointive positions in the government, were appointed by the king to the House of Nobles and were elected to the House of Representatives. From 1842 to 1880, out of a total of 34 different men who held cabinet positions, 28 were Europeans or Americans and only six were Hawaiian or part Hawaiian. Throughout this same period whites made up 28 percent of the legislature although they made up only 7 percent of the population.[10] Aupuni Hawai'i was no longer made up of just Lāhui 'Ōiwi. It became a multiethnic nation-state representative of both settler and Lāhui 'Ōiwi interests.

Lāhui 'Ōiwi seeking to protect the land and natural resources for subsistence of the people and to protect their cultural customs and practices coalesced when necessary through ad hoc or temporary organizations to express concern over the conduct of the king and his council of chiefs. For example, 5,790 Lāhui 'Ōiwi from Maui, Lāna'i, Moloka'i, and Hawai'i sent petitions to the king and the legislature in 1845 to preserve the traditional land system, not allow foreigners to become naturalized citizens, not let foreigners own land in Hawai'i, and not appoint foreigners to government positions.[11]

The distinction between the interests of Lāhui 'Ōiwi and Aupuni Hawai'i grew more apparent when the government pursued a reciprocal trade treaty with the United States. A nationalist movement calling themselves "Hawai'i for the Hawaiians" organized against the treaty. The movement persisted and grew after the treaty was consummated and implemented. The Reciprocity Treaty stimulated an unprecedented growth of the sugar industry and Hawai'i's economy. Between 1875 and 1882, thirty-eight new plantations were opened on twenty thousand acres of land through the work of forty thousand contract laborers who were imported to Hawai'i.[12] The displacement of Native Hawaiians from their traditional lands increased as the cultivation of sugar increased. By 1890, Hawaiians made up only 45 percent of the population because of the increase of immigrant laborers.[13]

In 1893, U.S. commissioner James Blount, in his report on the conditions that led up to the illegal overthrow of the Hawaiian monarchy, characterized the Reciprocity Treaty as follows:

> From it [the Reciprocity Treaty] there came to the islands an intoxicating increase of wealth, a new labor system, an Asiatic population, an alienation between the native and white race, an impoverishment of the former, an enrichment of the latter, and the many so-called revolutions, which are the foundation for the opinion that stable government can not be maintained.[14]

By 1886, nine-tenths of Hawai'i's exports were sold to the United States, and eight-tenths of Hawai'i's imports came from the United States.[15] The stage was set for the settler interests to take control of Aupuni Hawai'i and seek annexation by the United States.

When the U.S.-Hawai'i Reciprocity Treaty of 1875 expired, the U.S. Congress demanded exclusive use of and control over Pu'uloa (Pearl Harbor) as a condition of renewing the treaty. King Kalākaua refused. American planters and foreign business interests formed the Hawaiian League in alliance with the all-white, 500-man volunteer militia of the Hawaiian Kingdom called the Honolulu Rifles. Together, these groups carried out a coup d'état—forcing King Kalākaua to accept a constitution that became known as the "Bayonet Constitution."[16] The Bayonet Constitution took the executive power away from the king and transferred it to the cabinet. The king was forced to dismiss his own cabinet members and select men chosen by the Hawaiian League. The constitution enfranchised American and European settlers and disenfranchised all Asians.[17] Although King Kalākaua continued to reign as monarch, with all of the executive power in the hands of the cabinet, the white American and European settlers controlled Aupuni Hawai'i.

Once in power, the cabinet voted to turn over exclusive use of Pearl Harbor (Pu'uloa) to the U.S. government in return for the renewal of the U.S.-Hawai'i Reciprocity Treaty, and the King reluctantly signed the new treaty.[18] The "reform government," as it was called, did not represent the interests of Lāhui ʻŌiwi. Lāhui ʻŌiwi nationalists realized that they had to organize politically to protect and assert their interests. Immediately they organized mass meetings, circulated petitions, and sent delegations to the king asking him to abrogate the Bayonet Constitution and dismiss the cabinet. These efforts failed.[19]

Lāhui ʻŌiwi took up arms in 1889 to directly seize back control of Aupuni Hawaiʻi from the white settlers. Named for its leader, the Wilcox Rebellion was suppressed within eighteen hours by the reform government.[20] Following the failure of the rebellion, Lāhui ʻŌiwi organized the Hui Kālaiʻāina (Hawaiian Political Association) to contend for control of Aupuni Hawaiʻi through the legislature. The Hui Kālaiʻāina persisted as the primary political organization of Lāhui ʻŌiwi into the early twentieth century and represented an early form of self-governance.[21]

In 1891, when Liliʻuokalani succeeded her brother to the throne and took her position as queen, the Hui Kālaiʻāina launched a massive petition drive appealing to the queen to promulgate a new constitution. They succeeded in getting 6,500 registered voters, two-thirds of all registered voters, to sign. The queen felt both compelled and empowered to abrogate the 1887 constitution in favor of a new constitution that would restore her power as the chief executive of the government.[22] Lāhui ʻŌiwi now had a chance to regain control of Aupuni Hawaiʻi. However, the white settlers were determined to control Aupuni Hawaiʻi and sought annexation to the United States to advance their own economic interests.

Hawaiʻi and the U.S. Government

On January 17, 1893, American merchants, sugar planters, and missionary descendants, with the backing of the U.S. government and the landing of U.S naval forces (on January 16, 1893), proclaimed that a provisional government was in control of the Hawaiian Islands. Lāhui ʻŌiwi immediately organized to vigorously protest the overthrow and the proposed U.S. annexation of Hawaiʻi. Mass meetings were held, rallies were organized, and petitions were circulated. Political organizations and groups already in existence on every island, such as the Hui Kālaiʻāina and the newly formed Hui Aloha ʻĀina

(Hawaiian Patriotic League), advocated support for the queen and the constitutional monarchy. Their primary objectives were to maintain the independence of the Aupuni Hawai'i and to secure the civil rights and national resources of Lāhui 'Ōiwi. Under the leadership of Queen Lili'uokalani, a descendant of the ruling chiefs of Hawai'i, they sought to regain control of Aupuni Hawai'i and keep it independent of the U.S. government.[23]

The effort by American interests to annex Hawai'i in 1893 failed when U.S. president Grover Cleveland, who had succeeded Benjamin Harrison, withdrew the annexation treaty from consideration by the U.S. Senate and dispatched former Georgia congressman James Blount to Hawai'i to investigate the events of January 1893. The Hawaiian Patriotic League and others organized rallies and meetings and submitted testimonies and petitions to commissioner Blount, which had a significant influence on his findings, supporting the restoration of the Queen.[24]

After receiving Blount's report, President Cleveland determined that the United States had been responsible for the overthrow of the monarchy and that the queen should be restored to the throne. Cleveland referred the matter to the U.S. Congress. The Senate Foreign Relations Committee conducted its own hearings and concluded that the United States should annex Hawai'i.[25] Because annexation would not be possible as long as Cleveland was president, on July 4, 1894, the provisional government established the Republic of Hawai'i. The majority of Lāhui 'Ōiwi refused to participate in this government.[26]

In January of 1895, Lāhui 'Ōiwi nationalists organized an armed insurrection aimed at restoring the queen to the throne.[27] However, despite months of planning, the restoration effort was defeated just as it was about to be launched. In all, 220 Lāhui 'Ōiwi nationalists were arrested and charged as prisoners of war for treason and concealment of treason.[28] The queen herself was arrested, tried, and found guilty of misprision or concealment of treason.[29] On January 24, 1895, while imprisoned in 'Iolani Palace, Queen Lili'uokalani was forced to sign a statement of abdication in favor of the republic.[30] The arrests, trials, and imprisonment of the royalists effectively suppressed all armed efforts to restore the monarchy. Nevertheless, Native Hawaiians persisted in their opposition to annexation through rallies, meetings, petitions, newspapers, songs, and publications.[31]

In 1897, the McKinley administration submitted an annexation treaty to the U.S. Senate for ratification by the necessary two-thirds majority. Lāhui 'Ōiwi organized against the treaty. The Hui Kalai'āina launched a petition drive opposing annexation and calling for the restoration of the monarchy. They collected seventeen thousand signatures. Hawaiian nationalist leaders formed the Hui Aloha 'Āina of men and women, and their petition against annexation collected twenty-one thousand signatures.[32] Queen Lili'uokalani and a delegation of Lāhui 'Ōiwi carried the petitions to Washington, DC, and successfully convinced the majority of senators to defeat the treaty.

In 1898, the U.S. Congress claimed control over the islands through the Newlands Joint Resolution of Annexation with the agreement and support of the Republic of Hawai'i.[33] The constitutionality of the Annexation of Hawai'i through a joint resolution rather than by a treaty was hotly debated in Congress at the time and continues to be challenged by Lāhui 'Ōiwi scholars today.[34] The United States began to govern Aupuni Hawai'i as a territory from 1900 through 1959. Politically, the United States empowered a white oligarchy of Americans to govern the multiethnic Aupuni Hawai'i as an incorporated territory that eventually became a U.S. state.

Lāhui 'Ōiwi: An Indigenous Minority

The Lāhui 'Ōiwi population was estimated between four hundred thousand and eight hundred thousand inhabitants in 1778, the year that British explorer Captain James Cook arrived in Hawai'i. Throughout the years of foreign settlement of the islands, Lāhui 'Ōiwi, because of their lack of genetic immunity, succumbed to foreign continental diseases that grew to epidemic proportions. Such diseases included cholera, measles, whooping cough, influenza, leprosy, and tuberculosis.

In 1845, non–Kanaka 'Ōiwi were allowed to become naturalized citizens. By 1890, because of their continuing decline and the importation of immigrant contract labor primarily from China and Japan, Lāhui 'Ōiwi made up only 45 percent of the population of the islands. Nevertheless, as Asian residents were not allowed to become naturalized citizens, Lāhui 'Ōiwi still made up 85 percent of the citizens of the Hawaiian Kingdom.[35]

The demographic trend for Lāhui ʻŌiwi to become a minority in the homeland was already evident by the end of the nineteenth century. If the Hawaiian Kingdom had continued its governance of the islands, Lāhui ʻŌiwi would not only have become a minority of the population but also a minority of the citizens of the kingdom. They were devolving into an indigenous minority of Aupuni Hawaiʻi in much the same way that Fijians are an indigenous minority in Fiji and the Maori are the indigenous minority in New Zealand (Aotearoa). In each of these independent Pacific Island nation-states, the indigenous Pacific Islanders have sovereign rights that are distinct from those of the citizens as a whole.

By 1900, when Hawaiʻi began to be governed as a territory of the United States, Lāhui ʻŌiwi of full Hawaiian ancestry had declined to 29,800, and there were 7,800 Kanaka ʻŌiwi of mixed ancestry. In all, Lāhui ʻŌiwi made up 24 percent of the population. At the same time, because first generation Chinese and Japanese were barred from becoming naturalized citizens of the United States, Lāhui ʻŌiwi made up 69 percent of the registered voters.[36]

Lāhui ʻŌiwi actively participated in territorial politics and contended for political control over Aupuni Hawaiʻi with the oligarchy of American businessmen and planters. At the same time, Lāhui ʻŌiwi also recognized the need to organize new political, civic, and benevolent organizations in order to provide for the well-being of the Native Hawaiian people and to protect national and ancestral rights and trust assets. These organizations assumed the rudimentary functions of self-governance for Lāhui ʻŌiwi. Prominent among these organizations were Hawaiian Land Hui (Groups of Lāhui ʻŌiwi who jointly owned land), Hawaiian royal societies (Royal Order of Kamehameha I, Kaʻahumanu Society, Daughters and Sons of Hawaiian Warriors, and the Hale O Nā Aliʻi), Ahahui Puʻuhonua O Nā Hawaiʻi (Hawaiian Protective Association), the Hawaiian civic clubs, and associations of Hawaiian homesteaders.

Through the work of these organizations, the U.S. Congress acknowledged Lāhui ʻŌiwi as a distinct indigenous people with whom the United States had a special relationship. This was most evident in, but not limited to, the mandate of the U.S. Bureau of American Ethnology to research Lāhui ʻŌiwi, the passage of the Hawaiian Homes Commission Act in 1921, the Kalapana Extension Act in 1938, and the sections of the Hawaiʻi Admission Act in 1959 that identified Lāhui ʻŌiwi as beneficiaries of the Hawaiian Homelands and the Ceded Public Lands Trust.[37]

Throughout the 1970s and through the end of the twentieth century, Lāhui ʻŌiwi formed several organizations of self-governance, which included but were not limited to "The Hawaiians," which sought to expand the land distributed to Lāhui ʻŌiwi by the State of Hawaiʻi Department of Hawaiian Home Lands; the Congress of Hawaiian People, who sought to expand educational opportunities for Lāhui ʻŌiwi at the Kamehameha schools; Aboriginal Lands of Hawaiian Ancestry (ALOHA), which sought reparations for Lāhui ʻŌiwi from the U.S. Congress for the role of the United States in the overthrow of the Hawaiian monarchy; the Protect Kahoʻolawe ʻOhana, which sought to stop the U.S. Navy bombing of the island of Kahoʻolawe and restore the island; Alu Like, Inc., which attracted federal funds to support the social and economic self-sufficiency of Lāhui ʻŌiwi; and Ka Lāhui Hawaiʻi, which sought to reestablish a government-to-government relationship with the federal and state governments.

Lāhui ʻŌiwi also formed ʻāina, or land-based organizations, to protect their natural and cultural resources from tourist, commercial, and industrial development. On the Island of Hawaiʻi, Ka ʻOhana o KaLae organized against a planned spaceport, Mālama Ka ʻĀina Hana Ka Āina formed to claim Hawaiian homelands near the Hilo airport, and the Pele Defense Fund organized to protect the volcano deity, Pele, from geothermal energy development. On Molokaʻi, the Hui Alaloa, Ka Leo O Manaʻe, and Hui Hoʻopakela ʻĀina exercised traditional access rights through private lands to utilize ocean resources and worked against resort and tourist developments. On Maui, Hui Ala Nui O Makena formed to keep access to the ocean on Mauiʻs south shore open for fishing and gathering, Hāna Pōhaku started community-based economic development projects in Kipahulu, and Keʻanae Community Association worked to keep the water flowing into their taro pond fields. On Kauaʻi, Hawaiian Farmers of Hanalei initiated community-based projects at Waipā, and Ka Wai Ola sought to manage tour boat operations along the north shore. On Oʻahu, community-based economic projects were started in Waiʻanae (Kaʻala Farms and Opelu Project) and Waiahole Valley.

Lāhui ʻŌiwi leaders also formed organizations that sought the independence of Aupuni Hawaiʻi, separate from the U.S. government. These include but are not limited to ʻOhana O Hawaiʻi, which transformed into the Kingdom of Hawaiʻi founded by Aunty Peggy Haʻo Ross; the Institute for the Advancement of Hawaiian Affairs, founded by Pōkā Laenui; Ka Pākaukau, initiated by Richard Kekuni Blaisdell, MD; the Nation of Hawaiʻi, founded by Dennis "Bumpy" Kanahele; the Reinstated Hawaiian Kingdom, founded by Henry Noa; and the Acting Council of Regency of the Hawaiian Kingdom Government founded by Keanu Sai, PhD.

These political formations were paralleled by a renaissance and revival of traditional navigational arts through the Hōkūleʻa and Polynesian Voyaging Society; the expansion of the number of *hālau hula* (hula schools) evident in the increased participation in the annual Merrie Monarch Hula Festival in Hilo, Hawaiʻi; the revival of the Hawaiian language with the establishment of Hawaiian language immersion preschools, public schools and charter schools; and the overall flourishing of Hawaiian cultural and spiritual customs, beliefs, and practices in Hawaiʻi's rural communities.

At the beginning of the twenty-first century, the total population of Hawaiʻi numbered 1.2 million. The 239,655 Lāhui ʻŌiwi make up 20 percent of the population. Another 161,500, or 40 percent of the 401,162 Lāhui ʻŌiwi counted in the 2000 U.S. census, lived in the continental United States.[38] In sum, the minority position of Lāhui ʻŌiwi in Hawaiʻi has given rise to complicated issues and challenges related to rights and entitlements as compared to that of the larger general public. This led to a movement to re-establish a government for the Lāhui ʻOiwi (Native Hawaiian indigenous nation) and re-establish a government-to-government relationship with the U.S. government.

Reality Bites: Indigenous People or Racial Group?

The U.S. Supreme Court, in the *Rice v. Cayetano* case, ruled on February 23, 2000, that elections for the trustees of the State of Hawaiʻi Office of Hawaiian Affairs (OHA), in which only Lāhui ʻŌiwi were allowed to vote, used unconstitutional race-based qualifications, a violation of the Fifteenth Amendment of the U.S. Constitution, which states that the right to vote cannot be denied because of race or color.[39]

The U.S. Supreme Court in its ruling also stated that Lāhui ʻŌiwi have a shared purpose with the general public in the islands and that the Constitution of the United States has become the heritage of all the citizens of Hawaii, including Lāhui ʻŌiwi. In addition to suggesting that Lāhui ʻŌiwi have assimilated into the general settler society, the court raised questions about whether or not Lāhui ʻŌiwi are, in fact, a distinct and unique indigenous people with the right of self-governance and self-determination under U.S. law or whether they are, instead, an ethnic or racial minority.

The majority of the Supreme Court justices also seemed to open the door to future legal challenges on the indigenous status of Lāhui ʻŌiwi when it stated that it is a matter of some dispute, for instance, whether Congress may treat the native Hawaiians as it does the Indian tribes.[40] We can stay far off that difficult terrain, however.

Suddenly, the status, rights, and entitlements that Kanaka ʻŌiwi had enjoyed as an indigenous people throughout the twentieth century could be potentially challenged out of existence as race-based entitlements that violated the equal protection clause of the Fourteenth Amendment. In fact, in each year since the Rice decision, a group of Republican senators has filed an objection to special funding provisions for Lāhui ʻŌiwi.

What are these rights and entitlements? Beginning in 1906 and through 1998, the U.S. Congress, in effect, recognized a trust relationship with the enactment of 183 federal laws that explicitly included Kanaka ʻŌiwi in the class of Native Americans. Some of the laws extended federal programs set up for Native Americans for health, education, housing, elder care, and job training to Lāhui ʻŌiwi. The American Indian Religious Freedom Act includes the acknowledgement and protection of the religious customs, beliefs, and practices of Lāhui ʻŌiwi. The Native American Graves Protection and Repatriation Act extends protection to Lāhui ʻŌiwi graves and burials.[41] The U.S. Congress also created two public lands trusts for which Kanaka ʻŌiwi are beneficiaries—Hawaiian Home Lands and the Ceded Public Lands Trust.[42]

With so much at stake for Lāhui ʻŌiwi, Lāhui ʻŌiwi organizations, led by the OHA, began to work on a strategy for reorganizing a Lāhui ʻŌiwi government and reestablishing a formal government-to-government relationship with the U.S. government. They worked with Hawaiʻi's congressional delegation, led by Senators Daniel Akaka and Daniel Inouye, and the administration of President Bill Clinton. In March 1999, Senator Akaka asked the Departments of Interior and Justice to initiate the process of reconciliation that had been called for in the Public Law 103–150 Apology Resolution. Hearings were held in Hawai'i in December 1999, and a report was completed in October 1999. Based on the report, the Native Hawaiian Government Reorganization Act (called the Akaka Bill) was introduced in Congress in November 2000 to explicitly and unambiguously clarify the trust relationship between Lāhui 'Ōiwi and the United States.

Opponents of Lāhui 'Ōiwi recognition successfully lobbied Congress to oppose the bill. Calling themselves Aloha 4 All, the group is supported by the National Coalition for a Color Blind America. On their web page, which lists four members, they state,

> This legislation is dangerous to the people of Hawai'i and to the sovereignty of the United States. It is an attempt to divide the thoroughly integrated people of Hawai'i along racial lines. It would partition the State of Hawai'i by setting up an apartheid regime to which only kanaka maoli (the name Native Hawaiians prefer to call themselves) could belong. . . . One of the most troubling aspects of the Akaka bill is its attempt to create an Indian tribe where none currently exists. It would be the first time in history when Congress recognizes a currently non-existent political entity and then puts in place a procedure to populate it.[43]

The Aloha 4 All group claims that all residents of Hawai'i are Hawaiian and that the limitation of any benefits to those who are "racially Hawaiian" is discriminatory and violates the Fourteenth Amendment of the U.S. Constitution.[44] Litigation pursued by the group has taken the form of three civil suits: *Patrick Barrett v. State of Hawaii, et al*; *John Carroll v. James Nakatani, et al.*; and *Arakaki v. Lingle*.[45] Initially, the suits sought to dismantle the State Department of Hawaiian Home Lands and the OHA and to abolish the traditional and customary rights of Lāhui 'Ōiwi to gather for subsistence, cultural, and religious purposes on public and private lands. In June 2001, Patrick Barrett changed his strategy to that of seeking to open the benefits assured to Lāhui 'Ōiwi by the State of Hawai'i under these departments and the state constitution to all residents of the islands. The *Arakaki* case asserted that Lāhui ʻŌiwi are not indigenous people because they arrived here from other Polynesian islands and with contact and the importation of contract laborers, Lāhui ʻŌiwi have intermarried and thus assimilated into the mainstream Hawaiian society. Here is an excerpt from the brief filed with the federal court on April 11, 2003:

> No one can trace his or her ancestry back to the first canoe of immigrants. This long story of immigration—longer than the entire post-Columbian history of immigration to America—refutes the claim that the class of Hawaiians and native Hawaiians as defined by ancestry in HRS 10-2 and Hawaiian Homes Commission Act of 1920(7) are "indigenous" to Hawaiʻi. All groups came from outside and did not originate here.... Culturally, socially, economically and in every other material respect, that racial group [Native Hawaiians] manifests none of the elements of separate yet common culture, tradition, language, institutions or beliefs which could separate them as a group from the rest of Hawaiʻi's people.[46]

By 2015, federal recognition through congressional action appeared defeated, especially with the retirement of Senator Akaka from Congress in 2013 and the passing of Senator Inouye in 2012. OHA and Lāhui ʻŌiwi leaders have developed an alternate path for the sovereignty of Lāhui ʻŌiwi.

A New Pathway for Lāhui ʻŌiwi

In 2011, the Hawaiʻi state legislature passed a bill for the establishment of a roll of Lāhui ʻŌiwi to elect delegates to an ʻaha or convention to draft a governing document for the reestablishment of a government for Lāhui ʻŌiwi. In May 2015, there were 122,700 Lāhui ʻŌiwi registered on this roll.[47] The ʻAha convened February 1–26, 2016, and drafted a constitution for a government of, by, and for Lāhui ʻŌiwi.

In 2014, the U.S. Department of the Interior announced that it was considering the opening of a pathway to reestablish a government-to-government relationship with Lāhui ʻŌiwi. The announcement stated,

The Secretary of Interior (Secretary) is considering whether to propose an administrative rule that would facilitate the reestablishment of a government-to-government relationship with the Native Hawaiian community, to more effectively implement the special political and trust relationship that Congress has established between that community and the United States.[48]

The final rule to reestablish a government-to-government relationship with Lāhui ʻŌiwi became effective on November 14, 2016, and is entitled 43 CFR Part 50.[49]

Both initiatives have received strong support by Lāhui ʻŌiwi who advocate the reestablishment of Lāhui Hawaiʻi and a government-to-government relationship with the United States. At the same time, there has also been strong opposition by Lāhui ʻŌiwi who advocate for the complete independence of Aupuni Hawaiʻi from the U.S. government.

Strategies for the Independence of Aupuni Hawaiʻi

Lāhui ʻŌiwi opponents feel that the recognition of Lāhui Hawaiʻi as a separate political entity with internal self-governing authority will not resolve the principal claims of Aupuni Hawaiʻi for independence from the United States. More importantly, they fear that resolution of the claims of Lāhui Hawaiʻi with the U.S. government could actually prevent the case for independence from getting on to the agenda of the United Nations or international courts of law. These opponents reject a government-to-government relationship of Lāhui Hawaiʻi with the United States as demeaning and restrictive of full self-determination.[50]

A symposium on international recognition and Hawaiian sovereignty sponsored by the OHA on November 1, 2014, featured international law experts James Anaya and Robert Williams. Both panelists confirmed that the reestablishment of Lāhui ʻŌiwi with a government-to-government relationship with the United States would not harm the case for international recognition of Aupuni Hawaiʻi. Instead, they pointed out that the reestablished Lāhui ʻŌiwi could actually provide resources and a platform for the broader movement of independence for Aupuni Hawaiʻi.[51]

There are two main strategies for restoring the independence of Aupuni Hawaiʻi. The first is to seek the decolonization of Hawaiʻi through the United Nations. In 1946, Hawaiʻi was inscribed with the UN Committee on Non-Self Governing Territories. As a result of the plebiscite that resulted in statehood for Hawaiʻi, the United States removed Hawaiʻi from that list in 1959. Independence advocates charge that the plebiscite did not meet the standards of free and fair process for (1) neutrality of the plebiscite area, (2) freedom from foreign occupation, and (3) control of the administration of the plebiscite by a neutral authority. In addition, the voters were presented only with the choice of statehood and were not allowed the option of complete independence or free association. Like East Timor, Kanaky (New Caledonia), and French Polynesia, this strategy would reinscribe Hawaiʻi with the UN to hold a free and fair plebiscite.

The second strategy is to seek the deoccupation of Hawaiʻi under the international "law of war" process. The rationale is that the United States is effectively at war with the sovereign and independent Hawaiʻi nation-state (Aupuni Hawaiʻi) and has occupied the islands since 1893. Under international law an illegal occupation and annexation cannot pass lawful title to the occupying power. This strategy turns to the United Nations and other appropriate international forums to resolve the prolonged occupation of Hawaiʻi. The objective is to expose the occupation of the Hawaiian Kingdom (Aupuni Hawaiʻi) within the framework of the 1907 Hague Conventions IV and V and domestic statutes of the Hawaiian Kingdom in order to provide a foundation for a transition and the ultimate end of the occupation of the Hawaiian Kingdom.[52]

Two major challenges for the advocates of the strategies to achieve the independence of Hawaiʻi exist. First is the denial on the part of the United States that Hawaiʻi is still a nation-state with the right of sovereignty and self-determination. The United States is determined to protect the political status of Hawaiʻi as a state within U.S. borders. The second challenge is the task of organizing all the members of Aupuni Hawaiʻi, all those born and raised in Hawaiʻi (not just Lāhui ʻŌiwi), to support the independence of Hawaiʻi.

Table 4.1. Comparison of Lāhui Hawaiʻi and Aupuni Hawaiʻi

Entity	Root	Members	Legal framework	Pathways	Goal
Lāhui ʻŌiwi	District chiefs, Island Aha (Council of Chiefs), Island high chiefs, Hawaiian Kingdom and constitutional government	Persons of Native Hawaiian ancestry	Hawaiʻi state law, U.S. federal law, UN Rights of Indigenous Peoples	Reestablish Native Hawaiian government through Naʻi Aupuni election and Ratification of Aha Constitution, U.S. Department of the Interior rule provides option for government-to-government federal relation	Protect Native Hawaiian cultural customs, beliefs, practices, and language; manage Hawaiian lands and resources to provide for well-being of Native Hawaiians and ʻāina
Aupuni Hawaiʻi	District chiefs, Island Aha (Council of Chiefs), Island high chiefs, Hawaiian Kingdom and constitutional government	Multiethnic people of Hawaiʻi	Article 73 of UN charter, "law of nations"	Reinscription with UN and plebiscite, de-occupation by United States, international recognition of Hawaiʻi as nation-state	Self-determination of Native Hawaiians and the multiethnic peoples of Hawaiʻi under an independent Hawaiʻi nation-state

Ha'ina la Mai Ana Kapuana—The Story Continues . . . Let It Be Told

In this chapter I have attempted to provide a new perspective on the movements and strategies being pursued to achieve sovereignty. In Hawai'i, sovereignty for Lāhui 'Ōiwi is the primary social justice issue to address and resolve. Many newcomers to Hawai'i claim that they bear no obligation to reconcile with the descendants of Lāhui 'Ōiwi for the injustices that occurred decades ago by persons to whom they bear no relation. However, non–Lāhui 'Ōiwi in Hawai'i benefit from, while Lāhui 'Oiwi bear the burden of, the results of those historical injustices.

Aloha mai no, aloha aku (when love is given, love should be returned).[53] This *'ōlelo no'eau* means that *aloha* is reciprocal. Lāhui 'Ōiwi people have given *aloha* to newcomers and their descendants for generations. Now is the time for *aloha* to be acknowledged and returned to Lāhui 'Ōiwi and their descendants. The story of sovereignty continues, and it will be passed on. *Aloha nō*.

Notes

1. Lili'uokalani, *The Queen's Songbook* (Honolulu: Hui Hānai, 1999), 194.
2. *Kanaka 'Ōiwi* and *Kanaka Maoli* are two Hawaiian language terms that mean "Native Hawaiian." *Kanaka* means "person." *Maoli* means "native," "indigenous," "genuine," "true," and "real." *'Ōiwi* means native and can be literally translated as "of the ancestral bone." For Native Hawaiians, the bones of our ancestors and ourselves hold the essence of the soul and spirit of both predecessors and descendants and are the core of ancestral memory and knowledge passed on through the generations. In the 1878 and 1890 census of the Hawaiian Kingdom and Constitutional Government, Kanaka Maoli referred to someone of full Hawaiian ancestry. 1897 petitions of Hawaiian nationalists to the U.S. Congress in opposition to the annexation of Hawai'i used the term *Hawaii Oiwi* for Native Hawaiians. *Lāhui* means "nation," "race," "tribe," "people." *Lāhui 'Ōiwi* as used by

Queen Liliʻuokalani means "Native Hawaiian people" and as used in this article is inclusive of anyone who has Hawaiian ancestry.

3. See Liliuokalani, *Hawaii's Story by Hawaii's Queen* (Honolulu: Mutual, 1991).

4. The *Aliʻi* trusts are charitable trusts established by chiefly Hawaiian rulers for the benefit of Lāhui ʻŌiwi and include Kamehameha schools, the Lunalilo Trust, the Queen Liliʻuokalani Children's Center, and the Queen Emma Trust Estate. Native Hawaiians are also beneficiaries of two public trusts established by the U.S. Congress: Hawaiian Homelands (1921), and the Ceded Public Lands Trust (1959). Monies to benefit Lāhui ʻŌiwi from the Ceded Public Lands Trust is given to the Office of Hawaiian Affairs. Suits include Carroll v. Nakatani/Barrett v. State, 342 F.3d 934 (9th Cir. 2003); Arakaki v. Lingle, 477 F.3d 1088 (9th Cir. 2007).

5. Joint Resolution to Acknowledge the 100th Anniversary of the January 17, 1893 Overthrow of the Kingdom of Hawaiʻi, Pub. L. No. 103-150, 107 Stat. 1510 (1993).

6. This article is based on a larger manuscript written by the author in conjunction with Melody Kapilialoha MacKenzie, professor and director at the Center of Excellence in Native Hawaiian Law at the University of Hawaiʻi at Mānoa.

7. Carolyn Kehaunani Cachola Abad, *The Evolution of Hawaiian Socio-Political Complexity: An Analysis of Hawaiian Oral Traditions* (PhD diss., University of Hawaiʻi, Mānoa, 2000) and Samuel Mānaiakalani Kamakau, *Ruling Chiefs of Hawaii* (Honolulu: Kamehameha Schools Press, 1961).

8. Treaty with Hawaii on Friendship, Commerce and Navigation, 9 Stat. 977 (1850); Convention Between the United States and His Majesty the King of the Hawaiian Islands, 19 Stat. 625 (1875); Supplementary Convention Between the United States of America and His Majesty the King of the Hawaiian Islands to Limit the Duration of the Convention Respecting Commercial Reciprocity Concluded January 30, 1875, 25 Stat. 1399 (1884). The treaties entered into by the Hawaiian Kingdom included the following countries: Austria-Hungary (June 18, 1875), Belgium (October 4, 1862), Denmark (October 19, 1846), Japan (August 19, 1870), Portugal (May 5, 1882), Italy (July 22, 1863), The Netherlands (October 14, 1862), Russia (June 19, 1869), Switzerland (July 20, 1864), Spain (October 29, 1863), and Sweden (July 1, 1852).

9. Ralph S. Kuykendall, *The Hawaiian Kingdom*, vol. 1, *1778–1854: Foundation and Transformation* (Honolulu: University of Hawaiʻi Press, 1938).

10. Davianna McGregor-Alegado, "Hawaiian Resistance: 1887–1889" (MA thesis, University of Hawaiʻi, 1979), 5. In 1880, King David Kalākaua adopted the policy of appointing Hawaiians to fill cabinet level positions.
11. Davianna McGregor-Alegado, "Voices of Today Echo Voices of the Past," in *Mālama Hawaiian Land and Water*, ed. Dana Naone Hall (Honolulu: Bamboo Ridge Press, 1985), 44–58. Also in Lilikalā Kameʻeleihiwa, *Native Land and Foreign Desires: Pehea Lā e Pono ʻAi?* (Honolulu: Bishop Museum Press, 1992).
12. Merze Tate, *The United States and the Hawaiian Kingdom: A Political History* (New Haven, CT: Yale University Press, 1968). U.S. Department of State, "President's Message," in *Papers Relating to Mission of James H. Blount, United States Commissioner to the Hawaiian Islands* (Washington, DC: U.S. Government Printing Office, 1893), 105; U.S. House of Representatives, 53rd Congress, 2d Session, Ex. Doc. No. 47, *President's Message Relating to the Hawaiian Islands, December 18, 1893* (Washington, D.C.: U.S. Government Printing Office, 1893). U.S. House of Representatives, 53rd Congress, 3d Session, Ex. Doc. No. 1, Part 1, App. II, *Foreign Relations of the United States 1894, Affairs in Hawaii* (hereinafter *Affairs in Hawaii*) (Washington, DC: Government Printing Office, 1895), 571, http://libweb.hawaii.edu/digicoll/annexation/blount.php.
13. Census of the Hawaiian Islands, 1890.
14. Ibid.
15. David Kalākaua, *The Legends and Myths of Hawaii* (Rutland, VT: Tuttle, 1972), 63–64; William Adam Russ Jr., *The Hawaiian Revolution, 1893–1894* (Selinsgrove, PA: Susquehanna University Press, 1959).
16. Jon Van Dyke, *Who Owns the Crown Lands of Hawaiʻi?* (Honolulu: University of Hawaiʻi Press, 2008), 120–124.
17. Voting privileges were extended to American and European males *regardless* of citizenship. 1887 Constitution of the Hawaiian Kingdom.
18. Van Dyke, *Who Owns the Crown Lands*, 124–28.
19. Liliʻuokalani, Queen of Hawaii, 1838–1917, Bishop Museum Archives; *The Diary of Queen Liliʻuokalani* (Honolulu: Bishop Museum Archives, 1992), January 16–18, 1888; "Cabinet Meetings 1887–1890" entry for January 18, 1888; Lorrin Thurston, *Memoirs of the Hawaiian Revolution* (Honolulu: Advertiser, 1936), 180–83; R. W. Wilcox and Lorrin A. Thurston, *Reply of Hon. R.W. Wilcox to Statements of Minister Thurston Before the Hawaiian Legislative Assembly* (Honolulu: Hawaiian Gazette Steam Print, 1890), June 10, 1890.

20. Eight Native Hawaiian nationalists were killed, twelve were wounded, and seventy were arrested. Those nationalists charged with treason were subsequently acquitted by all-Native-Hawaiian juries. McGregor-Alegado, "Hawaiian Resistance," 76–107.
21. David William Earle, "Coalition Politics in Hawai'i 1887–90: Hui Kālai'āina and the Mechanics and Workingmen's Political Protective Union" (MA thesis, University of Hawai'i, Mānoa, 1993), 75.
22. Liliuokalani, *Hawaii's Story*, 231.
23. Noenoe Silva, *Aloha Betrayed: Native Hawaiian Resistance to American Colonialism* (Durham, NC: Duke University Press, 2004), 131, 136–63. Non–Lāhui 'Ōiwi citizens of Aupuni Hawai'i also supported these efforts to keep Hawai'i independent of the United States and these organizations are claimed as predecessors to the current movements for both the sovereignty of Lāhui Hawai'i and the independence of Aupuni Hawai'i.
24. Ibid., 130–34.
25. Joint Resolution to Acknowledge the 100th Anniversary of the January 17, 1893 Overthrow of the Kingdom of Hawai'i, Pub. L. No. 103-150, 107 Stat. 1510 (1993).
26. Only 509 Lāhui 'Ōiwi took the oath of allegiance to the republic's constitution, while 9,554 Lāhui 'Ōiwi had been regestered to vote in 1890. See "The Census of 1890 by Age and Nationality, Showing Number of Registered Voters," *Affairs in Hawaii*, cited in Thomas G. Thrum, *Hawaiian Almanac and Annual for 1893: A Handbook of Information* (Honolulu: Press, 1892).
27. See Russ, *The Hawaiian Revolution*, 55–57.
28. Twenty-one of the men who were Caucasian were given and took the option to leave Hawai'i to avoid serving prison sentences.
29. Allen, *Betrayal of Queen Liliuokalani, Last Queen of Hawaii, 1838–1917* (Glendale, CA: A. H. Clark, 1982), 331–50.
30. Subsequently, the queen renounced the statement, explaining that she had been coerced into signing it in order to save her arrested supporters from execution. Liliuokalani, *Hawaii's Story*, 274.
31. For one example, see F. J. Testa, *Buke Mele Lahui: Book of National Songs* (1895; repr. Honolulu: University of Hawai'i Press / Hawaiian Historical Society / Hawaiian Language Reprint Series, 2003), containing patriotic songs honoring the queen and those who defended her. In September and October 1897, Senator John Morgan, chairman of the Senate Foreign Relations Committee,

and four congressmen traveled to Hawai'i to rally support for a treaty of annexation that the Republic of Hawai'i had negotiated with President McKinley. They met mass opposition as thousands of Native Hawaiians rallied at Palace Square against the treaty.

32. Noenoe K. Silva, "Kanaka Maoli Resistance to Annexation," *'Ōiwi: A Native Hawaiian Journal* 1 (1998): 40–80; *Aloha Betrayed: Native Hawaiian Resistance to American Colonialism* (Durham, NC: Duke University Press, 2004).

33. Ibid.

34. The primary argument against the resolution was that only under the constitutional treaty-making power could the United States gain territory. To acquire Hawai'i by a legislative act, a joint resolution, would usurp the power of the Senate and executive branch to act in matters relating to acquisition of new territories and set a dangerous precedent. Although annexationists pointed to the acquisition of Texas in 1845 by joint resolution as precedent, most anti-annexationists believed that Texas had been brought into the Union legally under Congress's power to admit new states. Statehood was not proposed for Hawai'i, so the Texas acquisition had no precedential value. Moreover, in the Texas situation, the joint resolution was approved by a plebiscite held in Texas. No plebiscite was proposed for Hawai'i. One Senator offered an amendment to the Newlands measure providing for such a vote by all adult males, but it was defeated. See *Congressional Record*, 31st Congress (June 15, 1898): 6018; (June 20, 1898): 6149; (June 24, 1898): 6310; (July 6, 1898): 6709–12 for debate and vote on the resolution; also see Melody Kapilialoha MacKenzie, ed., *Native Hawaiian Rights Handbook* (Honolulu: University of Hawai'i Press, 1991), 24n100. For contemporary challenges, see Keanu Sai, "A Slippery Path Towards Hawaiian Indigeneity: An Analysis and Comparison Between Hawaiian State Sovereignty and Hawaiian Indigeneity and Its Use and Practice in Hawai'i Today," *Journal of Law and Social Challenges* 10 (Fall 2008): 68–133.

35. Robert Schmitt, *Demographic Statistics of Hawaii: 1778–1965* (Honolulu: University of Hawai'i Press, 1968), 74, table 16; "The Census of 1890 by Age and Nationality, Showing Number of Registered Voters," cited in Thrum, *Hawaiian Almanac*.

36. For percentage of the population, see U.S. Bureau of the Census, *15th Census of the United States: 1930, Population Second Series, Hawai'i: Composition and Characteristics of the Population and Unemployment* (Washington, DC: Gov-

ernment Printing Office, 1931), 48, table 2, for composition and characteristics of population. For voter registration data, see Hawai'i (Territory) Governor of the Territory of Hawaii, *Report to Secretary of Interior, 1931* (Washington, DC: Government Printing Office, 1931), 14.

37. Pub. L. No. 61-266, 26 Stat. 703, 718 (1910); Pub. L. No. 69-600, 44 Stat. 1069, 1079 (1927); Pub. L. No. 71-158, 46 Stat. 229, 241 (1930); Pub. L. No. 67-34, 42 Stat. 108 (1921), Hawaiian Homes Commission Act, Pub. L. No. 75-680, § 3, 55 Stat. 784, 784–85 (1938); Kalapana Extension Act, Pub. L. No. 86-3, 73 Stat. 4 (1959); Hawaii Admission Act, Sections 4 and 5 (f).
38. Office of Hawaiian Affairs, *Native Hawaiian Data Book*, table 1.19, "Native Hawaiian Population by Region in the United States: 1990, 2000, 2010," http://www.ohadatabook.com/T01-19-13.pdf.
39. Rice v. Cayetano, 485 U.S. 495 (2000). Kennedy delivered the opinion of the court, in which Rehnquist, O'Connor, Scalia, and Thomas joined. Breyer filed an opinion concurring in the result, in which Souter joined. Stevens filed a dissenting opinion in which Ginsburg joined as to Part II. Ginsburg filed a dissenting opinion.
40. Cf. John M. Van Dyke, "The Political Status of the Hawaiian People," *Yale Law and Policy Review* 17, no. 1 (1998): 95–147, and Stuart M. Benjamin, "Equal Protection and the Special Relationship: The Case of Native Hawaiians," *Yale Law Journal* 106, no. 3 (1996): 537 612.
41. Department of the Interior and Department of Justice, "From Mauka to Makai: The River of Justice Must Flow Freely: Report on the Reconciliation Process Between the Federal Government and Native Hawaiians" (Washington DC: Department of the Interior, Department of Justice, 2000), https://www.doi.gov/sites/doi.gov/files/migrated/ohr/library/upload/Mauka-to-Makai-Report-2.pdf.
42. Potentially, challenges could also be posed to provisions of the Hawai'i State Constitution that acknowledge and protect Lāhui 'Ōiwi entitlements.
43. *Rice v. Cayetano*, 528 U.S. 495, 520 (2000).
44. Ibid. KITV News, June 4, 2001; *Honolulu Advertiser*, June 5, 2001, B-2. Another group who opposes entitlements for Lāhui 'Ōiwi is the Grassroot Institute of Hawaii.
45. Patrick Barrett v. State of Hawaii, et al., Civil No. CV-00-00645 DAE-KSC (2000); John Carroll v. James Nakatani, et al., Civil No. CV00-00641 DAE-KSC (2001).

46. Arakaki v. Lingle, Civ. No. 02-00.139 SOM/KSC, Plaintiff's Opposition to Motion for Judicial Notice, 4-11-03 (2003).
47. "Frequently Asked Questions on the Advance Notice of Proposed Rulemaking (ANPRM) for Procedures for Reestablishing a Government-to-Government Relationship with the Native Hawaiian Community, June 2014," https://www.bia.gov/cs/groups/xopa/documents/text/idc1-027104.pdf.
48. Department of the Interior, Office of the Secretary, 43 CFR Part 50.
49. See https://www.regulations.gov/document?D=DOI-2015-0005-6341.
50. For an analysis of these international strategies, see Julian Aguon, "The Commerce of Recognition (Buy One Ethos, Get One Free): Toward Curing the Harm of the United States' International Wrongful Acts in the Hawaiian Islands," *'Ohia: A Periodic Publication of Ka Huli Ao Center for Excellence in Native Hawaiian Law* (2012), https://www.law.hawaii.edu/sites/www.law.hawaii.edu/files/content/Programs%2CClinics%2CInstitutes/108622%20L1%20Aguon%20r5.pdf.
51. https://www.youtube.com/watch?v=j4KwqoCus_A&list=PLnkIWTIznWSAG446Z98lL4BYKaVR5tTto&index=3.
52. http://www.hawaiiankingdom.org and http://www.hawaiiankingdom.org/pdf/HK_Strategic_Plan.pdf. See Convention (IV) respecting the Laws and Customs of War on Land and Its Annex: Regulations Concerning the Laws and Customs of War on Land, Oct. 18, 1907, 36 Stat. 2277, T.S. No. 539.
53. Mary Kawena Pukui, *'Ōlelo No'eau: Hawaiian Proverbs and Poetical Sayings* (Honolulu: Bishop Museum Press, 1983), p. 15, no. 113. Aloha mai no, aloha aku / o ka huhu ka mea e ola 'ole ai (When love is given, love should be returned / anger is the thing that gives no life).

II

Sovereign Bodies

5

Chairmen, Presidents, and Princesses

The Navajo Nation, Gender, and the Politics of Tradition

JENNIFER NEZ DENETDALE

In 1998, a woman by the name of LeNora Fulton announced her candidacy to become president of the Navajo Nation.[1] She immediately faced criticism from Navajo/Diné men and women who argued that Navajo women should not be leaders because it would lead to chaos in society, as a traditional narrative stipulated.[2] While Navajo women exert considerable influence within their families and in local community politics, they are discouraged from full political participation in the Navajo Nation sovereign government. Yet despite being generally absent from the political sphere, they are quite visible in government as Miss Navajo Nation, the official representative and ambassador of the Navajo Nation. These gender dynamics raise a number of important questions regarding the political project of Navajo Nation: What does it mean to valorize Navajo women as princesses and beauty queens to represent ideal Navajo womanhood? How are women signifiers of culture and tradition in the construction of the Navajo Nation and, at the same time, denied full political participation in the Navajo government? How has the establishment of a modern Navajo government shifted traditional gender roles in ways that have been detrimental to Navajo women?

Part of the answer lies in the concept of nation itself. As feminist scholars note, the idea of nation relies on the language of family and casts women as the mothers and the culture bearers of the nation.[3] Significantly, although many Navajo men, and even women, declare that Navajo women should not hold the highest office in Navajoland, both men and women draw on traditional narratives to challenge ideas about appropriate gender roles modeled on Western ideals. With the imposition of Western democratic principles, Navajo women find themselves confronted with new oppressions in the name of "custom and tradition." In this chapter, then, I examine the intersection of the Navajo nation and gender by considering women's presence in the governmental structure and how Navajo leaders, who are primarily men, reproduce Navajo nationalist ideology to reinscribe gender roles based on Western concepts even as they claim that they operate under traditional Navajo philosophy and conceptions of sovereignty.[4]

From Traditional Government to Navajo Nation

Before Euro-American invasion, the Diné, who by all accounts were an autonomous people, practiced their own system of government, albeit not one that was seen as rational or acceptable to Euro-Americans.[5] The fundamental Navajo political entity, called a "natural community," was composed of local bands that consisted of ten to forty families. The largest assembly, called a *naachid*, or regional gathering, met to address internal matters, intertribal affairs, hunting, and food gathering. Twenty-four headmen, twelve of whom were peace leaders and twelve of whom were war leaders, constituted the *naachid*. During years of peace, the peace leader presided, and during wartime the war leader presided. Anthropologist Aubrey W. Williams Jr. notes that the Diné political process was closely tied to their ceremonial life and that the *naachid* functioned to cure individuals, to bring rain, and to restore the fertility of the soil.[6] The last *naachid* was reportedly held around 1858, before the attack on Fort Defiance led by nineteenth-century Navajo chiefs and political leaders Manuelito and Barboncito.[7]

Headmen held their leadership based on their own abilities to serve the people. They were expected to ensure proper behavior, maintain moral injunctions such as prohibitions against incest and adultery, and enforce economic laws. Often medicine men themselves, headmen served as intermediaries between the People and the Holy People. They relied on the *hastói* (elder men) and the *hataali* (medicine people) for guidance. After a natural community selected a headman, he went through an initiation process that included a Blessingway. The initiation included the anointing of the new leader's lips with corn pollen.[8]

Although written reports do not mention women as leaders or chiefs, Navajo oral tradition and other accounts make note that it was not unheard of for women to serve as headmen or chiefs.[9] Further, early American accounts have noted Navajo women's presence in council proceedings between Navajo and American leaders.[10] In one of the first publications by a Diné woman, Ruth Roessel notes that Navajo women were not appointed as leaders of natural communities, but they influenced the decisions that male leaders made on behalf of their people.[11] My own research on Juanita, or Asdzáá Tł'ógi, the wife of Manuelito, draws on Navajo oral accounts and suggests that she was respected as an influential leader among her people and that her husband relied on her for counsel.[12]

During the Spanish and Mexican periods, the Diné retained their autonomy. However, with the American invasion in 1846, Navajos found it increasingly difficult to do so, particularly because the hostilities were heightened as slave raiders targeted Navajo women and children, leading to cycles of conflict and peace between Navajos, New Mexicans, and Americans.[13] Beginning in 1863, Navajos experienced dramatic transformations as their physical resistance to foreign invasion came to an end under American rule. Declaring that the Diné would either surrender or be exterminated, Brigadier General James Carleton conceived of a prison camp near Fort Sumner, New Mexico, where surviving Navajos would be refashioned in the image of the white man. Carleton then ordered frontiersman Kit Carson to force a Navajo surrender, which Carson accomplished through a scorch and burn campaign. Thousands of Navajos surrendered and were forcibly relocated at the Bosque Redondo camp, near Fort Sumner, from 1864 to 1868.[14]

The people suffered at Bosque Redondo for four long years. The land did not recognize them. The cornfields failed as droughts and pests took their toll. They starved and died from diseases. Women were sexually assaulted.[15] Indian agents became increasingly autocratic and appointed male Navajo leaders who answered to them.[16] Just at the camp alone, more than twenty-five hundred Navajos died. Navajos continually pressured their captors to allow them to return home. Carleton also came under public criticism, and tensions were further heightened when other public officials challenged his assimilation program. It soon became apparent to the prison officials that the program to assimilate the Navajos was a failure.

As the conditions at Bosque Redondo became known, especially with the dissemination of a joint House and Senate committee report, Navajos were closer to realizing their fervent wishes to return to their homeland.[17] According to oral tradition, medicine people played an important role in the Navajo impetus to return home.[18] Finally, to the joy of the Diné, their leaders negotiated a treaty with the United States that allowed them to return to their beloved homeland.[19] Although no Navajo woman signed the treaty, Ruth Roessel noted that "their thoughts and feelings were evident in the treaty."[20]

The Bosque Redondo experience dramatically transformed the Navajo political system. For example, the *naachid* was no longer performed. However, upon their return to their homeland, Navajo leaders conducted a ceremony to reaffirm the chiefs' roles as leaders of the People. The chiefs led the People to Window Rock, where a Blessingway was performed, sacred mountain soil bundles were tied, and each headman took a bundle and passed through Window Rock four times. The signing of the 1868 treaty proved a relative advantage for the Navajo people when we consider that so many other Native peoples were dispossessed of their lands and relocated to Indian territory in Oklahoma. The Navajo Nation's sovereign status was recognized by the United States in two treaties, of 1849 and 1868, although the Navajos were simultaneously considered to be wards of the U.S. government.[21]

With their return to their ancestral lands, Navajos rebuilt their herds to pre–Bosque Redondo levels and struggled to restore a measure of self-sufficiency to their lives. To a great extent, in the early reservation period, Navajo pastoral life, with its constant quest for grazing lands, meant isolation from American influences.[22] Thus, into the mid-twentieth century, Navajos still practiced many of their old ways and spoke their language almost exclusively.

In the 1920s, the U.S. government created the first Navajo "business" council for the express purpose of expediting tribal business because oil and natural gas companies were eager to drill on Navajo land.[23] The establishment of this council was part of the American assimilation process that emphasized patriarchal values. Henry Chee Dodge, Charlie Mitchell, and Daacha'-chii Bikiss were appointed to this first council in 1922.[24] Early council meetings were convened under the direction of the commissioner to the Navajos, Herbert Hagerman, who had the final word in all council proceedings. As the leader and Blessingway singer Frank Mitchell reported in his life story, "In Washington, they looked upon us as children, or minors who did not have a mind of our own."[25]

In the 1930s and 1940s, Navajos again suffered under U.S.-Indian policies when they were forced to reduce their livestock by 50 percent because of overgrazing. This mandate forced Navajos into the wage economy.[26] At the same time that federal officials forced livestock reduction, they also attempted to persuade Navajos to accept the Indian Reorganization Act (IRA). The IRA could be seen as beneficial because it halted land allotment to individuals rather than to the community and brought more Indian involvement into their governments; however, much to the disappointment of Indian commissioner John Collier, Navajos rejected the IRA because they linked it to livestock reduction. Despite the Nation's rejection of the IRA, Navajos were subjected to government rule based on the Western democratic model.

As anthropologist Christine Conte and Navajo attorney Genevieve Chato note, this Western form of government is patriarchal, looking only to men to fill leadership roles. The result was the undermining of Navajo women's traditional rights, including land-use rights, property and livestock rights, and primary care and control of children.[27] In addition, as Chato and Conte have observed, during the early reservation period and into the 1950s, Navajo children were sent off the reservation to attend boarding schools where they learned Western values, including notions of "proper" gender roles. Returning to the reservation, Navajo men took leadership roles in the Navajo government while women assumed secretarial positions. Like white American women, Navajo women were expected to relegate themselves to the domestic realm, which is associated with little political or economic power.

Even as the Navajo government took on the structure and patriarchal values of a Western government, male Navajo leaders claimed that their actions and decisions were rooted in traditional Navajo political thought. However, as political theorist David Wilkins points out, except for the peacemaker's court, there are few traditional elements of government evident in the present-day Navajo political structure.[28] Undoubtedly Navajo leaders do continue to rely on traditional ceremonies for affirmation and guidance; however, in many cases, these rituals are performed within their personal and kin networks rather than as part of general governance.

In 1968, Navajo leaders, with the assistance of whites, staged a number of cultural events to celebrate Navajo "progress." Events included the reenactment of the return from Bosque Redondo and culminated with the re-signing of the Treaty of 1868. Emphasizing Navajos' entrance into modern American society as demonstrated through the development of their natural resources, the establishment of a Western-style government, and the provision of educational opportunities for Navajo youth, the Navajo public was offered an opportunity to reflect on the past and celebrate one hundred years of Navajo progress. The staged events made Navajo men and federal officials the primary enactors and interpreters of Navajo progress.[29]

Like other Indian governments, the Navajo Nation has experienced political turmoil that pitted tribal members against each other and threatened to tear communities apart.[30] The Navajo nation relies on a number of strategies, such as staging cultural events and employing rhetoric about tradition, to draw links between a traditional Navajo political system and the modern government, and these have been met with Navajo suspicion and criticism. Oftentimes the Navajo government is seen merely as an arm of the federal government, and Navajos learned early on not to trust Navajo leaders who sometimes enforced federal Indian policies, however reluctantly. Western government structures imposed on Indigenous political structures have profoundly influenced gender relations in Indigenous communities.

Nation and Gender

Until fairly recently, Native women have been invisible in the historical record, although they have drawn the attention of scholars when they appeared in roles associated with men, such as the warrior or war woman, or as the wives and supposed collaborators of white American men.[31] The twentieth century saw a few Native women elected or appointed to leadership positions in federal and tribal governments. Yet Native women who assumed positions as principal chiefs, chairwomen, governors, and council delegates met with criticism and hostility from other tribal members, who often believe that women should not hold leadership positions in tribal governments.[32]

This was evident in LeNora Fulton's case. When she declared her candidacy for president of the Navajo Nation in 1998, becoming only the second woman to run for the highest leadership position in the Nation, Fulton came under strict Navajo public scrutiny.[33] Fulton had extensive experience working with the Navajo government, including her work as council delegate from Fort Defiance, Arizona. Yet her decision to run for president led some Navajo men to inform her that "the presidency is men's work" and that tradition dictates that women should not aspire to the highest tribal office.[34] In a letter to the *Navajo Times*, Fulton wrote,

> I've heard some remarks that Navajo women should not be leaders, but I know that we live in a time where every Navajo person is needed to fight for the survival of our Nation. Navajo women do have a place in politics, in the world of business, in education, in law and the judicial system, and it is time for Navajo women to take their place of leadership.[35]

Fulton's platform highlighted family and community issues and tied them to the Nation's survival. She insisted that she followed traditional dictates that acknowledge the importance of women to Navajo survival and continuity. She felt, like many other Navajo women who have been successful in carving out a career, that she was, "a sacred being [who was] raised to be a leader."[36]

Although no Navajo woman had yet been elected president of the Navajo Nation, women had served as council delegates and in various offices at the chapter levels. Annie Dodge Wauneka, the most prominent woman council delegate, served from 1951 to 1968. Her contributions to the betterment of Navajo family life and health reflect views that Native women in public leadership roles often bring "domestic" issues into the public forum.[37] Irene Stewart, a peer of Annie Wauneka, ran for a council delegate position in 1955 and 1959, both times unsuccessfully. Thereafter serving as a chapter officer for many years, Stewart noted that women are often discouraged from seeking leadership roles, and particularly that of chairperson (the office now known as president). She often heard criticism of women, and reports that "whenever there were difficulties some were quick to criticize. One man said, 'We should not allow women to take office in our Tribal council and chapters.'"[38]

Stewart related the traditional narrative that is cited to bar Navajo women from leadership.

> The Navajo have a legend about a woman leader. Her name was Asdzáá Naat'áani (Woman Chief). She was the queen of her people in the underworld before the Navajos came to this land. Her authority was mostly over women and girls. She became lax in her authority, especially in regard to moral principles, thus making it easy for other women to become loose in their morals.... There were many quarrels between the men and the women over who was to support whom. The women said they did not need men to support them and this made the men angry. They decided to leave the women all to themselves and to make a new home far across a big sea. In time, life became hard for both sexes but the queen and her daughter remained stubborn and would do nothing to bring the sexes back together. Finally, after four years, an old wise owl advised them there would be no more Diné if they continued with their foolishness. This made them admit that they were wrong, and ever since the men have taken over as rulers. My people have this story in mind when they criticize a woman leader. They say there will be confusion within the tribe whenever a Navajo woman takes office.[39]

This narrative is a variation on stories that detail what happens when men and women fail to recognize that both their roles are important to the survival and perpetuation of the People. It is a narrative that has been interpreted in different ways. For example, in the 1960s and 1970s, anthropologist Mary Shepherdson, who collaborated with Irene Stewart to produce Stewart's autobiography, commented on Stewart's retelling of the narrative and compared it to the Bible. Shepherdson allowed her white feminist perspective to interfere with her understanding of Navajo gender roles, saying, "I contend that neither of these sacred stories can do anything but lower the status of Navajo and Christian women."[40] In her study of women in Navajo society published in 1981, Ruth Roessel also declares that traditional women "usually refrain from wishing or believing that some day a woman will be a

Chairman of the Navajo Tribal Council." Yet Roessel adds that "in the early days of Navajo history it appeared that the men expected and welcomed the participation of women in roles of leadership and decision-making."[41]

Whatever the interpretation, the question that arises is why we arbitrarily declare that women should respect tradition by not vying for the top leadership of the Navajo Nation government and at the same time refuse to recognize that the hierarchical structure of the modern government itself is not traditional. It must be kept in mind that the concept of Navajo nationalism is a modern one and that the application of creation narratives to interpret the meaning of nation and women's roles in the political body needs to be handled critically.

Among Navajos, there are some characteristics and attributes that are not considered gender specific; thus, Navajo women are credited with intelligence, compassion, and the ability to speak well and persuasively. They also are said to have the community's interest foremost in mind. According to Navajo values, an individual is a leader if he or she has the necessary skills and qualifications. Since the 1990s, Navajo women have claimed the privilege of holding high political offices within the Navajo government and based their claims on traditional narratives that convey the importance of gender balance and women's contributions to the betterment, survival, and continuation of the Diné. Tradition becomes a tool that both Navajo men and women use to legitimate claims about appropriate gender roles.[42]

While tradition is cited to exclude women from full participation in the Navajo polity, an unabashedly nontraditional practice, that of conducting beauty pageants, is used to present an ideal Navajo womanhood to Navajos and the outside world. To illuminate how women are involved in the Navajo nationalist project, I turn to the Miss Navajo Nation pageant and discuss how the requirements reflect, on the one hand, traditionally ideal Navajo womanhood and, on the other, imposed notions of ideal Euro-American womanhood, which draw on Victorian ideals of purity, chastity, and domesticity. Scholars have begun to pay attention to Native beauty pageants and suggest that these contests, including photographs of them, reflect strategies where Natives are negotiating their relationships to their traditional cultures and, at the same time, are cognizant of their affiliation with Indian and American nations.[43] I intend to add to the emerging conversation by suggesting that we must also consider Native beauty contests as further evidence of the bifurcation of men's and women's roles wherein men participate fully in the public sphere while women are relegated to specific and limited participation in the same sphere.

As Miss Navajo Nation, Navajo women are simultaneously symbols of national pride that announce to the world that Navajos have successfully entered the mainstream and signifiers of cultural continuity with the Navajo past.[44] The first Navajo beauty pageants began in the 1950s as part of the tribal fairs. Indian agents of the U.S. government created these fairs to demonstrate successful Navajo assimilation to the outside world and to expose Navajos to modern American technologies. The beauty contests were important to the announcement that Navajos had successfully entered modern progressive society.[45] In the 1980s, the Navajo Nation created the Office of Miss Navajo Nation to administer the annual beauty pageant and to oversee Miss Navajo Nation's public appearances. In these contests, Navajo women dress in traditional outfits and must demonstrate a traditional skill, both of which evoke a sense of the timelessness of cultural values. "Traditional" Navajo women's purity, mothering and nurturing qualities, and morality are evoked by the Navajo Nation to extol Navajo honor and are in turn claimed on behalf of the modernizing project of Navajo nationalism. When a woman crowned Miss Navajo Nation does not conform to the dictates of ideal Navajo womanhood, she is subjected to harsh criticism intended to reinforce cultural boundaries. Her body literally becomes a site of surveillance that symbolically conveys notions about racial purity, morality, and chastity.

According to the official website of the Office of Miss Navajo Nation, the chosen young woman must have characteristics that reflect those of our female deities, particularly Changing Woman, who epitomizes the Navajo woman. Changing Woman was born to rid the world of chaos and darkness, and she did so by giving birth to the Hero Twins, Monster Slayer and Born for Water. As a mother, Changing Woman is nurturing, benevolent, and generous. She also created the original clans by rubbing skin from various parts of her body. In particular, Changing Woman is lauded for her powers of reproduction, for she alone has the power to produce the coming generations of Navajos.

As the model Changing Woman, Miss Navajo Nation must follow directives about a woman's appearance, morals, and virtue. A woman must be young, between the ages of eighteen and twenty-four, single and never have been married, and never have been pregnant. She must not be seen in a bar or publicly intoxicated; nor can she use tobacco (other than ceremonially). If she has a boyfriend, they must be discreet, and she must not be cohabiting with him. During her official appearances, Miss Navajo Nation must always be accompanied by two chaperones from the Office of Miss Navajo Nation. Yet the deity on whom Miss Navajo Nation models herself is acknowledged for her sexuality, her ability to procreate; it is these human qualities that make her one of the most revered of the Navajo Holy People.

If Miss Navajo Nation is accused of misconduct or violations of the ethical laws and/or codes of conduct, she must answer to the Government Services Committee of the Navajo Nation to address the allegations and clear her name; if found guilty, she must relinquish her crown. Ironically, while Miss Navajo Nation must be virtuous and have impeccable morals, every other week or so, the *Navajo Times* reports with relish the infractions of Navajo male leaders, including embezzlements, adultery, and domestic violence. These men are rarely brought before any committee of the Navajo Nation, although sometimes public airings of leaders' ethical violations bring about changes.

In 1997, Radmilla Cody from Grand Falls, Arizona, was named Miss Navajo Nation. Of Navajo and African American descent, Miss Cody was deemed by the judges to be the best representative of Navajo tradition and culture. Her beauty and grace and, in particular, her ability to sing traditional Navajo songs quickly pushed her into the Navajo public eye. Especially laudable from the perspective of an appreciative Navajo public was Cody's ability to "butcher a sheep with surgical precision" while dressed in a lavishly decorated velvet blouse and skirt that covered her almost completely from neck to ankles.

Journalist Debra Weyermann noted in an article she wrote on Cody that her crowning led to a display of racism from some Navajos who did not approve of a woman who was half Navajo and half African American representing them. According to Weyermann, Navajo Nation president Albert Hale "harangued pageant officials about the unseemliness of Cody being crowned Miss Navajo."⁴⁶ Two months after Cody was crowned Miss Navajo Nation, Orlando Tom, a Navajo from Blue Gap, Arizona, sent a letter to the *Navajo Times* complaining that Cody did not reflect the best characteristics of Navajos because of her mixed heritage. According to Tom, Cody's appearance is "clearly black, and thus representative of another race of people."⁴⁷ Tom went on to warn readers that tribal members of mixed heritage were a threat to the future of the tribe and suggested that Cody focus on her African American heritage and stay out of Navajo affairs.⁴⁸ A barrage of letters, many of which lambasted Tom for his prejudice and defended Cody, reflect Navajos' adoration of Cody.⁴⁹ Navajos like Tom have conveniently forgotten that Navajos claim an ancestry that includes the adoption of and intermarriage with neighboring Pueblos and Mexicans.

In the controversy over Cody's race and blood quantum, she was not only criticized for not looking like a Navajo but also for looking African American. Such concerns raise questions about Navajo responses to Navajos with African American ancestry. As anthropologist Circe Sturm has observed in her own studies of Cherokees and race mixing with African Americans, Cherokees have discriminated against Cherokee freedmen, refusing to acknowledge Cherokees with black blood as Cherokees for a number of reasons, including the creation of a Cherokee state apparatus modeled on the U.S. federal government that polices Cherokee identity on the basis of genealogy and race. Just as Cherokees have responded to U.S. racism in ways that are unique to their own history and nation building, so too have Navajos reproduced, reinterpreted, and redeployed dominant race thinking.⁵⁰

In January 2003, after she had completed her reign, Cody began serving a twenty-one-month sentence in an Arizona federal prison for knowing about and not reporting her ex-boyfriend's drug-smuggling operation and for strapping packets of cocaine to her body and slipping through airport security. In her letter of apology to the Navajo people and then in an interview, both of which were published in the *Navajo Times*, Cody explained that she became enmeshed in her boyfriend's drug operation because she feared for her life.⁵¹ Cody's story of domestic violence is a familiar one, for Navajos, and Native peoples in general, experience some of the highest rates of unemployment, homicide, poverty, domestic violence, and suicide.⁵² Once again, Cody was in the Navajo public eye. Her involvement with drugs raised questions about her morality and virtue, particularly as it appeared applicable to her being a former queen of the Nation. Once again, Navajo readers wrote letters to the *Navajo Times*, some condemning her, but many offering prayers and sending her messages of compassion and understanding.

Although Miss Navajo Nation embodies Navajo cultural values and ideal womanhood, we must also acknowledge that beauty pageants are rooted in white middle-class values that present femininity as embodied in chastity, Victorian morality, and virtue. The criteria for Miss Navajo are influenced and shaped by colonialist beliefs about the place of women and their symbolic value as representatives of the Nation. Introductions of Western-style governments have meant exposure to Western value systems, including ideas about proper gender roles. As feminist scholar Chandra Mohanty observes, male-led reforms in Third World nationalist movements have also been occupied with legislating and regulating the sexuality of women, particularly women from the emerging middle class, including the selective encouragement of women's entry into the public sphere by institutions that in turn controlled women's entry into the labor force and into politics.[53] In a similar manner, American notions of gender roles have been integral in the formation of the modern-day Navajo Nation, where women are symbolized as the culture bearers and the mothers of the Nation without having access to all sectors of society, particularly the political realm.

The Navajo Nation's claims to practice many of the traditions of their ancestors in the administration of the government must be seen in light of transformations under colonialism. While it is necessary for Native scholars to call on the intellectual community to support and preserve Indigenous sovereignty, it is crucial that we also recognize how history has transformed traditions and that we be critical about the ways tradition is claimed and for what purposes. In some cases, tradition has been used to disenfranchise women and to hold them to standards higher than those set for men. Tradition is not without a political context. As postcolonial critic Anne McClintock observes in her examination of how nations are gendered,

> all nations depend on powerful constructions of gender. Despite nationalisms' ideological investment in the idea of popular unity, nations have historically

amounted to the sanctioned institutionalization of gender difference. No nation in the world gives women and men the same access to rights and resources of the nation-state.[54]

In sum, First Nations scholar Taiaiake Alfred, in his critique of contemporary tribal governments, asserts that Native governments based on Western democratic models have not been successful and that a return to a traditional philosophy "will help us restore the lost harmony between indigenous people's social and political cultures."[55] Including an analysis of gender is crucial to transforming contemporary Native governments because women are primary actors in the configurations of Nation. Otherwise, as McClintock asserts, "if nationalism is not transformed by an analysis of gender power, the nation-state will remain a repository of male hopes, male aspirations, and male privilege."[56] Finally, as Cherokee scholar Andrea Smith insists, we must be willing and courageous enough to confront sexism, for "if we maintain these patriarchal gender systems, we will be unable to decolonize and fully assert our sovereignty."[57] Affirming tribal sovereignty challenges tribes to consider that the effect of colonization and Europeanization could influence the decisions our leaders make and programs they pursue in a manner that may ultimately undermine our sovereignty.[58]

Notes

1. This article came out of a lecture that I presented to several audiences composed of Diné, Natives, and non-Natives—community members, scholars, and students. Their comments and insights helped me to better articulate issues related to the complicated relations of Diné women, sexism, colonialism, and Diné sovereignty. Thanks to LeNora Fulton Johnson, Dorothy Lameman Fulton, and Leila Help-Tulley for their insights on Navajo women and leadership. My appreciation also for the Indigenous and Indian feminist scholarship and encouragement of Andrea Smith, J. Kehaulani Kauanui, and Sanjam Ahluwalia.

2. Throughout my discussion, I move back and forth between the terms *Navajo*, *Diné*, and *the People*, as they refer to my people, the Diné. Similarly, I use the terms *Native* and *Indigenous* to refer to the original inhabitants of this conti-

nent. I have tried to avoid the term *Indian* as it does not describe who we are as Native peoples but rather refers to people from India.

3. Nira Yuval-Davis, *Gender and Nation* (Thousand Oaks, CA: SAGE, 1997), 29. See also Chandra Talpade Mohanty, Ann Russo, and Lourdes Torres, eds., *Third World Women and the Politics of Feminism* (Bloomington: Indiana University Press, 1991); Anne McClintock, Aamir Mufti, and Ella Shohat, eds., *Dangerous Liaisons: Gender, Nation, and Postcolonial Perspectives* (Minneapolis: University of Minnesota Press, 1997); Ann Laura Stoler, *Carnal Knowledge and Imperial Power: Race and the Intimate in Colonial Rule* (Berkeley: University of California Press, 2002); Micaela di Leonardo, ed., *Gender at the Crossroads of Knowledge: Feminist Anthropology in the Postmodern Era* (Berkeley: University of California Press, 1991); Lata Mani, *Contentious Traditions: The Debate on Sati in Colonial India* (Berkeley: University of California Press, 1998); Mrinalini Sinha, "Gender in the Critiques of Colonialism and Nationalism: Locating the 'Indian Woman,'" in *Feminists Revision History*, ed. Ann-Louise Shapiro (New Brunswick, NJ: Rutgers University Press, 1994), 246–75; Anne McClintock, "Family Feuds: Gender, Nationalism and the Family," *Feminist Review* 44 (1993): 61–80; Margaret Jolly, "Motherland? Some Notes on Women and Nationalism in India and Africa," *Australian Journal of Anthropology* 5 (1994): 41–59.

4. There are many studies of how Native women have fared under colonialism. See the following for examples: Paula Gunn Allen, *The Sacred Hoop: Recovering the Feminine in American Indian Traditions* (Boston: Beacon Press, 1986); Patricia Albers and Beatrice Medicine, *The Hidden Half: Studies of Plains Indian Women* (Lanham, MD: University Press of America, 1983); Mona Etienne and Eleanor Leacock, eds., *Women and Colonization: Anthropological Perspectives* (New York: Praeger, 1980); Karen Anderson, *Changing Woman: A History of Racial Ethnic Women in Modern America* (New York: Oxford University Press, 1996); Theda Perdue, ed., *Sifters: Native American Women's Lives* (New York: Oxford University Press, 2001); Elizabeth Cook-Lynn, *Why I Can't Read Wallace Stegner and Other Essays: A Tribal Voice* (Madison: University of Wisconsin Press, 1996); M. Annette Jaimes with Theresa Halsey, "American Indian Women: At the Center of Indigenous Resistance in North America," in Jaimes, *State of Native America: Genocide, Colonization, and Resistance* (Boston: South End Press, 1992), 311–44; Lee Maracle, *I Am Woman* (North Vancouver: Write-On Press, 1988); Michelene E. Pesantubbee, *Choctaw Women in a Chaotic World: The Clash*

of Cultures in the Colonial Southeast (Albuquerque: University of New Mexico Press, 2005); and Andrea Smith, *Conquest: Sexual Violence and American Indian Genocide* (Cambridge, MA: South End Press, 2005).

5. There are many studies of Native American governments, including the following: Vine Deloria Jr. and Clifford Lytle, *The Nations Within: The Past and Future of American Indian Sovereignty* (New York: Pantheon 1984); Sharon O'Brien, *American Indian Tribal Governments* (Norman: University of Oklahoma Press, 1989); Vine Deloria Jr., *We Talk, You Listen: New Tribes, New Turf* (New York: Macmillan, 1970); Don L. Fixico, *Termination and Relocation: Federal Indian Policy, 1945–1960* (Albuquerque: University of New Mexico Press, 1986); Francis Paul Prucha, *American Indian Policy in the Formative Years: The Indian Trade and Intercourse Acts, 1790–1834* (Lincoln: University of Nebraska Press, 1970); Rebecca L. Robbins, "Self-Determination and Subordination: The Past, Present, and Future of American Indian Governance," in *The State of Native America: Genocide, Colonization, and Resistance*, ed. M. Annette Jaimes (Boston: South End Press, 1992), 87–121; Marjane Ambler, "The Rights and Responsibilities of Sovereignty," *Tribal College Journal of American Indian Higher Education* 16, no. 1 (Fall 2004): 8–9; and Paul Boyer, "The Rhetoric v. The Reality," *Tribal College Journal of American Indian Higher Education* 16, no. 1 (Fall 2004): 10–13.

6. Aubrey W. Williams Jr., *Navajo Political Process* (Washington, DC: Smithsonian Institution Press, 1970), 5. See also Richard Van Valkenburgh, "Navajo Common Law I: Notes on Political Organization, Property and Inheritance," *Museum Notes: Museum of Northern Arizona* 9, no. 4 (1936): 17–22, and "Navajo Naat'aani," *Kiva* 13, no. 2 (1948): 14–23.

7. David M. Brugge, "Documentary References to a Navajo Naachi'id in 1850," *Ethnohistory* 10, no. 2 (1963): 186–88.

8. Office of Navajo Government Development, *Navajo Nation Government* (Window Rock, AZ: Office of Navajo Government Development, 1998), 2–10.

9. David E. Wilkins, *The Navajo Political Experience* (Tsaile, AZ: Diné College Press, 1999), 71.

10. Carol Douglas Sparks, in an effort to illuminate Navajo women's roles in the nineteenth century, notes that in 1846, the Navajo leader Narbona's wife was present at a meeting between Navajo and American men where she so moved the Navajo men with her speech against the Americans that the Navajo warriors escorted her out

of the meeting at Narbona's bidding. See Carol Douglas Sparks, "The Land Incarnate: Navajo Women and the Dialogue of Colonialism, 1821–1870," in *Negotiators of Change: Historical Perspectives on Native American Women*, ed. Nancy Shoemaker (New York: Routledge, 1995), 135–56. See also John T. Hughes, *Doniphan's Expedition: Containing an Account of the Conquest of New Mexico and California*, ed. William Elsey Connelly (Topeka, KS, 1907), 166–85; and Jacob S. Robinson, *A Journal of the Santa Fe Expedition Under Colonel Doniphan* (Princeton, NJ: Princeton University Press, 1932; repr., New York: Da Capo Press, 1972), 42–51.

11. Ruth Roessel, *Women in Navajo Society* (Rough Rock, AZ: Navajo Resource Center, 1981), 132–35.

12. For an account of Juanita, see Jennifer Nez Denetdale, "'One of the Queenliest Women in Dignity, Grace, and Character I Have Ever Met': Photography and Navajo Women—Portraits of Juanita, 1868–1902," *New Mexico Historical Review* 79, no. 3 (Summer 2004): 288–318.

13. Recently, scholars have built on the work of David Brugge, who examined Catholic Church records in New Mexico and discovered that the number of Native and particularly Navajo baptisms corresponded with raids on Navajos. See David M. Brugge, *Navajos in the Catholic Church Records of New Mexico, 1694–1875* (Tsaile, AZ: Navajo Community College Press, 1985). See also Frank McNitt, Navajo Wars: Military Campaigns, Slave Raids, and Reprisals (Albuquerque: University of New Mexico Press, 1990), and James F. Brooks, *Captives and Cousins: Slavery, Kinship, and Community in the Southwest Borderlands* (Chapel Hill: University of North Carolina Press, 2002).

14. Clifford E. Trafzer, *The Kit Carson Campaign: The Last Great Navajo War* (Norman: University of Oklahoma Press, 1982).

15. John Wilson, "Prisoners Without Walls: Fort Sumner in 1854," *El Palacio* 74, no. 1 (Spring 1967): 10–28.

16. Louise Lamphere, "The Internal Colonization of the Navajo People," *Southwest Economy and Society* 1 (1976): 6–8.

17. U. S. Congress, Joint Special Committee, *Condition of the Indian Tribes: Report of the Joint Special Committee, Appointed Under Joint Resolution of March 3, 1865: With an Appendix* (Washington, DC: Government Print Office, 1867).

18. Broderick H. Johnson, ed., *Navajo Stories of the Long Walk Period* (Tsaile, AZ: Navajo Community College Press, 1994).

19. Martin A. Link ed., *Treaty Between the United States and the Navajo Tribe of Indians with a Record of the Discussions That Led to Its Signing* (Las Vegas, NV: KC, 1968).
20. Roessel, *Women in Navajo Society*, 132.
21. Mary Shepardson, *Navajo Ways in Government: A Study in Political Process*, Memoirs of the American Anthropological Association, no. 96 (Menasha, WI: American Anthropological Association, 1963), 12.
22. Richard White, *The Roots of Dependency: Subsistence, Environment, and Social Change Among the Choctaws, Pawnees, and Navajos* (Lincoln: University of Nebraska Press, 1983), 212–90.
23. Kathleen P. Chamberlain, *Under Sacred Ground: A History of Navajo Oil, 1922–1982* (Albuquerque: University of New Mexico Press, 2000).
24. Peter Iverson, *The Navajo Nation* (Albuquerque: University of New Mexico Press, 1981).
25. Frank Mitchell, *Navajo Blessingway Singer: The Autobiography of Frank Mitchell, 1881–1967*, ed. Charlotte J. Frisbie and David P. McAllester (Tucson: University of Arizona Press, 2003), 225.
26. Colleen O'Neill, "The Making of the Navajo Worker: Navajo Households, the Bureau of Indian Affairs, and Off-Reservation Wage Work, 1948–1960," *New Mexico Historical Review* 74, no. 4 (October 1999): 375–403.
27. Genevieve Chato and Christine Conte, "The Legal Rights of American Indian Women," in *Western Women: Their Land, Their Lives*, ed. Lillian Schlissel, Vicki L. Ruiz, and Janice Monk (Albuquerque: University of New Mexico Press, 1988), 229–46.
28. Wilkins, *Navajo Political Experience*.
29. Martin A. Link, ed. *Navajo: A Century of Progress, 1868–1968* (Window Rock, AZ: Navajo Tribe, 1968). In 1968, a number of cultural events that included a fair, essay contests, a contest to create a Navajo Nation flag, and several publications were part of yearlong events to celebrate one hundred years since Navajos returned from Bosque Redondo in 1868.
30. David Wilkins describes some of the turmoil that the Navajo government has experienced, particularly during Peter MacDonald's fourth term, when a struggle for power resulted in the deaths of several Navajos and prison terms for others, including MacDonald himself. After MacDonald's resignation, a host of other Navajo men served as president and were removed for various violations.

See Wilkins, *Navajo Political Experience*. See also Donald Grinde and Bruce Johansen, "The Navajos and National Sacrifice," in *The Multicultural Southwest: A Reader*, ed. A. Gabriel Melendez, M. Jane Young, Patricia Moore, and Patrick Pynes (Tucson: University of Arizona Press, 2001), 204–17; and Peter Iverson, *Diné: A Navajo History* (Albuquerque: University of New Mexico Press, 2002).

31. See, e.g., Laura Jane Moore, "Lozen: An Apache Woman Warrior," in *Sifters: Native American Women's Lives*, ed. Theda Perdue (New York: Oxford University Press, 2001), 92–107.
32. See, e.g., Wilma Mankiller and Michael Wallis, *Mankiller: A Chief and Her People* (New York: St. Martin's Griffin, 1994).
33. Marley Shebala, "The Race Has Begun! Fulton to Run for President in '98," *Navajo Times*, June 26, 1997, A-1. Kay Curley Bennett ran in 1986 and then in 1990. In the 1990 election, she was disqualified as a candidate because of a tribal law that required all candidates running for tribal chairman to have served in an elective position before or to have been an employee of the tribe. After a ruling by the Navajo Supreme Court, she was allowed to run as a write-in candidate because the ballots had already been printed. See Bill Donovan, "First Woman to Run for Tribal President Had Many Talents," *Navajo Times*, November 20, 1997, A-5.
34. Patrisia Gonzales and Roberto Rodriguez, "Women's Leadership Is Re-emerging in Indian Country," *Column of the Americas* (blog of Gonzales and Rodriguez, Universal Press Syndicate), July 10, 1998, http://www.voznuestra.com/Americas/_1998/_July/10_I (no longer posted).
35. LeNora Y. Fulton, "Women Can Lead," *Navajo Times*, May 7, 1998, A-4; Gonzales and Rodriguez, "Women's Leadership Is Re-emerging."
36. Marley Shebala, "Wanted: More Women Leaders," *Navajo Times*, February 6, 1997, A-7.
37. Carolyn Niethammer, *I'll Go and Do More: Annie Dodge Wauneka, Navajo Leader and Activist* (Lincoln: University of Nebraska Press, 2001); Virginia Hoffman and Broderick H. Johnson, "Annie Dodge Wauneka," in *Navajo Biographies* (Chinle, AZ: Rough Rock Demonstration School, 1974), 2:90–105; Melanie McCoy, "Gender or Ethnicity: What Makes a Difference? A Study of Women Tribal Leaders," in *Readings in American Indian Law: Recalling the Rhythm of Survival*, ed. Jo Carrillo (Philadelphia: Temple University Press, 1998), 235–41.

38. Irene Stewart, *A Voice in Her Tribe: A Navajo Woman's Own Story*, ed. Lowell John Bean and Thomas C. Blackburn, with the foreword by Mary Shepardson (Socorro, NM: Ballena Press, 1980), 61.

39. Ibid. Published accounts of the Navajo creation narratives include Paul G. Zolbrod, *Diné Bahane': The Navajo Creation Story* (Albuquerque: University of New Mexico Press, 1984); Washington Matthews, *Navajo Legends* (New York: American Folklore Society, 1897); Aileen O'Bryan and Sandoval, *The Diné: Origin Myths of the Navaho Indians* (Washington, DC: Bureau of American Ethnology, 1956); and Ethelou Yazzie, ed., *Navajo History* (Rough Rock, AZ: Rough Rock Demonstration School, 1984).

40. Mary Shepardson, "The Status of Navajo Women," *American Indian Quarterly* 6, no. 1/2 (Spring/Summer 1982): 160. Deborah Gordon, in her examination of relationships between white women scholars and their Native subjects, notes that Mary Shepardson claimed a friendship with Irene Stewart as opposed to being in a hierarchical relationship where Shephardson as the anthropologist exerted her authority and power to interpret the meaning of Stewart's life and culture. See Deborah Gordon, "Among Women: Gender and Ethnographic Authority of the Southwest, 1930–1980," in *Hidden Scholars: Women Anthropologists and the Native American Southwest* (Albuquerque: University of New Mexico Press, 1993), 129–45.

41. Roessel, *Women in Navajo Society*, 133.

42. In yet another interesting twist on the meaning of women's traditional roles in Navajo society, Diné writer Laura Tohe asserts that Navajo women do not claim *feminism* as a term or as a way to describe who they are and what they do because they have always enjoyed authority and autonomy. Such a position fails to name the colonial space in which Navajo women find themselves and the ways in which a history of colonialism has wreaked havoc in their lives while they also struggle to reclaim their lives, culture, and history. See Laura Tohe, "There Is No Word for Feminism in My Language," *Wicazo Sa Review* 15, no. 2 (Fall 2000): 103–10.

43. See Wendy Kozol, "Miss Indian America: Regulatory Gazes and the Politics of Affiliation," *Feminist Studies* 31, no. 1 (Spring 2005): 64–94. A couple of former Miss Navajos have noted their experiences in the pageants, calling them positive and culturally affirming. See, e.g., Ellen McCulloguh-Brabson and Marilyn Help, *We'll Be in Your Mountains, We'll Be in Your Songs: A Navajo Woman*

Sings (Albuquerque: University of New Mexico Press, 2001). Marilyn Help is a former Miss Navajo who today is a prominent Navajo cultural teacher and performance artist.

44. There are many studies devoted to the emergence of ethnic beauty pageants and their significance to nation building. See, e.g., Huma Ahmed-Ghosi, "Writing the Nation on the Beauty Queen's Body: Implications for a 'Hindu' Nation," *Meridians: Feminism, Race, Transnationalism* 4, no. 1 (2003): 205–27; Colleen Ballerino Cohen, Richard Wilk, and Beverly Stoeltje, eds., *Beauty Queens on the Global State: Gender, Contests, and Power* (New York: Routledge, 1996); Maxine Leeds Craig, *Ain't I a Beauty Queen? Black Women, Beauty, and the Politics of Race* (New York: Oxford University Press, 2002); Sarah Banet-Weiser, *The Most Beautiful Girl in the World: Beauty Pageants and National Identity* (Berkeley: University of California Press, 1999); Elwood Watson and Darcy Martin, *"There She Is, Miss America": The Politics of Sex, Beauty, and Race in America's Most Famous Pageant* (New York: Palgrave Macmillan, 2004); and Judy Tzu-Chun Wu, "'Loveliest Daughter of Our Ancient Cathay!' Representations of Ethnic and Gender Identity in the Miss Chinatown U.S.A. Beauty Pageant," in *Western Women's Lives: Continuity and Change in the Twentieth Century*, ed. Sandra K. Schackel (Albuquerque: University of New Mexico Press, 2003): 389–426.

45. In contrast to my findings, Wendy Kozol places the phenomenon of Native beauty contests in the Red Power movement and names them as yet another strategy for cultural survival. I found that the Navajo beauty contests occurred within an atmosphere where Navajo leaders were extolling Navajo progress within the Western meaning of progress and as it could be evidenced by the development of natural resources, entrance into Western education, and the attainment of Western-style homes and all of their comforts. See Wendy Kozol, "Miss Indian America."

46. Debra Weyermann, "Little Big Woman: Meet the Real Miss America, the Queen of the Navajo Nation," *Mirella* (October 1999): 166.

47. Orlando Tom, "Sense of Identity," *Navajo Times*, December 23, 1997, A-4. See also Leona R. Begay, "Times Are Changing," *Navajo Times*, March 26, 1998, A-4.

48. Leslie Linthicum, "Queen of Two Cultures," in *The Multicultural Southwest Reader*, ed. A. Gabriel Melendez, Patricia Moore, Patrick Pynes, and M. Jane Young (Tucson: University of Arizona Press, 2001), 262–66.

49. For examples of letters to the editor, see Ryan Battles and Nathan J. Tohtsoni, *Navajo Times*, April 2, 1998, A-4; Ivis Daniel Peaches and Tish Ramirez, *Navajo Times*, April 16, 1998, A-4; Shirlee James-Johnson, "Bring Healing Not Hate," *Navajo Times*, April 9, 1998, A-4; and Priscilla Bahe, "Amount of Navajo Blood Shouldn't Matter," *Navajo Times*, January 8, 1998, A-4.

50. Circe Sturm, *Blood Politics: Race, Culture, and Identity in the Cherokee Nation of Oklahoma* (Berkeley: University of California Press, 2002), 204, 205.

51. Radmilla Cody, "A Message to the Navajo People," *Navajo Times*, December 5, 2002, A-4. See also Marley Shebala, "Fall from Grace: Ex-Miss Navajo Radmilla Cody Recounts Story That Led to Drug-Related Charges and Prison," *Navajo Times*, December 12, 2002, A1, A3, and "'She'll Be Back Singing Like a Bird, Healed from a Broken Wing,'" *Navajo Times*, December 12, 2002, A3; Rick Abasta, "Award-Winning Singer Plans to Keep Public Schedule," *Navajo Times*, December 12, 2002, A1, A3.

52. Luana Ross, "Imprisoned Native Women and the Importance of Native Traditions," in *States of Confinement: Policing, Detention, and Prisons*, ed. Joy James (New York: Palgrave, 2002), 132–43.

53. Chandra Talpade Mohanty, "Cartographies of Struggle," in Mohanty, Russo, and Torres, *Third World Women*, 1–47.

54. Anne McClintock, "'No Longer in a Future Heaven': Gender, Race, and Nationalism," in McClintock, Mufti, and Shohat, *Dangerous Liaisons*, 89.

55. Taiaiake Alfred, *Peace, Power, Righteousness: An Indigenous Manifesto* (Don Mills, ON: Oxford University Press, 1999), 44.

56. McClintock, "'No Longer in a Future Heaven,'" 109.

57. Smith, *Conquest*, 139.

58. Andrea Smith, "Native American Feminism, Sovereignty, and Social Change," *Feminist Studies* 31, no. 1 (Spring 2005): 123, 124; Jennifer Nez Denetdale, "Representing Changing Woman: A Review Essay on Navajo Women," *American Indian Culture and Research Journal* 25, no. 3 (2001): 1–26.

6

Same-Sex Marriage in the Cherokee Nation

Toward Decolonial Queer Indigeneities

JESSICA A. F. HARKINS

In 2004, Kathy Reynolds and Dawn McKinley, two Cherokee women in a committed relationship, decided they wanted to pursue a legal marriage through the Cherokee Nation. With support from Cherokee and gay rights activist David Cornsilk, Reynolds and McKinley determined that they wanted more rights as a couple after McKinley was barred from visiting Reynolds's hospital room. They applied for and received a marriage license from the Cherokee Nation, got married, but were then unable to file their license because a Cherokee Tribal Council attorney (though acting as a private citizen) had challenged the validity of the marriage. In the time between these two events (and indeed spurred by Reynolds and McKinley's actions), the tribal council had unanimously approved a constitutional amendment defining marriage as between a man and a woman.

Following this, though, the couple had multiple wins. First, in August of 2005, the judicial appeals tribunal of the Cherokee Nation rejected the attorney's petition to block the marriage, arguing that he lacked standing to bring a suit against the couple. In December of 2005, the tribunal also rejected an attempt by tribal council members to invalidate the couple's marriage "because the council members could not show that they were individually harmed or affected by the marriage in any way."[1] A third suit was brought against the couple in 2006 by the Cherokee court administrator, but the Cherokee court once again ruled in favor of the couple. Since these decisions, however, Reynolds and McKinley have decided not to file their marriage certificate or pursue any other legal action in the Cherokee courts. The law itself has remained in place, and furthermore, in December of 2014, the Eastern Band of Cherokees in North Carolina voted to reaffirm the ban.[2]

This case took place alongside and within the larger context of a sex panic across the United States focused on same-sex marriage.[3] At the federal level, the Defense of Marriage Act (DOMA, passed in 1996 by President Bill Clinton) banned the recognition of same-sex marriages until its recent overturning in 2013. The state level has been more divided; since Massachusetts legalized same-sex marriage over a decade ago, thirty-six other states and the District of Columbia have gradually followed suit. The issue has played a central role in political campaigns, and it has sparked debates from the Christian right, gay and lesbian rights organizations, queer leftists, and academics alike. Sovereign territories within U.S. borders have not been immune to this panic either; while movement began with the Navajo and Cherokee Nations' 2004 and 2005 respective bans of same-sex marriage, currently the tribes that have legalized it outweigh those that do not recognize it twenty-one to twelve, a shift that in some cases has been spurred by DOMA's overruling.[4]

In this chapter, I focus on these two interrelated panics: same-sex marriage in the mainstream United States and same-sex marriage in Native America, specifically in the Cherokee Nation. Discourses surrounding both of these sites point to a number of tensions, including the rhetoric of tradition, histories of regulation, the structural continuation of settler colonialism, and relationships between gender, sexuality, and sovereignty. I contend with each of these issues in order to unpack how the mainstream United States has made and continues to make efforts to regulate Native communities and individuals through heteronormative strategies tied to racialized and indigenized sexuality as well as simultaneous Native resistance through practices of distinct naming and refusal of norms.

The Cherokee Nation's ongoing struggle over same-sex marriage offers a unique view of the relationship between the mainstream United States and Native America. Reynolds and McKinley's case has garnered the involvement of multiple other actors: Todd Hembree, a legal counselor for the Cherokee

National Council; the Cherokee Tribunal Council; the couple's lawyer at the National Center for Lesbian Rights (NCLR); David Cornsilk, introduced above; and Cherokee anthropologist Brian Gilley. Each of these players has a different stake in the issue, and therefore the case offers a complex, multilayered window into the relationship between marriage, sexuality, indigeneity, the U.S. state, and Native nations. Within this setting, I develop a queer analysis of settler colonialism, drawing on concepts of U.S. sexual exceptionalism, heteronormativity, liberalism, and regulatory U.S. colonialism.

This methodology has been particularly informed by Andrea Smith's call for a subjectless critique in the field of queer Native studies, thus centering settler colonialism and positioning the U.S. state, the objectification of Native people, non-Native subjects, and academia as sites of settler colonial violence as well as Qwo-Li Driskill's Two-Spirit doubleweaving critique.[5] Driskill describes this approach through a number of points of focus, the most salient of which for this chapter include seeing "Two-Spirit people and traditions as both integral and a challenge to nationalist and decolonial struggles," engaging "in both intertribal and tribally specific concerns," being "woven into Native feminisms by seeing sexism, homophobia, and transphobia as colonial tools," being "informed by and mak[ing] use of other Native activisms, arts, and scholarship," and seeing "Two-Spirit identities in relationship with spirituality and medicine."[6] By aiming to attend to each of these objectives, I trace the ways through which sexuality has been a tool of U.S. colonization of Native peoples, resulting in the adoption of U.S. heteronormative values by Native nations in some ways though resisted and destabilized in others.

Looking at the interplay between tradition and the temporality of settler colonialism, I argue that progressive politics grounded in liberalism have shaped both the mainstream and Native United States in a way that positions Native nations in the popular imaginary as regressively backward and have also reinforced the ongoing project of settler colonialism by locating certain practices and peoples safely in the past. Additionally, I focus specifically on the discursive function of tradition and the temporal distinction between past and present. I argue that Native traditions of Two-Spirit identities, while used as evidence for the legitimacy of Cherokee same-sex marriage by the couple's representation and other supporters, are relegated to the past, while contemporary Cherokees, specifically Reynolds and McKinley, are discursively constructed as liberal, mainstream LGBT individuals and thus aligned with national LGBT rights activism. This distinction functions within the larger context of settler colonialism in which a "logic of elimination" necessitates the disappearance (physically and culturally and the intersection thereof) of Native peoples in order for the land to appear fully settled.[7] At the same time, I also raise questions of sovereignty, pointing to the ways a distinct Native gender and sexuality can be an important component of sovereignty making as well as allowing for a potential revisioning of liberal values within an indigenous context.

Heteronormativity and Tradition Within U.S. Settler Colonialism

Heteronormativity can be traced as a tool of colonialism since the onset of European occupation of the present-day United States. Through different government sanctions, laws, and norm-producing practices, the U.S. state and culture has long functioned to set standards intended to exclude and eliminate those who have not fit those norms. While this applies to many marginalized groups, such as immigrants, people of color, and poor people, the tool of heteronormativity takes on a related yet unique role in the context of colonialism. As Andrea Smith explains, settler colonization in the Americas historically rested on heteropatriarchal methods that included the targeting of indigenous peoples who did not conform to gender binary models.[8] Scott Morgensen terms this process the "colonial biopolitics of modern sexuality," in which discourses of racial, sexual, and gender transgression of indigenous individuals directed colonial endeavors of death and population management.[9]

Detailing the specifics of this history and continued project of heteronormativity, Mark Rifkin examines its manifestation through impositions of straightness, heteroconjugality, monogamous coupledom, nuclear families, private home ownership, and reproduction.[10] Rifkin further describes how these practices have been unique to the colonial project: "U.S. imperialism against native peoples over the past two centuries can be understood as an effort to make them 'straight'—to insert indigenous peoples into Anglo-

American conceptions of family, home, desire, and personal identity."[11] Some of these specific practices include a restructuring of families to fit Western norms, the enforcement of blood-quantum percentages to determine tribal membership, and the imposition of Western concepts of gender and sexuality.[12] Thus, in the context of colonialism, heteronormativity is taken up as a governing eliminatory technique using imposed normativities related to kinship and family structures, gender and sexual identities, reproduction, and racial formations to further marginalize Native peoples to the ultimate objective of nonexistence.

This heteronormative colonial logic has encouraged an adoption of Western values and practices by Native peoples in the United States in a way that has sometimes led to an obscuring and possible erasing of previous ways of life. Western family and marriage practices, for example, have often so thoroughly displaced previous Native practices that concepts of tradition are not always easily defined. Smith describes this as a process of "internalization," arguing that, through colonialism and U.S. empire, Native peoples have internalized self-hatred, patriarchy, and patterns of violence, an internalization that is manifested in the rhetoric of tradition.[13] Tradition takes multiple forms, with different people turning to various sources or periods of time from which to draw their understanding of its meaning. While new instantiations of tradition can take benign or even positive forms, there have also been harmful constructions of tradition, such as Smith's example in which sexual violence in Native communities is depicted as "traditional" in order to justify its occurrence.[14] In addition, because tradition is a necessarily important site within Native discourse in the United States because of its crucial ties to history, culture, and place, it becomes a particularly loaded concept within certain debates. A case can certainly be made that truer or better forms of tradition surely exist, and indeed part of my argument about tradition rests on the idea that when it manifests as discrimination, this is neither a true nor good version of tradition, though my analysis of tradition avoids sifting through different interpretations to find the one underlying, authentic truth.

Contradictory rhetorical strategies point to difficulties that often arise when turning to tradition as proof in present-day political debates both because it may be impossible to access perfectly and because it may not be directly applicable to contemporary ways of life. Tradition can be configured to suit specific and even oppositional objectives, and broader Native practices have sometimes been universalized to construct narratives about specific tribes. Interpretations of tradition are further complicated by the change in context between centuries ago and today in which, for example, same-sex marriage has become a politicized issue. Native feminists have also argued that gender oppression and power differentials currently exist between indigenous men and women and that focusing on false, constructed, or antiquated notions of tradition that emphasize gender equality only serves to obscure further the present-day conditions of gender oppression within indigenous communities.[15] For example, Joanne Barker's work on the landmark tribal sovereignty cases *Martinez v. Santa Clara* and *Santa Clara v. Martinez* challenges the way participation in gender discrimination by Native communities gets coded as an issue of sovereignty and thus excused and permitted.[16]

In the context of the Navajo Nation, Jennifer Nez Denetdale similarly argues that gender operates as a disciplinary mechanism in which heteropatriarchal logics get deployed under the auspices of tradition.[17] She explains that the leaders of the Navajo Nation, the majority of whom are men, have been invested in reproducing a "Navajo nationalist ideology" that "re-inscribe[s] gender roles based on Western concepts even as they claim they operate under traditional Navajo philosophy."[18] Denetdale asserts that any adoption of Native "tradition" that upholds discrimination is, in effect, a blurring of American and Navajo values, displaying an uncritical acceptance of American values and aligning contemporary Navajo beliefs and practices with tradition.[19] Thus, claims of tradition can be manifestations of present-day beliefs (which have often been shaped by colonial processes and their responses) and may manipulate knowledge of traditional practices in order to construct legitimacy. These rhetorical uses of tradition affirm Western ideas and deny the existence of respect and acceptance in Native cultures.[20] In her work, Denetdale turns to Smith, who asserted in a 2006 keynote address that "we cannot decolonize without addressing sexism, and attempting to do so ignores the fact that it has been precisely through gender violence that we have lost our lands in the first place."[21] In other words, turning to tradition to justify inequality and discrimination relies on a false understanding of tradition and furthermore serves to obscure the reality of present-day sexism and homophobia.

The Reynolds and McKinley Case
Tradition and Two-Spirit

Native individuals who oppose or support the banning of same-sex marriage within the Cherokee Nation similarly draw on notions of tradition to support their claims. In Reynolds and McKinley's trial, briefs have been filed with the court that argue that same-sex marriage is "inconsistent with Cherokee Nation culture, heritage, and tradition."[22] In the vein of many of the other court documents, one petition submitted by Todd Hembree asserts that "same sex marriages were not part of Cherokee history or tradition. Cherokee society in 1892 did not allow nor contemplate same sex marriage. This Court should determine that same sex marriage is not allowed under today's laws."[23] And on the other side of the debate, there are equivalent examples of a reliance on tradition to uphold the argument in favor of same-sex marriage. Gilley, for example, who submitted an affidavit in support of Reynolds and McKinley, said that "there is overwhelming evidence for the historic and cultural presence of multiple gender roles and same-sex marriage relations among most if not all Native North Americans, including the Cherokee, and . . . they historically shared in the institution of marriage."[24]

Within the proceedings of the trial, Reynolds and McKinley officially responded to Hembree with the following reliance on tradition: "Tradition is an outgrowth of culture and culture is reflected in the native language. Respondents have asserted and can show that the terms for spouse in the Cherokee language are translated into English as, 'my companion,' 'the one I live with,' and 'my cooker.' These terms are gender neutral."[25] Of course, there are a number of rhetorical strategies being drawn on in these statements, including a national body that needs protection, notions of a proper family structure, and nonbinary gender identities. However, each of these statements also points to the definition of Cherokee traditional practices, arguing that because practices happened in a certain way in the past, their continued practice is justified. These statements thus point to difficulties that often arise when turning to tradition as proof and the ways tradition can be shaped to suit specific and even oppositional objectives. Different components of history, such as language and customs, are being drawn on, which allows for further variation in interpretation.

Two-Spirit, a term raised by Denetdale above in the context of same-sex marriage in the Navajo Nation, plays a particularly salient role in conversations that engage with gender, sexuality, and tradition. The term, which refers to Native gender and sexual identities that reside outside the white, mainstream binaries, was first introduced by academics and activists in the early 1990s. It recognizes a diversity across tribes and a need for contextualization, and it has also been utilized within queer Native studies as a way to point to and discuss non-Western embodiments of gender and sexuality. As Driskill explains, Two-Spirit resists colonial definitions and expresses "sexual and gender identities as sovereign from those of white GLBT movements" in a decidedly nonmonolithic understanding of Native traditions.[26]

Two-Spirit critiques also provide an alternative for anthropology's use of the word *berdache*; white, mainstream GLBTQ categorizations; and both Native and non-Native constructions of gender identities.[27] Morgensen adds that within Native activism, Two-Spirit functions as a form of anticolonialism that forces a recognition of the role of Native queer people's knowledge production, resists the invocation of cultural authenticity by highlighting "a link among diverse traditions and contemporary identities and activisms," and works against indigenous universality by recalling diversity though potentially interconnected histories.[28] For example, NativeOUT, an activist group whose goal is "to create social change in rural and urban communities that benefit Indigenous Lesbian, Gay, Bisexual, Transgender, Queer, and Two-Spirit people," draws on a "Two-Spirit history" to support its mission.[29] The group is part of a larger Two-Spirit movement "whose primary focus is [to] reestablish their traditional roles within their respective tribes, as, historically, most Two-Spirit individuals, including not-men, not-women, gays and lesbians (and those who fell in between genders and sexualities), fulfilled a spiritual, if not sacred, purpose within specific tribes."[30] The Two-Spirit movement recognizes that this is a contemporary categorization, but despite the newness of the term, the movement nevertheless draws on traditional histories of practices and social values. By explicitly bringing traditional practices into the present, this work unsettles the eliminatory historicization of Native peoples, and it allows for shifts in tradition over time and space.

In Reynolds and McKinley's case, Gilley draws from his more substantial academic work that looks at Two-Spirit peoples and their roles in Native societies to develop an academic/legal/activist argument. In an affidavit in support of Cherokee same-sex marriage, he writes, "Gender (and, for that matter, marriage) were traditionally seen by Native Americans in complex, sometimes fluid ways that bear little resemblance to the binary biological categories favored by Westerners. Your gender . . . was traditionally determined by a person's role in a community, not your biological sex."[31] Although Gilley does not use the term *Two-Spirit* explicitly here, his characterization directly refers to the ways scholars and activists define it, as evidenced in his own scholarly text, *Becoming Two-Spirit*.[32] A Two-Spirit tradition in Native communities, then, has been utilized in order to argue for a more accepting and nondiscriminatory attitude regarding Native gender and sexual diversity.

In addition to supporting a more general acceptance of nonnormative gender and sexuality, these different arguments concerning Native Two-Spirit identities also shape discourses specific to same-sex marriage. As quoted above, Gilley points to "multiple gender roles" and "same-sex marriage practices" in numerous Native societies in order to validate the legalization of same-sex marriage in present-day Native nations.[33] Traditions of Two-Spirit practices and identities, then, are being drawn on in order to present a history of Native gender and sexual fluidity as well as to specifically support the legalization of same-sex marriage within Native nations. Driskill and Daniel Heath Justice have addressed these complexities in the Reynolds and McKinley case nicely. Driskill, for example, demonstrates how Two-Spirit histories and contemporary existence have been marginalized by Cherokee nationalism during tribal council meetings concerning same-sex marriage.[34]

Justice complicates this notion by pointing out that there is no documented history of queer acceptance within the Cherokee Nation specifically, and to assert it as such based on a broader Native American history is universalist, though this lack of documentation should also not be interpreted as definitive proof of queer nonexistence or nonacceptance either.[35] Despite these qualifications, Justice nevertheless critiques the Cherokee tribal council's "queerphobic" response to Reynolds and McKinley, arguing that the council was acting as a policing agent by attempting to pathologize same-sex relationships and effecting social control over the couple by discursively locating them outside the Cherokee Nation.[36] Rather than abandoning the importance of tradition, though, Justice proposes an approach that is historicized and contextualized, that values adaptation and inclusivity of difference, that engages with diverse kinship values, and that adheres to historical and contemporary realities.[37]

The Role of U.S. Liberalism

In a way contrasting with the rhetorical function of Two-Spirit in the case, liberal values of equality, individualism, and private, nuclear family structures also fundamentally inform the discourse of Reynolds and McKinley's case, coming from both the couple and their various legal representation. The narrative of the case is that the couple simply wanted the same rights as any other couple, specifically, the right of recognition of their marriage. In interviews, McKinley repeatedly clarified that she and Reynolds are not activists; rather, they are fighting for the recognition of the marriage for which the Cherokee Nation has given them a marriage license.[38] Thus, the strategy of the case is not questioning the validity of laws that prevent the marriage of same-sex couples or even arguing against a law that is discriminatory against gays and lesbians. Instead, the case is depicted as one couple simply fighting for its own individual rights. And while the larger potential for the dismissal of their case could possibly be the legalization of same-sex marriage in the Cherokee Nation, the actual strategy playing out is an important site of discourse, for it demonstrates what, in the current moment, is the most viable method for winning this type of case.[39]

This overall narrative in the case manifests in a variety of places. According to Cherokee law, an individual can only bring a suit against the tribal court if he or she is being personally harmed, and this restriction has helped define the contours of the strategies on both sides.[40] For example, commenting on an initial victory of the case in 2005, National Council of La Raza staff attorney Lena Ayoub stated, "Permitting same-sex couples to marry does not individually harm or affect other people. The court's ruling protects people's right to conduct their lives in privacy and peace, without being hauled into court by third parties who have no relationship to them and no direct interest in the matter being litigated."[41] In other words, because the couple is not infringing on any other individual's personal rights, Reynolds and McKinley should be able to conduct their lives however they want. Similar appeals to privacy are also present in Reynolds's response to the December 2005 ruling in her favor, in which she stated, "Dawn [McKinley] and I are private people, and we simply wish to live our lives in peace and quiet, just as other married couples are permitted to do. We are grateful to the Court for applying the law fairly and for protecting our privacy and our rights as equal citizens of the Cherokee Nation."[42]

Here, Reynolds avoids advocating for her right to be part of a same-sex marriage in any sort of public way, in effect speaking directly to Hembree's initial complaint against the legal union of the couple. She is fighting for a private enactment of equality, one that would take shape within the space of hospital rooms or, perhaps, wills and adoption, aspects of life that are relegated to the domestic sphere of the family. As McKinley stated before the first ruling, "We don't bother anyone, we mind our own business . . . stick to ourselves. How would our marriage hurt anyone?"[43] This overriding strategy, then, places the issue on the level of individuals: Reynolds and McKinley, as an individual couple, maintain a private life and therefore have no effect on other individuals' lives.

These liberal strategies of turning to equality, individualism, and privacy, not surprisingly, align with mainstream methods of achieving gay and lesbian rights. As one particularly relevant example, many scholars have looked at the terms of the *Lawrence and Garner v. Texas* case that overturned antisodomy laws on the federal level in 2003.[44] Although this Supreme Court decision was, undoubtedly, a positive change within the realm of queer rights, the tactic through which the case was successfully argued rested on the notion of individuals' rights to privacy. The majority opinion in the case, written by Justice Anthony Kennedy, reads, "The question before the Court is the validity of a Texas statute [*Bowers v. Hardwick*] making it a crime for two persons of the same sex to engage in certain intimate sexual conduct."[45]

Thus, rather than granting gays and lesbians protection under the law or arguing that antisodomy laws are discriminatory, the argument seen to be most valid by the judges was that every individual has the right to privacy within the intimate/domestic realm.

The Human Rights Campaign (HRC) offers another example of liberalism within LGBT organizing. The HRC, which is "America's largest civil rights organization working to achieve lesbian, gay, bisexual and transgender equality . . . works to secure equal rights for LGBT individuals and families at the federal and state levels by lobbying elected officials, mobilizing grassroots supporters, educating Americans, investing strategically to elect fair-minded officials and partnering with other LGBT organizations."[46] Two of the organization's largest campaigns have been fighting for the legalization of same-sex marriage as well as the elimination of the U.S. military's "Don't Ask Don't Tell" policy. These areas of focus have been targeted at individuals and families while obscuring other issues, such as violence against queers, U.S. militarism/colonialism, and pervasive heteronormativity more generally. Overall, then, despite the radical queer movements that were growing in the 1980s and early 1990s, which fought for AIDS activism, anticonsumerism, queering normative spaces, and antiassimilationism (such as Queer Nation and ACT UP), the recent trends have focused on a more assimilationist agenda, fighting for the right to be treated "just like straight people."[47]

Therefore, placing the terms of Reynolds and McKinley's case within a liberal framework, the proliferation and enforcement of values such as individualism and privacy can in part be interpreted as techniques of settler governance. Rather than taking a more radical approach to their case or the issue of same-sex marriage, the couple and their lawyers have defaulted to what can be read as normative liberal ideologies that ultimately align with heteronormative values, thus excluding many others from the benefits of their potential victory and also helping to constitute the process of settler colonialism by discursively distinguishing between past traditions and present-day positionalities or identities. By calling on individualism and privacy, they are asking for change to their own personal lives, thus releasing the Cherokee Nation or the U.S. state from any culpability in perpetuating discrimination. Therefore, this strategy, developing out of current conditions of political possibility, leads to the adoption of liberal values by the couple and also promotes the restriction of the couple's nonnormativity to the terms determined by mainstream society.

To develop this idea further, Jasbir Puar's concept of "queer as regulatory," in which she argues that "a generative project of liberalism, the purportedly liberating process of deregulation inaugurates yet again the multiplication of pools of knowledge—particularization, minutiae . . . 'heightened scrutiny'—of queer bodies," proves useful.[48] Applying this to the case of marriage, the legalization of same-sex marriage (which could be read as a "deregulation" of the institution of marriage) is, in effect, a folding of queer bodies into the nation's normative citizenry through prescriptive terms, thus subjecting those people to increased scrutiny. In other words, by fighting for the recognition of same-sex marriage through "acceptable," normative terms, the Reynolds and McKinley case only serves to incorporate the couple into the nations that nevertheless continue to operate through a heteronormative framework. Perhaps, then, as other queer theorists argue, same-sex marriage may not be the pinnacle of progress for gay rights.[49]

U.S. Sexual Exceptionalism and Settler Colonialism

These issues of tradition and liberal values contribute to the ways in which Reynolds and McKinley's case can be read through the terms of sexual exceptionalism. U.S. sexual exceptionalism, according to Puar, is a concept that brings together queerness and U.S. exceptionalism in order to position the United States as more progressive than others relative to the acceptance of sexual minorities.[50] Because the United States is more liberal, progressive, open minded, and so forth, it is well positioned (in fact it is the country's duty) to correct other people's behavior. Additionally, part of Puar's discussion of sexual exceptionalism is about the way queers have been temporarily folded into the U.S. nation-state in order for the country to actively project an image of progressivism, a process she terms "homonationalism."[51] She sees U.S. queers being incorporated into the nation so that other (in her argument, specifically Arab and Muslim) bodies can fill the position of "others." Therefore, queers become part of the United States so that they can aid in the exclusion of Arabs and Muslims and the ever-present position of "others" is strategically filled by another group.

This theoretical framework presents a useful way of analyzing Reynolds and McKinley's case specifically through terms of liberalism, indigeneity, and temporal modernity. By working within the current possible strategies of achieving same-sex marriage rights, Reynolds and McKinley are, in one interpretation, arguing to be incorporated into the mainstream heteronormative United States. Notably and importantly, Reynolds and McKinley are discursively placed in distinction to the Cherokee Nation through contradicting discourses of tradition. Even though the women themselves are not claiming a Two-Spirit identity, the media and the couple's legal team have partially placed them in this tradition of Native Two-Spirit gender and sexual fluidity (partially, in that they fail to explicitly categorize the women as Two-Spirit, but they nevertheless draw direct connections between the women and this historical tradition). Therefore, the couple has been folded into the U.S. national body in part because of this past while at the same time the Cherokee Nation has been constructed as regressively backward. The left mainstream United States is able to support the couple (which can most clearly be seen through their representation by the NCLR) while simultaneously otherizing the Cherokee Nation as a whole and perhaps, in light of the Navajo Nation's and other tribes' similarly timed bans on same-sex marriage, all contemporary Native peoples as a whole.

In this specific context, the interplay between tradition and liberalism adds a more nuanced and explicitly colonial perspective to the notion of U.S. sexual exceptionalism. According to the leftist discourses surrounding the case, Native tribes have had a long history of gender and sexual fluidity, as is substantiated by the neologism *Two-Spirit*. However, continuing on this time line, Native peoples have purportedly often become homophobic through processes of colonialism and Western cultural influence. As Gilley has stated, "What many Cherokees in this instance failed to recognize, and what is often the case with native peoples, is that the things they are calling traditional values are things that came about through interactions with Euro-Americans."[52] And furthermore, through this narrative, Reynolds and McKinley's marriage should be recognized by the Cherokee Nation if they are to stay true to their traditions. While Gilley's statement recalls Smith's, Denetdale's, and

Barker's arguments that I outline above, my emphasis is that by asserting that Cherokees have "failed to recognize" their misunderstanding of tradition while this couple has somehow been able to recognize this, as evidenced by their adherence to mainstream U.S. liberalism, the message is that proper manifestations of tradition take the shape of mainstream liberalism.

What this narrative structure fails to recognize is the distinction between a Two-Spirit history and Reynolds and McKinley's present apparent alignment with mainstream liberal values and LGBT rights prescriptives. The current societal constraints disallow rights struggles that do not conform to a certain set of values. Similar to *Lawrence and Garner v. Texas*, rather than taking a more radical approach (such as arguing for a recognition of Two-Spirit identities instead of for the same right to live together in peace, "just as other married couples are permitted to do"), the most viable tactic has been to be folded into the U.S. national body through rhetorics of individualism, privacy, and family.[53]

In the case of same-sex marriage in the Cherokee Nation, then, U.S. sexual exceptionalism can be read as a technique of colonial governance that follows the same logic of cultural genocide as laid out by Smith, Morgensen, and Rifkin above. Although purportedly espousing a recognition of and respect for Two-Spirit peoples, through the terms of Reynolds and McKinley's case, in reality only heteronormative notions of gender and sexuality are given recognition and legitimacy within the U.S. nation-state. Two-Spirit identities are discursively relegated to history and tradition while liberal same-sex marriage rights are depicted as the modern manifestation of that past (despite, of course, *Two-Spirit* being a contemporary term that allows for the diversity and malleability of tradition). Thus, Native peoples who follow mainstream heteronormative scripts are folded into the U.S. nation once their Native culture has been safely secured in the past, while those "conservative" Native peoples who are unable to "get over" the heteronormative patriarchal effects of colonialism are positioned as backward and not yet includable into the U.S. nation.

Proscribing sexual and gender identities can be even further understood as a constraint on sovereignty. Indeed, Justice and Driskill argue that gender and sexual expressions are intimately tied to Native sovereignty.[54] Justice asserts, "a place of legitimized queerness matters to Native cultures and . . .

it matters to both tribal politics of sovereignty and a sovereignty of aesthetic (and erotic) expression," thus making space for the connection between gender and sexual nonnormativities and Native sovereignty.[55] In other words, the ability to define and express one's sexual and gender identities in terms that are not delineated by white, mainstream categories is an important component of Native sovereignty. As Morgensen points out, "Native GLBTQ people argued that their place within Native societies cannot be explained as that of a sexual minority," as this logic is embedded in colonial origin.[56] This potential for Native sovereignty by way of Two-Spirit inclusion is thus foreclosed by the terms of the political debate over Cherokee same-sex marriage.

Discourse of Native "Regression"

This colonial perspective of U.S. sexual exceptionalism also relies on a teleological notion of progress so that the mainstream United States is positioned as forward moving while the colonial Native other is contrasted as backward moving. Puar explains ideas contained within this as a "discourse attached to immigrant populations and communities of color about a more overt disapproval of homosexuality and a more deeply entrenched homophobia, this homophobia cast as properly conservative and traditional when it serves the political right and the state, cast as uncosmopolitan and hopelessly provincial when it can fuel anti-immigrant, counterterrorist, and antiwelfare discourses," or in this case, anti-same-sex marriage discourses.[57] However, for Native peoples, discursive tension exists between being traditionally conservative and being regressively conservative, or in other words, disavowing their accepting and open-minded past in order to embrace a conservative moralism (whereas populations of immigrants and people of color are depicted as having always been homophobic).

This teleological progress narrative and Native "regression" is exhibited in multiple discourses concerning same-sex marriage in the Cherokee Nation. As one example, on a segment of the liberal talk radio show *Democracy Now!* titled "Gay Marriage in Native America," journalist Amy Goodman begins by pointing to the divisive nature of same-sex marriage in the United States, the prohibition of same-sex marriage in a number of states, as well as how "some states have moved forward in granting legal rights to gay and lesbian couples."[58] Later in the interviews, Goodman takes a similar tactic with both Joe Shirley, president of the Navajo Nation at the time, and David Cornsilk, Dawn McKinley's counsel. In these interviews, Goodman emphasizes that despite her interviewees' acceptance of same-sex marriage, both tribes voted unanimously against it. Additionally, in Gilley's comments concerning Reynolds and McKinley's case, he remarks that he finds it ironic that many Native American communities today are homophobic despite their histories of fluid gender and sexual identities.[59] Through these different statements, the mainstream United States is upheld for its "mastery of linear teleologies of progress" while Native nations are contrasted with this unwavering direction through their "ironic" regression to homophobia.[60]

Sexual exceptionalism and its reliance on a progress narrative of liberal leftist values also serve to position the mainstream United States as the pinnacle of progressiveness and, therefore, well situated to judge others. Gayatri Spivak's notion of "white men saving brown women from brown men" takes on a slightly modified version here, with white lesbians (from NCLR) saving Native lesbians from Native men.[61] Although I am not arguing against the legal recognition of Reynolds and McKinley's marriage, I am critiquing the conditions of possibility that have led to a reliance on liberal progressive notions of sexuality as well as pointing to the ways through which these conditions can be read as heteronormative methods of colonialism.

Another area of critique can be directed at the way in which this move of U.S. sexual exceptionalism serves to elide a number of important issues, including the colonial imposition of heteronormativity that has led to homophobia within Native communities (as outlined most clearly by Smith, Morgensen, and Rifkin above); the possibility that heteronormativity may be a survival mechanism for racial and national others within the United States; the fact that marriage, normativity, and acceptance of nonnormativities can take on different meanings within indigenous groups; and the discrimination and heteronormativity that continues to shape the composition of the mainstream United States. This effectively erases discrimination that is still legally sanctioned in the country, such as housing, employment, and healthcare discrimination that still persists to various degrees both federally and across the states. This level of U.S. sexual exceptionalism is productive in that it not only presents the United States as progressive and accepting of sexual minorities, it also actively masks its own sanctioned injustices that would otherwise contradict its liberal façade.

Mainstream U.S. values rely on a notion of belonging that has been enforced in Native communities through a variety of strategies, and the contemporary panic over Native same-sex marriage laws can also be read through this history of belonging. Within U.S. history, a variety of peoples have been successively excluded, including, for example, African American slaves, Chinese immigrants (in accordance with the Page Act of 1875), people of Japanese descent, and, less formally but still effectively, those who fall outside of a classed, racialized heteronormative framework. For Native peoples, belonging to the U.S. national body entails a cultural erasure (supplanting a real inclusion of Two-Spirit identities with liberal gay rights rhetoric) and a simultaneous censure of Native communities as a whole that are seen as deeply, unchangeably homophobic. Therefore, similar to a homonationalist framework, the folding in of heteronormative Native queers is dependent on the exclusion of another group—in this case, "conservative" Native peoples.[62] What is unique in this case, however, is the division between a small section of Native peoples and the remaining entirety of Native peoples in the United States.[63]

Conclusion

In sum, I have argued the following: (1) On the one hand, through the rhetoric of tradition, Two-Spirit practices are used as proof that same-sex marriage should be allowed within the Cherokee Nation and are also used as evidence of Native peoples' inherently "progressive" pasts. (2) This past gets tied to Reynolds and McKinley, despite their self-positioning as seemingly ideal liberal subjects, and thus they have properly adhered to a Two-Spirit tradition precisely because of their unobtrusive version of an LGBT rights stance. (This, of course, points to clear contradictions.) (3) In light of the Cherokee Nation Council's unanimous ban on same-sex marriage, the Cherokee Nation as a whole is depicted as regressively backward in contrast to

Reynolds and McKinley. (4) Finally, because Two-Spirit is used as proof of past practices, and the contemporary instantiation of sexual nonnormative practices aligns more so with mainstream LGBT rights, this discourse furthers settler colonialism by safely securing traditional practices in the past and producing proper Native peoples as assimilated through mainstream progressive politics. Most importantly, these discourses further settler colonialism.

This analysis raises two concluding questions: can individualism and privacy be differently read as embodiments of Native sovereignty, and, a decade later, what does the landscape look like?

Liberal individualism has long been a component of U.S. colonialism through the granting of citizenship, economic incentive, tribal dismemberment, and land privatization, all dating back to the Indian Citizenship Act of 1924 and the Indian Reorganization Act of 1934.[64] Indigenous groups have also often been discussed in ways that are distinct from or at least have a complex relationship to individualism, usually in favor of the collective or the betterment of the people.[65] The ways in which individualism manifests in the Reynolds and McKinley case can be seen in relation to this longer history and discourse, a perspective I have focused on thus far, though alternatively the importance the couple has placed on privacy and individualism could be read in a way that is unique to Native sovereignty or perhaps as a refusal to engage in the mainstream activism in support of same-sex marriage.

Morgensen's discussion of settler homonationalism—which describes ways non-Native queers have appropriated a history of Native gender and sexual variation, discursively placing Native peoples in the realm of history and contributing to larger discourses (or silences) about the absence of contemporary Native peoples—offers a reason why supporters of Cherokee and Native Two-Spirit or same-sex marriage rights may be wary of how their own activism gets taken up by the mainstream United States.[66] Reynolds and McKinley's call to individual privacy may indeed be a refusal to provide fodder for the mainstream same-sex marriage rights movement rather than an unwavering adherence to liberal values. This resistance can thus be seen as an enactment of an alternative sovereignty, one that is not invested in recognition from non-Native groups and is perhaps more attuned to mutual responsibility.[67] While the complexities of this positioning are important to acknowledge, the ways the couple has been taken up within the public still remain. Regardless of the reason behind their focus on privacy, they are still understood in contrast to the Cherokee Nation's regressive conservatism.

Finally, as the number of tribes that allow same-sex marriage increases, while both the Cherokee and Navajo Nations' bans remain in place despite continued resistance by Native Two-Spirit organizations, how has the mainstream United States been reconciling this? As one example, recent attention given to the Diné Marriage Act in the *New York Times* engages in similar conversations of tradition both in favor of and against the continued tribal ban on same-sex marriage, highlights the role of a small few in a battle against the discriminatory law, and notes how the ban contrasts with the laws in the neighboring states of New Mexico, Arizona, and Utah.[68] While same-sex marriage trends may be shifting across both the state and tribal governments, it seems that the practice of including those deemed representative of the forward-moving tide and rejecting those who are "stuck in the past" or have moved backward remains consistent.

Notes

1. National Center for Lesbian Rights (NCLR), "Cherokee High Court Rules in Favor of NCLR and Same-Sex Couple: Holds that Tribal Council Members Lack Standing to Challenge Couple's Marriage" (press release), January 4, 2006.
2. Joanne Barker, *Native Acts: Law, Recognition, and Cultural Authenticity* (Durham, NC: Duke University Press, 2011), 205; Holly Kays, "Cherokee Affirms Gay Marriage Ban," *Smoky Mountain News*, January 14, 2015, http://www.smokymountainnews.com/news/item/14943-cherokee-affirms-gay-marriage-ban.
3. I use the language of same-sex marriage to adopt the terminology that has popularly been used within the past two decades in legal and political debates both within the mainstream United States and among Native American tribes, but there are complex and multiple understandings of gender and sexual identities within Native American pasts and presents, which I address in my later discussion on Two-Spirit identities. While "same-sex marriage" often serves as a catchall phrase in contemporary discourse, it functions within heteronormative frameworks of gender binaries, gay and lesbian identities, and liberal marriage

4. E.g., see the discussion of Jason Pickel and Darran Black's marriage through the Cheyenne and Arapaho tribes, which issued a marriage license to the same-sex couple only after DOMA was struck down; Lisa De Bode, "Native American Tribes Challenge Oklahoma Gay Marriage Ban," *Al Jazeera America*, October 22, 2013, http://america.aljazeera.com/articles/2013/10/22/native-american-tribes challengeoklahomagaymarriageban.html. A number of other tribes also began permitting same-sex marriages following the end of DOMA as well, such as the Keweenaw Bay Indian Community, Fort McDowell Yavapai Nation, and the Confederated Tribes of the Colville Reservation, among others.
5. Andrea Smith, "Queer Theory and Native Studies: The Heteronormativity of Settler Colonialism," *GLQ* 16, no. 1/2 (2010): 42–68; Qwo-Li Driskill, "Doubleweaving Two-Spirit Critiques: Building Alliances Between Native and Queer Studies," *GLQ* 16, no. 1/2 (2010): 69–92.
6. Driskill, "Doubleweaving Two-Spirit Critiques," 81–85.
7. Patrick Wolfe, "Settler Colonialism and the Elimination of the Native," *Journal of Genocide Research* 8, no. 4 (2006): 387–409.
8. Smith, "Queer Theory and Native Studies," 61.
9. Scott Lauria Morgensen, "Settler Homonationalism: Theorizing Settler Colonialism Within Queer Modernities," *GLQ* 16, no. 1/2 (2010): 105 31.
10. Mark Rifkin, *When Did Indians Become Straight?: Kinship, the History of Sexuality, and Native Sovereignty* (New York: Oxford University Press, 2011).
11. Ibid., 8.
12. Ibid.
13. Andrea Smith, *Conquest: Sexual Violence and American Indian Genocide* (Cambridge, MA: South End Press, 2005), 13.
14. Ibid.
15. Joyce Green, ed., *Making Space for Indigenous Feminism* (New York: Zed Books, 2007).
16. Barker, *Native Acts*.
17. Jennifer Nez Denetdale, "Chairmen, Presidents, and Princesses: The Navajo Nation, Gender, and the Politics of Tradition," *Wicazo Sa Review* 21, no. 1 (2006): 9–28.
18. Ibid., 9.

19. Jennifer Nez Denetdale, "Securing Navajo National Boundaries: War, Patriotism, Tradition, and the Diné Marriage Act of 2005," *Wicazo Sa Review* 24, no. 2 (2009): 131–48.
20. Ibid.
21. Ibid., 136.
22. NCLR, "Cherokee High Court Rules in Favor of NCLR."
23. Todd Hembree, Petition for Declaratory Judgment, In Re: The Marriage License of Kathy Reynolds and Dawn McKinley, June 16, 2004 (No. CV-04-36).
24. NCLR, "Cherokee High Court Rules in Favor of NCLR."
25. Kathy Reynolds and Dawn McKinley, Response to Petitioner's Response to Motion to Dismiss, Kathy Reynolds and Dawn McKinley, pro se, September 2, 2004.
26. Qwo-Li Driskill, "Stolen from our Bodies: First Nations Two-Spirits/Queers and the Journey to a Sovereign Epic," *Studies in American Indian Literatures* 16, no. 2 (2004), 52.
27. Driskill, "Doubleweaving Two-Spirit Critiques," 73.
28. Scott Morgensen, *Spaces Between Us: Queer Settler Colonialism and Indigenous Decolonization* (Minneapolis: University of Minnesota Press, 2011), 85–86.
29. Louva Hartwell, "About NativeOUT," accessed May 2, 2011 (no longer posted), http://www.nativeout.com/home/about-nativeout.html.
30. Dan Napelee, "Two-Spirit History," accessed May 2, 2011 (no longer posted), http://www.nativeout.com/digital-library/ts-history.html.
31. Kevin Foley, "Professor Brian Gilley's Expertise in Gender and Sexuality Among Native Americans Part of Cherokee Same-Sex Marriage Case," *Anthropologist on the Case*, University Communications, University of Vermont, January 18, 2006, http://www.uvm.edu/~uvmpr/?Page=article.php&id=1881.
32. Brian Joseph Gilley, *Becoming Two-Spirit: Gay Identity and Social Acceptance in Indian Country* (Lincoln: University of Nebraska Press, 2006).
33. NCLR, "Cherokee High Court Rules in Favor of NCLR."
34. Qwo-Li Driskill, "Cherokee Two-Spirit People Reimagining Nation," in *Queer Indigenous Studies*, ed. Qwo-Li Driskill, Chris Finley, Brian Joseph Gilley, and Scott Lauria Morgensen (Tucson: University of Arizona Press, 2011), 106–7.
35. Daniel Heath Justice, "Notes Toward a Theory of Anomaly," *GLQ* 16, no. 1/2 (2010): 213.
36. Ibid., 222.
37. Ibid., 214.

38. Amy Goodman, "Gay Marriage in Native America," *Democracy Now!*, May 31, 2005, https://www.democracynow.org/2005/5/31/gay_marriage_in_native_america; Lois Romano, "Battle over Gay Marriage Plays Out in Indian Country," *Washington Post*, August 1, 2005, http://www.washingtonpost.com/wp-dyn/content/article/2005/07/31/AR2005073100885.html.

39. When I first began this work, Oklahoma, within which the Cherokee Nation is located, and North Carolina, within which the Eastern Band of Cherokee Indians is located, did not permit same-sex marriage. The potential passage of same-sex marriage in these tribes therefore had significant implications on the relationship between state, federal, and tribal laws. Currently, however, same-sex marriage is allowed in both Oklahoma and North Carolina.

40. See Phillips v. Eagle, Judicial Appeals Tribunal of the Cherokee Nation, JAT 98-09-B, 1998.

41. National Center for Lesbian Rights (NCLR), "Cherokee Court Rejects Petition to Block Same-Sex Marriage" (press release), August 3, 2005.

42. NCLR, "Cherokee High Court Rules in Favor of NCLR."

43. Quoted in Romano, "Battle over Gay Marriage."

44. David Eng, *The Feeling of Kinship: Queer Liberalism and the Racialization of Intimacy* (Durham, NC: Duke University Press, 2010); Jasbir Puar, *Terrorist Assemblages: Homonationalism in Queer Times* (Durham, NC: Duke University Press, 2007).

45. Lawrence and Garner v. Texas, Justice Kennedy's opinion of the court, Court of Appeals of Texas, 14th District (2003), http://law2.umkc.edu/faculty/projects/ftrials/conlaw/lawrencevtexas.html (emphasis added).

46. Human Rights Campaign (HRC), "Mission Statement," http://www.hrc.org/hrc-story/mission-statement.

47. See Lisa Duggan's *Twilight of Equality: Neoliberalism, Cultural Politics, and the Attack on Democracy* (Boston: Beacon, 2003), esp. the chapter "Equality, Inc." for further discussion of neoliberal gay rights movements and the HRC.

48. Puar, *Terrorist Assemblages*, 114.

49. See, e.g., Michael Warner, *The Trouble with Normal: Sex, Politics, and the Ethics of Queer Life* (Cambridge, MA: Harvard University Press, 2000), and Amy Brandzel, "Queering Citizenship? Same-Sex Marriage and the State," *GLQ* 11, no. 2 (2005): 171–204.

50. Puar, *Terrorist Assemblages*.

51. Ibid.
52. Quoted in Foley, "Professor Brian Gilley's Expertise."
53. NCLR, "Cherokee High Court Rules in Favor of NCLR."
54. Justice, "Theory of Anomaly"; Driskill, "Stolen from our Bodies."
55. Justice, "Theory of Anomaly," 208.
56. Scott Lauria Morgensen, "Unsettling Queer Politics: What Can Non-Natives Learn from Two-Spirit Organizing," in Driskill et al., *Queer Indigenous Studies*.
57. Puar, *Terrorist Assemblages*, 29.
58. Goodman, "Gay Marriage in Native America" (emphasis added).
59. Foley, "Professor Brian Gilley's Expertise."
60. Puar, *Terrorist Assemblages*, 3.
61. Gayatri Spivak, "Can the Subaltern Speak?" in *Marxism and the Interpretation of Culture*, ed. Lawrence Grossberg and Cary Nelson (Urbana: University of Illinois Press, 1988), 271–313.
62. Puar, *Terrorist Assemblages*.
63. While the Cherokee and Navajo Nations have maintained their bans on same-sex marriage along with ten other tribes, the twenty-one that have now legalized it may be leading to a discursive shift in the way Native peoples are understood in relation to gender, sexuality, and homophobia. These more recent changes, though, are not within the scope of this chapter.
64. See Jessica Cattelino, "The Double Bind of American Indian Need-Based Sovereignty," *Cultural Anthropology* 25, no. 2 (2010): 235–63; and Rifkin, *When Did Indians Become Straight?*
65. E.g., see Cindy Holder and Jeff Corntassel, "Indigenous Peoples and Multicultural Citizenship: Bridging Collective and Individual Rights," *Human Rights Quarterly* 24, no. 2 (2002): 126–51, and the discussion of Cherokee towns in Scott Richard Lyons, "Rhetorical Sovereignty: What Do American Indians Want from Writing?," *College Composition and Communication* 51, no. 2 (2000): 447–68.
66. Morgensen, *Spaces Between Us*.
67. Smith, "Queer Theory and Native Studies," 60.
68. Julie Turkewitz, "Among the Navajos, a Renewed Debate About Gay Marriage," *New York Times*, February 21, 2015, http://www.nytimes.com/2015/02/22/us/among-the-navajos-a-renewed-debate-about-gay-marriage.html?smid=nytcore-iphone-share&smprod=nytcore-iphone&_r=0.

7

Bloodline Is All I Need?

Sovereignty and Hawaiian Hip-Hop

STEPHANIE NOHELANI TEVES

I'm Filipino. I'm Hawaiian.
Who are you to judge what I am?
This is what I am. Defiant.
KRYSTILEZ, "WHO I AM"[1]

On August 19, 2005, well-known 1990s black-nationalist rap group Public Enemy performed before a small crowd at Kapiʻolani Community College on the island of Oʻahu. Diamond Head Crater loomed in the distance, looking like a picture postcard, dwarfing the stage, and framing the half-empty field in which the concert was held. It was Admission Day, a day to commemorate Hawaiʻi's statehood, but no mention was made of statehood by any of the local opening acts.[2] The event was billed as "The First Annual Hawaiʻi Hip Hop Festival," with Public Enemy headlining and supported by local opening acts J-Bird, Spookahuna, Parc Cyde, Emirc, and Krystilez. As I watched these young Pacific Islander men jump and gesticulate across the stage, rapping about chasing *punanis* (a slang term for vagina), I yawned and sighed. The performance felt indicative of hip-hop's mainstreaming impulses in which the contradictions and possibilities of hip-hop, political consciousness and misogyny, were laid bare on stage.[3] Rather than dismissing these men as inauthentic sexist hip-hop wannabes who are damaging and undesirable representatives of Pacific masculinity or hip-hop writ large, in this article I investigate the conditions under which these performances of modern Kanaka Maoli, or Native

Hawaiian, identity is performed through Hawaiian hip-hop in the context of wider sovereign cultural and political discourses.[4]

Hip-hop came to Hawai'i as quickly as it spread across the continental United States.[5] Since the early 1980s, black-identified American popular culture has proliferated all over the world.[6] Due to the rise of globalized mass media, hip-hop has been adopted and produced by disenfranchised youth through what Halifu Osumare has referred to as "connective marginality," a social and historical context that informs youth participation in hip-hop outside the United States.[7] Youth in places such as Palestine, Japan, Ireland, Cuba, and Hawai'i share experiences of cultural displacement, a connection with black-identified culture, and the desire for self-representation.

Fantasies about Hawai'i, one of the most geographically isolated places on earth, are built from an archive of imagery dating back to the late eighteenth century. Representations proliferate in drawings and paintings, photographs, films, literary works, and perhaps most prominently in widely disseminated images of Kanaka Maoli women dancing hula.[8] Since the early twentieth century, this has been the most common representation of Kānaka Maoli, who, as "soft primitives," were often called on to be "ambassadors of aloha" and to promote Hawai'i's charms.[9] Such performances continue to produce an imagined sense of intimacy between Americans and Hawai'i, with Hawai'i's femininity supposedly welcoming the incorporative thrusts of American heteropatriarchy.[10] Stock imagery of Kānaka Maoli, embodied in the hula maiden, the carefree surfer boy, and numerous incarnations of the lazy Native, remains iconic in the American imaginary.[11] The global circulation of these representations forever marks Hawai'i as the land of grass shacks, palm trees, hula girls, and beautiful beaches.

Kānaka Maoli have struggled to push back against these representations, offering a rewriting of Hawaiian history, quite literally.[12] Infused by Hawaiian nationalism, a growing library of works investigates the naturalization of American colonialism in Hawai'i, producing innovative Kanaka Maoli representations in the realms of visual arts, music, dance, and film in an attempt to increase visibility and combat stereotypes. Narratives of resistance, resilience, and revitalization have become common, but as evidenced by Krystilez and the other performers at the Hawai'i Hip Hop Festival, the internalization of heteropatriarchy is business as usual, and it reenacts Kanaka Maoli subjection in gendered and problematic ways. To push back against commodified and feminized versions of Hawaiian culture, the discursive performances of Kanaka Maoli men walk a fine line in their attempt to reaffirm Kanaka Maoli identity, often perpetuating misogyny in the process.[13] Scholarship in Pacific studies has been attentive to these gendered dynamics, analyzing representations that render Kanaka Maoli or Polynesian men as nothing more than hypermasculinized professional athletes or, in the case of military service, as modern-day "warriors."[14] One wonders, whose sovereignty is promoted in these assertions? Which bodies are put at risk? Whose indigeneity is affirmed, and what perspectives are normalized in order for these expressions of resistance to be possible?

In this chapter I map out the ways in which these performances of Kanaka Maoli identity can be liberatory and deeply contradictory, and I address a Hawaiian hip-hop performer's navigation of these conditions and the media he employs. Through a close reading of Krystilez's album *The "O,"* I examine contemporary Kanaka Maoli cultural production in order to articulate the contradictory intersection of indigeneity and performance in modern Hawai'i. In his performance of "defiant indigeneity," Krystilez insists on an identity that is simultaneously amorphous, disarticulated, and conceptualized through state logics, yet it perpetually defies its own construction. I begin by introducing Krystilez and conceptualizing defiant indigeneity as an expression of sovereignty. I then contextualize the emergence of Hawaiian hip-hop and Krystilez's particular narrative. Finally, I analyze *The "O"* from a Native feminist perspective and assess the broader political stakes of contemporary Kanaka Maoli cultural production.

Kānaka Maoli Representing: Krystilez

> *Where the palm trees is where you want to be*
> *but paradise is not what it seems*
> *This is the O!*
> *Where you get hustled*

> *tourists get mobbed*
> *and if you start a fight*
> *bitch you'll get mobbed*[15]

One of Hawai'i's most well-known and respected MCs, Krystilez is a Kanaka Maoli hip-hop artist from a Hawaiian homestead on a rural part of O'ahu who performs in urban Honolulu.[16] In 2006, his first release, *The Greatest HI*, won the Hawai'i Music Award for Best Hip Hop Album, and in the same year, it was nominated for an Nā Hōkū Hanohano Award for Best Hip Hop/R&B Album. Krystilez is also a disc jockey on a popular local radio station (owned by media conglomerate Clear Channel) and is recognized on the underground hip-hop freestyle circuit. His second album, *The "O"* (2006) features thirteen professionally recorded original tracks with lyrical content that reflects Krystilez's desire to be respected as an MC on a U.S. national level. His songs range in content from aspiring "club banger" hits to stories about Hawai'i that differ greatly from the one in the global imagination.

The "live" music scene in Honolulu privileges Hawaiian music and limits opportunities for other types of performers. Krystilez, therefore, does not receive mainstream attention on local radio or television and in general has to promote himself online and in the streets, utilizing YouTube, MySpace, Facebook, and Twitter to post videos speaking directly to the viewers, whoever or wherever they may be. The comments sections or posting walls of these online interfaces contain posts by users who represent where they come from, praise Krystilez, call him out, critique him, and often promote their own agendas (e.g., albums, clothing lines, or events).[17] Ironically, the very technology that produces the corporatized conditions that prevent Krystilez's mainstream circulation also bears a radical promise, as corporations must contend with the unruly and emergent participatory culture represented by Krystilez and his fans.[18]

Advertisements for the release of *The "O"* were plastered all over O'ahu streets and light posts throughout December 2006.[19] To generate hype, Krystilez posted videos of himself on YouTube counting down the days to the album's release. He expresses his vision of *The "O"* in a series of videos posted on YouTube in which he acknowledges his usage of subliminal messages and welcomes multiple interpretations of his music.[20] He asserts that *The "O"* sig-

Figure 7.1. Still of *West Side*, music video by Krysteliz, released in 2012.

nifies who he is but is also open to interpretation. He explains that *The "O"* can represent a bag of drugs, the circle of life, a freestyle cipher, or the island of Oʻahu.[21] At first the album appears to imitate perceptions of hip-hop music as nothing more than violent and misogynistic commentary, but the richness of Krystilez's rhymes should not be underestimated. Although Krystilez in many ways subscribes to the rampant sexism, endorsement of illegal activity, and glorification of violence (particularly on the tracks "Shake," "How Bad Do You Want It," and "The Way It Is") that mainstream hip-hop is known for, he also presents a narrative of life in Hawaiʻi that is conveniently ignored and dismissed. Tracks such as "The 'O,'" "Diamonds," and "Bloodline" present glaring counternarratives to the mythic representation of Hawaiʻi as paradise.

"The 'O'" and "Bloodline" contain expressions of personal and political sovereignty, representing the necessity of creative performance spaces away from the tourist gaze. Krystilez conveys a common sentiment within Hawaiian and local communities, that is, a desire for Hawaiian culture to be autonomous from the tourist-driven capitalist markets that structure performance and in many ways, life in Hawaiʻi. These sentiments may not take a definitive political stance on sovereignty, but they speak to the tensions that underlie the ongoing question of who Hawaiʻi belongs to and who belongs in Hawaiʻi.

This is especially evident in the album's title track, "The 'O.'" The song begins with an A half note played on a synthesizer. Then the beat drops as the sound of a woman chanting fades in. The sound conjures up imagery of a *kumu hula* (hula master) commanding their *hālau* (troupe) to take the stage. Instead, Krystilez forcefully interjects, "Where the palm trees is where you want to be but paradise is not what it seems." Accompanying his aggressive rapping style is the sound of the woman, which alludes to Hawaiian chanting, or the performance of an *oli* in the *hoʻāeae* style. The *oli*, an unmetered Indigenous Hawaiian chanting style, repeats throughout the song as a foil to Krystilez's often-brutal rhymes. The chorus, "This is the O!" is shouted continuously over the synthesizer and the woman's voice. Her voice rises in prominence as Krystilez leads into each chorus with a vamp in which he charges, "Where the. . . ." He fills in something different each time—from pounding beers to having sex with "bitches," making hits, and hustling.

The song continues by detailing what happens on "the West" (referring to the west side of the island of Oʻahu, the perceived "bad" part of the island known for its Kanaka Maoli population). He addresses this explicitly: "Where you're told not to go when you come off the plane. At the beaches proceed with caution." In keeping with the Hawaiian music and hip-hop traditions of representing where you come from, Krystilez firmly locates himself in his hometown, Nānākuli Homestead. He widens the reach of Kanaka Maoli indigeneity through the invocation of the *oli* and the song's lyrical content.[22] Lyrically, *The "O"* is filled with sensationalistic imagery that narrates the positions of power—party promoter, bouncer, rapper, drug dealer, DJ, pimp—that Krystilez and his friends occupy. The combined video for the songs "The 'O'" and "Won," originally posted on YouTube, offers visuals that differ from the song's lyrical content.[23] The video begins with "Won": Krystilez is shown in the middle of palm trees; the next shot is in front of the Koʻolau mountain range, green and lush behind a raised SUV with an advertisement for *The "O"* and Krystilez painted on it in blue and green. When the camera spins around, Krystilez and his crew are in the SUV, sometimes standing next to it, hanging out of the side, or hanging off the back. IZ Real is notably shirtless, kneeling on top of the truck's roof, singing and punching the air, jerking and snapping his head toward the sky. The truck is driving slowly as "Won" starts.

The song has a decidedly more critical tone than the others, expressing the problems in the "melting pot," in which cultures are supposed to blend but instead continuously conflict. Krystilez remarks that being raised in Hawai'i, he was "raised in the middle of racism" in stark contrast to the perception that Hawai'i is a multiracial paradise. The video, which is a mash-up of "Won" and "The 'O'" ends with a Hawaiian flag filling the screen. The camera pans back to a shot of the SUV in front of the Ko'olau mountains again. A man in green and brown baggy fatigues holds a Hawaiian flag in the air. Throughout *The "O"* Krystilez emphasizes his humble beginnings growing up on a Hawaiian homestead. He is part of a Hawaiian musical tradition of *mele kū'ē* (resistance songs) that communicates social realism in a local media environment that lacks public space to assert numerous perspectives, particularly viewpoints that support sovereignty.[24]

Hawaiian Sovereignty

It is not surprising that Krystilez's narrative emerges precisely as sovereignty debates intensified in Hawai'i during the last decades. Since the overthrow of the Hawaiian Kingdom in 1893, Native Hawaiians have actively resisted American colonialism and attempted cultural genocide. After a century of struggle, Kanaka Maoli cultural resistance and activism obtained an official acknowledgment of the role that the U.S. military played in the illegal overthrow of the Hawaiian Kingdom. The "Hawai'i Apology Resolution" brought mainstream attention to the Kanaka Maoli sovereignty movement, opening the door to a federal process to recognize Native Hawaiians as an Indigenous group with claims to self-determination. As a backlash against these efforts, by 1996, lawsuits attacked Native Hawaiian organizations and entitlements such as the Office of Hawaiian Affairs (OHA), the Department of Hawaiian Homelands (DHHL), and the Kamehameha Schools Bishop Estate (KSBE).[25] These lawsuits, particularly *Rice v. Cayetano* (1996), which challenged OHA's Hawaiian-only voting policy, invoked the Fifteenth Amendment and civil rights acts in order to justify claims of racial discrimination against non–Kānaka Maoli.[26] The lawsuits, relying on U.S. racial classifications rather than Indigenous genealogical distinctions, questioned who is "entitled" to what in Hawai'i, thereby delegitimizing Indigenous claims, racializing Native peoples, and normalizing white subjectivity.[27]

To fight against these lawsuits, the first version of the Native Hawaiian Government Reorganization Act, known as "the Akaka Bill," named after U.S. Senator Daniel Akaka, was introduced in the U.S. Congress in 2000. Supporters of the bill, such as OHA and KSBE, argued that it would protect Hawaiian entitlements by recognizing Kānaka Maoli as an Indigenous people rather than as an ethnic minority, which would in turn protect OHA, federal programs for Native Hawaiian health, education, gathering rights, and the DHHL. The Akaka Bill became a rallying point for many within the Kanaka Maoli community, who view federal recognition or a "nation within a nation" structure as necessary to protect our Hawaiian entitlement programs as well as a strategy to rebuild our communities and to combat our ongoing colonization.

Proindependence activists and scholars have warned, however, that growing federal and state support for Hawaiian recognition are indicative of the settler colonial forces that seek to further incorporate Hawaiian indigeneity, settle Hawaiian ceded land claims, and solidify military control of Hawai'i and the rest of the Pacific. While federal recognition would grant Kānaka Maoli specific rights as a domestic dependent nation under U.S. federal jurisdiction, allowing us to form our own government as well as a number of other protections, it would simultaneously obfuscate Kanaka Maoli rights to self-determination under the UN Declaration on the Rights of Indigenous Peoples and on our own terms. Over the past decade, many Kānaka Maoli have become critical of federal recognition, favoring to think of Hawai'i—as it is framed by legal scholars and activists—as illegally occupied by the U.S. military. Perhaps most importantly, the Akaka Bill does not give back one inch of land.[28]

Public apologies, like forms of reconciliation or recognition processes, operate as neoliberal efforts to "move forward" from the damage wrought by settler states (allegedly in the past) but do little to assist Indigenous peoples living in the present. A rejection of these accommodationist processes became evident in the summer of 2014, when the Department of the Interior (DOI) held hearings to solicit "feedback" from the Kanaka Maoli community about the United States' role in "helping" to "organize" a Hawaiian governing entity. During these meetings, Kānaka Maoli overwhelmingly voiced their opposition to federal recognition and U.S. federal intervention in Hawaiian nation building altogether. Perhaps noncoincidentally, the DOI meetings were announced shortly after OHA CEO Kamanaʻopono Crabbe wrote a letter to Secretary of State John Kerry inquiring about the status of the Hawaiian Kingdom under international law.[29] It became abundantly clear that there was a rising tide of defiance directed at U.S. colonial forces or any agents who attempted to compromise Hawaiian sovereignty. Notably, many of the testifiers against federal recognition were young people, and a recurrent theme in their testimonies was that Hawaiian sovereignty was never ceded and that in order for us to move forward we should focus on our own visions of the future by taking care of one another rather than focusing on recognition from our colonizer.

Indigenous peoples assert and articulate their sovereignties in a manner that is not wholly reliant on the state or Western political discourse in general. Taiaiake Alfred has called for a return to traditional forms of governance that are generated through culture, community, and the land rather than Western understandings of sovereignty that are linked to the ability to exercise power through coercion and domination. Native feminists have discussed that sovereignty begins in the home, in the way that we raise future generations, and that governance does not come from a document but in how we maintain our relations. Sovereignty is an expression of responsibility to our nations as self-disciplined individuals committed to our survival as a people.[30] Similarly, as Audra Simpson describes, sovereignty and nationhood can be expressed differently from the essentialized modes of expectation—that is, the performance of bounded culture—and this different mode of expression pushes against narrow forms of judicial interpretation.[31] Krystilez's music brings forth assertions of sovereignty that sometimes problematically draw on state-based forms but also simultaneously asserts a defiance of those very structures that prioritizes Hawaiian forms of belonging in the face of colonialism.

Hawaiian culture has a concept known as *Ea*, which distinguishes sovereignty as a way of life that is built on relationships with other beings, animals, and landscapes. As described in *A Nation Rising* (2014), the Hawaiian word *Ea* translates as life, breath, and sovereignty. Sovereignty is life and breath in *Ea*, which is an active state that cannot be achieved or possessed because it is in constant action.[32] *Ea* then represents the experiences of people on the land that prioritize caring for and restoring these relations on the land. Sovereignty in *Ea* is not about a supreme authority over territory but about sacred connections that can be shared.[33] The latter is imperative in Hawai'i, where the multiethnic and Indigenous Hawaiian population overlaps in precarious ways. Therefore, movements for *Ea* in Hawai'i also coincide with a movement for "kuleana consciousness." "Kuleana consciousness" has emerged as a way of thinking and living that centers how individual sovereignty should connect with the land and thinking of those connections to place that are not only about Indigenous political sovereignty in the "West." As poet, activist, and scholar ku'ualoha ho'omanawanui writes, "Kuleana consciousness is a recognition of responsibility and a call to action that extends to all, even settlers can interrogate themselves and others and ask what their kuleana to Hawai'i can be or should be."[34] An expansion of thinking about sovereignty thus also requires a rethinking of belonging and responsibilities to place that are necessary to decolonial projects that extend to all aspects of Native life and to all the groups that live in these places.

These conflicts and debates have completely altered the discourse of Hawaiian sovereignty and the future of Hawai'i, indicating the power and vulnerability that influences and circulates through Kanaka Maoli cultural productions. Extinguishing Hawaiian independence claims through the recognition process coincides with efforts to articulate certain forms of Hawaiian culture that do not challenge settler colonialism and can be easily accommodated. In "Bloodline" Krystilez affirms Hawaiian homesteads as enduring sites of Hawaiian indigeneity and pride despite the precariousness of homesteads themselves or the state formation that underlies them, which I explain in the next section. There are no simple answers to these contradictions. Krystilez's music presents a challenge to state-based forms of recognition and commodified Hawaiian culture, using it against itself. In a Kanaka Maoli context where the question of federal recognition pervades much of the public political discourse among Kānaka Maoli, it is critical for artists, filmmakers, and performers to express their politics in multiple genres, in ways that the settler state may not even be able to *see*.

Defiant Indigeneity

Through "defiant indigeneity" Krystilez performs a configuration of indigeneity that constantly deconstructs, resists, and recodifies itself against and through state logics. Defiant indigeneity is a method and theory of the ways that Kānaka Maoli mobilize performance (in both quotidian and aesthetic realms) to survive the annihilating conditions of colonization and occupation and also to affirm and reproduce collective forms of Indigenous being, belonging, and becoming. Defiant indigeneity is a form of performative sovereignty that is required of Indigenous peoples alongside an awareness of the precarity of such requirements. Krystilez is about representing where he comes from, but he does so in a way that explicitly appropriates state logics of racialization: by crafting a narrative based on blood that (paradoxically) operates against the Kanaka Maoli epistemological belief that we are genealogically descended from specific places. In "Bloodline," the standout final track on the album that encapsulates the entire album's intent, Krystilez performs a tribute to Hawaiian homesteads, remaking homestead space through listener identification with "Bloodline" in order to traverse the colonial taxonomies that demarcate homestead space. By shouting out multiple homestead names and referring to them as "bloodlines," Krystilez invites Kānaka Maoli to "rep your bloodline." Even if listeners are not from the homestead, the deep connections remain. Krystilez's greatest defiance is that his narrative is based on legislation that was intended to manage a declining Kanaka Maoli population.

The 1920 Hawaiian Homes Commission Act (HHCA) affirmed the special relationship between the United States and Kānaka Maoli by sanctioning two hundred thousand acres of Hawaiian homestead land—lands that belonged to the Hawaiian Kingdom before it was illegally overthrown in 1893. Passed by the U.S. Congress in 1921, when Hawaiʻi was a territory, the HHCA conferred the responsibility of administering the homestead lands to the state of Hawaiʻi when it was admitted to the Union in 1959. In 1978, responsibility for homestead lands was transferred to the newly created OHA, a semiautonomous state agency that manages Hawaiian entitlements.[35] The administration of these lands has come under considerable scrutiny because of the 50 percent blood-quantum requirement that prevents many Kānaka Maoli from qualifying for lands.[36] As explained by J. Kēhaulani Kauanui, the blood-quantum requirement for Hawaiian homesteads was created because the U.S. government thought that high rates of intermarriage would eventually cause the number of Kānaka Maoli who could qualify for lands to dwindle (and it did). Within this logic was the hope that the "pure" or "real" Kānaka Maoli would eventually disappear. The language used at this time was that of "rehabilitation." Kānaka Maoli were encouraged to return to the land, participate in agriculture, and reembody their natural state rather than navigate the worlds of technology and industry.[37] Framed in such a manner, Kānaka Maoli are viewed as welfare recipients, not as genealogical descendants of the lands in question. The blood-quantum regulations built into the HHCA are particularly damaging for Kānaka Maoli because, in contrast to U.S. policies and understandings about race and blood, it is genealogy that connects us to each other, to place, and to land.[38]

Just as Christian morality became law during the nineteenth century in Hawai'i, the early twentieth century saw the adoption of the so-called truth in the science and technologies of the body, which influenced the blood-quantum laws that were used to racialize the Kānaka Maoli. These laws, enacted on the bodies of Kānaka Maoli, encouraged Christian modes of heteronormativity that would supposedly prepare Kānaka Maoli for wage labor and capitalist agriculture. They disciplined Kanaka Maoli bodies by relegating them to particular lands, places, and spaces.[39] Kanaka Maoli identity thus became measurable through blood quantum rather than through Kanaka Maoli cultural affiliations and genealogy, which exacerbates land dispossession and the devaluation of Kanaka Maoli epistemologies. During the late twentieth century, using blood to claim an identity was somewhat indicative of a reductive racialized logic whereby the residues of biological racism that marked certain bodies as less desirable than others is personified, conjuring histories of the "one-drop rule" transposed on African Americans and the blood-quantum restrictions still exercised by many Native American tribes.

The narrative Krystilez presents in "Bloodline" walks a tightrope by basing itself on an identity claim that is in turn based on land claims, which are based on scientific discourses embedded in settler colonial processes aimed at displacing Indigenous peoples. Such assertions of Indigenous sovereignty unfortunately work to also marginalize many within our community who do not measure up to colonial determinants of membership. In a recent legal case, *Day v. Apoliona* (2008), five Native Hawaiian men sued the Office of Hawaiian Affairs for failing to restrict homesteads and other social programs to the definition of half-Hawaiian blood. As Maile Arvin explains, white supremacy, heteropatriarchy, and settler colonialism underlie "calling the law" on your own community to enforce a legal definition, which represents a problematic division within the Hawaiian community.[40] Most recently there has also been a proposal to reduce the blood-quantum qualification to 25 percent, which has produced much opposition, because while it would expand access to more Hawaiians, it will continue to base qualification on blood quantum rather than Hawaiian forms of genealogical identification. Throughout "Bloodline" Krystilez challenges the politics of recognition that reduce racial politics to visual markers and the biological discourses used to justify it while subverting and reifying the discourse about blood and authenticity for his own advancement. In his assertion of defiant indigeneity, Krystilez performs on multiple registers to disrupt the mainstream imaginings of Kanaka Maoli identity, thus revealing the fabrication of Kanaka Maoli identity.

The video for "Bloodline," posted on YouTube, begins with Krystilez in front of a black background singing "I can't deny it I'm fucking Hawaiian none of y'all can beef with me." As the lens pans back, Krystilez steps away from the camera, and a crowd walks up behind him.[41] The video is set in the evening, and the predominantly male crowd members behind him are holding shirts that say "Made in Nānākuli." Others wear "3RD" shirts, in reference to Nānākuli Third Road Homestead housing, and make a "W" with their hands to represent the west side of Oʻahu as well as the number three, for their homestead road. As the video continues, Krystilez (and the others in the video) look directly at the viewer, sporadically punching the air and pointing at the camera.

The crowd sings along with him, and IZ Real, who is particularly aggressive in his rapping style, frequently steps forward, using his hands to articulate his lyricism. The video ends with Krystilez and IZ Real in a boxing ring, as a thin, brown woman in black, tiny shorts, tube top, and platform stilettos—and whose face is never shown—circles the ring holding a sign in the air that says "bangers 4 bangers." As the camera fades out, Krystilez and IZ Real jump around the ring shouting, "Nānākuli Bloodline," "Waiʻanae Bloodline," and "Waimānalo Bloodline" in reference to some of the more well-known homesteads. Throughout the video, the crowd makes visible the community that Krystilez is representing. They sing,

> Seein through a thug's eyes
> We ride all night till sunlight
> All because I love my muthafuckin bloodline.
> I rather die on my feet
> than ever live on my knees
> till I face defeat bloodline is all I need.[42]

The community presence shown in the video exemplifies the importance of "bloodline," or homestead lands, for the wider community, despite the colonial processes that have named them. "Bloodline" allows the Kānaka Maoli to generate meaningful *moʻolelo* (stories) and *mele* (songs) about homesteads in a generative process that expresses the shifting meanings of lands that are consistently remade by historical conditions and by the people who inhabit these lands.

Hawaiian homesteads have deep-rooted meaning as well as other types of significance that existed before homestead land was demarcated. These meanings will continue to exist even if homesteads no longer do. Hawaiian lands are "storied places" that have always played a crucial role in narrating Hawaiian tradition—traditions that are still active today.[43] The Kānaka Maoli weave *moʻolelo* in order to narrate the history of these lands in a dialogue that enacts a transformative recognition of place. As Cristina Bacchilega explains, the Kānaka Maoli produce *nā wahi pana*, or storied places, that draw on cultural memory and activate history in the present moment and location.[44]

"Bloodline" does this by producing new forms of cultural memory through Krystilez's narration of what his homestead means to him, his listeners, and his viewers. Within hip-hop, representing place is about recognizing the support that community brings and acknowledging the grim conditions of "the ghetto." Rather than telling a story about economic decline, racial segregation, and criminal activity, hip-hop can explore the ways in which spaces and places are made meaningful.⁴⁵ Hawaiian homesteads are often called "ghetto" because they are recognized as profoundly Kanaka Maoli spaces and, by extension, are perceived as economically depressed and ridden with crime. The story Krystilez tells throughout *The "O"* draws on hip-hop's desire to represent place as well as on Kanaka Maoli practices of *nā wahi pana*, which offer a narrative of the homestead that, although grim, asserts pride in Kanaka Maoli resilience. In "Bloodline," this is represented visually as well as in the lyric, "till I face defeat, bloodline is all I need."

The visual and sonic re-creation of homestead space in "Bloodline" allows Kānaka Maoli to identify with homesteads through song. Hawaiian music has always served the purpose of honoring place, a need that is amplified in the present as the Kanaka Maoli diaspora continues to grow. To feel a connection to a place, even though you may have never been there (or even if you are there), is increasingly negotiated through cultural production and the global digital-media formats through which hip-hop circulates. As this diaspora grows, thinking about indigeneity as "belonging to a place" rather than "belonging in a place" might better contextualize the lives of the Kānaka Maoli.⁴⁶ In this vein, as Vicente Diaz and J. Kēhaulani Kauanui have noted, indigeneity is both routed and rooted, moving, evolving, and gesturing toward its past and its future.⁴⁷ In a capitalist economy that has pushed many Kānaka Maoli off island out of economic necessity, this is necessary.⁴⁸ Kanaka Maoli indigeneity, therefore, must allow movement. As Kauanui has pointed out, one of the biggest problems with the Kanaka Maoli diaspora is that Kānaka Maoli living off island are invisible to each other and to Kānaka Maoli living in Hawai'i.⁴⁹

The call and response at the end of "Bloodline" combats this. When IZ Real shouts "Rep your bloodline! Nānākuli Bloodline!," a cacophony of voices replies, "Nānākuli get!" The song slowly fades out as a long list of places on O'ahu—all communities with large Kanaka Maoli populations—are shouted and repeated.⁵⁰ "Bloodline" pays tribute to homesteads and the other places mentioned while expressing the complexities of Kanaka Maoli connections to place, because many Kānaka Maoli living in the islands (and elsewhere) do not meet the blood-quantum requirements.⁵¹ By shouting out these places, "Bloodline" makes visible an affirmation of pride in the homestead that viewers can experience in spite of the tension that exists between the Kānaka Maoli who can make claims to homestead land and those who cannot. Hawaiian homesteads continue to serve as sites of cultural ownership and pride even if these sentiments are experienced alongside highly charged political debates about how Kanaka Maoli enduring existence is quantified by the federal government. Krystilez's defiant indigeneity emerges out of his narrative of life on the homestead. "Bloodline" performs a tribute to Hawaiian homesteads, a tribute to the promise of Hawaiian sovereignty. Through a complex combination of nostalgia for a romanticized precolonial Hawaiian past and an affirmation of Kanaka Maoli enduring presence on these lands, Krystilez manages to weave together—lyrically and visually—the ways in which homesteads remain sources of Kanaka Maoli ownership and pride.

Keeping It Maoli

At the same time, Hawaiian hip-hop is structured by the corporatization of hip-hop production. The hierarchal inequities that plague mainstream societies are undeniably present in hip-hop, and sexism, heteronormativity, and colonialism are replicated, endorsed, and normalized within these discourses, sometimes to an alarming degree. I say this not to discredit the work of Krystilez completely but to argue that we must document the complexities of Hawaiian hip-hop rather than just proclaiming its existence. As Stuart Hall writes, "The danger arises because we tend to think of cultural forms as whole and coherent: either wholly corrupt or wholly authentic. Whereas, they are deeply contradictory; they play on contradictions, especially when they function in the domain of the 'popular.'"[52] Notably, the majority of scholarship on Native hip-hop solely focuses on coherent narratives of resistance rather than artists who challenge Native communities to grapple with the often contradictory expressions of sovereignty that are unfortunately at the core of what it means to be a Native person today.

Expectations of indigeneity are informed by social meanings and popular representations. Many people think they know what indigeneity looks like and is, which is an affront to Indigenous self-determination and sovereignty. Depending on the context, this might invoke the image of the crying Indian or the hula girl. Both of these tropes do damage that I need not rehearse here, but we must be cognizant of the arbitrariness of authenticity and the dangers of foreclosing possibilities. These are largely performative enactments that Native people carry out in their daily lives and are especially crucial for performers. Throughout Krystilez's songs he expresses the necessity of complicating representations at the same time he straddles claims of authenticity. Native Studies scholars have argued that it is more useful to look at the way Indigenous people deploy "authenticity" as a shifting set of ideas that work for certain ends, not as a measuring stick.[53] "Authenticity," then, is always tentative and contingent on context. As Scott Richard Lyons explains, we must turn our attention to the social processes that create identities, which means a move away from conceptions of Natives as "things" that can be studied.[54] We do, at times, as a reaction to colonialism, privilege notions of purity and authenticity because it offers us a sense of stability, but when that stability is exposed as a colonial-necessitated desire, we should turn our focus to the multitude of strategies employed to survive.

This space is tricky to talk about. As hip-hop critics have noted, hip-hop thrives because it offers something "real" or "authentic" in a materialistic world. Hip-hop's magic is its ability to connect with the powerless and give them a voice in a world that sees little, if any, value in them. Krystilez must insist on his authenticity when he raps "Is he real? Yes, he is. Fucka!" ("The 'O'") because of the pervasive imagery of tourism that markets Hawai'i as paradise. Krystilez's narrative of the "savage" or criminal Native man in this sense must always be read in contrast to the "happy Native" because of the commodified conditions that structure any performance of Kanaka Maoli identity. Krystilez might be narrating the realities surrounding him; alternately, he is the "savage" who is actually aware of the image he presents and purposely sells what he thinks will appeal to an audience.

Through Hawaiian hip-hop, Kānaka Maoli (youth) are making and claiming their own spaces; they are not waiting for the government to recognize them or to define wholly who they are. This is an expression of *Ea*, of sovereignty and life. Advocating for a reframing of the essentialist/nonessentialist debate, Brendan Hokowhitu reanalyzes performance through Indigenous sovereignty as a "way Indigenous Peoples choose to represent their worlds, whether that be through hybrid or essentialist notions of culture, both forms remain critical to strategic decolonization and fluid epistemologies."[55] Instead of fearing dilution and a loss of the "authentic," he focuses instead on the sovereignty of Indigenous peoples and communities to represent themselves alongside a commitment to be self-reflexive.[56] While affirming authenticity and realness can sometimes be a necessary tactic to push back against stereotypical imagery of Kānaka Maoli, it reembeds a belief that our "real" selves existed before colonization, and it is dangerously similar to imperialist ideas of the noble savage. This is also a reinvestment in the notion that the "real" Native exists in their natural state somewhere, uncorrupted by the ills of the West. We must dislodge the flattening of "the Native" as the prediscursive foundation upon which modern subjectivity asserts itself.

Despite hip-hop's mass commercialization, many audiences are still attached to a real, authentic hip-hop that existed before or exists somewhere outside of capitalist production. People often insist on the realness of particular performers (people hold on to "Native" this way, too). Performers play into this. They are aware that some things sell and others do not. The poster advertising *The "O"* featured Krystilez as "Wanted" for "Blowing up Hawai'i." Alluding to the "wanted" outlaw posters made famous by the Western film genre, Krystilez positions himself as inherently criminal. This criminality references the Western outlaw who is bound up in assertions of American masculinity and the conquering of the Western frontier. The phrase "Blowing Up Hawai'i" is derived from the expression to "blow up," a common hip-hop phrase that usually suggests someone is rising to stardom. "Blow up" also comes from "blowing up someone's spot," meaning that in the action a secret is revealed. The wording also denotes a criminal act of breaking something open through an explosion. This play on words is taken further in YouTube videos of Krystilez on the streets of Waikīkī proclaiming to "blow up Hawai'i one way or another" and laughing while saying it.[57] Even if the viewer recognizes that Krystilez is just a performer, the specter of Kanaka Maoli criminality, fears about terrorism, and imagery of Kanaka Maoli activists occupying space ('Iolani Palace, for example) are invoked[58] (the latter being a common stereotype in Hawai'i that is associated with sovereignty activists). By referencing this trope, Krystilez pushes against dominant tourist representations of Kānaka Maoli as welcoming, docile, and lazy, aligning himself with the imagery associated with sovereignty and a general sense of defiance. At the same time, it also lends support to the perception that Kanaka Maoli men are unable to survive in the modern world because they are trapped in a cycle of violence, drug abuse, and criminal behavior.[59]

Reconciling these conflicts or finding the "truth" of Krystilez's narrative is beside the point. What these representational moves do show us is that a system exists that normalizes these representations and limits other more nuanced expressions. As a performer, Krystilez must constantly balance social expectations and cultural identity. Although Kānaka Maoli have always actively resisted flat constructions of ourselves, more complicated representations do not circulate as much as mainstream ones. This plays out in the realm of cultural production and everyday practice in which debates about authenticity permeate public discourse as Kānaka Maoli struggle to hold on to the one thing that we are recognized for: our culture. As a whole, Krystilez's goal is to put Hawai'i on the hip-hop map, getting it recognized, making it visible, and letting its voice be heard. It is also about reclaiming places and spaces—particularly digital space, given the laws and policies that prevent reclamation of lands. Although aggressively claiming space is crucial for cultural resistance, it is also fraught, as the video for "Bloodline" features misogynistic and aggressive imagery throughout. Hawaiian hip-hop has taken on similarly gendered politics as an avenue through which Indigenous self-determination is performed in tandem with the production of capitalist heteropatriarchy that objectifies women and positions men of color as violent criminals. The considerable amount of attention paid to the cultural production of Kanaka Maoli men in musical forms (such as reggae and hip-hop in academic and nonacademic spaces) indicates a desire to understand and make space for male Kanaka Maoli narratives that have heretofore been hidden behind the hypervisibility of the hula girl and its mirror image, the angry activist Kanaka Maoli woman.[60]

The Double Colonization of a Hawaiian Hip-Hop Feminist

Kanaka Maoli women have labored hard to ensure the survival of the Kānaka Maoli, but this labor has often been criticized, especially when the women are publicly critical of the men.[61] Haunani-Kay Trask's landmark article "Fighting the Battle of Double Colonization: The View of a Hawaiian Feminist" is instructive when analyzing Hawaiian hip-hop.[62] In this article, she explains the conflicts she faced as a woman in the Hawaiian nationalist movement and the racism she experienced among white women in feminist circles. The genus of her argument is similar to that of arguments advanced by feminists of color who call out the racism expressed in some feminist groups and the heteropatriarchy implicit in many nationalist movements, civil rights movements, and community struggles. Turning a blind eye to the absence or misogynistic portrayal of women in Hawaiian hip-hop is a current manifestation of these conflicts. Being a Kanaka Maoli feminist and a fan of Krystilez, I find myself in this bind.

Native feminists, like women of color feminists, constantly have their authenticity and loyalty challenged.[63] As an intellectual project, Native feminism offers a way to assess the internalization of Western ideas about gender roles. It insists on critiquing heteropatriarchy when working toward decolonization and favors models of nationhood that are not based on exclusion or secondary marginalization. Native feminism aspires instead to build nations that are not heteronormative or patriarchal and do not use the nuclear family as their building block.[64] Kauanui has encouraged the Kānaka Maoli to question male domination and sexism aggressively when doing the political work that ensures their collective survival.[65] This perspective applies directly to a critique of Hawaiian hip-hop wherein the aspirations for sovereignty or nationhood do not overshadow the rampant sexism and its relationship to heteropatriarchy in the music. Such a critique draws attention to the fact that certain artists still benefit from male privilege in a system that normalizes and rewards sexism.

I cannot turn away from the imagery of women being lyrically and visually possessed, merely ornamental in videos. As Krystilez poignantly asserts, "I'm one of the best when it comes to peaches jumping on my penis. Just ask Jaz Trias damn near broke my dick, pussy so tender" ("Come On Get It"). This song references Jasmine Trias, a Filipino American recording artist and aspiring actress from Hawai'i who was the third-place finalist on *American Idol* in 2004. At the time, she was only seventeen. She quickly rose to local stardom and has found considerable success in the Philippines. Turning a blind eye to these expressions, perhaps because they do not explicitly express something "Hawaiian" or are not representative of Hawaiian hip-hop as a whole, ignores the fact that they are nonetheless generated in Kanaka Maoli communities. They articulate sentiments that circulate within Kanaka Maoli lives, are internalized through an enduring investment in heteropatriarchy, and are infused by corporate hip-hop. Surely, as many interpretations of *mele* might suggest, Kānaka Maoli have always talked about women and sexuality in complex and sometimes very sexual terms. The digital-media networks through which Hawaiian hip-hop now moves, however, give these lyrical and visual representations of sexuality a much wider circulation.

When Krystilez implies in "Bloodline" that he will beat someone like a "fag" if they step to him on his homestead, he exhibits his own entrenchment in heteropatriarchy: he threatens to brutalize a man physically who steps on his land to the point that he is an emasculated man—even less than a woman. Krystilez is not alone in this performance. Shown with him in "Bloodline" is a crew of "bangers," personified in his lyricism and in the video's visual imagery. While this could be read as an assertion of sovereignty, in which a Native man is warning possible intruders (settlers) that he will defend his land—or the homestead—to the death, there is more to it. Krystilez articulates sovereignty and cultural pride through violent misogynistic homophobic discourse, demonstrating how failing to critique heteropatriarchy undermines interrogations of the violence that we enact on one another—even when that violence might be done in the name of "sovereignty" or protecting one's homestead.

In another song, he raps, "Where we raise bangers. Where the *māhūs* will fuck your ass up and suck your cock too" ("The 'O'"). *Māhū* is a Hawaiian term used to describe everything from gay men to drag queens to transwomen, and although Krystilez's reference to the *māhū* seems homophobic at first, something else is going on.[66] In this lyric, Krystilez is allowing *māhūs* a space of agency in their performance of a feminized masculinity, something unexpected in hip-hop. Krystilez actually recognizes *māhū* in Hawaiian culture and modern Hawaiian society as forces to be reckoned with. In the phrasing, the *māhū* is part of "The 'O'" and is crucial to its setting. The *māhū* will "fuck your ass up" too, along with "the bangers." The *māhū* in this song also have a serious stake in protecting Hawaiian lands and indigeneity and indeed, personal sovereignty and gender expression. Krystilez presents a different type of masculinity through an engagement of nonheteronormative gender roles that can be linked to Kanaka indigeneity.

At the same time, it appears that Krystilez's lyricism perpetuates violence on anyone who does not heed the masculinity that he promotes—one that is fundamentally linked to male-gendered bodies with little space allowed for a diverse gender expression of masculinity. Overall, he characterizes women as being disposable and makes homophobic remarks, almost to the point of exhaustion. Because Krystilez performs much of mainstream hip-hop's heteropatriarchal capitalist agenda, this music is not only influenced by Hawaiian sovereignty. It also reproduces the sovereignty in imaginative, albeit problematic, ways. Neglecting to analyze these processes critically thus sustains a heteronormative and patriarchal vision of Hawaiian sovereignty.

Defiant indigeneity necessitates looking at how the Kānaka Maoli were made into disciplined subjects—looking to the spaces in which marginal voices get incorporated, co-opted, and recolonized into a unitary discourse. It also requires us to recognize that Kanaka Maoli sovereignty is contested in unexpected performance spaces such as hip-hop. Talking about Kanaka Maoli resistance and resilience through cultural innovation is without a doubt vital, but we must advance criticism of Kānaka Maoli as well rather than constructing a binary logic of colonizer (evil) versus colonized (good). Jasbir Puar writes, "It is easy, albeit painful, to point to the conservative elements of any political formation; it is less easy and perhaps more painful, to point to ourselves as accomplices of certain normalizing violences."[67] As Kānaka Maoli, we know that we have always engaged in cultural performance in order to retain our living culture in remarkably innovative ways, but it is time to discuss resistance and agency alongside deeply embedded forms of heteropatriarchy, violence, and racist sentiments found in some forms of contemporary Hawaiian performance and in the way that people think about sovereignty and the Hawaiian future. We must confront a Hawaiian cultural production that is as messy and violent as colonization, and we must force ourselves to assess the costs of the violence enacted through some of the narratives that Krystilez performs. Taking up this charge is crucial, for as long as Kanaka Maoli cultural production focuses all its attention on excavating a "lost" past—even if only to invigorate and grow contemporary struggles for political autonomy—as a means to make ourselves "whole," we miss the opportunity to attend to those spaces in which expressions of Kanaka Maoli identity are complicated, less explicit, and built on the subjugation of other groups.

In a climate in which Native Hawaiian federal recognition is presented as the only option left for the Kānaka Maoli, and thousands of Kānaka Maoli are increasingly living on beaches because of the astronomically high cost of living in Hawai'i, charting the future of the Kānaka Maoli appears at times to be a grim endeavor. The Hawaiian sovereignty movement, once thought to be the brainchild of "crazy Hawaiians," has now become mainstream discourse in Hawai'i. Government support of Native Hawaiian federal recognition is widespread, while the Hawaiian community itself appears to continue to be divided. The attacks on Native Hawaiian entitlement programs are a testament to the threat that Kanaka Maoli self-determination poses, particularly to the *haole* and Asian elite in Hawai'i. The political realities that face the Kānaka Maoli today get interrogated and invigorated through the performance of various types of cultural resistance that ironically lay bare the legacies of racialized and gendered subjection while reconstituting them.

As Hawaiian sovereignty is negotiated in classrooms, on beaches, and in boardrooms, we recognize all the work that has made it a possibility rather than a fantasy of Kanaka Maoli activists. We must also realize how much remains to be done. A key step in this process is being critical of ourselves. Kanaka Maoli identity is vast and at times disjunct. It bears repeating that the insistence on coherent Kanaka Maoli identities presumes that we are fully known, collapsed in all our complexity, and closed off to connections and transformations that might be libratory. In order to generate insights into the multilayered realities visible in Kanaka Maoli cultural production, we must critically examine the performances of Kanaka Maoli identity and the motivations behind such celebrations and elisions. In an unapologetic embodiment of Kanaka Maoli indigeneity, Krystilez makes visible and possible our ongoing defiance as we reclaim performance space in our homeland. As Krystilez spits,

> This is reality
> This is not a movie
> Protect my family it's my common duty

You like war
Say no more
Bring your drama to me
Third Road Homestead fucka Nānākuli EA!⁶⁸

Notes

1. "Who I Am" will be on Krystilez's forthcoming album. Krystilez e-mailed me this song and others in December 2009. The song was available on Krystilez's MySpace page, http://www.myspace.com/krystiles, accessed June 29, 2011 (no longer posted).
2. Hawai'i became a state on August 21, 1959. For details on the debates regarding Hawai'i's status as a state, see Dean Itsuji Saranillio, "Seeing Conquest: Colliding Histories and the Cultural Politics of Hawai'i Statehood" (PhD diss., University of Michigan, 2009).
3. Commonly used in Caribbean patois and popularized by rap music. *Punani* is used frequently in Hawai'i because *pua nani* translates to "beautiful flower." It is often used to refer to female genitalia.
4. The state of Hawai'i distinguishes between the terms *Hawaiian* and *Native Hawaiian*, each of which has a contested legality based on blood quantum. In this work, I will use the term *Kanaka Maoli* to refer to the Native peoples of the Hawaiian archipelago. It is a reference to any person descended from the Indigenous people inhabiting the Hawaiian Islands before 1778. *Kanaka Maoli* has recently been taken up by the Kanaka Maoli; it translates into "true people" or "real people" in relation to Hawaiian indigeneity. *Kānaka Maoli*, with the macron over the *ā* is the plural of *Kanaka Maoli*. Please also note, I will use the term *Hawaiian* to refer to categories such as "Hawaiian music" or "Hawaiian culture" and will refer to legislation under their official names, such as "Native Hawaiian Governmental Reorganization Act" and "Native Hawaiian Entitlement," because of their common usage.

    The definition of *Hawaiian hip-hop* varies. In this article, *Hawaiian hip-hop* refers to a hip-hop performer or group that identifies as Kanaka Maoli and produces hip-hop music that addresses issues that pertain to Hawai'i and the Kānaka Maoli.

5. As Osumare notes, a hip-hop scene started to coalesce in Honolulu during the early 1980s, evidenced in mainstream acknowledgment on a local television show called "Breakin Hawai'i" in 1984. For more see Halifu Osumare, "Props to the Local Boyz: Hip Hop Culture in Hawai'i," in *The Africanist Aesthetic in Global Hip Hop: Power Moves* (New York: Palgrave, 2007), 105–48.
6. See Robin D. G. Kelley, foreword to *The Vinyl Ain't Final: Hip Hop and the Globalization of Black Popular Culture*, ed. Dispannita Basu and Sidney Lemelle (Ann Arbor, MI: Pluto Press, 2006), xi–xvii; Tony Mitchell, "Kia Kaha! (Be Strong): Maori and Pacific Islander Hip Hop in Aotearoa/New Zealand," in *Global Noise: Rap and Hip Hop Outside the USA*, ed. Tony Mitchell (Middlesex, CT: Wesleyan University Press, 2001), 280–304; and Neal Ullestad, "Native American Rap and Reggae: Dancing to the Beat of a Different Drummer," in *Ethnomusicology: A Contemporary Reader*, ed. Jennifer Post (New York: Routledge, 2006), 331–50.
7. Osumare, "Props to the Local Boyz," 69.
8. See Patty O'Brien, *The Pacific Muse: Exotic Femininity and the Colonial Pacific* (Seattle: University of Washington Press, 2006); Houston Wood, *Displacing Natives: The Rhetorical Production of Hawai'i* (Lanham, MD: Rowman and Littlefield, 1999); and Jane Desmond, *Staging Tourism: Bodies on Display from Waikiki to Sea World* (Chicago: University of Chicago Press, 2001).
9. Adria Imada, "Hawaiians on Tour: Hula Circuits Through the American Empire," *American Quarterly* 56, no. 1 (2004): 111–49.
10. Ibid.
11. See Wood, *Displacing Natives*, 103–22. Examples of film include *Bird of Paradise* (1932), *Waikiki Wedding* (1938), *Song of the Islands* (1944), *Blue Hawai'i* (1961), and more recent titles such as *50 First Dates* (2004), *Forgetting Sarah Marshall* (2008), and the remake of the television series *Hawai'i Five-O* (2010–).
12. See Lilikalā Kameʻeleihiwa, *Native Land and Foreign Desires: Pehea La E Pono Ai?* (Honolulu: Bishop Museum Press, 1992); Noenoe Silva, *Aloha Betrayed: Native Hawaiian Resistance to American Colonialism* (Durham, NC: Duke University Press, 2004); J. Kehaulani Kauanui, *Hawaiian Blood: Colonialism and the Politics of Sovereignty and Indigeneity* (Durham, NC: Duke University Press, 2008); and Jonathan Osorio, *Dismembering Lahui: A History of the Hawaiian Nation to 1887* (Honolulu: University of Hawai'i Press, 2002).

13. Ty Kawika Tengan, *Native Men Remade: Gender and Nation in Contemporary Hawai'i* (Durham, NC: Duke University Press, 2008), 66.
14. Work in Pacific studies has been especially attentive to the way that Pacific masculinity is figured. In sports, see the work of Vicente M. Diaz, "'Fight Boys til the Last': Football and the Remasculinization of Identity in Guam," in *Pacific Diasporas: Island Peoples in the United States and Across the Pacific*, ed. Paul Spickard, Joanne Rondilla, and Deborah Hippolyte Wright (Honolulu: University of Hawai'i Press, 2002), 169–94; and Brendan Hokowhitu, "Tackling Maori Masculinity: A Colonial Genealogy of Savagery and Sport," *Contemporary Pacific* 16, no. 2 (2004): 259–84. In terms of military service, see also Tengan, *Native Men Remade*; Ty Kawika Tengan, "Re-Membering Panala'au: Masculinities, Nation, and Empire in Hawai'i and the Pacific," *Contemporary Pacific* 20, no. 1 (2008): 27–53; and Jennifer Nez Denetdale, "Securing Navajo National Boundaries: War, Patriotism, Tradition, and the Diné Marriage Act of 2005," *Wicazo Sa Review* 24, no. 2 (2009): 131–48. Denetdale also notes how the word *warrior* is used to motivate Navajo participation in U.S. wars. Denetdale raises questions about how Navajo participation in U.S. wars becomes aligned with a Navajo warrior tradition, making the link between family values and recent legislation, such as the Diné Marriage Act of 2005.
15. Krystilez, "The 'O,'" in *The "O,"* Tiki Entertainment, 2006, compact disc.
16. The 1920 Hawaiian Homes Commission Act (hereinafter referred to as HHCA) affirms the special relationship between the United States and Native Hawaiians. Two hundred thousand acres of land are set aside for Native Hawaiian homesteads. Annual lease rent is $1 per year with a ninety-nine-year lease, and a lease term can be extended for an additional one hundred years. As of 1998, only 40,703 acres were under lease to 6,547 homesteaders, with 29,702 applicants still waiting. Applicants must be of at least 50 percent blood quantum in order to qualify or be the descendant of someone on the waiting list.
17. In the summer of 2007, I posted a review of Krystilez on my "summer fieldwork" blog (a requirement of my Center for World Performance Studies residency at the University of Michigan), which he found and reposted on his MySpace page soon after. The comments posted in response to my blog (posted on his site) charged me with being overly critical and speculated regarding who I was to make such comments. The details aside, this is evidence of how the Internet serves as vital space for Krystilez and his fans.

18. Jean Burgess and Joshua Green, *YouTube: Online Video and Participatory Culture* (Malden, MA: Polity Press, 2009), 76.
19. Produced by Tiki Entertainment, a full-service promotional one-stop shop that produces music, prints banners, builds websites, and does car detailing.
20. http://www.youtube.com/user/tikient, accessed February 24, 2011 (no longer posted).
21. Krystilez expresses his feelings about the *The "O"* in a video, http://www.youtube.com/user/tikient#p/u/11/huirRxquPKg, accessed June 29, 2011 (no longer posted). See also Gary C. W. Chun, "Nanakuli's in the House," *Honolulu Star-Bulletin*, January 26, 2007, music sec.
22. Place songs are frequent in Hawaiian music. Contemporary place songs include Olomana's "Ku'u Home o Kahalu'u," Ehukai's "Moloka'i Slide," and Bruddah Waltah's "Kailua-Kona."
23. Unfortunately, the video for "The 'O'" and "Won" has been taken down from YouTube (originally accessed November 13, 2009).
24. Patricia L. Gibbs, "Alternative Things Considered: A Comparative Political Economic Analysis of Honolulu Mainstream and Alternative Print News Communication and Organization" (PhD diss., University of Hawai'i, 1999).
25. President Bill Clinton signed into law the Hawai'i Apology Resolution, US PL 103-50, on November 23, 1993. The Apology Resolution was signed into law on the one hundredth anniversary of the overthrow, expressing a commitment to provide support for the reconciliation process between the United States and the Native Hawaiian people. Many see this bill as the first step to Native Hawaiian federal recognition.
26. Rice v. Cayetano (1996). Big Island rancher Freddy Rice sued the Office of Hawaiian Affairs (and the State of Hawai'i, which administers the Office of Hawaiian Affairs, hereinafter referred to as OHA) for racial discrimination because he could not vote in Hawaiian-only OHA trustee elections. Rice was financed in part by the Campaign for a Color-Blind America, a neoconservative think tank. Arakaki v. State of Hawai'i (2000) sued the state of Hawai'i because at the time, a requirement of OHA trustee eligibility was Hawaiian ancestry. Other lawsuits target Kamehameha School's Hawaiian-ancestry admissions preferences.
27. See Judy Rohrer, "'Got Race?': The Production of Haole and the Distortion of Indigeneity in the *Rice* Decision," *Contemporary Pacific* 18, no. 1 (2006): 1.

28. J. Kehaulani Kauanui, "Native Hawaiian Decolonization and the Politics of Gender," *American Quarterly* 60, no. 2 (2008): 280. The most recent version of the Akaka Bill (S. 3945) was presented to the U.S. Congress on November 15, 2010.
29. Kamana'opono Crabbe's letter was published in *Star-Advertiser*, "OHA Trustees Rescind Letter to Feds on Hawaiian Kingdom's Status," *Honolulu Star-Advertiser* May 9, 2014, http://www.staradvertiser.com/news/breaking/20140509 _oha_seeks_clarity_on_hawaiian_kingdom_status.html?2i, accessed July 25, 2014 (no longer posted). Response from OHA board of trustees chair College Machado can be found in Andrew Walden, "OHA Chaos: Machado, Crabbe Dueling Statements," *Hawai'i Free Press*, May 13, 2014, http://www.hawaiifreepress.com/ArticlesMain/tabid/56/ID/12611/OHA-Chaos-Machado-Crabbe-Dueling-Statements-full-text.aspx.
30. Leeanne Betaamosake Simpson website, http://leannesimpson.ca/niimtoowaad-mikimaag-gijiying-bakonaan-dancing-on-the-back-of-our-turtle-re-creating-nishnaabeg-governance, February 2, 2011, accessed July 20, 2016 (no longer posted).
31. Audra Simpson, *Mohawk Interruptus: Political Life Across the Borders of Settler States* (Durham, NC: Duke University Press, 2014), 20.
32. Noelani Goodyear-Ka'ōpua, Ikaika Hussey, and Erin Kahunawaika'ala Wright, *A Nation Rising: Hawaiian Movements for Life, Land, and Sovereignty*, Narrating Native Histories (Durham, NC: Duke University Press, 2014), 3–4.
33. Ibid., 7.
34. ku'ualoha ho'omanawanui, *Voices of Fire: Reweaving the Literary Lei of Pele and Hi'iaka*, First Peoples: New Directions in Indigenous Studies (Minneapolis: University of Minnesota Press, 2014), xxxix. Noelani Goodyear-Kaopua, "Kuleana Lahui: Collective Responsibility for Hawaiian Nationhood in Activists Praxis," *Affinities* 5, no. 1 (2011): 130–63.
35. The OHA was created in 1978 to develop, coordinate, and watch over programs and activities relating to Hawaiians.
36. The HHCA, created by the U.S. Congress during the territory period, was later transferred to the state of Hawai'i in 1959 as a precondition of statehood. Since 1959, the Department of Hawaiian Home Lands has administered the program, verifying applicants' eligibility based on 50 percent blood quantum. You may also qualify for lands if you are descended from someone who is no longer

living but was on the list and the name comes up. In addition to this requirement, because obtaining the necessary documents and making a formal claim is mired in various levels of bureaucracy, many Kānaka Maoli have difficulty qualifying for these lands and are deterred from the application process, with thousands still on the waiting list. Similarly, the awarded homestead plot could be located where a Kanaka Maoli might not want to live, e.g., far away from their workplace or, in some cases, on a different island than the one on which they live.

37. Kauanui, *Hawaiian Blood*.
38. Ibid.
39. Sally Engle Merry, *Colonizing Hawai'i: The Cultural Power of Law* (Princeton, NJ: Princeton University Press, 2000).
40. Maile Arvin, "Still in the Blood: Gendered Histories of Race, Law, and Science in *Day V. Apoliona*." *American Quarterly* 67, no. 3 (September 2015): 681–703.
41. The video for "Bloodline," http://www.youtube.com/watch?v=LXJKsvGiS5Y. These lyrics are sung in the same rhythm as Tupac's song "Ambitionz Az a Ridah" (1996).
42. Krystilez, "Bloodline," *The "O,"* Honolulu: Tiki Entertainment, 2006, compact disc.
43. Cristina Bacchilega, *Legendary Hawai'i and the Politics of Place* (Philadelphia: University of Pensylvania Press, 2007).
44. Ibid.
45. Murray Forman, *The 'Hood Comes First: Race, Space, and Place in Rap and Hip-Hop* (Middletown, CT: Wesleyan University Press, 2002).
46. Graham Harvey and Charles D. Thompson, eds., *Indigenous Diasporas and Dislocations* (Surry, UK: Ashgate, 2005).
47. Vicente M. Diaz and J. Kehaulani Kauanui, "Native Pacific Cultural Studies on the Edge," *Contemporary Pacific* 13, no. 2 (2001): 315–42. Diaz and Kauanui build on James Clifford's *Routes: Travel and Translation in the Late Twentieth Century* (Cambridge, MA: Harvard University Press, 1997).
48. Office of Hawaiian Affairs, Planning and Research Office, *Native Hawaiian Data Book* (Honolulu: Planning and Research Office, Office of Hawaiian Affairs, 1994), 17.
49. J. Kehaulani Kauanui, "Diasporic Deracination and 'Off-Island' Hawaiians," *Contemporary Pacific* 19, no. 1 (2007): 139.

50. The comments section for the "Bloodline" video is telling of the different interpretations that the video yields. Some comments represent their own "bloodline," or where someone is from, whereas other comments mock Krystilez and others in the video as gangsta wannabes or shameful examples of Hawaiianness.
51. According to the Empowering Pacific Islander Communities (EPIC), *Native Hawaiians and Pacific Islanders: A Community of Contrasts 2014 Report*, http://empoweredpi.org/wp-content/uploads/2014/06/A_Community_of_Contrasts_NHPI_US_2014-1.pdf, the Kānaka Maoli population living outside of Hawai'i has increased 40 percent since 1990 because of the cost of living and limited economic opportunities. Sixty percent of the Kānaka Maoli population lives in Hawai'i, followed by large populations in California, Washington, Nevada, and Texas.
52. Stuart Hall, "Notes on Deconstructing the Popular," in *People's History and Socialist Theory*, ed. Raphael Samuel (London: Routledge, 1981), 223.
53. Paige Sylvia Raibmon, *Authentic Indians: Episodes of Encounter from the Late-Nineteenth-Century Northwest Coast* (Durham, NC: Duke University Press, 2005), 3.
54. Scott Richard Lyons, *X-Marks: Native Signatures of Assent* (Minneapolis: University of Minnesota Press, 2010), 59–61.
55. Brendan Hokowhitu, "Haka: Colonized Physicality, Body-Logic, and Embodied Sovereignty," in *Performing Indigeneity: Global Histories and Contemporary Experiences*, ed. L Graham and G Penny (Lincoln: University of Nebraska Press), 293.
56. Ibid.
57. See "Tiki's Takin It to the Streets," http://www.youtube.com/user/tikient#p/a/u/0/DeHlkA34VB4.
58. See Mark Niesse, "Native Hawaiians Occupy Iolani Palace Grounds," *Maui News*, May 1, 2008; B. J. Reyes, "Akaka Bill Opponents Occupy Iolani Palace," *Honolulu Star-Bulletin*, June 8, 2006.
59. Tengan, *Native Men Remade*, 9.
60. See Fay Akindes, "Sudden Rush," in *Grove Dictionary of American Music*, 2nd ed. (New York: Oxford University Press, 2013); ku'ualoha ho'omanawanui, "From Ocean to O'shen: Reggae, Rap, and Hip Hop in Hawai'i," in *Crossing Waters, Crossing Worlds*, ed. Tiya Miles and Sharon P. Holland (Durham, NC: Duke University Press, 2006), 273–308; Adria Imada, "Head Rush: Hip Hop and a Hawaiian Na-

tion 'on the Rise,'" in *The Vinyl Ain't Final*, ed. Dipannita Basu and Sidney Lemelle (Ann Arbor, MI: Pluto Press, 2006), 85–99.

61. Kanaka Maoli women have always publicly deployed power. Historically, Kanaka Maoli women were noted for their powerful roles in Hawaiian Kingdom affairs, as organizers in the Hui Aloha 'Aina, and their roles in other Hawaiian civic organizations that assembled the antiannexation petitions during the late nineteenth century. Throughout the twentieth century, as some Kanaka Maoli women found agency performing on "hula circuits," others voiced opposition to statehood during the territory period, and as the Hawaiian Renaissance germinated during the 1970s, Kanaka Maoli women were active organizers in the Protest Kahoʻolawe Ohana. Throughout the 1980s and 1990s, they were prominent leaders within the Hawaiian sovereignty movement.

62. Haunani-Kay Trask, "Fighting the Battle of Double Colonization: The View of a Hawaiian Feminist," *Annual Journal of Ethnic Studies* 2 (1984): 196–213.

63. Joyce Green, ed., *Making Space for Indigenous Feminism* (London: Zed Books, 2007).

64. Andrea Smith and J. Kehaulani Kauanui, "Native Feminisms Engage American Studies," *American Quarterly* 60, no. 2 (2008): 271.

65. Ibid.; Kauanui, "Native Hawaiian Decolonization."

66. Māhū was a hermaphrodite in precolonial Hawaiian society. Contemporary usage generally refers to gay men, transidentified people, and drag queens. Very rarely does it refer to lesbians.

67. Jasbir Puar, *Terrorist Assemblages: Homonationalisms in Queer Times* (Durham, NC: Duke University Press, 2007), 24.

68. Krystilez, "Bloodline."

8

Of Shadows and Doubts

White Supremacy, Decolonization, and Black-Indian Relations

BRIAN KLOPOTEK

Since 1998 I have been doing ethnological and historical research in the southeastern United States that revolves around federal recognition of Indian tribal sovereignty. One of the thorniest trails to navigate with people I interview has been the place of blackness in Southern Indian communities. The subject raises hackles quickly because of the ways in which the presence of African ancestry undermines claims to a distinct Indian identity. As a result of this and other factors, antiblack racism remains as an unresolved internal and external conflict among tribes in the South. As a Choctaw with roots in Louisiana and as an activist for racial equality, I seek here to explore and dissect these issues in an effort to counter antiblack racism and reveal the ways indigenous communities have at times embraced what is ultimately a self-defeating support of white supremacy.

Racial theory that encompasses more than the Indian-white or black-white context is crucial in this effort. In many ways, the Native-white relationship is unique, based not just in race but also in the indigenous and sovereign status of Native American nations in relation to a settler colonial state. As an example, spearfishing rights for Chippewas in northern Wisconsin are not *racially* based rights—they are rights of citizens of the sovereign bands of Chippewas who reserved those rights in treaties (which racial minorities cannot enter into under current legal frameworks in the United States). If these were *racial* rights, *all Indians* would be entitled to spearfish in northern Wisconsin, but such is not the case.[1] We need to be mindful of this contrast, because ethnic studies as a field and the U.S. public more generally do not understand or make useful distinctions between indigenous groups and racial minorities, and they typically fail to recognize how the colonizer-indigenous relationship is central to understanding and enabling other racial projects. Much has changed over the ten-odd years since I originally drafted the ideas for this essay: the structure of settler colonialism has become firmly established in the ethnic studies and American studies lexicon, and the Native American and Indigenous Studies Association has fostered an exponential increase in the volume and visibility of new Native studies scholarship. Still, the many iterations and implications of indigenous-colonial relations and their relationship to race have only just begun to be mapped out.[2]

That is to say, Native American studies has focused so intently on what sets indigenous nations apart from other racial minorities that we have not fully acknowledged our common experiences as racialized minorities in a racialized world. This is not an argument to collapse these disciplines into one but rather a reminder to attend to the imbrications of the distinct vectors of indigeneity and race in each field. Indians are part of a racial system that transcends the binary racial relationship with whites and our colonial relationship with them; we are part of a dynamic constellation, an entire system of race, privilege, and power, and every node in that system affects Native people to some degree. We understand, for example, that white racializations of *Indian* people affect everything from government-to-government relationships to the way Indian youths are socialized/conditioned in educational systems. But Indians are part of and participate in a national discourse about race, and we need to better understand how racial formations and indigeneity are *tied together*, too. How do ideas about whiteness, Indianness, *and* blackness, for example, shape tribal identities? How were shifting attitudes toward Indians in the 1920s tied to the classification of Mexicans as a distinct category in the 1930 census?[3] How have Japanese-American and Anglo-American myths of racial equality in Hawai'i undermined indigenous Hawaiian sovereignty efforts?[4]

Stories from my experiences in Louisiana Indian communities exemplify the complex historical relations among black, white, and Indian peoples, but this pattern of antiblack racism is evident in many Indian communities in the southeastern United States, as other scholars have documented extensively. James Merrell, for example, makes the starkly illustrative statement in a 1984 article that "as recently as 1981, informants on the reservation called avoidance of and contempt for blacks 'a Catawba tradition.'"[5] Similarly, Arica Coleman discusses the Rappahannock identity of Mildred Loving, one of the plaintiffs in *Loving v. Virginia*, the famous court case that struck down Virginia's antimiscegenation laws. While widely regarded solely as an African American woman, Loving herself denied having any African ancestry at all in a 2004 interview, arguing that "the Rappahannocks never had anything to do with Blacks."[6] Helen Rountree discusses the ways Virginia's "racial purity" laws, instituted immediately after the Civil War, became "a veritable cornerstone" of Indian self-identity in Virginia because they distinguished the legal rights of Indians with no African ancestry from those with African ancestry.[7] The Mississippi Choctaws, a tribe notable for its high degree of language and cultural conservatism, historically refused to associate with blacks.[8] The Lumbees, a tribe whose status as such is called into question by some who think they are "mulattos" masquerading as Indians, have historically exhibited some of the same behavior, refusing to send their children to black schools when they were not allowed to enroll in white schools under Jim Crow.[9] Each of the so-called Five Civilized Tribes of Oklahoma (Cherokee, Chickasaw, Choctaw, Creek, Seminole) has, in varying degrees, excluded people from tribal enrollment because of their African ancestry, leading some of the remaining tribal members with African ancestry to hide their heritage behind particularly loud antiblack rhetoric.[10]

This list could go on, but it should suffice to establish the broad and deeply set pattern of antiblack racism among Southern Indians that reaches beyond the borders of any individual tribe or state. In fact, the pattern reaches beyond the southeastern United States and beyond indigenous communities, to be sure, but I will limit the conversation here to Louisiana tribes to provide a focus that allows me to make the arguments most effectively. I state this at the outset to help frame the following discussion and to shield tribes I am specifically discussing from being singled out for special contempt. I hope the fact that we are all in this narrative together provides some consolation to the fact that I am discussing here what many would rather bury. This is our common heritage as colonized subjects of a racist nation, and I hope this discussion can lead us toward healing and decolonization.

Research in Louisiana Indian Communities

While the stories of every tribal community in Louisiana could provide ample material for discussion on this topic, I will focus on the Clifton-Choctaws presently because their story reveals critical iterations of the triangular relationship among Indianness, whiteness, and blackness. The Clifton-Choctaws are a state-recognized tribe in the process of petitioning for federal recognition. Some local tribes and tribal members support the Clifton-Choctaws' bid for recognition while others oppose it. A substantial part of the opposition to their recognition can be traced to the fact that some of the members of the community have African ancestry, which makes them automatically "black" regardless of any other ancestry under legal and popular U.S. racial codes. As a result, the issue of blackness becomes central to Clifton-Choctaw identity construction.

When I visited the community between 1998 and 2000, the tribal member serving as the federal recognition liaison and unofficial office manager looked to be of Native, African, and European descent, as did her son and several other family members. Her name was Theresa Clifton Sarpy, and she occupied a position of visibility and power, a diplomatic position that in many ways made her the face of the tribe, so I assumed her presence in that position meant the Clifton-Choctaws were uninterested in downplaying their African ancestry despite reports to the contrary from outsiders.

I can remember asking Sarpy about Clifton-Choctaw relations with surrounding black and white communities during my first interview with her. She said the Clifton-Choctaws have good relations with some blacks, such as the state representative from Alexandria, but that typically, distrust flavors the relationship. She quickly added that distrust also typifies Clifton-Choctaw attitudes toward whites. They have good relations with some, bad with others, she said, citing conflicts with the sheriff's office and the school board as examples of the latter. She asserted that perceptions depended on the individuals involved in the relationship, because many Clifton people distrust outsiders in general, regardless of race. There is an element of truth to her statement about distrust of all outsiders, but after about ten seconds of silence, another truth burst out from its place just beneath the surface: "But on the whole," Sarpy told me, "they trust whites more than they trust blacks."[11]

Setting aside for a moment her use of the word *they* rather than *we*, it is clear that Sarpy was abundantly aware of antiblack racism among fellow community members and trying to convey it—for a number of reasons both personal and political, I am sure—in an understated way. Other community leaders tiptoed around antiblack racism, too, distancing themselves from it, feeling me out, without necessarily performing an overt display of contempt for blacks. Consider, for example, the words of a Clifton man in his seventies, a man who might pass for white in many places. In his youth, he recalled, "they'd call you Redbone, they'd call you mulatto, they'd call you everything but probably what you are. So, we always, it was a fight with us when they'd call us all these other names, because we always had been taught that we was from Indian people."

The narrative implies that the *inaccuracy* of the labels "mulatto" and "Redbone" was at issue; antipathy remains in the subtext, where it is clear that the *blackness* of the labels caused the offense. The element of Indian identity that depended on not only a lack of black ancestry but also antipathy toward blacks, it seemed to me, was a holdover from the older generations, a fading tradition, verging on becoming covert even in this older man's statement about his childhood. I recognized that it was a part of community history, but I categorically separated it from the "modern" community. I later realized it was a mistake to tie these attitudes to specific generations and assume declining acceptance of these "traditions" merely because of Sarpy's central and visible position in the community.

After I had been away for three years, a series of incidents made me realize that I had been underestimating the importance of antiblack racism and the extent of community denials of black ancestry. In December of 2003, as part of the collaborative process mandated by indigenous methodologies, I resent a draft of the Clifton-Choctaw chapter from my dissertation to Sarpy so that tribal members could read and comment on it before it was finalized. Sarpy had left the position shortly after I sent the original draft, and apparently no one had seen it the first time around. The new recognition coordinator was a white spouse of a tribal member who was eager to read the chapter. I sent off two copies and waited for the marked-up copy to arrive in the mail. I waited and waited, but nothing came.

I called a couple of times in the intervening two months and left messages but never heard back. Finally, one day, I reached her by phone and asked her what she and others thought of it. I was anxious, because community approval presents a hurdle at least as significant as academic approval and infinitely more challenging and fraught with danger. More than mere courtesy, collaboration makes for more rigorous academic work because it makes us accountable to the expertise and authority of community members as lifelong participant-observers. The new coordinator was hesitant, and I could sense that a significant critique was about to emerge. She told me "all this information" was new to her and that she was shocked by it. I asked what information specifically was so shocking. She started talking in a tone that let me know she was choosing her words carefully. "You know, the stuff about the [*pause*] . . . *mulattos*."

She was referring to my discussions of blackness in the community's ancestry, to the fact that many of the ancestors of community members were identified as "mulattos" in the 1910 census, to the history of intermarriage with the nearby Cane River Creoles of Color, to the fact that I had called the community mixed Indian, black, and white in my draft chapter. She said her husband was angry about this characterization but that he acknowledged that the perception of his people as "mulattos" had been ongoing for a number of years. She guessed that many other community members would be similarly angry but only about the issue of mixing with blacks—mixing with whites was completely acceptable.

As it turns out, she was right. When I next visited the Clifton-Choctaw community in 2004, she was no longer working for the tribe, so I talked with the new tribal recognition coordinator. I brought two copies of my completed dissertation on this trip: one to give to the tribal chair and one to the tribal council. While I made some minor adjustments in phrasing to indicate that some of the community had African ancestry and some potentially did not,

I did not remove discussions of blackness altogether. I talked with the new coordinator, who was a tribal member in her late forties or so, and told her about the concerns of her predecessor. She concurred that it certainly would go over poorly with many tribal members, and it did not sit well with her, either. She said that *blacks had always been excluded from the community* and that if she had any say in the matter, *the tribe would uphold that tradition*. She told me that Sarpy had always, in fact, been marginal to the community because of her blackness, a troubling statement that gave me a new window into Sarpy's experiences of belonging in her community.

I had a conversation with the tribal chair about the issue later that week, and she used the more diplomatic tones that I had heard from other officials, although she, like others, expressed concern that I had suggested that the community had black ancestry and black cultural influences. Perplexed, I told her I thought it was commonly acknowledged that some members of the Clifton-Choctaw community had black ancestry, in particular through ties to the Cane River Creoles of Color. Her eyes brightened with recognition and what appeared to be relief, and she said, "Oh, well, yes, the Cane River Creoles, we do share ancestry with them." In local terms, the Cane River Creoles, who have African, French, and Native ancestry, were distinguished from blacks by their large percentage of European ancestry, their history as free people of color and slaveholders themselves (which carries connotations about both race and class), their Francophone traditions, and their celebrity as bearers of a unique tradition that sets Louisiana apart from the rest of the United States. In central Louisiana, they were "a race apart from Blacks" in their own minds and to a significant degree in local custom as well.[12] These were not the "blacks" that many Clifton-Choctaws were loath to be affiliated with. French- and Latin American–style racial gradations still operate in the area to the extent that the terms *black* and *Creole of Color* connote different sets of people and different levels of prejudice in contrast with the "one-drop rule" of Anglo America. This clarifies to some extent Clifton resistance to the suggestion that they had "black" ancestry.

Though the tribal chair acknowledged connections with the Cane River Creoles of Color, she insisted that whatever racial ancestry the community had, they had been largely isolated from mainstream black and white influences and intermarriage for many years. That is, while there was intermarriage with Creole of Color and white outsiders at various points, the community had been largely insular, marrying among themselves for the better part of 150 years. Certainly there was white influence and (less so, she points out) black influence on the community, but on some level, she believes a discussion of black influences in particular diminishes their distinctive Indian identity. In terms of perceptions of the community and in terms of the *federal recognition process* (which is at its heart about perceptions), she may be right.

Regulating Racial Categories

The origin of antiblack racism among Southern Indians clearly rests in Anglo-American racism and colonialism, two phenomena that are so closely related that they might be better accounted for if we understand them as behavior resulting from an ideology of white supremacy—an ideology in which white people and their ancestors are understood to be morally, intellectually, politically, and spiritually superior to nonwhites, and therefore entitled to various forms of privilege, power, and property.[13] This ideology was forced on Southern Indian communities gradually but surely under the twin hammers of military conquest and assimilationism.

A number of scholars have documented Southern Indian adoption of Anglo systems of racial thinking as one component of a multifaceted response to U.S. aggression. In mirroring the peculiar notions of civility held by Anglos around race and gender, tribes hoped to protect themselves against conquest based on constructions of Indian savagery.[14] Claudio Saunt suggests that as a result, race became "a central element in the lives of southeastern Indians, not just as a marker of difference between natives and White newcomers but as a divisive and destructive force within Indian communities themselves."[15] Though there was conflict within tribes over the issues of slavery and blackness, southeastern tribes increasingly adopted Anglo-American racializations of African-descended people through the course of the nineteenth century.

Conversely, subconsciously, and equally destructive was the progressive tribal acceptance of Anglo-American racializations of whites, since every stereotype about people of color and indigenous nations also contains a hidden stereotype about whites, what I call a *shadow stereotype*.[16] If Indians adopt the idea that blacks are inherently suited to labor, inherently immoral, and inherently unentitled, they also adopt the unspoken, hidden corollary that whites are inherently intellectual, moral, and entitled. In a system of dichotomous oppositions, if whites are inherently intellectual, moral, and entitled and Indians are not whites, then what are Indians? If we start thinking of race as centered not around the imagined deficiencies of people of color but instead around the myth of white people's inherent superiority, it becomes a much simpler system to understand, and the seemingly "unique" racializations of people of color and indigenous groups cease to be unique or perplexing. Rather, they become permutations of the same basic idea of white supremacy, entitlement, and domination.

For much of the twentieth century, segregation policies were the arena in which the boundaries of race and privilege were officially policed, and because of this history in educational policy specifically, Indians in the South typically defined themselves in ways that distanced them from blacks as much as possible. While there were simultaneous impulses toward isolationism from whites, when they wanted access to education, Southern Indians (with and without African ancestry) fought to have their children enrolled in white schools and refused to send them to black schools. Rather than challenging the existence of the color line, most tried to position themselves on the right side of it. By saying they would not go to school with blacks, an act of self-defense taken with the intention of ameliorating racial discrimination against Indian people and maintaining a distinct Indian identity (with its attendant legal, moral, and political claims), Indians were complicit in the segregation and oppression of blacks.[17] Consequently, antiblack racism seeped deeper still into the construction of Indian identity.

The Clifton-Choctaws followed this pattern, establishing a community elementary school for themselves in the late 1910s. By the early 1920s, the Rapides Parish school district had begun to pay for a teacher for the school rather than having community members fill that role themselves. The Parish designated the school as white, and the teacher assigned to the school was always white, but the Clifton-Choctaws were not allowed to attend white high schools in nearby Boyce or Simpson after they had completed all eight grades available at the community school. They refused to attend "colored" schools, and when the community school was closed in 1971, they were bussed to white schools in Alexandria (despite the 1954 ruling in *Brown v. Board of Education*, Alexandria schools did not officially desegregate until 1973).[18] The Clifton-Choctaws, like other Southern Indians, continue to grapple with the legacy of this history today.

More recently, federal Indian policy that determines whether previously nonfederal tribes should qualify for federal recognition has been a clearer venue for the regulation of the boundaries of Indian identity, and by extension in this case, black, white, and Creole of Color identities as well. Created in 1978, federal recognition criteria demand that nonfederal tribes establish their continuing existence as a tribe with clear social and political bounds from historical times to the present in order to be acknowledged or recognized as a sovereign indigenous nation with all the political and financial commitments that entails.[19] The criteria seem reasonable at first glance, but significant problems have emerged in their implementation. Specifically, for the purposes of this discussion, blackness and its absence come into the federal recognition discussion in several ways. The first is the significance of previous recognition from governments, surrounding communities, and social scientists, each of which helps establish tribal persistence under federal regulations.[20] Because of Anglo-American conceptions of race and the one drop rule, anyone with visible or known African ancestry ("one drop" of African "blood") was considered black or colored for most purposes. An Indian community with even a small degree of black ancestry, then, is much less likely historically to have been acknowledged as an Indian community by governments, social scientists, or surrounding populations than a community with even greater degrees of white ancestry, making it much more difficult for the former to establish present claims.[21]

A look at the census provides a good example of this bias in historical records. The 1910 census for Rapides Parish, for example, lists many of the families in the Clifton community as "mulattos,"[22] and the special "Indian Schedule" for Rapides Parish in 1910 lists none of the seven family surnames represented in the Clifton community in recent years despite the fact that at least one of the Clifton-Choctaw ancestors had contacted an Alexandria attorney in 1898 in an apparent attempt to secure an allotment of land in the Choctaw Nation.[23] The census enumerators in 1910 were instructed to use the Indian Schedules "principally for the enumeration of Indians living on reservations or in tribal relations, and also by the enumerators in certain counties containing a considerable number of Indians."[24] They were given further instructions on deciding how to group mixed communities. "Detached Indians living either in white or negro families outside of reservations should be enumerated on the general population schedule as members of the families in which they are found; but detached whites or negroes living in Indian families should be enumerated on this special Indian schedule as members of the Indian families in which they are found. In other words, every family composed mainly of Indians should be reported entirely on this special schedule, and every family composed mainly of persons not Indians should be reported entirely on the general population schedule."[25]

This presents a problem for the Clifton community. People of mixed black, white, and Indian ancestry were classified as mulattos by the census undifferentiated from people of solely white and black ancestry. The surrounding population did acknowledge Indian ancestry in the Clifton community when they called them Redbones, a derogatory term that connotes Indian, black, and white ancestry, but the official census record did not have a category to reflect that distinction, which would allow people to conclude that the record stated they were solely black and white instead of Indian.[26]

The census enumerator's decision also reflected the broader American understanding that the presence or absence of Indian ancestry did not usually alter a designation as *mulatto*, a term that could mean any mix of black and nonblack ancestry in the United States. The presence of African ancestry among any of the Clifton families may very well have closed the enumerator's eyes to the possibility that this might be an Indian community as much as anything else, particularly if any links to the Cane River Creoles were known to the enumerator.[27] Moreover, Jack Forbes's research into Virginia census records at the very least suggests that we need to use caution in assigning *any* African ancestry to people listed in historical records as mulatto. Certainly people of visible African ancestry were classified as such, but so were people of undetermined racial ancestry. A designation as mulatto is not in itself confirmation of African ancestry and certainly is not confirmation of a lack of Indian ancestry.[28] The only strong conclusion that we can draw is that the enumerators believed that the people they listed as mulatto should not be considered white.

Similarly, in terms of previous federal acknowledgment of Indian communities, the Bureau of Indian Affairs of the 1930s was extremely disinclined to serve communities with black ancestry because of the one-drop rule. Considering that previous acknowledgment from the federal government is the gold standard and is supposed to establish tribal existence at every point prior (unlike acknowledgment from social scientists or surrounding communities), African ancestry becomes a considerable barrier to recognition. Bureau officials expressed concern in 1934, for example, that they might be called on to serve Louisiana Indians who were "mixed with negroes" like other "so-called Indians in Louisiana particularly in Terrebonne Parish [in reference to the Houma tribe], such people being of various racial mixtures."[29] Bureau records indicate that black ancestry among *some* members of *some* Louisiana Indian groups made officials less inclined to serve *any* of the Louisiana tribes, but they did briefly serve those who could demonstrate that they had not mixed with blacks, such as the Jena Choctaws and the Coushattas. Thus, tribes with African ancestry or intermarriage are clearly at a disadvantage in this aspect when petitioning for federal recognition, as well.

Perhaps the most difficult rejection to deal with comes from other Indians. While several Tunica-Biloxi tribal leaders have expressed support for Clifton-Choctaw tribal status, including longtime tribal chairman Earl Barbry Sr., some of the neighboring and now federally recognized Jena Choctaws have been fairly critical of the Clifton-Choctaws' claims to tribal status. Individuals within the Jena Band respond to the Clifton-Choctaws in different ways, though, so any impression that they uniformly reject Clifton-Choctaws because of African ancestry in the community would flatten and compress the range of opinions other Indian people have about Clifton.

Tribal Chief Cheryl Smith and former chief Christine Norris have argued that there certainly are Indian individuals in the Clifton-Choctaw community but that the presence of Indian ancestry in some of the members does not make them a tribe. Smith noted after attending a Louisiana Inter-Tribal Council–sponsored festival in Clifton in the late 1990s that "one of the new leaders or council members or something, he looked just like a perfect old Choctaw Indian man would look like, you know just Indian. I mean, he's *Indian*." She feels the same way about other state-recognized tribes, acknowledging that some members clearly have Indian ancestry but withholding support for their federal recognition. If the community as a whole could demonstrate more social, cultural, and—frankly—racial markers of Indian identity, they would seem more like a cohesive Indian community to her, one that could be classified as a tribe.

A Jena Choctaw elder who is now deceased, Mary Jackson Jones, added that it is unfair to withhold recognition from the "real" Indians at places like Clifton and Houma, but by the same token, it would be unfair to recognize non-Indians with them. Her definition of what constitutes a "real" Indian was not terribly complex—she believed anyone with any Indian ancestors, no matter how remote, could be a "real" Indian. Any relation is real, she said, and that ancestry cannot be cut off or erased. While she was a "full blood," her own tribe's minimum blood quantum was one-eighth at the time of the interview, and she correctly predicted that it would drop lower still since most of the young people were marrying whites at the time. The Clifton-Choctaws may meet her standards for being Indian, at least, and perhaps for tribal recognition if they can document that they all have at least one Indian ancestor.

Former Jena Choctaw chief Jerry Jackson, also deceased, believed that the Clifton-Choctaws had no Indian ancestry at all, and that they should have had their state recognition revoked. His opinion relied on—and contributed to—a genealogical argument that erupted in 1988 between the Clifton-Choctaws and Sharon Brown, a specialist in Indian genealogy who worked for both Jena and Clifton. Brown concluded after researching Clifton genealogy for six months that they were not Indians but were "really" blacks with just some Indian ancestry. Apparently after an argument with the spouse of the Clifton tribal chair in 1988, Brown went to the newspapers with her "revelation," leading to articles that publicly declared them as non-Indian poseurs.[30] Jena Choctaw chief Cheryl Smith described the articles as "horrible." The articles were supposed to say that the Clifton-Choctaws were primarily mixed black and white with only a little Indian ancestry, but that ended up being distorted to say that they were not Indian at all, she contends.

During another formal interview with Theresa Clifton Sarpy, I asked her about accusations made in those articles that the Cliftons were "really" black and not Indian at all. She bristled.

> Sharon Brown came up with that, who also worked for the tribe. As a matter of fact, she's the one that started training me to do genealogy. And she and [a former recognition coordinator] got in it about something, I don't really know. And next thing we knew, she did have two articles in the paper about it.... I would put it this way. We have documented our Indian ancestry. Now, whether—and I'm not going to say there's no black blood in the tribe, because quite a few people in the community are triracial. But the majority are—I mean, it all goes back to Native Americans. We have been able to document that. And I really don't think there's a tribe in Louisiana that can say that they did not have maybe a drop of black blood or Caucasian or anything else within them.

Members of the Clifton-Choctaw community who appear to have black ancestry, people such as Sarpy, bear a unique burden in being discriminated against within the tribe and within their families. Doubts about tribal authenticity that are linked to accusations of blackness are placed on their shoulders—or more accurately, on their faces. I contend that it would help their recognition case if they dealt with African ancestry directly; skirting around it or distancing themselves from it, as in the days of de jure educational segregation, gives the impression that they are trying to hide the truth, which is never productive in a legal proceeding such as the acknowledgment process. It would also help ease their sense of shame over the issue and take some of the burden off of phenotypically black tribal members.

But this situation brings up an ethical and scholarly dilemma: how do I push Clifton-Choctaws to embrace or at least acknowledge African ancestry in their community when there is a strong sentiment in the community to deny it altogether? What is my responsibility as a Louisiana Choctaw researcher to this other Louisiana Choctaw community of which I am not a member but with whom I share a common Choctaw heritage? How do I implement the supportive, collaborative model of indigenous methodologies without undermining my personal responsibilities as an activist? If the

Clifton-Choctaws know that talking about African ancestry in the community has caused them problems in the past, I am putting myself in a position of betraying their trust and saying that I know better than they do about how and when to talk about these things.

Robert Warrior's discussion of American Indian intellectual activism has been instructive in this regard. In his essay in *American Indian Literary Nationalism*, he develops further his arguments from earlier work in which he suggests that intellectual interrogation of our most pressing social and political problems is a vital contribution to the full realization of tribal sovereignty. Rather than giving in to every whim of tribal councils, he says, "When researchers cede control or are expected to cede control of the conclusions they draw in their work, I can't imagine what good end is being served. Clearly, indigenous people have suffered at the hands of unscrupulous, biased research for generations, but I would suggest that those same people stand to suffer nearly as much or more from scholarly work that, by fiat, reflects the prescribed points of view of appointed research police."[31] Thus, in service to a conception of indigenous sovereignty that embraces and relies on dissent in support of tribal vitality, we have to move forward with these uncomfortable conversations.

In *Ties That Bind: The Story of an Afro-Cherokee Family in Slavery and Freedom*, Tiya Miles notes that various individuals, black and Indian, discouraged her from discussing the history of Cherokee slaveholding, of Cherokees as colonized and colonizing subjects. The desire to "disremember" these painful shared histories among communities of color is entangled with contemporary desires and anxieties about imagined histories of "natural affinity" or "natural animosity" among communities of color, the ways we construct race and righteousness, and the ways we draw connections or construct boundaries. But there is a story to tell, even if it is "not a story to pass on," not a story anyone wants to remember or address publicly.[32] However, as Miles wrote, drawing on the theoretical underpinnings of Toni Morrison's *Beloved*, "the void that remains when we refuse to speak of the past is in fact a presence, a presence both haunting and destructive."[33] When we examine these histories alongside contemporary realities, we gain knowledge and discover ways to work through theoretical and emotional conflicts. We need healing and redemption around this issue. And we need decolonization.

One of the foundational racializations of Indians (of all indigenous peoples, really) suggests that tribes are tradition bound and that any deviation from tradition means that a tribe is somehow less Indian. Called a *declension model*, a reference to the idea that any cultural *change* is equivalent to cultural *decline*, this idea keeps Indians locked in a "conceptual prison."[34] But in reality, all people—including Indian people—are dynamic, and we have the power to change and adapt our strategies as new information comes to light. The ability to choose whether to change, when to change, and how to change is, in fact, the essence of sovereignty. When we understand that the ideology of white supremacy performs multiple tasks, diverting multiple resources away from oppressed groups and toward whites through multiple kinds of behavior, we can see more clearly that antiblack racism, even when performed by Indians, confirms a racial formation that places whites at the top of a racial hierarchy.[35] Such an ideology hardly seems to be in the best interests of Indians.

Rather than pathologizing Indians, though, we need to recognize the source of Indian antiblack racism within a broader colonial project and acknowledge its hidden effect not only on Indian resources but also on Indian senses of self. As the root of both colonialism and racism, white supremacist racial formations undermine Indian well-being through a number of practices that funnel land, resources, culture, and sovereignty away from indigenous peoples.[36] But without a broader understanding of how racism and colonialism work together, we do not always see how white supremacy twists through all of our communities.

Alternative Futures, Alternative Sovereignties

Choctaw cultural anthropologist Valerie Lambert, who previously worked for the Office of Federal Acknowledgment, puzzles a bit over the "widespread fetishization" of federal acknowledgment in the late twentieth century, because growing up in the Choctaw Nation, she writes, "it was often taken for granted by those around me that the United States did not respect tribal sovereignty."[37] While federal recognition of tribal sovereignty is extremely valuable in some ways, it also undermines tribal sovereignty before a tribe even enters the acknowledgment process by powerfully limiting their vision of what an Indian or a tribe can be. That is to say, the existence of the acknowledgment process—and of the divide it indicates between formally acknowledged and formally unacknowledged tribes—challenges the rights of tribes to be who they are without apology. Many tribes and individual Indians *already* think about how well they fit into a variety of conceptions of authenticity on a regular basis. What does it mean if I speak or do not speak my tribe's language or if my tribe no longer speaks its language? How will my claims to be an Indian be received if I tell people I am enrolled or not enrolled? Will I be perceived as a struggler, as worthy or unworthy of a place at the table because I am an Indian?[38] When tribes try to fit themselves into the mold the Bureau of Indian Affairs (BIA) has set for tribal recognition policy, they face even greater scrutiny and doubt than tribes usually endure, and it is absolutely critical at that juncture to see the ways that conceptions of race—not just of Indianness and whiteness but also of blackness—factor into the calculus of tribal identity and belonging.

Chickasaw/Choctaw cultural anthropologist Shannon Speed suggests that Zapatistas in Mexico have learned, after failing to achieve protection of indigenous rights in Chiapas from the Mexican government, that "rights exist in their exercise, not their establishment in the legal regimes of the state."[39] Following this logic, tribes should be careful not to surrender their sovereignty in the process of trying to have their sovereignty validated by the federal government, whether through federal acknowledgment procedures, court cases, or other legalistic pursuits. An activist vision of indigenous sovereignty has to include a sense that the very position of indigeneity is harnessed to resist encroachment by an outside imperial or colonial force (otherwise, why invoke the term *indigenous* at all?). As such, tribes need to resist the racial hierarchies that undergird colonialism in every instance, and antiblack racism is clearly one of the foundational tenets of that system.

When the Clifton-Choctaws began organizing for federal recognition in the mid-1970s, it was at the urging of Joe Pierite Sr., the last traditional chief of the Tunica tribe, who had met a Clifton elder by chance in an Alexandria hospital. At the time, the Tunicas did not allow anyone with African American ancestry on their tribal rolls. They had even banished from the reservation tribal members who married African Americans, but that rule had been loosened in recent years. In fact, Herman Pierite, a full brother of the last tribal chief, was able to serve on the newly organized tribal council in the late 1970s despite having an African American wife. At the time, however, his children and grandchildren were still not allowed on the tribal rolls because they were also African American. The tribe was in the middle of the process of petitioning for federal recognition, and the non–African American tribal members felt it would be best for their case if they had only "Indian-looking" Indians on the rolls—those of one quarter Indian ancestry or more and with no African American ancestry—because that was what they thought the BIA would accept most easily. Before he died, Herman Pierite secured a promise from Earl Barbry Sr., a young tribal member who had recently been elected to his first of many terms as tribal chairman, to enroll his children and grandchildren once the tribe had secured federal recognition. Barbry followed through with his promise after the Tunica-Biloxi tribe was recognized in 1981, and the tribe no longer makes any official distinction between those with and those without African American ancestry.

Marshall Sampson, a grandson of Herman Pierite and a member of the Tunica-Biloxi tribal council since 1997, recalls that only a few non–African American tribal members would even visit with his family in his youth in the 1970s. While he acknowledges that some antiblack racism remains in the tribe, he offers the repeated elections of several of Herman Pierite's descendants to the tribal council as evidence of racism's declining prevalence there. "You have people that made some bad decisions," he says, "but it doesn't mean that we have to continue making bad decisions or that we have to make the same decisions that they made."

Antiblack racism in Indian communities is hardly uniform, but it is a significant presence that affects the ways people think of themselves and others, whether they are aware of it or not. While the inherent challenges of the federal acknowledgment process put pressure on communities like the Clifton-Choctaws to distance themselves from individuals and communities with African ancestry, a different future can take shape. White supremacist racial projects divide Indian tribes from other communities of color, from other tribes, and even from other members of our own tribes. But a more equitable future—one paralleling developments among the Tunica-Biloxi tribe—can emerge as we interrogate our past, sort out our present, and strive toward a future where the idea of sovereignty can be harnessed to free us all from both colonialism and racism. Imagine that.

Notes

1. On Chippewa spearfishing rights, see the remarkable documentary *Lighting the 7th Fire*, directed by Sandra Sunrising Osawa (Seattle: Upstream Productions, 1994).
2. For an excellent example of scholarship using a settler colonial frame to understand race outside of the indigenous-settler relations, see Juliana Hu Pegues, "Interrogating Intimacies: Asian American and Native Relations in Colonial Alaska" (PhD diss., University of Minnesota, 2014). Patrick Wolfe's formulation of settler colonialism as a persistent structure remains central to much of the emerging work; Patrick Wolfe, *Settler Colonialism and the Transformation of Anthropology: The Politics and Poetics of an Ethnographic Event* (London: Bloomsbury Academic, 1998).
3. See Neil Foley, "Becoming Hispanic: Mexican-Americans and Whiteness," in *White Privilege: Essential Reading on the Other Side of Racism*, ed. Paula S. Rothenberg (New York: Worth, 2002), 49–59.
4. See Haunani-Kay Trask, "Settlers of Color and 'Immigrant' Hegemony: 'Locals' in Hawai'i," *Amerasia Journal* 26, no. 2 (2000): 1–24.
5. James H. Merrell, "The Racial Education of the Catawba Indians," *Journal of Southern History* 50, no. 3 (August 1984): 374.
6. Arica L. Coleman, "'Tell the Court I Love My [Indian] Wife': Interrogating Race and Self-Identity in *Loving v. Virginia*," *Souls* 8, no. 1 (2006): 75. She expands this discussion in *That the Blood Stay Pure: African Americans, Native Americans, and the Predicament of Race and Identity in Virginia* (Bloomington: Indiana University Press, 2013).
7. Any Indian person there with more than one-quarter African "blood" (later one-sixteenth) would be classified as "colored" and thus have access to fewer rights and resources than those classified as Indians, who were those of more

than one-quarter Indian blood (later one-sixteenth). Helen C. Rountree, *Pocahontas's People: The Powhatan Indians of Virginia Through Four Centuries* (Norman: University of Oklahoma Press, 1990), 200, 211.

8. Bobby Thompson and John H. Peterson Jr., "Mississippi Choctaw Identity: Genesis and Change," in *The New Ethnicity: Perspectives From Ethnology*, ed. John W. Bennett (St. Paul: West, 1975), 180.

9. Karen Blu, *The Lumbee Problem: The Making of an American Indian People* (Cambridge: Cambridge University Press, 1980, repr. Lincoln: University of Nebraska Press, 2001), 62–65. Generally, see Malinda Maynor Lowery, *Lumbee Indians in the Jim Crow South: Race, Identity, and the Making of a Nation* (Chapel Hill: University of North Carolina Press, 2010).

10. On Cherokees, see Circe Sturm, "Blood Politics, Racial Classification, and Cherokee National Identity: The Trials and Tribulations of the Cherokee Freedmen," *American Indian Quarterly* 22, no. 1/2 (Winter/Spring 1998): 230–258, and Tiya Miles, *The Ties That Bind: The Story of an Afro-Cherokee Family in Slavery and Freedom* (Berkeley: University of California Press, 2004). On Creeks, see Claudio Saunt, *Black, White, and Indian: Race and the Unmaking of an American Family* (Oxford: Oxford University Press, 2005). On Seminoles, see Kevin Mulroy, *The Seminole Freedmen: A History* (Norman: University of Oklahoma, 2007). On Choctaws and Chickasaws, see Barbara Krauthamer, *Black Slaves, Indian Masters: Slavery Emancipation, and Citizenship in the Native American South* (Chapel Hill: University of North Carolina Press, 2013). Generally, see Tiya Miles and Sharon P. Holland, eds., *Crossing Waters, Crossing Worlds: The African Diaspora in Indian Country* (Durham, NC: Duke University Press, 2006); James F. Brooks, ed., *Confounding the Color Line: The Indian-Black Experience in North America* (Lincoln: University of Nebraska Press, 2002).

11. A close reading of this statement would note her use of the word *they* to refer to the Clifton community when it would seem more appropriate for her to use the word *we*. This seems like evidence of discomfort in including herself in that opinion by saying "we trust Whites more than we trust Blacks." But it also seems to be a long-standing reflex to distance the community "on the whole" from blacks and blackness even while she is unwilling to ally herself with such thinking.

12. Gary B. Mills, *The Forgotten People: Cane River's Creoles of Color* (Baton Rouge: Louisiana State University Press, 1977), xiv. Lalita Tademy, a Cane River Creole

herself, wrote a best-selling novel and Oprah's Book Club selection about her people, giving perhaps the most visible moment in recent Cane River history; Lalita Tademy, *Cane River: A Novel* (New York: Warner, 2002).

13. While in its common use outside the academy the term *white supremacy* conjures images of Klan robes and neo-Nazi skinheads, the term as it is used in contemporary ethnic studies also refers to the everyday ideology of white racial superiority and domination carried even by people who do not consider themselves racist and even by people of color. For a general discussion of white supremacist ideology and material advantages in the United States, see P. S. Rothenberg, ed., *White Privilege: Essential Readings on the Other Side of Racism* (New York: Worth, 2002), and George Lipsitz, *The Possessive Investment in Whiteness: How White People Profit from Identity Politics* (Philadelphia: Temple University Press, 1998; rev. ed., 2006).

14. Saunt, *Black, White, and Indian*; *A New Order of Things: Property, Power, and the Transformation of the Creek Indians, 1733–1816* (Cambridge: Cambridge University Press, 1999); Miles, *Ties That Bind*; *The House on Diamond Hill: A Cherokee Plantation Story* (Chapel Hill, NC: University of North Carolina Press, 2010); Theda Perdue, *Slavery and the Evolution of Cherokee Society, 1540–1866* (Knoxville: University of Tennessee Press, 1979); *Cherokee Women: Gender and Culture Change, 1700–1835* (Lincoln: University of Nebraska Press, 1999); and Daniel F. Littlefield, *Africans and Seminoles: From Removal to Emancipation* (Westport, CT: Greenwood Press, 1977).

15. Saunt, *Black, White, and Indian*, 4.

16. Patricia Hill Collins, building on the work of bell hooks, calls this set of dualities "dichotomous oppositional differences" and notes that they structure many kinds of dominating relationships: race, class, gender, sexuality, and even reason over emotion; Patricia Hill Collins, "Learning from the Outsider Within: The Sociological Significance of Black Feminist Thought," special issue, *Social Problems* 33, no. 6 (December 1986): S20. I develop the concept of shadow stereotypes in Brian Klopotek, *Recognition Odysseys: Indigeneity, Race, and Federal Tribal Recognition Policy in Three Louisiana Indian Communities* (Durham, NC: Duke University Press, 2011), 268.

17. Neil Foley draws heavily on Toni Morrison's ideas about southern European immigrants becoming white in the United States by demonstrating their hatred of blacks as he grapples with similar racial formation issues in Mexican Ameri-

can integration activism in Texas in the 1930s. Neil Foley, "Becoming Hispanic: Mexican Americans and Whiteness," in Rothenberg, *White Privilege*, 49–59.

18. For more in depth discussion of this history, see Klopotek, *Recognition Odysseys*, 216–19.

19. Office of Federal Acknowledgment, United States Bureau of Indian Affairs, "Procedures for Establishing That an American Indian Group Exists As a Tribe," Fed. Reg. 3934 (February 25, 1994). 25 C.F.R. §83, previously 25 C.F.R. Part 54.7(e)(4), Fed. Reg. 39363 (September 5, 1978). The most recent revisions to acknowledgment procedures attempt to reduce reliance on outsider assessments of tribes but still require contemporaneous historical evidence of internal self-identification as Indians in the petitioning process. Department of the Interior, Bureau of Indian Affairs, "Federal Acknowledgment of American Indian Tribes," Fed. Reg. 37862 (July 1, 2015), https://www.gpo.gov/fdsys/pkg/FR-2015-07-01/pdf/2015-16193.pdf.

20. Susan Greenbaum adeptly and precisely addresses this matter, though others have addressed it elsewhere. Susan Greenbaum, "What's in a Label? Identity Problems of Southern Indian Tribes," *Journal of Ethnic Studies* 19, no. 2 (Summer 1991): 107–26; Rachael Paschal, "The Imprimatur of Recognition: American Indian Tribes and the Federal Acknowledgment Process," *Washington Law Review* 66 (1991): 209–28; William Starna, "'We'll All Be Together Again': The Federal Acknowledgment of the Wampanoag Tribe of Gay Head," *Northeast Anthropology* 51 (1996): 3–12; Jack Campisi, *The Mashpee Indians: Tribe on Trial* (Syracuse, NY: Syracuse University Press, 1991); James Clifford, "Identity in Mashpee," in *The Predicament of Culture: Twentieth-Century Ethnography, Literature, and Art* (Cambridge, MA: Harvard University Press, 1988), 277–346. A number of significant contributions can be found in Miles and Holland, *Crossing Waters, Crossing Worlds*, and Brooks, *Confounding the Color Line*.

21. Circe Sturm discusses this issue in the Cherokee Nation of Oklahoma; Sturm, "Blood Politics."

22. 1910 Census, Rapides Parish, Louisiana, lists many Clifton, Tyler, and Smith families as mulatto. This is clearly not a complete and diagnostic genealogical connection, but it is obvious that these are the ancestors of at least some of the modern Clifton families.

23. James Andrews to Paul Thomas, February 11, 1898, original in possession of Norris Tyler, Clifton-Choctaw tribe.

24. U.S. Census Bureau, *Measuring America: The Decennial Censuses from 1790 to 2000* (Washington, DC: U.S. Department of Commerce, Economics and Statistics Administration and U.S. Census Bureau, 2002), 55.
25. Ibid., 56.
26. See also W. L. Williams, "Patterns in the History of the Remaining Southeastern Indians, 1840–1975," in *Southeastern Indians Since the Removal Era*, ed. Walter L. Williams (Athens: University of Georgia, 1979), 193–210.
27. U.S. Census Bureau, *Measuring America*, 56. "Proportions of Indian and other blood. —If the Indian is a full-blood, write 'full' in column 36, and leave columns 37 and 38 blank. If the Indian is of mixed blood, write in column 36, 37, and 38 the fractions which show the proportions of Indian and other blood, as (column 36, Indian) 3/4, (column 37, white) 1/4, and (column 38, negro) 0. For Indians of mixed blood all three columns should be filled, and the sum, in each case, should equal 1, as 1/2, 0, 1/2; 3/4, 1/4, 0; 3/4, 1/8, 1/8; etc. Wherever possible, the statement that an Indian is of full blood should be verified by inquiry of the older men of the tribe, as an Indian is sometimes of mixed blood without knowing it."
28. Jack Forbes, *Africans and Native Americans: The Language of Race and the Evolution of Red-Black Peoples*, 2nd ed. (Urbana: University of Illinois Press, 1993).
29. A. C. Hector to W. Carson Ryan Jr., September 12, 1934, File 68776-1931-800, Part I, National Archives Record Group 75.
30. Kathy Calongne, "Genealogist Says Clifton-Choctaws Are Not Indians," *Alexandria Daily Town Talk* (Alexandria, LA), August 7, 1988, A1-2; "Jena Tribe: Cliftons Should Prove Ancestry to Get Grant," same issue, A2. "La. Tribe Fights to Prove Its Heritage," *Times-Picayune*, August 14, 1988, C8.
31. Robert Warrior, "Native Critics in the World: Edward Said and Nationalism," in *American Indian Literary Nationalism*, Jace Weaver, Craig S. Womack, and Robert Warrior (Albuquerque: University of New Mexico Press, 2006), 214.
32. Miles, *Ties That Bind*, xv, citing Toni Morrison, *Beloved* (New York: Plume, 1987; repr. 1988), 274–75.
33. Miles, *Ties That Bind*, xvi. Miles and many others witnessed the calamity and pain of this ghostly presence at a conference she organized on black-Indian relations at Dartmouth in 1998 called "'Eating Out of the Same Pot': Relating Black and Native (Hi)stories." Several pieces have been written about the dramatic conflicts that surfaced throughout: Valerie J. Phillips, "Epilogue: Seeing

Each Other Through the White Man's Eyes," in Brooks, *Confounding the Color Line*, 371–85; Saunt, *Black, White, and Indian*, 6–9; Tiya Miles, "Preface: Eating Out of the Same Pot?," in Miles and Holland, *Crossing Waters, Crossing Worlds*, xv–xviii; Robert Warrior, "Afterword," in Miles and Holland, *Crossing Waters, Crossing Worlds*, 321–25.

34. Vine Deloria Jr., *Custer Died for Your Sins: An Indian Manifesto* (New York: Macmillan, 1969; repr. with new preface, Norman: University of Oklahoma Press, 1988), chap. 4; Paige Raibmon, *Authentic Indians: Episodes of Encounter from the Late Nineteenth-Century Northwest Coast* (Durham, NC: Duke University Press, 2005).

35. George Lipsitz suggests the value of this formulation in his work; George Lipsitz, *American Studies in a Moment of Danger* (Minneapolis: University of Minnesota Press, 1998), 138.

36. Following Omi and Winant's definition of racial formation as "the sociohistorical process by which racial categories are created, inhabited, transformed, and destroyed," and a racial project as "simultaneously an interpretation, representation, or explanation of racial dynamics, and an effort to reorganize and redistribute resources along particular racial lines." Michael Omi and Howard Winant, *Racial Formation in the United States from the 1960s to the 1990s*, 2nd ed. (New York: Routledge, 1994), 55–56.

37. Valerie Lambert, "Choctaw Tribal Sovereignty at the Turn of the 21st Century," in *Indigenous Experience Today*, ed. Marisol de la Cadena and Orin Starn (New York: Berg, 2007), 154–55.

38. For an excellent examination of the psychology of belonging and authenticity among Gros Ventres and other Indians, see Joseph P. Gone, "Mental Health, Wellness, and the Quest for an Authentic American Indian Identity," in *Mental Health Care for Urban Indians: Clinical Insights from Native Practitioners*, ed. Tawa Witko (Washington, DC: American Psychology Association, 2006).

39. Shannon Speed, *Rights in Rebellion: Indigenous Struggle and Human Rights in Chiapas* (Palo Alto, CA: Stanford University Press, 2008), 37.

9

The Look of Sovereignty

Style and Politics in the Young Lords

FRANCES NEGRÓN-MUNTANER

The day was October 18, 1970, and a young man by the name of Pablo "Yoruba" Guzmán was doing all the talking. Armed with an Afro, U.S. military fatigues, and Cuban shades, Guzmán—the Minister of Information for a radical group called the Young Lords—was demanding that any police officer who came into the East Harlem Methodist Church step aside. The Young Lords had occupied the church after a funeral march to protest the suspected murder of one of their members, Julio Roldán. To make sure that firearms would not be planted on the premises, Guzmán styled his actions with great care: dressed as a commander himself, he body searched the captain in charge of the operation, forcing him "to assume the position spread."[1] The order produced the desired results. Not only did the police fail to find any weapons, the very next morning one New York newspaper headline read "Policemen Frisked by the Young Lords."[2]

The Lords' road to citywide recognition had been both long and short. Launched on July 26, 1969, the New York Lords were initially a branch of the Young Lords Organization of Chicago, a street gang turned political group led by José "Cha Cha" Jiménez. In existence since 1959, the group's primary goals were to defend Puerto Rican neighborhoods and demand respect from rival Italian, Appalachian, and Latino gangs.[3] The Chicago Lords, however, underwent a process of radicalization after Jiménez received a sixty-day sentence on a drug possession charge over the summer of 1968. While in prison, Jiménez read works by Thomas Merton, Martin Luther King Jr., and Malcolm X. He also became familiar with the thought of Puerto Rican nationalist leader Pedro Albizu Campos and the Black Panthers' concept of self-defense.[4]

Perhaps as a sort of poetic justice, the founding Lords, who had initially carved a name for themselves as a turf gang, invested much of their political capital in fighting gentrification in Chicago's Puerto Rican communities. Yet from the outset, the New York Lords were different.[5] For one, many had little association with street gangs.[6] In fact, a number of the Lords' core leadership had some college education and had belonged to traditional left groups before joining the organization. Furthermore, if the Chicago Lords had tense relations with the media and in the eyes of the public never quite shed their gang origins, the New York Lords were another story. In the words of former Lord Miguel "Mickey" Meléndez, "We had different working methods [from Chicago] and the New York media at our disposal."[7] The groups' divergence eventually became official when, in May 1970, the New York group broke off from the Young Lords Organization of Chicago to become the Young Lords Party.

To this day, scholars debate how and to what extent the New York Lords changed public institutions in the city or achieved revolutionary goals. Often overlooked, however, are the ways in which the Young Lords significantly disrupted a symbolic economy founded on the stigmatization of Puerto Ricans as criminally prone if politically docile and in the process transformed not only how the world saw Puerto Ricans but also how they saw themselves. Equally critical, they equipped an already upwardly mobile sector of the community to fully participate in New York's political and cultural spheres. In more ways than one, the Lords' afterlife has shown—and this is an important choice of words—that Puerto Ricans could "make it" at the same level as New York's other historic ethnic minorities, particularly European Jews and Italians. In Guzmán's terms, "The concept of winning, right, that is the number one contribution of the Young Lords Party—that is what we are, man, the concept of winning."[8]

But how did the Young Lords' leadership turn what one former Chicago Lord called a "ragtag army" into a winning (political) party? After all, they identified and were identified with one of the most politically disempowered communities in New York. In addition, their core leadership comprised five to ten people who could typically mobilize only a few hundred members to demonstrations even if they claimed a membership of a thousand.[9] Just as significant, the organization's median age was close to eighteen, with some prominent members, such as deputy minister of finance Juan "Fi" Ortiz being as young as fifteen.

Historian Mervin Mendez regarded the Young Lords' youth as one of the reasons for their success. "The eyes of children are not hypocritical," Mendez remarked in an interview. "They're very honest, deadly honest."[10] While many, including the Young Lords, saw their youth as more of a political liability, I concur with Mendez on one thing: looking and being looked at are at the center of the New York Lords' story. A major part of the Young Lords' achievements relied on what could be called the "look of sovereignty"—that is, a way to style, display, and move the body to denote that a political actor is willing and able to exercise self-governance and full citizen rights at any time he or she determines. This look was likewise a part of an evolving visual vocabulary that could be recognized by the state, mainstream media, and radical groups in and outside the city.

At another level, the Lords' successful deployment of style underscores that although the concept of sovereignty is commonly understood in relation to the prerogative of states to control national territory, it is not solely a matter of law; sovereignty is also a performative and aesthetic act. As Michel Foucault, one of the few theorists to consider the close relationship between style and sovereignty, observed, "If I want people to accept me as king, I must have the kind of glory which will survive me, and this glory cannot be disassociated from aesthetic value."[11] The Lords' stylized performance further implies that given how the identity of racialized and colonized groups is routinely shamed by dominant cultural discourses, their political mobilization often requires the act of refashioning or restyling the public self. For style, as scholar Jesús D. Rodríguez Velasco has argued, is intimately linked to how citizens "express their will to form an active part of . . . sovereign power."[12]

That the Young Lords fully understood the importance of style to politics makes their trajectory a rich archive to inquire into the effects and limits of both practices. An engagement with Lords style also partly explains why they remain the most widely recognized of New York Latino radical organizations of the late 1960s and early 1970s. Whereas other contemporary groups, such as the Real Great Society (RGS), were similarly pivotal and generative—it was RGS, after all, that incubated the Young Lords in their East Harlem offices—the Lords and their iconography have come to signify radical politics itself for subsequent generations of activists.[13] Additionally, the Young Lords' sartorial history accentuated that style is not an afterthought to political action but rather a practice that materializes at the exact moment when dissent is articulated and a new political body brought forth. Or as Guadeloupian writer Maryse Condé once put it, "The revolution starts with new clothes."[14]

Change of Clothes

The struggle to refashion Puerto Ricans in New York did not, of course, begin with the Young Lords. New York Puerto Ricans have historically been aware of their low status in the city's symbolic and political economies and have pursued ways to redress it. During the post–World War II period, for instance, many young men tried to valorize themselves by belonging to gangs and styling themselves accordingly. In the words of former Young Lord chairman Felipe Luciano, "My first models of resistance were Puerto Rican men. I saw Puerto Rican men stand up to the Italian gangs, oblivious to the fact that these guys might put a hit on them. I saw them stand up . . . in T-shirts, with pegged pants and curly hair coming down their foreheads."[15] Those who played the politics of respectability also sought redress by means of style, wearing the standard suit and tie in the hope of gaining access to the U.S. party machineries, the island's Commonwealth's Office in New York, or the War on Poverty programs.[16]

But coming onto the scene at a time of global political radicalization and the expansion of visual media technologies, the Young Lords opted for a different strategy to alter the perception of Puerto Ricans and their conditions. They seized the very site of shame and subordination—the body—and restyled it to maximize its potential as a mobile political sign that staged and anticipated their liberation from colonial, racist, and patriarchal structures of power. In this way, "costume," as Daphne A. Brooks has suggested in another context, was a path for self-transformation and freedom.[17] That the Young Lords specifically focused on the body was not a coincidence. Similar to other groups in the United States and Puerto Rico, the Lords understood that the violence visited on Puerto Ricans through inferior health services, mass sterilization, poor nutrition, substandard housing, and inadequate education was political. Moreover, an emphasis on the body spoke to the colonial stereotype of Puerto Ricans as incapable of sovereign action because of their individual and body politic's presumable weakness. Since the start of U.S. rule in 1898, officials routinely dismissed Puerto Ricans' self-governance claims and demands for political participation by alluding to the community's sickness, ignorance, poverty, and lack of hygiene.

To counter a politico-symbolic economy that barred Puerto Ricans from resources and visualized them as disposable, the Young Lords worked hard to produce a different body for *boricuas*: well fed, well dressed, and well educated as well as drug and lead free. This was a body guided by a new consciousness that could "stand up" to the system and take control of the Puerto Rican nation's destiny by discipline, organization, and coordinated action.[18] By restyling and beefing up the body, the Lords aimed to shed what former Young Lord Mickey Meléndez called the "colonial pathology of docility" and replace it with "an image of Puerto Ricans as tough and inventive defenders of their rights as citizens."[19] In this and other ways, the Young Lords fashioned a public body that moved U.S. Puerto Ricans into political modernity, which, as Wendy Parkins has written, "depends on the concept of an individual who is not subject to the authority of any other except by consent and who is also free to withdraw this consent."[20]

In a broader sense, the Young Lords' desire to improve their political performance is linked to how shame is constitutive of Puerto Rican ethnonational identity in a modern colonial context. As I have argued elsewhere, U.S. colonial discourses have historically imagined Puerto Ricans as black, poor, and lacking national subjects. Not surprisingly, many of their forms of survival, including escape, avoidance, or unarmed resistance, have been considered "queer" in the sense of both odd (nonnormative) and effeminate (weak, cowardly).[21] Given this context, Puerto Ricans' performances as national subjects are often aimed at the American gaze, a "dirty look" that not only deems Puerto Ricans low, criminal, and "other" in relation to first-class, upstanding, normative American subjects but demeans them in the eyes of other groups as well. Insisting on being seen otherwise, the Lords asserted that Puerto Ricans had nothing to be ashamed of; on the contrary, what was shameful was the racist, colonial, and patriarchal gaze.

Equally significant, in contrast to the island Puerto Rican elites who emphasized their racial, class, and gender-normative identities, the Young Lords engaged with, rather than denied, the racialized and queer cast of Puerto Rican identity. On the one hand, they embraced feminism and at times overtly identified with the stigmatized political location of LGBT people, particularly gay men. On the other hand, in a manner different from how mainstream political leaders frequently deployed a national discourse of ambiguity toward U.S. sovereignty, the Young Lords' sovereign acts offered an oppositional (if problematic) masculinist alternative: one that challenged American imperial "muscular" style with the muscle of national liberation aesthetics deployed by African American, Cuban, and Vietnamese revolutionaries.

In sum, to contest multiple sites of symbolic and political dispossession, the Young Lords developed a range of "self-actualizing performance[s]" that were striking in their economy.[22] A group without major financial or institutional support, the Young Lords promoted low-cost imaginative practices such as symbolic disruption, sartorial reinvention, and dramatic storytelling to stage a radical alternative to the status quo. In these ways, the Young Lords built on Felix Padilla's observation that "the only significant resource Puerto Ricans possessed was the capacity to make trouble ... and force authorities to respond."[23] With style and stunts, the Lords set out to conquer New York.

Lords of Style

As the Young Lords themselves have noted, the Black Panthers largely inspired their style. From the party's founding in 1966, Black Panther imagery and gestures such as the raised fist became a widely cited shorthand to signify empowerment and revolution for radicalized minorities. The Black Panthers' strategic use of style and the media's tendency to cover primarily the organization's most spectacular actions often made Panther fashion better known than their platform or programs. Media consumers, for instance, may not have been aware that the Black Panthers wanted a United Nations–sponsored referendum on black self-determination or a general amnesty for all imprisoned black men. But the majority of TV viewers knew what the Panthers looked like: "They were splendidly outfitted . . . black leather jacket, slacks, shoes, and beret . . . turtleneck shirts; dark glasses optional," in the words of historian William L. Van Deburg.[24]

A cross between urban street style, outlaw fashion, and Third World revolutionary aesthetics, the male Panther's look accentuated the wearer's power. This is evident in the use of the black leather jacket, a garment that since its origins in early twentieth-century Germany enclosed a complex history that signified military power, rebellious masculinity, outsider status, and social disaffection.[25] Long firearms, military formation choreography, and the display of "scowling facial expressions" similarly defined the Panther look.[26] Whereas Black Panther women could also be seen carrying guns and wearing black leather jackets, their style was less regulated and habitually regarded by critics as a statement of high fashion instead of political practice. In the notorious terms of "Radical Chic" chronicler Tom Wolfe, Panther women were more inclined to wear "tight pants and Yoruba-style headdresses, almost like turbans, as if they'd stepped out of the pages of Vogue, although no doubt Vogue got it from them."[27]

For the Young Lords, drawing from the Black Panthers was an effective way to make Puerto Ricans visible. Different from African Americans, Puerto Ricans at the time were mostly concentrated in a few neighborhoods in the Northeast, Illinois, and Ohio, and seemed racially ambiguous according to American racial schemes. Fashioning themselves as "a kind of Puerto Rican equivalent to the Black Panthers"[28] allowed the Lords to be readily identified as a desirable ally to other radical groups and as a revolutionary organization that would take the rights of Puerto Ricans by any means necessary. In citing the Black Panthers through the use of berets, leather jackets, and/or Afros, the Lords were engaging in what style theorist Nathan Joseph has called "sartorial metaphor": "borrowing . . . the social characteristics of another—status, relationships, and attribute—by adopting his dress."[29]

Identifying with the Black Panthers was also about challenging racism among Puerto Ricans. If race is nearly always downplayed in Puerto Rican national politics, many Young Lords wore their blackness literally on their sleeve by dressing in African and African American–inspired fashions. This trend was embodied in the style of Young Lords such as Guzmán, who sported a Malcolm X look, Afro, and occasional dashiki. In addition, while the Young Lords remained a Puerto Rican majority organization, black style signaled its openness to accepting all groups within their organization and communicated its desire to work on behalf of the "people" rather than narrowly defined communities. This is evident in that a significant number of Young Lords—from 25 to 30 percent—were not Puerto Ricans, and many were African Americans.[30] Importantly, this practice of inclusion went beyond the rank and file. Some of the top Lords like Guzmán were "halfies" (in his case, of Cuban and Puerto Rican parents), and Denise Oliver, who went on to serve as minister of economic development, was African American.

Simultaneously, the Young Lords knew that to be taken seriously as Latino revolutionaries, they could not be perceived as just an imitation of black groups. At the level of style, the Young Lords addressed this by infusing their Panther-inspired attire with accessories that accentuated Puerto Rican identity. For instance, whereas the Panther beret was black, the Lords' own was purple, a detail that is easy to miss if looking at black-and-white footage or photographs. Purple explicitly referenced the Young Lords' Chicago gang origins since this was their distinct color as a street gang. Moreover, the Lords adopted Chicago's "YLO button," which showed a "fist holding a rifle and a Spanish phrase, 'Tengo Puerto Rico en mi corazón'—'I have Puerto Rico in my heart'—against a silhouette of the island."[31] The beret was arguably the item that most identified the New York Lords: "People knew us by the beret and the buttons that we wore on them," recalls former Lords leader Iris Morales. "If we did not want to be seen or engage as a Young Lord, we would take off our beret."[32]

An equally significant addition was the Puerto Rican flag, a key accessory. During the first half of the twentieth century, the flag emerged as a symbol of defiance to U.S. colonial authority in large part because of its suppression by the local government. Proindependence groups such as the Nationalist Party led by Pedro Albizu Campos often displayed the flag at public events despite its being outlawed (or precisely because it was). Although the Estado Libre Asociado officially adopted the banner in 1952, the fact that it could still not be legally flown "alone"—without the American flag—carried its oppositional meanings well into the 1970s.[33] After Puerto Ricans migrated to the United States and expanded their participation in American institutions, the flag came to signify ethnonational identity in multiple locations, from New York's Puerto Rican Day Parade to war zones in Korea. Whether they intended to call attention to the "national question" and/or underscore their ethnic difference,[34] many Young Lords wore the Puerto Rican flag on their heads, chest, and hands—anywhere that they could hang it.

A good number of Young Lords similarly wore "U.S. Army-issued field jackets, combat fatigues,"[35] and black boots. While wearing U.S. military garments may appear incongruous given the Young Lords' opposition to American colonial policies and foreign interventions, these sartorial choices communicated a range of ideas regarding their aspirations, experience, and form of organization. Army attire, for example, connoted the Young Lords' paramilitary structure, which included a central committee consisting of five people: a chairman and the ministers of information, education, defense, and finance. Fatigues likewise referenced the contradictory experience of Puerto Rican service in the U.S. military and opposition to the Vietnam War. "We had a lot of Vietnam vets and they wore their uniform," adds Morales. "They were proud that they had fought in Vietnam but ambivalent about the fact that they had killed Vietnamese."[36] In wearing the uniform, the Lords aimed to remove the stigma of passivity and weakness and be seen as warriors, an image associated with heroism, strength, and honor in the American popular imagination.

The common use of olive green clothing further emphasized the Young Lords' identification with Third World revolutionary movements and projected their actions as those of revolutionary soldiers against the state and its representatives. This affinity was present from the very beginning, starting with the date chosen by the Young Lords to stage their first public event:

July 26, 1969. The day overtly referenced the Cuban July 26 Movement, which became the military arm of the anti-Batista forces that eventually propelled Fidel Castro to power in 1959. Honoring their key political genealogies—nationalist, black, and Third World—the Young Lords introduced themselves to New York "clad in fatigues resembling the BPP [Black Panther Party] and holding aloft a banner of a rifle over the Puerto Rican flag as their insignia."[37]

The Young Lords' constant citation of the basic Third World guerrilla uniform also explicitly signified their aspiration of combating U.S. colonialism in Puerto Rico. According to Meléndez, "We began to believe in the possibility that we could become an independent and self-governing nation, controlling our own economy and our own destiny. We redefined ourselves in this tradition of struggle and resistance against powerful foreign intervention."[38] Yet the rare display or use of the ultimate sovereignty accessory—guns—suggested that even if they identified with liberation movements in the United States and abroad, defended their own right to armed struggle, and in print constantly included drawings and photos of guns, theirs was a conflict fought primarily in the symbolic rather than the military arena.

This reality is evident in the sole New York action in which guns were widely wielded in public: the aforementioned funeral of Young Lord Julio Roldán. Arrested on October 15, 1970, for allegedly trying to set an East Harlem apartment on fire, Roldán was taken to the Manhattan House of Detention for men, otherwise known as the Tombs.[39] A few days after his arrest, Roldán was found dead in his jail cell, hanging by a belt. Although the police labeled the death a suicide, the Young Lords believed that Roldán was murdered. In response, the Lords occupied what they had renamed the "People's Church" for a second time. On this occasion, both female and male Lords entered the building carrying arms in a show of force designed to signal that their organization would not tolerate the killing of its members.[40] But because the Lords were not interested in confronting the police or being arrested, they devised a magnificent exit strategy: before leaving, they broke down the guns and hid them in the clothes and purses of seemingly harmless neighborhood doñas leaving the church.

The Young Lords' downplaying of guns is in contrast to the Black Panthers and speaks to different histories and contexts despite significant affinities. The Panthers initially became visible as the Black Panther Party for

Self-Defense to confront police brutality and "a law-and-order culture" in California.[41] Arms also stood for the Black Panther rejection of nonviolence as a resistance strategy and frustration with the limitations of the Civil Rights Movement. Fittingly, the Black Panthers' first statewide action, on May 2, 1967, was an armed entrance into the California state capitol at the same time that the legislature was considering the Mulford Act, a gun control bill that would have barred residents from carrying concealed weapons. At the end, even after dropping "self-defense" from their name to avoid being perceived as "a paramilitary organization" and emphasizing service programs,[42] guns remained a loaded symbol of empowerment for the Black Panthers.[43]

In this sense, while both groups displayed guns for symbolic reasons, and the Young Lords similarly recognized police brutality and prison conditions as a threat to Puerto Rican well-being, much of the Lords' core politics emerged from being marginalized and unrecognized rather than targeted and attacked. In addition, through their close study of past Puerto Rican nationalist armed revolts, the Young Lords were arguably aware of the risks of these actions, the potential for state violence against community members, and the high price paid by proindependence militants who often enjoyed little support. Not surprisingly, even on the occasions when he advocated armed struggle, the Young Lords' minister of defense Juan González underscored the importance of coalescing with other allies, particularly blacks and radicalized workers, and the tactical need to "divide up the work necessary to destroy amerikkan power."[44]

When going it alone, the Young Lords tended to carry weapons under circumstances regarded as extreme and only to stress that Puerto Rican political will and/or citizenship had to be respected. In this sense, the Young Lords were generally unwilling to engage in the definitive sovereign action: determining who lives and who dies. Even Mickey Meléndez, one of the Lords' highest-ranking military members, who at one time was given the task of building up an "underground armed branch,"[45] described the scene at the Methodist Church in exclusively performative terms: "For the first time, we would brandish weapons. They were meant to be symbolic; we wanted to force the city to negotiate with us for prison reforms. We were angry and wanted to show how serious we were, publicly and on TV."[46] This is consistent with Nathan Joseph's observation that in certain contexts, "the importance of weapons may derive less from their actual efficacy than their associated cultural values. The right to weapons has long symbolized the wellborn or even the ordinary adult male in a warlike society."[47]

Inherent in Joseph's gendered comment is that looking like the Young Lords had different implications for men and women. As a visual sign, the male Young Lords' armed image signaled that Puerto Rican men were capable of violence. In writer José Yglesias's view, the Lords' look was about "being a macho, a real male, means standing up to the Man."[48] Or, in the more explicit terms of former Young Lord Richie Perez, "When we integrated campuses . . . we got to [kick ass] too . . . throw racists down the stairs. We did non-violent actions—but it was a TACTICAL question, not a matter of PRINCIPLE. It was important that our antagonists knew this."[49] The idea was to make it clear that Lords men could—and would—defend themselves and their rights by force if they so decided.

Though the male Lords' look projected a sovereign masculinity and women sometimes carried arms to connote that they also were "warriors and defenders of the community,"[50] dressing as a "Lady Lord" had as much, if not more, to do with power differentials between genders. By wearing clothing associated with men and war such as combat boots in private and public spaces, women signified a rejection of the traditionally defined gender roles of housewives and mistresses so closely associated with the "macho" culture some men were attempting to uphold. In the succinct words of Iris Morales, who was married to Chairman Felipe Luciano at the time, "War begins at home."[51] Women's adoption of the Young Lords uniform was ultimately a sign of discontent in relation to gender expectations and a demand that women be treated as equals in and out of the organization.

Although women may have valued military dress, their style, like that of female members of the Black Panthers, was generally less regimented than the men's. In addition to the fact that many women embraced fashion choices that affirmed their sexual autonomy, such as the miniskirt, there was another important reason: it did not take long for Lords women to figure out that dressing the part was not enough to be recognized as sovereign or equal. As the Young Lords increasingly thought of themselves as a paramilitary organization, sexist ideologies arguably became more dominant in day-to-day operations, and women's discomfort with their low status grew apace.[52] Consequently, eight months into the life of the Young Lords, the women members staged the first transformative insurrection experienced by the organization. And, not coincidentally, in one of the most colorful accounts of the Lords' feminist revolt, Denise Oliver narrates the inciting incident via dress metaphors.

The triggering event took place at the home of poet and activist Amiri Baraka (LeRoi Jones). Chairman Luciano, who was intrigued by Baraka's strand of nationalism, went to meet him accompanied by several Lords men and Denise Oliver. According to Oliver, when she arrived at Baraka's home, she noticed that women "crawled into the room on their hands and knees wearing elaborate headdresses decorated with fruit"[53] while "Baraka's coterie of male guards and supporters . . . wore dashikis and gave power handshakes to the male Lords." Uncomfortable with the scene, Oliver reportedly asked Baraka about the role of women in his organization but was ignored throughout the gathering. After Oliver left, she called a meeting with other Lords women and urged them to pressure the male leadership for greater inclusion in the top command. Oliver succinctly summed up the reason that this course of action was pressing: "[because] if we didn't do something we would end up on our hands and knees with fruit on our heads."[54]

To bring the point home, the Lords women proceeded to create their own caucus, formally pressured for change, and threatened to stop working on behalf of the organization.[55] Some women also reportedly refused to have sex with the men until the central committee met their demands. (Lord internal regulations prohibited sex outside of the group for fear of government infiltration.) By June of 1970, the Lords women had won a series of victories that substantially altered their status.[56] Among these were the elevation of two women to the central committee and other positions of power and the complete overhaul of point 5 in the party program, the only item that the Young Lords amended while an active organization. Whereas before the Young Lords argued in their platform that "machismo must be revolutionary and not oppressive," the new point 5 read: "We want equality for women. Down with machismo and male chauvinism."[57] For the Lords women, the rationale for the amendment was simple. In the words of Oliver, "machismo was never gonna be revolutionary. Saying 'revolutionary machismo' is like saying . . . 'revolutionary racism.' "[58]

Ready for Their Close-Up

Arriving at the right look and mending the gendered splits, however, was only the first step. Once refashioned, the Young Lords had to move their bodies and their audience by telling compelling stories in which they were the protagonists of a political drama about the city's failure to serve and protect its people. Importantly, these performances were directed not only at the state or like-minded radical groups but also at Puerto Ricans and other community members. According to *New York Times* journalist Joseph Fried, one of the first reporters to cover the Young Lords, their main goal was "to show the people of El Barrio, East Harlem's Puerto Rican slum, that such activity was necessary to get city action to meet community needs."[59] Aiming to inspire respect among some and fear in others, the group captured the imaginations of thousands of people who had never met a Young Lord in person or directly benefited from Lord actions.

Because a wide base of support was crucial to challenge institutions, offer services, and "awaken" Puerto Ricans to their own political potential, the Young Lords heavily promoted their corporeal movements to the often-criticized mass media, effectively recruiting them to act as their coproducers. "Look, you know," wrote Guzmán, "the media is gonna have to be used. Until we can put out the *Daily News* regularly, until we have a TV station and a radio station, chalk it up. Everybody on welfare got a TV set, everybody got a radio, everybody buys the *Daily News* and *El Diario*, so as long as the people got access to these things, we might as well use them to the best of our advantage."[60] Moreover, as New Journalist Tom Wolfe once observed, "Without publicity it has never been easy to rank as a fashionable person in New York City."[61] In other words, politics required publicity and publicity required that you make news. And to make news you had to not only "look good" but also tell a moving story.

The Young Lords' discovery of the importance of effective (and entertaining) media representation to contemporary politics was not met with universal approval. The traditional left deeply disliked the Lords' style and tactics. The leaders of the Movement for Puerto Rican Independence (MPI), for instance, were particularly clear when they called the Young Lords "a group of immature young people looking for publicity" and a "bunch of crazy exhibitionists."[62]

Despite the Left's bad reviews, the Young Lords' emphasis on the media was not arbitrary. The group came into being at a time when media outlets were significantly expanding and there was an unprecedented hunger for television news. News programs were similarly changing into more stylish and dramatic presentations that sought to build audiences rather than promote traditional journalistic values such as "content and social responsibility."[63] In addition, city residents increasingly constituted their social and political identities via their interaction with mass media products. Knowing how to attract and grasp media attention was at this time paramount to any disruption of hegemonic discourses around race, colonialism, and citizenship.

Furthermore, although the Young Lords were not the first Puerto Rican group to recognize the importance of performance to politics—anarchists like Luisa Capetillo and the Nationalists under Albizu Campos understood it, too—they were the first U.S.-based organization to do so in a context where the mass media had become a major political power as great as, and at times greater than, the state in allocating the cultural capital of groups seeking support for their claims. In this sense, improving Puerto Rican looks through style, performance, and choreography was both a mode of "self-defense" as the Black Panthers would have it and a means to quicken the pace of political empowerment and accumulation of cultural capital.

In attempting to capture media attention, however, the Young Lords faced structural obstacles. Different from affluent whites who can access news and media infrastructure, Puerto Ricans had few resources to call attention to their concerns. In contrast to African Americans, who despite marginalization had a more sustained presence in media and greater prominence in American national discourse, Puerto Ricans were rarely recognized as either a U.S. ethnic minority or a separate national group; consequently, their claims were regularly dismissed as irrelevant and/or anti-American. Moreover, they were often confused with immigrants and blacks and required additional effort to gain separate notice. It is thus not a coincidence that Puerto Rican activists and organizations are known for extreme stunts, such as the Nationalist Party's 1954 shooting on Congress to bring attention to Puerto Rico's colonial situation or twice climbing the Statue of Liberty and unfurling Puerto Rican flags in support of various causes, including evicting the U.S. Navy from Vieques.

To counter their limitations, the Young Lords developed two key performances with a "sense of drama . . . and a flair."[64] The first was the well-coordinated stunt, exemplified by their first mass action in July of 1969, known as the "Garbage Offensive." According to Mickey Meléndez, the Lords picked garbage, no pun intended, because that is what barrio residents identified as their number one neighborhood problem. This was an astute choice because, as historian Johanna Fernández has observed, not only were barrio residents concerned with the issue; it had also become a sensitive matter for the city at large. The fact that New York's sanitation infrastructure was outdated, city workers underpaid, and the growing volume of waste increasingly difficult to manage was on the minds of many New Yorkers.[65] But a third account that is particularly fitting for my argument is that the Young Lords decided to concentrate on the overwhelming problem of trash in East Harlem because, as Yoruba Guzmán put it, "garbage is visible and everybody sees it."[66]

In addition, "garbage" was what many New Yorkers considered Puerto Ricans to be. A 1948 travel book, *New York Confidential*, by Jack Lait and Lee Mortimer, minced no words in describing the new immigrants: "They are mostly crude farmers, subject to congenital tropical diseases, physically unfitted for the northern climate, unskilled, uneducated, non-English-speaking, and almost impossible to assimilate and condition for healthful and useful existence in an active city of stone and steel."[67] Even after decades of living in New York, Puerto Ricans continued to be largely seen as unassimilable to the city's values and norms. Former congressman Herman Badillo, for instance, once commented that when he began registering Puerto Ricans to vote in the late 1950s, he heard a man say, "We have to do something about that guy Badillo. He's been bringing all this garbage to register and to vote."[68] Ten years later, Guzmán would similarly conclude that "[the] D.O.G [Department of Sanitation] looks upon Puerto Ricans and Blacks as though they are something lower than garbage."[69] So, making the garbage visible—and purposefully representing it as a sign of how "dirty" the system was rather than as a measure of Puerto Rican worth—was a highly effective way of prompting New Yorkers to look at Puerto Ricans in an entirely different light.

Influenced by prior RGS actions and named after the 1968 Vietnamese Tet Offensive, the Young Lords and other community members decided to meet every Sunday to clean up the garbage. To this end, the Lords requested supplies from the city and were summarily ignored. After experiencing similar treatment more than once and seeing that the trash was not collected or, if it was, remained "strewn in the street," the Lords changed their tactics.[70] For over a month, the Lords and other residents pushed the garbage farther and farther onto 110th Street and Third Avenue and made piles that partly obstructed traffic. On August 17, something unexpected happened: the protesters decided to set the garbage on fire.

Setting garbage on fire was, according to political scientist José Ramón Sánchez, a turning point in relations between Puerto Ricans, the state, and New York City at large.[71] Whereas residents had piled up garbage and swept the streets before the Young Lords came onto the scene, the style deployed by the Lords suggested that this was not business as usual. The idea was no longer to ask the authorities for help but to make their failure to help visible, thus deflecting shame onto a system that did not live up to its self-proclaimed standards of cleanliness, efficiency, and order. And, from the Young Lords' point of view, what the garbage made evident was at least twofold: that "the system does not serve them [Puerto Ricans]" and that Puerto Ricans, while they were surrounded by garbage, were not responsible for the conditions they lived in.[72]

Yet to establish themselves as prime-time players and to be widely recognized as sovereign political actors—that is, subjects who did not require state or church approval to act on their desires—the Young Lords needed to dramatize their movements and capture New York's attention on a grander scale. To achieve this, they began making use of a second tactic—the "kidnapping" building crisis—an open-ended dramatic performance that invited spectators to join and assist in changing existing conditions.[73] The first action to embody the new tactic was the takeover of the First Spanish Methodist Church on the corner of 111th Street and Lexington. The impasse began when the pastor, Reverend Humberto Carranza—a Cuban exile to whom the Young Lords must have seemed like miniature Che Gueveras—repeatedly refused the Lords' request for space to house several programs, including a day care center and a popular free breakfast program over a four-month period. Frustrated with the lack of progress, the Young Lords decided to take the church. On December 29, 1969, they began an eleven-day occupation during which hundreds of people participated in their programs.

The Young Lords' biggest victories may have been at other levels. The Garbage Offensive and the takeover of First Spanish Methodist had instituted the Lords as representatives of Puerto Ricans in what they perceived as a global revolution and had decisively transformed Puerto Rican expectations of themselves. In Guzmán's words, "Before the Young Lords Party began—people used to walk with their heads down like this, and the pigs would walk through the colonies, man, like they owned the block. They'd come in here with no kind of respect in their eyes. But after the Garbage Offensive and the People's Church it was a whole new game."[74] In the end, the longer-term effect of these actions had less to do with whether the city picked up the garbage in East Harlem somewhat more frequently than before or offered church space. Rather, it had to do with how they transformed Puerto Ricans from spectators into political actors, unhinging enduring stereotypes of Puerto Rican passivity and ineffectiveness.[75]

Emboldened by their accomplishments, the Young Lords went on to organize other, similar high-profile actions such as the "liberation" of an X-ray truck to conduct community tuberculosis tests on June 17, 1970, and the occupation of Lincoln Hospital, nearly a month later, on July 14.[76] Prompted by the outrage of proposed budget cuts and inhumane treatment of patients, the Lincoln takeover was a classic Young Lords action: it included the occupation of an unpopular hospital that most agreed was a "butcher shop." In addition, the siege lasted only twelve hours, attracted news cameras, and made no use of physical force. Notably, even the hospital's chief administrator, Dr. Antero Lacot, described the action as "helpful" in "trying to dramatize a situation which is critical."[77]

Ultimately, the Young Lords offered a familiar and popular storyline to the media featuring disempowered youth with a just cause that was likely to end well for all involved. In Guzmán's terms, "The people dig an underdog, that was the great appeal of the Mets at one time, and you have to understand that that's exactly what we are, underdogs."[78] Despite the Lords' revolutionary rhetoric, they chose relatively easy targets that could lead to tangible improvements. According to Sánchez, "They appeared dangerous yet used church space for a free breakfast program and free medical care."[79] This is one of the main reasons that the Young Lords generally had the sympathy of journalists and broad sectors of the public, including some individuals and organizations that they targeted. Similarly, their New York actions did not seek military control or revolutionary overthrow of the state but access to resources, self-transformation, and expansion of the political imagination.

Heart of Lords

For over a year, the Young Lords won nearly every publicity battle if not every political fight. Some may have disagreed with their look or tactics, but few disagreed with their reasoning. This is evident in that the Lords were often arrested for trespassing and other offenses, but the charges would eventually be dropped. Still, the Young Lords began losing momentum after 1972, when they engaged in a series of public actions and internal debates that began to alter their image and strategy. Their first political turn arguably had taken place earlier, on June 8, 1970, when they marched in the annual Puerto Rican Day Parade alongside members of the Movement for Puerto Rican Independence and the Puerto Rican Students Union. During the parade, the group embarrassed a number of participants and organizers when they pelted officials and Puerto Rico's pro-statehood governor Luis A. Ferré with tomatoes, oranges, and eggs.[80]

Moreover, while bringing guns to Julio Roldán's funeral in 1970 was a symbolic gesture that did not end in armed confrontation, it anticipated a move toward more traditional nationalist military politics, one that boomeranged. As journalist Ansel Herz has argued, "Unlike previous building occupations, the second takeover of the 'People's Church' did not achieve any tangible victory for the community of El Barrio. No one was ever held responsible for Roldán's death. The open display of weapons did, however, agitate the FBI and lead to increased surveillance and repression."[81] In other words, as the Lords went from dramatic actions focused on community needs toward a proindependence agenda, the political ground began to shift. Not only did this new orientation deeply polarize the Young Lords and community members, it also made the media lose interest. All that the Lords had achieved seem to fade away.

Yet from the start the Young Lords had a constitutive duality that came to undo them as a political force. They may have been bent on being recognized as an integral if distinct part of New York and in solidarity with other anti-imperialist movements at home and beyond, but, as the Young Lords' button proclaimed, they had "Puerto Rico en el corazón," and it started weighing heavily. The Lords came to believe that acts of political imagination and community service in East Harlem did not go to the heart of Puerto Rican subordination and therefore could not free Puerto Ricans, decolonize the island, or confer the dignity of nation-state status.[82] After all, point 1 in the Young Lords' platform was "We want self-determination for Puerto Ricans, liberation on the island and inside the United States," and point 6 stated, "We want community control of our institutions and land."[83]

In contemplating growth for the organization within a context of declining mass activity, the Young Lords made a fateful decision. In March 1971, they launched Ofensiva Rompecadenas and started to develop a presence in Puerto Rico. This decision was not unanimous. It was, however, largely founded on a shared analysis that rested on two assumptions: one, that Puerto Ricans made up a single nation and therefore the occupied island was every boricuas' national land base, and two, that the origin of Puerto Rican disempowerment and stigmatization in the United States was the colonial status of Puerto Rico. In the succinct words of Felipe Luciano, "Puerto Rico is oppressed as a nation, it is a colony of the united states and the colonial status of Puerto Ricans follows them from the countryside to New York City."[84]

Based on this assessment, the Young Lords decided that they should reallocate energies and resources to winning independence and liberate the "two-thirds of our people [who] are in chains in Puerto Rico."[85] If Puerto Ricans were an "internal" colony of the United States, the only path to liberation was to externalize it through formal decolonization. "And this is why we must rise up together," wrote Lord leader Gloria Gonzalez. "Boricuas in the u.s. and Boricuas on the island, to put an end to yankee abuse . . . we must re-unite our Nation."[86] Only then would the new body and the old heart produce a truly free and sovereign Puerto Rican.

The Young Lords proceeded to open branches in Ponce, Aguadilla, and San Juan. Dressed in full Lords uniforms, their first major appearance was on March 21, 1972, as part of a commemorative march for the Ponce Massacre of 1937. But their presence was generally not welcome. Although the Lords' commitment to national sovereignty did not go unnoticed by sectors of the independence movement and later prompted outreach campaigns on the mainland,[87] most island nationalists felt little need for the "Nuyorican" warriors on their own turf. Counting on nationalist and left traditions over a century old and apparently feeling that the Young Lords had come to "show the other *independentistas* how to make revolution," many dismissed the new arrivals.[88] While there is limited research on this part of the Young Lords history, anecdotes from political activists of this period suggest that the New York Lords were seen as similar to other U.S.-born Puerto Ricans: low-class, non-Spanish-speaking, *atrevido* (brazen) Americans.[89]

In listening to their hearts, the Young Lords had come face-to-face with a nearly unbearable truth: if a great part of their transformation into revolutionaries had to do with realizing that they were Puerto Ricans and not Americans, the "real" Puerto Ricans did not think that they were Puerto Ricans at all, much less that they were needed to win any political battle.[90] In Juan González's words, "One of the biggest mistakes . . . the Young Lords ever made was . . . [to think] that we could figure out how to organize an independence movement on the island. Because the reality is that we're U.S.-raised Puerto Ricans, and the experience that we knew was the urban ghettoes of the United States."[91] This realization had great implications.

During more than a year of strenuous work, the Young Lords had fashioned themselves into a disciplined body ready for political power. Style was a form of discipline, and discipline was a way to produce a sovereign self: "We stressed self-discipline . . . we attempted to remake ourselves—change our thinking and behavior—while we fought to change the world."[92] But, one could say, Puerto Rico broke the Lords' heart, in some ways severing the heart from the body. And this severance revealed the tensions between two different conceptions of sovereignty. The first emphasized symbolic disruption, recognition as citizens, and the politicization of class, ethnicity, gender, race, sexuality, and colonial subordination. The second understood self-determination in nation-state terms and ultimately could be fought only in—and over—Puerto Rico. The gap exposed a fissure between the potentially sovereign body of the "Nuyorican" and her nonsovereign heart, Puerto Rico, one that would eventually make the Young Lords Party implode.

At the exact moment that the Young Lords aimed to overtly challenge U.S. sovereignty in Puerto Rico by migrating part of their operation to the island, the state moved to disassemble the organization's potential success by stepping up surveillance, increasing the number of infiltrators, and intensifying police harassment of individuals and property.[93] Equally important, the move south literally dislocated rather than stretched the Lords' body politic. In Iris Morales's words, "We started to lose the relationship with the community, which was what had kept us and made us strong. . . . People then didn't have a place where they would come and talk to us about the police brutality issues, they didn't have a place where there could be a free breakfast program or a free clothing drive."[94] In addition, the embrace of more conventional goals such as national sovereignty displaced other fundamental political objectives that had so defined the politics of the Young Lords, including dismantling racism and sexism.[95]

Finally, this dislocation became a deep fracture when Marxist-Maoist members led by Gloria Fontanez transformed the party into the Puerto Rican Revolutionary Workers Organization (PRRWO) in July 1972. The PRRWO's leadership, which included former core Lords, derided the Lords' previous nationalist analysis in favor of revolutionary proletarianism, arguing that only a working-class revolution in the United States would eliminate the threat of American imperialism. Some of the Lords were now even accused of being "rightist" and "reactionary." As the PRRWO's new leaders saw it, "Puerto Rico is not a divided nation. Puerto Rico is a nation in Puerto Rico, and the Puerto Ricans inside the U.S. are an oppressed national minority part of the North American working class."[96] Significantly, a measure of the proof that PRRWO offered for the Lords' political errors was sartorial: "Left extremism was being developed and this was seen in the way we dressed, as if we were an army, our way of talking, of living, so different from the rest of the working people."[97] In time, the PRRWO's dogmatism led to violent internal struggle, authoritarianism, and ineffectiveness.

Still, whereas the PRRWO is almost universally regarded as the Young Lords' "darkest hour," and their stance that the working class was the only possible revolutionary class was misguided, its leaders were not altogether wrong in assessing the Lords' project as that of an already upwardly mobile group ("lower petty bourgeoisie" in their terms). This is evident in their reasons for cutting off their ties to Chicago to become the Young Lords Party—the original Lords were considered too "street" and not sophisticated enough—and in their urgent quest for a base once social movements began to shift in the early 1970s.[98] Called the "intellectuals" by the Chicago group, the New York Lords' leadership composition also implied a distrust of, or at least a distance from, the masses: although the leadership stressed service to "the people," all decisions were made by a central committee, mostly composed of college-educated young men, who shared Che Guevara's assumption that a small group of militants could bring about structural change and foster revolutionary conditions.

Not surprisingly, one of the most tangible long-term effects of the Young Lords' political practice was the ways in which it enabled Puerto Rican upward mobility and greater participation in New York's mainstream institutions and mass media structures. As Guzmán summed up, "Ask any Latino professional in Nueva York who advanced in government or the corporate world between, say, 1969 and 1984, and you'll be told they owe part of their opportunity to the sea change of perception that Young Lords inspired."[99] Similarly, not a few Young Lords went on to careers inside the legal system, government, and mass media as producers, radio personalities, judges, organizers, administrators, nonprofit directors, and/or lawyers. For instance, Felipe Luciano was a radio personality on Fox 5 and WLIB radio. At present, Yoruba Guzmán is a newscaster for WCBS/Channel 2, Juan González is a *Daily News* columnist and cohost of the show *Democracy Now!*, and Iris Morales is a lawyer and filmmaker.

In the end, the Lords did not bring liberation to Puerto Rico or Puerto Ricans in the United States in the conventionally sovereign terms they envisioned. Their "look of sovereignty" paradoxically exposed the limits of style, of nationalist Puerto Rican politics, and of sovereign discourse itself in a context of global economic restructuring and enduring colonial power relations. Yet regardless of the Young Lords' internal struggles, by becoming lords of style, they upended the premise of Puerto Rican identity as inherently low, passive, and disposable and displaced the stigmatizing shame of racialization and colonialism from their bodies to state and media structures. Furthermore, the Young Lords' trajectory, including its failures, freed U.S. Puerto Ricans to inhabit different and multiple political locations as New Yorkers, blacks, Latinas, queers, and/or global citizens, among others. In the process, the Lords left behind a rich record of imaginative acts in challenging times. They also showed—and this is an important word—the possibility of thinking about politics as a daily practice of self-fashioning and transformative action rather than a utopian state somewhere beyond our reach.

Notes

1. Pablo Guzmán, "La Vida Pura: A Lord of the Barrio," in *The Puerto Rican Movement: Voices from the Diaspora*, ed. Andrés Torres and José E. Velázquez (Philadelphia: Temple University Press, 1998), 165.
2. Quoted in Mickey Meléndez, *We Took the Streets* (New Brunswick, NJ: Rutgers University Press, 2005), 186.
3. For additional context on the Young Lords of Chicago, see Lilia Fernandez, *Brown in the Windy City: Mexicans and Puerto Ricans in Postwar Chicago* (Chicago: University of Chicago Press, 2012); Jakobi Williams, *From the Bullet to the Ballot: The Illinois Chapter of the Black Panther Party and Radical Coalition Politics in Chicago* (Chapel Hill: University of North Carolina Press, 2013); and Jeffrey O. G. Ogbar, "Puerto Rico en mi Corazón: The Young Lords, Black Power and Puerto Rican Nationalism in the U.S., 1966–1972," *Centro Journal* 18, no. 1 (2006): 154.
4. Johanna Fernández, "The Young Lords and the Postwar City: Notes on the Geographical and Structural Reconfigurations of Contemporary Urban Life," in *African American Urban History Since World War II*, ed. Kenneth L. Kusmer and Joe W. Trotter (Chicago: University of Chicago Press, 2009), 66.
5. Although beyond the scope of this essay, the differences between the trajectory of the Chicago, New York, and other branches of the Young Lords were at times substantial. These involved differences not only in membership composition and goals but also in relationships to city structures, level of support

from the media, effect of counterintelligence programs such as COINTELPRO, the presence of other radical organizations, and public discourse around key issues.
6. Some Lords, however, had been part of gangs or related to gang members before joining the Lords. See Young Lords Party and Michael Abranson, *Palante: Young Lords Party* (New York: McGraw-Hill, 1971; repr. Chicago: Haymarket Books, 2011).
7. Meléndez, *We Took the Streets*, 136.
8. Pablo "Yoruba" Guzmán, "Before People Called Me a Spic, They Called Me a Nigger," in *Palante: Young Lords Party*, Michael Abramson and Young Lords Party (New York: McGraw-Hill, 1971; repr. Chicago: Haymarket Books, 2011), 82–83. Citations refer to the Haymarket edition.
9. Johanna Fernández, "Between Social Service Reform and Revolutionary Politics: The Young Lords, Late Sixties Radicalism, and Community Organizing in New York City," in *Freedom North: Black Freedom Struggles Outside the South, 1940–1980*, ed. Jeanne Theoharis and Komozi Woodard (New York: Palgrave Macmillan 2003), 261.
10. "Interview with Puerto Rican Historian Mervin Mendez: The Young Lords and Early Chicago Puerto Rican Gangs," January 27, 2002, http://www.uic.edu/orgs/kbc/latinkings/lkhistory.html.
11. Michel Foucault, interviewed by Paul Rabinow and Hubert Dreyfus, "On the Genealogy of Ethics: An Overview of Work in Progress," in *The Foucault Reader*, ed. Paul Rabinow (New York: Pantheon Books, 1984), 334.
12. Jesus D. Rodríguez-Velasco, *Citizenship, Monarchical Sovereignty, and Chivalry in the Iberian Late Middle Ages* (Philadelphia: University of Pennsylvania, 2010).
13. For further discussion of the Real Great Society, including its relationship with the Young Lords, see Luis Aponte Parés, "Lessons from El Barrio—The East Harlem Real Great Society/Urban Planning Studio: A Puerto Rican Chapter in the Fight for Urban Self-Determination," *New Political Science* 20, no. 4 (1998): 399–420.
14. Maryse Condé, *Heremakhonon* (Boulder, CO: Three Continents, 1985).
15. Quoted in Ed Morales, *Living in Spanglish: The Search for Identity in Latino America* (New York: St. Martin's Press, 2002), 83.

16. Amílcar Antonio Barreto, *Vieques, the Navy, and Puerto Rican Politics* (Gainsville: University Press of Florida, 2002).
17. Daphne A. Brooks, *Bodies in Dissent: Spectacular Performances of Race and Freedom, 1850–1910* (Durham, NC: Duke University Press, 2006), 5.
18. Che Ja, "Free the Hungry System," *Palante* 2, no. 13 (1970): 10.
19. José Ramón Sánchez, *Boricua Power: A Political History of Puerto Ricans in the United States* (New York: New York University Press, 2007), 196.
20. Wendy Parkins, "Introduction: (Ad)dressing Citizens," in *Fashioning the Body Politic: Dress, Gender, Citizenship* (Oxford: Berg, 2002), 1.
21. Frances Negrón-Muntaner, *Boricua Pop: Puerto Ricans and the Latinization of American Culture* (New York: New York University Press, 2004).
22. Brooks, *Bodies in Dissent*, 3.
23. Quoted in Fernandez, *Brown in the Windy City*, 173.
24. William L. Van Deburg, *New Day in Babylon* (Chicago: University of Chicago Press, 1992), 156.
25. Mick Farren, *The Black Leather Jacket* (Medford, NJ: Plexus, 2007).
26. Jane Rhodes, *Framing the Black Panthers: The Spectacular Rise of a Black Power Icon* (New York: New Press, 2007), 107.
27. Tom Wolfe, *Radical Chic and Mau Mauing the Flak Catchers* (New York: Picador 2009), 5.
28. "Militants Vow to Continue Protest at Harlem Church," *New York Times*, January 4, 1970.
29. Nathan Joseph, *Uniforms and Nonuniforms: Communication Through Clothing* (New York: Greenwood Press, 1986), 13.
30. Johanna Fernández, "Denise Oliver and the Young Lords Party: Stretching the Boundaries of Struggle," in *Want to Start a Revolution: Radical Black Women in the Black Freedom Struggle*, ed. Dayo F. Gore, Jeanne Theoharis, and Komozi Woodard (New York: New York University Press, 2009), 271.
31. Joseph P. Fried, "East Harlem Youths Explain Garbage-Dumping Demonstration," *New York Times*, August 19, 1969.
32. Iris Morales, phone interview with author, April 28, 2015.
33. Nancy Morris, *Puerto Rico: Culture, Politics, and Identity* (Westport, CT: Praeger, 1995), 50–52.
34. Guzmán, "Before People Called Me a Spic," 75.

35. Meléndez, *We Took the Streets*, 94.
36. Morales, phone interview.
37. Fernández, "Between Social Service Reform and Revolutionary Politics," 264.
38. Meléndez, *We Took the Streets*, 81.
39. "Young Lords Take Over Church, Protest Death," *Jet*, November 26, 1970, 52.
40. Richie Perez, "Julio Roldán Center Opens," *Palante* 2, no. 14 (1970): 4.
41. Amy Abugo Ongiri, *Spectacular Blackness: The Cultural Politics of the Black Power Movement and the Search for a Black Aesthetics* (Charlottesville: University of Virginia Press, 2009), 42.
42. Alondra Nelson, *Body and Soul: The Black Panther Party and the Fight Against Medical Discrimination* (Minneapolis: University of Minnesota Press, 2011), 62.
43. Jane Rhodes, *Framing the Black Panthers: The Spectacular Rise of a Black Power Icon* (New York: New Press, 2007), 106.
44. Juan González, "Armed Struggle," *Palante* 3, no. 13 (1971): 8.
45. Ansel Herz, "The Young Lords: Examining Its Deficit of Democracy and Decline," lib.com, June 13, 2012, https://libcom.org/library/young-lords-party-examining-its-deficit-democracy-decline. Originally published September 1, 2009, http://athomehesaturista.wordpress.com.2009/09/01-the-young-lords-party-examining-its-deficit-of-democracy-and-decline/ (no longer posted).
46. Meléndez, *We Took the Streets*, 182.
47. Joseph, *Uniforms and Nonuniforms*, 22.
48. José Yglesias, "Right On with the Young Lords," *New York Times*, June 7, 1970.
49. Richie Perez, "A Young Lord Remembers," lib.com, June 7, 2010, http://libcom.org/library/young-lord-remembers. Originally published May 2000, http://www.virtualboricua.org/Docs/perez_00./htm (no longer posted).
50. Iris Morales, e-mail to author, September 2, 2015.
51. Judy Klemesrud, "Young Women Find a Place in High Command of Young Lords," *New York Times*, November 11, 1970.
52. Denise Oliver in *Palante, Siempre Palante*, directed by Iris Morales, 1996.
53. Jennifer A. Nelson, "'Abortions Under Community Control': Feminism, Nationalism, and the Politics of Representation Among New York City's Young Lords," *Journal of Women's History* 13, no. 1 (2001): 162.
54. Ibid.
55. Morales, phone interview.

56. Nelson, "'Abortions Under Community Control,'" 159.
57. Young Lords Party, "Palante," in *The Puerto Rican Experience: A Sociological Sourcebook*, ed. Francesco Cordasco and Eugene Bucchioni (Totowa, NJ: Littlefield, Adams, 1973), 272.
58. Abramson and Young Lords Party, *Palante*, 52.
59. Joseph P. Fried, "East Harlem Youths Explain Garbage-Dumping Demonstration," *New York Times*, August 19, 1969.
60. Young Lords Party, "Palante," 261.
61. Wolfe, *Radical Chic*, 30.
62. "¿Young Lords o 'landlords'?: Ex miembros hablan de lo que hacen hoy," *El Diario-La Prensa*, March 4, 1989, 46.
63. Rhodes, *Framing the Black Panthers*, 63.
64. Guzmán, "Before People Called Me a Spic," 75.
65. Fernández, "Between Social Service Reform and Revolutionary Politics," 269.
66. Young Lords Party, "Palante," 258.
67. Jack Lait and Lee Mortimer, *New York Confidential* (New York: Crown, 1948), 126.
68. Adriana Bosch, executive producer, *Latino Americans* (PBS and WETA, 2013).
69. "Young Lords Block Street with Garbage," in *The Young Lords: A Reader*, ed. Darrel Enck-Wanzer (New York: New York University Press, 2010), 185.
70. Fernández, "Between Social Service Reform and Revolutionary Politics," 265.
71. Sánchez, *Boricua Power*, 207.
72. Fried, "East Harlem Youths," 86.
73. In the TV film *Palante, Siempre Palante* (1996), Felipe Luciano's describes taking the first building in this way: "We literally kidnapped the church."
74. Guzmán, "Before People Called Me a Spic," 82.
75. Perez, "Young Lord Remembers."
76. Fernández, "Young Lords and the Postwar City."
77. For more details, see Alfonso A. Narvaez, "Young Lords Seize Lincoln Building: Offices Are Held for 12 Hours—Official Calls Points Valid," *New York Times*, July 15, 1970, and Fernández, "Young Lords and the Postwar City," 76.
78. Guzmán, "Before People Called Me a Spic," 78.
79. Sánchez, *Boricua Power*, 203.
80. Yglesias, "Right On."

81. Herz, "Young Lords."
82. For further discussion of the relationship between sovereignty and political modernity, see Yarimar Bonilla, *Non-Sovereign Futures: French Caribbean Politics in the Wake of Disenchantment* (Chicago: University of Chicago Press, 2015).
83. Young Lords Party, "13 Point Program and Platform," in Cordasco and Bucchioni, *Puerto Rican Experience*, 272.
84. Felipe Luciano, "On Revolutionary Nationalism," *Palante* 2, no. 2 (1970): 10.
85. "Beat Is Gettin' Stronger," *Palante* 3, no. 4 (1971): 2.
86. Gloria Gonzalez, "Why Ponce?," *Palante* 3, no. 3 (1971): 18.
87. Andrés Torres, "Introduction: Political Radicalism in the Diaspora—The Puerto Rican Experience," in *The Puerto Rican Movement: Voices from the Diaspora*, ed. Andrés Torres and José E. Velázquez (Philadelphia: Temple University Press, 1998), 7.
88. "Resolutions of the Puerto Rican Revolutionary Workers Organization," in Enck-Wanzer, *Young Lords: A Reader*, 240.
89. Carmen Teresa Whalen, "The Young Lords in Philadelphia," in Torres and Velázquez, *Puerto Rican Movement*, 107–23.
90. Angela Carrasquillo and Ceferino Carrasquillo, *The Neorican: Unwelcomed in Two Worlds* (New York: Ediciones Puerto Rico de Autores Nuevos, 1979), 12–13.
91. *Palante, Siempre Palante*.
92. Perez, "Young Lord Remembers."
93. *Palante, Siempre Palante*.
94. Ibid.
95. Morales, phone interview.
96. "Editorial," in Enck-Wanzer, *Young Lords: A Reader*, 234.
97. "Ibid., 234.
98. Fernandez, *Brown in the Windy City*, 202–3.
99. Guzmán, "La Vida Pura," 165.

III

Life Without Sovereignty

10

Sovereignty Still?

MADELINE ROMÁN

In her article "Sovereignty and the Return of the Repressed," political theorist Wendy Brown writes that sovereignty is the new Viagra of politics.[1] That is, a device to provide a booster to contemporary politics and an object of desire shared by sovereign and nonsovereign countries alike. Yet what is the theoretical and political solvency of sovereignty as a concept? Can we "still" speak of sovereignty? The main contention of this essay is that it is not possible, not even desirable, to speak of sovereignty, either in terms of nation-states or in terms of singular lives. One way of making sense of the above contention is through an examination of the relations between nation and sovereignty, global society and nation-states, sovereignty's implications for certain political imaginaries and distinctions (center/periphery, metropoles/colonies), and the relation between sovereignty and contemporary theorizing on the subject.

Some would argue that prosovereignty struggles by nonsovereign countries (or "people") constitute alternative and even radical political proposals on the part of historically subjected and subaltern populations. Nonetheless, these alternatives suppose a refoundation (represented as "good" and "positive") of the nation similar or nearly equivalent to the proposed substitution of the bourgeois family by the "workers" and/or "feminist family." Still . . . it was family. Signifiers such as *nation* and *sovereignty* have a historical, political, and social load that is activated regardless of who invokes them.

The signifiers of national sovereignty, the sovereign as well as the national, must be deconstructed, for the attributes associated with sovereignty, that is, supremacy of power and authority, self-government, and the capacity for independent action and autonomous agency, among others, cannot be conferred to nation-states or to subjects in their singular character. Moreover, if we are to understand the increasing complexity of the contemporary world—and of social space in relation to our understanding of sovereignty—the present conditions demand if not a radical change at least a substantive modification of our conceptual toolboxes. This deconstructive task must be assumed at various levels: historical, political, and theoretical.

Nation/Sovereignty/Global Biopolitics

Despite its presumed timelessness, the phenomenon of sovereignty is related to the historical consolidation of nation-states and the violence that accompanies this process. The relationship between nation and sovereignty is registered in the modern political imaginary of the nation (understood as a political subject in which the constituent state sovereignty resides). Eligio Resta has observed that we are encouraged to regard as inevitable "the relationship between violence and sovereignty."[2] Sovereignty, in fact, is not a natural or "progressive" attribute of nations but a process that allows the winners of political conflicts to represent the latest arrangements of power as the "new law."[3] That is, sovereignty is the point of "indistinction" between violence and law. In a sovereign state, the sovereign is, as philosopher Giorgio Agamben has written, simultaneously in and outside of the juridical order; the ability to suspend the law is a privilege of the sovereign itself. Examples of this process at work, either through the activation of a state of exception and/or a state of emergency, abound. In the 2007–2008 period alone, Bangladesh, Pakistan, Thailand, and the United States, to name a few nations, had either declared states of emergency to control unrest or explicitly delineated spaces as above the law, as is the case of Guantánamo's detainee camp.[4]

In addition to this violence, notions of sovereignty founded on nation-state membership confront additional challenges in the present context, such as a growing number of noncitizens living within a nation's borders. As Agamben elaborates, the citizen-subject, who emerges as the counterpart of the sovereign, is a figure who has rights only according to a particular territorial demarcation (or nation-state). The exception—historically embodied in the figure of the refugee, illegal immigrant, or stranger—is, however, "truly the man of rights," in Hannah Arendt's words. He/she is the subject that embodies the limits of sovereignty and thus the limits of the rule/state of law. Symbolic expropriations of citizenship are also effected whenever x segment of the population cannot be accommodated or subsumed either under an identity that is considered mainstream or that is represented as the majority. In Puerto Rico, for instance we have witnessed the symbolic expropriation of citizenship of HIV-positive people, the homeless, transgender people, addicts, and others. In this regard, if sovereignty is also predicated on the political exclusion of a growing number of the population, how can one account for the desire and legitimation of sovereignty when, structurally, it is impossible? And how can one defend national sovereignty when significant segments of the population of all latitudes are deprived of any juridical shelter in its name?

The inherent limitations of sovereign power (embodied in the figure of the nation-state) are not the only matters to consider. Linked to a growing mass of noncitizens within and in between national boundaries, sovereignty is also currently challenged by the process of globalization. In his work, anthropologist Néstor García Canclini has identified the paradox of nationhood and globalization in the following terms.

> At the same time that globalization is conceived as the expansion of markets, and therefore, of the economic capabilities of societies, globalization diminishes the capacity of action of nation-states, political parties, unions, and classic political actors in general. It both produces more transnational exchange and shakes the certainties of belonging to a nation.[5]

For Arjun Appadurai, a global society acquires a rhizomatic dimension either by the continuous migration flows and the ways these foster all sorts of cultural reconversions or by the emergence of a world culture or by the economic and political opacity produced by deterritorializations, reterritorializations, and capital mergers. This leads Appadurai to suggest that the historical distinction center/periphery cannot make sense of what is currently happening and, I add, neither can the binary metropolis/colonies.[6] The intensification of these *transformations* raises urgent questions. For instance, how can we reconcile a desire for national sovereignty in an eminently globalized world where transnational capital is in command of the entire planet? The relative decline of nation-states in a planetary context, which reproduces itself by virtue of the whims of capital, has provoked more than one social critic to propose that people might benefit more from voting for the presidents of big corporations than from voting for the presidents of different nation-states, particularly in peripheral countries.

In addition to the erosion of national power in relation to transnational capital, capital also produces infra- and supranational movements that reorganize and divide political communities beyond nation-states.[7] These developments not only destabilize power relations inside nation-states but also are sometimes accompanied with an increase of "tribal" violence that expresses itself in the growth of ethnic and minority struggles throughout the world. As stated by Amartya Sen, the violence of illusion, that is, the violence provoked by the illusion of identity as destiny has repeatedly activated the requirement of killing in the name of "my people."[8] Unable to control these forces, nation-states have often responded by insisting on the validity of old political frontiers and cultural identities such as the nation or the ethnic or religious community[9] even if these presumed certainties produce and reproduce further violence. This is evident in multiple national contexts, including the United States, where anti-immigrant legislation has produced not only deportations but a sharp rise in hate crimes against Mexicans, and in Italy, where the state's focus on curbing "undesirable" immigration has also energized neo-Nazi gangs that attack both legal and illegal immigrants alike.

As it has been denounced over and over again, the nation constitutes a device of occlusion and exclusion of a whole range of identities based on ethnic, racial, gender, and sexual orientation. But in the current juncture, these exclusions are even more untenable as the subject's self-determination takes on political centrality. In the context of what sociologist Niklas Luhmann has called the "modernity of Modernity,"[10] the most important objective for the majority of people is the realization of their potential as individuals. The nation is thus relativized, even diffused. In most countries, the right to collective self-determination has been replaced with the right to the subject's self-determination in the sense of desires and rights of autonomy. This desire is, in fact, partly responsible for people moving across the globe in search of a "better life" rather than staying to build a "better country." This does not cancel the legitimacy of collective agencies and struggles for the rights to recognition that occur within a particular nation/state and the ways in which these struggles can open relevant spaces within the juridical system itself around what has been named the rights of the difference, nor does it cancel the ways in which these collective struggles can contribute to the production of other political imaginaries. However, more often than not, most of these struggles focus on efforts to be recognized within the imaginary of the nation-state rather than promoting a cosmopolitan political imaginary, therefore perpetuating, sharing, or desiring an imaginary of sovereignty entirely decoupled from contemporary social and political trends. In Puerto Rico, for instance, the semantic around Puerto Rican women and Puerto Rican gays and lesbians focuses on their Puerto Ricanness, as if this name marks its political legitimacy and/or singularity.

It could be argued that given the struggles of significant segments of the population for self-determination in terms of singular lives as well as the lack of effective sovereignty for actual sovereign states in a globalized world, formal political independence (in nonsovereign countries) becomes irrelevant. The idea that sovereignty is capable of producing a difference at any level is highly questionable. In this regard, as Luhmann expands, Modernity exists through its individualizing activity and the increasing impossibility of homogenizing lives, experiences, or positions. This is why it is no longer possible to produce common grounds and/or common denominators that could legitimize collective agency even in neocolonial contexts such as Puerto Rico, where political domination of one country by another would seem to demand it. The difficulty lies, to paraphrase Jacques Lacan, in that "the Puerto Rican" does not exist; Puerto Ricans are many and very different. Therefore, how can the idea that national sovereignty produces difference—either for sovereign or nonsovereign countries—be sustained? Perhaps the question has to be why political agencies have to be thought from and within imaginaries of sovereignty?

Another way of posing this question is by alluding to what philosopher Michel Foucault called "governmentality" or governance in the sense of managing and administering populations.[11] According to Foucault, since early to late Modernity, three forms of governability have emerged: the power of sovereignty, of normalization, and of biopower. The specific form of governmentality called biopower that dominates today attempts to rule over the totality of life, biologically and socially. Biopower takes life itself (bare life), population in its biological sense, as the object of domination. As one of the characters in the film *V for Vendetta* puts it, "Nuclear power is meaningless in a world where a virus can kill an entire population."[12] Although the dominance of one form of governmentality, such as biopower, does not entail the cancellation of others (e.g., in this case the power of sovereignty), the ascendance of biopower raises the question of how sovereignty can be possible when "real," actual power is not necessarily located in the state apparatus or in official government structures.

Although Giorgio Agamben proposes that at present, sovereign power is exercised biopolitically, what can sovereignty do when biopolitical forms of governance make it impossible to separate state/civil society and state and extrastatal spaces? Presently, as politics has become biopolitics, the real question of power has to do with establishing the form of organization that best serves to control bare life—a bare life that in Agamben's terms is increasingly pushed to the margins of nation-states, where people have no legal rights as citizens.[13] Note also that for Agamben, bare life understood as nonprotection from the law is expanding as Modernity evolves.

In biopolitics, the management and administration of bare life is displaced to an ambiguous terrain where doctors, laboratories, and biotechnological industries take on the position of the sovereign. This shift is evident in the centrality of biotechnological industries as governance techniques in popular culture products such as *V for Vendetta*, where "the worst biological attack . . . was not the work of religious extremists" but that of government in complicity with a pharmaceutical company controlled by several party members. Foucault contends that biopolitics rests on both a new kind of racism and on subjectivity similar to that of a war: some people need to be killed in order for some other people to live, to have a certain quality of life. As a character in *V for Vendetta* put it, "immigrants, Muslims, homosexuals, terrorists . . . disease-ridden degenerates . . . they had to go." What is the sense in a struggle for formal national sovereignties in a context where the power of sovereignty seems to be displaced to intangible and nonterritorial domains?

Sovereign Subjects

The shift to the biopolitical has great implications for how we think about the subject or agent of action. Traditional understandings of sovereignty are rooted in a Cartesian view of the subject; there is an assumption of the existence of the subject as an autonomous unit who is author of his/her own discourse and in control of his/her acts. Nonetheless, as contemporary debates suggest, the subject is neither a unit nor an autonomous entity. The subject is a multiplicity, or many persons, or in the succinct words of philosopher Fernando Savater, "the lover of tolerance in me upsets the intolerant part, which is/are also me."[14]

To the extent that subjectivity is the conjunction of all the identifications of the subject, it appears as a completely social and open-ended problem. As feminist theorist Rosi Braidotti has observed, in psychoanalytical praxis and theory, the idea of "differences within" is fundamental to understanding subjectivity as a point of intersection of different speaking registers.[15] Similarly, the subject cannot be considered an autonomous unit because the choices the subject makes and the domain of the personal are entirely traversed by the social sphere. In other words, all the choices that appear to be made by "individual people" are mediated by social discourses and technologies such as advertising, the two-party system, or the subjection of people to capital as labor. Because there is no speaking sovereignty or sovereignty of the speaking subject, agency cannot be defined as the restoration of the sovereign speaker.

Also, as philosopher Judith Butler suggests, agency is not the same as control; agency begins where sovereignty (i.e., the illusion of control of the subject) wanes.[16] We are encouraged, from different theoretical fields, to abandon the metaphysics of the subject, to forget the illusion of a foundation. For instance, there is no need to liberate the "national being" because the subject does not have a constitutive being to be emancipated. The correlation between liberation and nation-state status is also highly problematic from another point of view, as the vast majority of "peoples" do not live in nation-states of their own making. As Fernando Savater has written, "there are approximately two hundred States and three thousand languages or cultures; therefore, the majority of state political subjects in existence are plurilingustic and pluricultural."[17]

In addition, the nation is a historical construct associated with a specific context and a particular political project. According to the work of Eric J. Hobsbawm, first there was the production of territorial demarcations, then the corresponding feeling of belonging to that space.[18] What has been forged around sovereignty as a signifier is a will to power (such as "either I govern myself or I am governed by others") in which the subject has been imagined with all the attributes that the Western philosophical tradition ascribed to it and as if subjects were "final metaphysical points."[19]

In contrast to the understanding of a world of solid identities or sovereign subjectivities (e.g., a "national being"), another approach is to consider the subject as a flux of multiple becomings that is, however, produced by a series of discourses that inscribe subjectivity in a network of power devices (or technologies of the self). Rephrasing Braidotti, the question when trying to understand national sovereignty is not how the subject expresses its desire for liberation but rather what self is present in the expression of "national being." While the national being is the subject of citizenship, citizenship has been historically linked to the imaginary of patriotism, and it can be argued that this has resulted in passion for the mob, and occlusion of singularity and difference.[20] When the sovereign is collapsed within the national (being), there is no way to rescue singularity because this collapse is invariably produced to function as a homogenized people.

Another way to consider the impossibility of sovereign subjectivity is through an analysis of what philosopher Georges Bataille called eroticism.

As Bataille has theorized, there is no way to both concede to the erotic and consider the subject as a sovereign being. Eroticism presupposes the impossibility of sovereignty as it pushes subjectivity to its very limit, therefore canceling the possibility of a self-contained and/or self-determined subject:

> I said that I regarded eroticism as the disequilibrium in which the being consciously calls his own existence into question. In one sense, the being loses itself deliberately, but then the subject is identified with the object losing his identity. If necessary I can say in eroticism: I am losing myself.

The transition from the normal state to that of erotic desire presupposes a partial dissolution of the self, as he or she exists in the realm of discontinuity. The whole business of eroticism is to destroy the self-contained character of the participants as they exist in their normal lives.[21] Nonetheless, there is also in Bataille a resignification of sovereignty in his book *Lo que entiendo por soberanía* that seems to be related to a postmetaphysical view of the subject: the subject becomes sovereign departing from being, in the "being there" or the immediacy of life to which one only comes to not from knowledge but from nonknowledge (absence of knowledge):

> Only by annihilating or at least neutralizing in ourselves all operation of knowledge can we be in the instant without avoiding it. That is possible under the impression of strong emotions that break, interrupt, or leave in a second level the continuous development of knowledge.[22]

The sovereign, for Bataille, is the enjoyment of the present (time) without having to take into account anything but the present. Sovereignty, for Bataille, is linked not to transcendence (or to the assumption of the existence of the well-built subject of Modernity) but to immanence or just being there. Notice that it is a sovereignty that is closer perhaps to a state of "autosubjectivity," comparable to the possibility of self-subjectivation proposed by Foucault, that is, the possibility that the subject makes him- or herself a subject apart from the subjection proper to a specific system of domination. For Foucault, ethics are defined in relation to the care of the self in which the subject becomes ruler of herself and explores the possibility of fashioning herself in such a way that she produces her own center of gravity without the need for recognition or legitimization by the sovereign.

Also, and following systems theorist Niklas Luhmann, it is always possible to consider that the semantics of sovereignty could emerge as a component of all sorts of collective agencies (feminist, queer, indigenous, etc.), which could provoke certain political efficacies. But it is one thing to participate in those semantics in a performative way and another thing to portray them as either the truth of the social, the truth of the politics, or the truth of a specific group.

Finally, as Luhmann suggests, to the extent that Modernity is characterized by a principle of self-erosion, that in itself is the reflection of a process. In this sense, why not assume that to the extent that sovereignty as a signifier is attached to early Modernity and is contemporaneously activated within a diversity of power devices or technologies, it also erodes, getting out from a conceptual straightjacket to make way for a political *avenir* (future)? As it is also stated by Luhmann, in its initial stages, Modernity produces certain figures of thought that in time could not resist the social onslaught ("el embate social") of Modernity itself. Perhaps this has been the destiny of sovereignty as a signifier.

Notes

1. Wendy Brown, "Sovereignty and the Return of the Repressed," in *The New Pluralism: William Connolly and the Contemporary Global Condition*, ed. David Campbell and Morton Schoolman (Durham, NC: Duke University Press, 2008), 250–71.
2. Eligio Resta, *La certeza y la esperanza: Ensayo sobre el derecho y la violencia*, Paidós estado y sociedad 27 (Barcelona: Paidós Ibérica, 1995), 102.
3. Walter Benjamin, *Reflections: Essays, Aphorisms, Autobiographical Writings* (New York: Harcourt Brace Jovanovich, 1978), 283.
4. See Giorgio Agamben, *Homo Sacer: Sovereign Power and Bare Life* (Stanford, CA: Stanford University Press, 1998).
5. Néstor García Canclini, *La globalización imaginada* (México: Paidós, 1999), 21.

6. Arjun Appadurai, *Modernity at Large: Cultural Dimensions of Globalization* (Minneapolis: University of Minnesota Press, 1996).
7. Gilles Lipovetsky, *El crepúsculo del deber* (Barcelona: Anagrama, 1994), 197.
8. Amartya Sen, *Identity and Violence: The Illusion of Destiny* (New York: Norton, 2007).
9. Emilio González, "¿Ciudadanía sin polis, democracia sin demos?," *Bordes* 8 (2000): 4.
10. Niklas Luhmann, *Observaciones de la modernidad* (Barcelona: Paidós, 1977).
11. Michel Foucault, *Society Must Be Defended* (New York: Picador, 1997).
12. *V for Vendetta*, directed by James McTeigue (Warner Bros. Pictures, 2006).
13. Agamben, *Homo Sacer*, 122.
14. Fernando Savater, *Perdonen las molestias* (Madrid: Ediciones El País, 2001), 307.
15. Rosi Braidotti, *Sujetos nómades* (Buenos Aires: Paidós, 2000), 196.
16. Judith Butler, *Excitable Speech: A Politics of the Performative* (New York: Routledge, 1997), 16.
17. Fernando Savater, "El tiempo y la tempestad," in *Sobrevivir* (Barcelona: Ariel, 2001), 192 (my translation).
18. Eric J. Hobsbawm, *Nations and Nationalism Since 1780: Programme, Myth, Reality* (Cambridge: Cambridge University Press, 1990).
19. Butler, *Excitable Speech*.
20. Toby Miller, *The Well-Tempered Self: Citizenship, Culture, and the Postmodern Subject* (Baltimore: John Hopkins University Press, 1993).
21. Georges Bataille, *Eroticism, Death and Sensuality* (San Francisco: City Lights Books, 1986), 17.
22. Georges Bataille, *Lo que entiendo por soberanía* (Barcelona: Paidós, 1996), 70 (my translation).

11

Indigenizing Agamben

Rethinking Sovereignty in Light of the "Peculiar" Status of Native Peoples

Mark Rifkin

But the relation of the Indians to the United States is marked by peculiar and cardinal distinctions which exist nowhere else.

...

Though the Indians are acknowledged to have an unquestionable, and, heretofore, unquestioned right to the lands they occupy . . . ; yet it may well be doubted whether those tribes which reside within the acknowledged boundaries of the United States can, with strict accuracy, be denominated foreign nations. They may, more correctly, perhaps, be denominated domestic dependent nations.
CHEROKEE NATION V. GEORGIA (1831)

The relation of the Indian tribes living within the borders of the United States, both before and since the Revolution, to the people of the United States has always been an anomalous one and of a complex character.

...

They were, and always have been, regarded . . . not as States, not as nations, not as possessed of the full attributes of sovereignty, but as a separate people, with the power of regulating their internal and social relations, and thus far not brought under the laws of the Union or of the State within whose limits they resided.
U.S. V. KAGAMA (1886)

Protection of territory within its external political boundaries is, of course, as central to the sovereign interests of the United States as it is to any

other sovereign nation. But from the formation of the Union and the adoption of the Bill of Rights, the United States has manifested an equally great solicitude that its citizens be protected by the United States from unwarranted intrusions on their personal liberty. . . . By submitting to the overriding sovereignty of the United States, Indian tribes therefore necessarily give up their power to try non-Indian citizens of the United States except in a manner acceptable to Congress.
OLIPHANT V. SUQUAMISH INDIAN TRIBE, ET AL. (1978)

What does *sovereignty* mean in the context of U.S.-Indian policy? Looking at the statements above, all from U.S. Supreme Court decisions focused on the status of Native peoples, sovereignty at least touches on questions of jurisdiction, the drawing of national boundaries, and control over the legal status of persons and entities within those boundaries.¹ While one could characterize the concept of sovereignty as a shorthand for the set of legal practices and principles that allow one to determine the rightful scope of U.S. authority, it seems to function in the decisions less as a way of designating a specific set of powers than as a negative presence, as what Native peoples categorically lack, or at the least only have in some radically diminished fashion managed by the United States. Further, the decisions cited seem less to extend existing legal categories and precedents than to indicate the absence of an appropriate legal framework in which to consider the political issues and dynamics at hand. Native peoples appear as a gap within U.S. legal discourse. These passages suggest that the available logics of U.S. jurisdiction are unable to incorporate Native peoples comfortably, that continued Native presence pushes against the presumed coherence of the U.S. territorial and jurisdictional imaginary.

While the decisions seem to be grasping to find language adequate to the disturbing legal limbo in which Native nations appear to sit, they also insist unequivocally that such peoples fall *within* the bounds of U.S. sovereignty, and the oddity attributed to U.S.-Indian policy is offered as confirmation of that fact. Typifying "the relations of the Indians to the United States" as "peculiar" and "anomalous," while also consistently presenting Native peoples as unlike all other political entities in U.S. law and policy, indexes the failure of U.S. discourses to encompass them while speaking as if they were incorporated via their incommensurability. In *Homo Sacer: Sovereign Power and Bare Life*, Giorgio Agamben has described this kind of dialectic as the "state of exception," suggesting that it is at the core of what it means for a state to exert "sovereignty."[2] He argues, "the sovereign decision on the exception is the originary juridico-political structure on the basis of which what is included in the juridical order and what is excluded from it acquire their meaning," and "in this sense, the exception is the originary form of law."[3] What appears as an exception from the regular regime of law actually exposes the rooting of the law itself in a "sovereign" will that can decide where, how, and to what the formal "juridical order" will apply. The narration of Native peoples as an exception from the regular categories of U.S. law, then, can be seen, in Agamben's terms, as a form of "sovereign violence" that "opens a zone of indistinction between law and nature, outside and inside, violence and law."[4] The language of exception, of inclusive exclusion, discursively brings Native peoples into the fold of sovereignty, implicitly offering an explanation for why Native peoples do not fit existing legal concepts (they are different) while assuming that they should be placed within the context of U.S. law (its conceptual field is the obvious comparative framework).[5]

In using Agamben's work to address U.S.-Indian policy, however, it needs to be reworked. In particular, his emphasis on biopolitics tends to come at the expense of a discussion of geopolitics, the production of race supplanting the production of space as a way of envisioning the work of the sovereignty he critiques, and while his concept of the exception has been immensely influential in contemporary scholarship and cultural criticism, such accounts largely have left aside discussion of Indigenous peoples. Attending to Native peoples' position within settler-state sovereignties requires investigating and adjusting three aspects of Agamben's thinking: the persistent inside/outside tropology he uses to address the exception, specifically the ways it serves as a metaphor divorced from territoriality; the notion of "bare life" as the basis of the exception, especially the individualizing ways that he uses that concept; and the implicit depiction of sovereignty as a self-confident exercise of authority free from anxiety over the legitimacy of state actions.[6] Such revision allows for a reconsideration of the "zone of indistinction" produced by and within sovereignty, opening up analysis of the ways settler states regulate not only proper kinds of embodiment ("bare life") but legitimate modes of collectivity and occupancy—what I will call *bare habitance*.

If the "overriding sovereignty" of the U.S. is predicated on the creation of a state of exception, then the struggle for sovereignty by Native peoples can be envisioned as less about control of particular policy domains than of *metapolitical authority*—the ability to define the content and scope of "law" and "politics." Such a shift draws attention away from critiques of the particular rhetorics used to justify the state's plenary power and toward a macrological effort to contest the "overriding" assertion of a right to exert control over Native polities. My argument, then, explores the limits of forms of analysis organized around the critique of the settler-state's employment of racialized discourses of savagery and the emphasis on cultural distinctions between Euro-American and Indigenous modes of governance. Both of these strategies within Indigenous political theory treat sovereignty as a particular kind of political content that can be juxtaposed with a substantively different—more Native-friendly or Indigenous-centered—content, but by contrast, I suggest that discourses of racial difference and equality as well as of cultural recognition are deployed by the state in ways that reaffirm its geopolitical self-evidence and its authority to determine what issues, processes, and statuses will count as meaningful within the political system.

While arguments about Euro-American racism and the disjunctions between Native traditions and imposed structures of governance can be quite powerful in challenging aspects of settler-state policy, they cannot account for the structuring violence performed by the figure of sovereignty. Drawing on Agamben, I will argue that "sovereignty" functions as a placeholder that has no determinate content.[7] The state has been described as an entity that exercises a monopoly on the legitimate exercise of violence, and what I am suggesting is that the state of exception produced through Indian policy creates a monopoly on the legitimate exercise of legitimacy, an exclusive uncontestable right to define what will count as a viable legal or political form(ul)ation. That fundamentally circular and self-validating, as well as anxious and fraught, performance grounds the legitimacy of state rule on nothing more than the axiomatic negation of Native peoples' authority to determine or adjudicate for themselves the normative principles by which they will be governed. Through Agamben's theory of the exception, then, I will explore how the supposedly underlying sovereignty of the U.S. settler state is a retrospective projection generated by and dependent on the "peculiar"-ization of Native peoples.

The Domain of Inclusive Exclusion: The Camp and the Reservation

In introducing his argument in *Homo Sacer*, Agamben marks, while seeking to trouble, the distinction between *zoē* and *bios*—"the simple fact of living common to all living beings (animals, men, or gods)" versus "the form or way of living proper to an individual or a group."[8] He suggests that in classical antiquity the former was excluded from the sphere of politics and that part of what most distinguishes modernity, particularly the structure of the state, is the effort to bring the former into the orbit of governmental regulation, in fact to see it as the animating principle of political life ("the politicization of bare life as such"[9]). The first articulation of the book's central thesis, then, is as follows: "*It can even be said that the production of a biopolitical body is the original activity of sovereign power.*"[10] In other words, modern sovereignty depends on generating a vision of the "body"—of apolitical natural life—that is cast as simultaneously exterior to the sphere of government and law and as the reference point for defining the proper aims, objects, and methods of governance ("placing biological life at the center of its calculations"[11]). That "body" is divorced from politics per se while simultaneously defining the aspirational and normative horizon of political action. "Bare life," therefore, serves as an authorizing figure for decision making by self-consciously political institutions while itself being presented as exempt from question or challenge within such institutions.

Further, and more urgently for Agamben, the generation of "bare life" makes thinkable the consignment of those who do not fit the idealized "biopolitical body" to a "zone" outside of political participation and the regular working of the law but still within the ambit of state power. Describing this possibility, he observes, "The relation of exception is a relation of ban. He who has been banned is not, in fact, simply set outside the law and made indifferent to it but rather *abandoned* by it, that is, exposed and threatened on the threshold. . . . It is literally not possible to say whether the one who has been banned is outside or inside the juridical order."[12] For Agamben, the Nazi concentration camp serves as the paradigmatic example of the biopolitical imperatives structuring modern sovereignty, described as "the hidden matrix and *nomos* of the political space in which we are still living."[13] The existence of the camps disrupted the "functional nexus" on which the modern nation-state was "founded": "the old trinity composed of the state, the nation (birth), and land" in which "a determinate localization (land) and a determinate order (the State) are mediated by automatic rules for the inscription of life (birth or the nation)."[14] The camp opens up a location within the state in which persons who are linked to the space of the nation by birth can be managed as "bare life," as mere biological beings bereft of any/all legal protections of citizenship.

Yet if that denial of political subjectivity and simultaneous subjection to the force of the state confuses or perhaps conflates "exclusion and inclusion," to what extent is that blurring predicated on the reification of the boundaries of the "sovereign power" of the nation? Put another way, if the person in the state of exception is considered "bare life" and thus neither truly "outside [n]or inside the juridical order," how does one know that the "abandoned" comes under the sway of a given sovereign? How might the "irreducible indistinction" enacted by sovereignty that Agamben describes itself depend on a prior geopolitical mapping that is also produced through the invocation of sovereignty, differentiating those people and places that fall within the jurisdictional sphere of a given state from those that do not?

That process of *distinction*, I contend, draws on the logic of exception Agamben theorizes but in ways that cannot be reduced to the creation of a "biopolitical body." In describing how modern sovereignty appears to found itself on the will of the people, Agamben locates a biopolitical problematic at the core of that claim:

> It is as if what we call "people" were in reality not a unitary subject but a dialectical oscillation between two opposite poles: on the one hand, the set of the People as a whole political body, and on the other, the subset of the people as a fragmentary multiplicity of needy and excluded bodies; or again, on the one

hand, an inclusion that claims to be total, and on the other, an exclusion that is clearly hopeless; at one extreme, the total state of integrated and sovereign citizens, and at the other, the preserve—court of miracles or camp—of the wretched, the oppressed, and the defeated.[15]

The "People" stands less for the actual assemblage of persons within the state than for the set of those who fit the ideal "body," and who consequently will be recognized as "citizens," with the rest of the resident population consigned to the realm of "bare life"—the people who are not the People and thus are excluded from meaningful participation while remaining the objects of state control. However, when reflecting on the status of Indigenous populations in relation to the settler state, a third category emerges that is neither people nor People—namely *peoples*. The possibility of conceptualizing the nation as "a whole political body" requires narrating it as "a unitary subject" rather than a collection of separate, unsubordinated, self-governing polities. Conversely, for "inclusion" to be articulated as "total," it needs to have a clear domain over which it is extended. In critiquing the approach of previous theorists to the issue of sovereignty, Agamben notes, "The problem of sovereignty was reduced to the question of who within the political order was invested with certain powers, and the very threshold of the political order itself was never called into question."[16] However, Agamben's account itself assumes a clear "within" by not posing the question of how sovereignty produces and is produced by place, how the state is realized as a spatial phenomenon as part of "the very threshold of the political order itself."

I am suggesting, then, that the biopolitical project of defining the proper "body" of the people is subtended by the geopolitical project of defining the territoriality of the nation, displacing competing claims by older/other political formations as what we might call *bare habitance*. Agamben notes, "The camp is a piece of land placed outside the normal juridical order, but it is nevertheless not simply an external space,"[17] but that definition also seems to capture rather precisely the status of the reservation, a space that while governed under "peculiar" rules categorically is denied status as "external," or "foreign." Examining the reservation—and more broadly the representation of Native collectivity and territoriality in U.S. governmental discourses—through the prism of Agamben's analysis of the state of exception helps highlight the kinds of "sovereign violence" at play in the (re)production and naturalization of national space.[18] The effort to think biopolitics without geopolitics, bare life without bare habitance, results in the erasure of the politics of collectivity and occupancy: what entities will count as polities and thus be seen as deserving of autonomy; what modes of inhabitance and land tenure will be understood as legitimate; and who will get to make such determinations and on what basis?[19]

Focusing on the fracture between "the People" and "the people" imagines explicitly or implicitly either a reconciliation of the two (restoring a version of the "trinity" of state, land, and birth) or the proliferation of a boundaryless humanness unconstrained by territorially circumscribed polities. These options leave little room for thinking indigeneity, the existence of *peoples* forcibly made domestic whose self-understandings and aspirations cannot be understood in terms of the denial of (or disjunctions within) state citizenship.[20]

While in the next section I will address how biopolitical and geopolitical dynamics work together, specifically in the translation of Native peoples into aggregates of individual domestic subjects (as either a race or a culture), I first want to explore in greater detail how the production of national space depends on coding Native peoples and lands as an exception. Administrative mappings of U.S. jurisdiction remain haunted by the presence of polities whose occupancy precedes that of the state and whose existence as collectivities repeatedly has been officially recognized through treaties. The Supreme Court decisions with which I began all register this difficulty. In *Cherokee Nation v. Georgia*, the court explicitly finds that the "acts of our government plainly recognize the Cherokee nation as a state," indicating that it is "a distinct political society, separated from others, capable of managing its own affairs and governing itself."[21] Yet the majority opinion also insists, "The Indian territory is admitted to compose a part of the United States," adding, "They occupy a territory to which we assert a title independent of their will."[22] Following a similar line of reasoning, *U.S. v. Kagama* insists, "the colonies before the Revolution and the States and the United States since, have recognized in the Indians a possessory right to the soil, . . . But they asserted an ultimate title in the land itself,"[23] and Justice Rehnquist in *Oliphant v. Suquamish* argues, "Indian tribes do retain elements of 'quasi-sovereign' authority after ceding their lands to the United States," although "their exercise of separate power is constrained so as not to conflict with the interests of [the United States'] overriding sovereignty."[24] Each of these formulations acknowledges a tension between the kinds of political identity and authority suggested by the ability to enter into formal agreements with the United States and the claim that such otherwise (or previously) "distinct political societ[ies]" are fully enclosed within the boundaries of the state and thus subject in some fashion to its rule.

Presenting U.S.-Indian relations as "peculiar" or "anomalous" marks that tension, but such a description depicts the treaty system and the workings of federal Indian law as neither regular domestic law nor foreign policy. The oddity can seem to inhere in the treaties themselves, a supposed irregularity that U.S. lawmakers sought to remedy in the late nineteenth century by ending the practice of treaty making.[25] The "peculiar"-ity of the treaty system, though, is less a function of the constitutional status it confers on Indian policy (enacting it through documents that in the words of Article VI make it "the supreme law of the land") than the underlying contradiction to which the treaty system points. Treaties register and mediate a structural disjunction between the continuing existence of autochthonous Native collectivities, which predate the formation of the United States, and the adoption of a jurisdictional imaginary in which such collectivities are imagined as part of U.S. national space.

More than merely recognizing Native peoples as "distinct political societ[ies]" with whom the United States must negotiate for territory, however, the treaty system also seeks to interpellate Native polities into U.S. political discourses, presupposing (and imposing) forms of governance and occupancy that facilitate the cession of land.[26] While in one sense acknowledging Native peoples as "separate" entities from the United States, the treaty-based Indian policy of the late eighteenth and nineteenth centuries also sought to confirm the United States' "ultimate title in the land itself," thereby indicating the stresses generated by the narration of Native nations as domestic. Dispensing with treaties, though, does not eliminate such strain or the normative difficulties it creates for validating U.S. authority over Native populations and lands, instead simply trying to displace the problem of legitimacy, which still returns insistently to trouble U.S. legal discourses.[27]

The potential disjuncture in U.S. jurisdiction opened by the presence of nonnational entities with claims to land ostensibly inside the nation is sutured over by proclaiming a "sovereignty" that supposedly alleviates the potential "conflict" between U.S. and Native mappings. Presented as simply logically following from Native peoples' residence on "territory admitted to compose a part of the United States,"[28] the invocation of sovereignty casts them as exceptional, an aberration from the normal operation of law but one contained within the broader sphere of U.S. national authority. "Indian tribes" have only a "possessory right" or "quasi-sovereign" claims, but "ultimate title," the decisions reassuringly indicate, lies with the United States. Yet rather than providing an underlying framework in which to situate Indigenous populations, sovereignty instead appears as a mutable figure that enables their occupancy to be portrayed as "peculiar." Discursively, it bridges the logical and legal chasm between the political autonomy indexed by the treaty system and the depiction of them as domestic subjects. United States political discourses seek to contain the instability of the settler state by repeatedly declaring the nation's geopolitical unity, but at moments when that avowal is brought into crisis by the continuing presence and operation of Native polities, the topos of sovereignty emerges as if it exists before and beyond the specific legal questions at stake in any particular case or act of policy making. As Judith Butler suggests, "it is not that sovereignty exists as a possession that the US is said to 'have.'...Grammar defeats us here. Sovereignty is what is tactically produced through the very mechanism of its self-justification."[29] The citation of sovereignty in this completely open ended but rhetorically foundationalizing way suggests a potentially unlimited capacity to (re)define what will count as the organizing framework of political order.

The performative citation of sovereignty by the United States depends on the creation of a state of exception for Native peoples. The content of "sovereignty" in the decisions is the assertion of the authority to treat Native peoples as having constrained, diminished political control over themselves and their lands, and such a contention rests on the assumption that despite their existence before and after the founding of the United States as "separate people[s], with the power of regulating their internal and social relations,"[30] they somehow do not have equivalent status to "foreign" nations. As

Agamben observes, "the state of exception is . . . the principle of every juridical localization, since only the state of exception opens the space in which the determination of a certain juridical order and a particular territory first becomes possible."[31] The jurisdictional imaginary of the U.S. is made possible only by *localizing* Native peoples, in the sense of circumscribing their political power/status and portraying Indian policy as an aberration divorced from the principles at play in the rest of U.S. law, and that process of exception quite literally opens the *space* for a legal geography predicated on the territorial coherence of the nation.

While it rhetorically appears to validate or underwrite U.S. law, the figure of sovereignty results from the exception, making possible the founding of the regime of domestic policy. United States authority over Native peoples cannot be derived from the constitutional order of law, instead, in Agamben's terms, "tracing a threshold . . . on the basis of which outside and inside, the normal situation and chaos, enter into those complex topological relations that make the validity of the juridical order possible."[32] Those political collectivities whose occupancy does not fit the geopolitical ideal/imaginary of the state are left abandoned by it, "exposed and threatened on the threshold" of the juridical order that is made possible and validated by their exception.[33] From that perspective, settler-state sovereignty can be viewed less as an expression of the nation's rightful control over the land within its boundaries than as the topological production of the impression of boundedness by banning—rendering "peculiar," "anomalous," "unique," "special"—competing claims to place and collectivity.[34] This line of thought further suggests that if the validity of national policy is presented as being derived from the underlying fact of sovereignty, such a claim to legitimacy itself relies on the promulgation of an exception that rests on nothing more than the absoluteness with which it is articulated and enforced.

Dependence, Race, and the Tabooing of Culture

Representing Native populations and lands as occupying an "anomalous" position allows the U.S. government to validate its extension of theoretically unlimited authority over them, rendering them external to the normal functioning of the law but yet internal to the space of the nation. The dominance perpetuated through the ongoing re-creation of this state of exception, though, inheres not merely in the exercise of unhampered jurisdiction over Native peoples but in the ways that jurisdiction enables a metapolitical scripting of the terms of collectivity itself. More than circumscribing or disciplining the autonomy of Native peoples, Indian policy recodes their identities, defining and redefining the threshold of political identity and legitimacy and determining how Native peoples will enter that field, including what (kinds of) concepts and categories they will inhabit.[35] The representation of Native peoples as an exception makes possible their incorporation into U.S. administrative discourses in any number of ways along a wide spectrum ranging from polity to bare life. In that process of inscription, the biopolitical and the geopolitical dynamics of nation-statehood discussed above enter into a dialectical relay, the former serving as a way of resolving the threatened incoherence of the latter by providing a set of tactics through which to recast Native peoples as people.[36] In seeking to cope with the presence of preexisting polities on what it seeks to portray as domestic space, the United States often translates autochthonous, self-governing Native polities as populations; as either collections of bodies in need of restraint/protection or cultural aggregations. In being interpellated into U.S. political discourses in this way, they are managed as residents—as a kind of racialized, endangered, or enculturated body—on land that self-evidently constitutes part of the nation.

Turning again to the Supreme Court cases with which I began, this dynamic can be seen in the mobilization of the figure of dependence. The decision in *Cherokee Nation v. Georgia* invents the notion of "domestic dependent nation," and in justifying the fabrication of this unheard of status, the court articulates what would become a (if not *the*) central trope of federal Indian law, saying of Native peoples that "their relation to the United States resembles that of a ward to his guardian." The opinion adds, "They look to our government for protection; rely upon its kindness and its power; appeal to it for relief to their wants; and address the president as their great father."[37] That vision of superintendence depends on infantilization, casting the same group referred to earlier in the decision as a "distinct political society" as a child in need of guidance and safeguarding. This description, however, appears just in the wake of the court's insistence that "those tribes which reside within the acknowledged boundaries of the United States" cannot "with strict accuracy, be denominated foreign nations."[38] The image of Native nations as hapless minors, "ward[s]," appears retroactively to justify their status as "domestic," but their apparent dependency *follows from* their location "within the acknowledged boundaries" of the nation-state, "dependent" providing a content for "domestic" belonging other than simply the absence/disavowal of "foreign"-ness. A particular jurisdictional mapping, "within," then, comes to appear through the prism of dependence as a qualitatively different kind of relation; Native polities' call for the acknowledgment of their boundaries and autonomy is transfigured instead as a mass of *wants*—a term suggestive of persistent bodily need.

This discursive transmutation of Indigenous peoplehood into bare life is even more pronounced in *U.S. v. Kagama*. Rehearsing the language of "ward"-ship, the decision expands the scope and deepens the sense of the dependency cited in the earlier opinion: "These Indian tribes are the wards of the nation. They are communities dependent on the United States. Dependent largely for their daily food. Dependent for their political rights."[39] Dispensing with the rhetoric of nationhood from the previous decision, the court here envisions "Indian tribes" as groups whose continued existence is utterly contingent on federal care. They are an undifferentiated mass of flesh with no "political" existence apart from whatever "rights" may happen to be granted (or withheld) by the United States. Once again, though, this corporealization of Indians is brought back to the problems they potentially pose for national spatiality:

> The power of the General Government over these remnants of a race once powerful, now weak and diminished in numbers, is necessary to their protection, as well as to the safety of those among whom they dwell. It must exist in that government, because it never has existed anywhere else, because the theatre of its exercise is within the geographical limits of the United States, because it has never been denied, and because it alone can enforce its laws on all the tribes.[40]

While reinforcing the impression of an assemblage of exposed and endangered bodies—"remnants" whose frailty leaves them on the verge of extinction—the passage ends up justifying U.S. "power" by reference to the supremacy that is understood to be a necessary corollary of the coherence of "the geographical limits of the United States." The sheer vehemence of the statement that control over Indians "must exist in that government" intimates a profound anxiety, the phrase "anywhere else" suggesting a fear that the space of the nation might somehow be(come) alien to itself—an *elsewhere* to which U.S. jurisdiction explicitly is "denied" by the Indigenous inhabitants. The categorization of Indians as "weak and diminished" bodies or a murderous threat to "the safety" of neighboring white communities (a savage "race") appears to provide a reason, in a biopolitical key, for the exertion of authority over them, but it occupies the space of the exception already produced by the encompassing insistence that Native peoples fall within the "theatre" of U.S. governance.

Presenting Indians as bare life—dying "remnants," helpless children, and/or vicious savages—addresses their status within the regime of U.S. policy as if it were a function of natural facts, prepolitical or apolitical conditions to which U.S. institutions respond,[41] but the biopolitical figure of dependence also presumes a vision of geopolitical incorporation that precedes it, the latter appearing as merely background for the former. Yet the background keeps coming to the fore, invested in the decisions with a force that rhetorically exceeds and logically disjoints its apparent role as simply setting as opposed to focus or aim. Viewed in this way, the critique of Indian policy as racist only addresses biopolitical tactics without dislodging the geopolitical structure of exception. In *Like a Loaded Weapon: The Rehnquist Court, Indian Rights, and the Legal History of Racism in America*, Robert A. Williams takes such an approach, arguing that the vision of Indians as "uncivilized, unsophisticated, and lawless savages" enshrined in numerous nineteenth-century Supreme Court opinions continues to serve as the basis for Indian law, given the ongoing citation of those cases as precedent: "The stereotypes or images that the Court has thus legitimated and expanded can now be used to legally justify a rights-denying, jurispathic form of racism against those groups."[42] Through the term *jurispathic*, Williams, following the legal theorist Robert Cover, refers to the power of the court to make one tradition of law or legal interpretation the exclusive, authoritative one, thereby eliminating alternatives or denying them institutional validity by refusing to sanction them as legally/politically viable options. However, casting that dynamic in Indian policy as primarily one of a "racism" that denies access to "rights" leaves aside not only the question of territoriality but of Native peoples' status as independent polities. According to Williams, the Supreme Court refuses to apply the "egalitarian principles of racial equality normally applied to all other groups and individuals in post-*Brown* America," instead "deciding . . . Indian rights case[s] according to an overarching metaprinciple of Indian racial inferiority."[43] Yet if such "egalitarian principles" were applied so that Indians were deemed no different than any other "groups and individuals" in "America," that disposition in and of itself still would not reverse the linked dynamics of internalization and individualization through which Indians are understood as subjects of U.S. domestic law and policy, as firmly *within* the nation and thus subjected to its metapolitical authority. While no longer positioned as savages or "dependent" children, cast as fully rights-bearing individuals rather than bare life, Native peoples still would signify as collections of persons within the ambit of U.S. jurisdiction rather than as autonomous political collectivities whose identity and status cannot be managed by U.S. institutions.

Thus, although Williams recognizes the difference between Native peoples and those minorities whose horizon of legal aspiration is framed as full inclusion in the nation as citizens, offering what he describes as a "singularity thesis" that acknowledges "the unique types of autochthonous rights that tribal Indians want protected under U.S. law,"[44] his indictment of U.S. modes of racialization cannot fully capture the political work performed by sovereignty, or rather the work that the citation of sovereignty performs in (re)defining and regulating the terms of "political" identity. Inasmuch as the biopolitical discourse of race helps dissimulate the violence at play in the domestication of Native peoples by depicting the terms of U.S. rule as due to the "natural" qualities of Indians, the kind of antiracist challenge Williams suggests can help disqualify the bodily as a basis for Indian law, thereby clearing conceptual and discursive ground so as to draw attention back to the issue of territoriality.[45] Having done so, however, one still needs to contest not so much the "metaprinciple of Indian racial inferiority" as that of the jurisdictional coherence of national space.

In his interpretation of *Oliphant v. Suquamish*, for example, Williams claims that the court's denial of the defendant's authority to prosecute non-

Indians depends on little more than a rehearsal of demeaning nineteenth-century stereotypes of Indians from previous decisions, including *Cherokee Nation* and *Kagama*, that have been sanitized by the removal of most of the overtly denigrating language. Yet *Oliphant* asserts, "Upon incorporation into the territory of the United States, the Indian tribes thereby come under the territorial sovereignty of the United States and their exercise of separate power is constrained so as not to conflict with the interests of this overriding sovereignty."[46] Even if the Indian/non-Indian distinction were eliminated as a vestige of a noxious regime of racial hierarchy, the "territorial sovereignty of the United States" would remain, along with the dangerously amorphous, infinitely expansive, and uncontestable "interests" that are said to follow from it and that provide the means of "overriding" any initiative by Native populations to represent and assert themselves as autonomous collectivities.

If antiracist resistance remains urgent but still insufficient to the task of breaking the stranglehold on the "political" held by the United States as a result of its exceptionalization of Indigenous polities, might the notion of "culture" better serve to challenge settler-state authority? Agamben's argument inadvertently signals the limit of such a strategy. In sketching the notion of bare life, he offers the example of *homo sacer*, a status from Roman law for a person who has been convicted of a crime and as such may be killed without prosecution for homicide but who also cannot be sacrificed as an offering to the gods. Agamben asks, "In what, then, does the sacredness of this sacred man consist," and he answers that the "sacred" is the life that has been abandoned "outside both human and divine law," further suggesting that "*homo sacer* presents the originary figure of life taken into the sovereign ban."[47] What particularly interests me in his formulation is that in connecting the sacred to sovereignty, Agamben rails against the ways "the ethnological notion of taboo" works "to dissolve the specificity of *homo sacer*,"[48] suggesting that the "ambivalence" surrounding the "ethnographic concept of taboo" (as that which generates both awe and horror)

> cannot explain the juridico-political phenomenon to which the most ancient meaning of the term *sacer* refers. On the contrary, only an attentive and unprejudiced delimitation of the respective fields of the political and the

religious will make it possible to understand the history of their intersection and complex relations.[49]

The clear distinction between social "fields" is blurred by the tendency of "ethnological"/"ethnographic" analysis to smuggle in alien ideas and categories into discussion of the "political." Yet if *homo sacer*, freed from the confusion of "taboo," is exemplary of the political work of sovereignty, what defines the field of politics? It appears as that which is left once one has stripped away "ethnographic" excess, creating a threshold between "the political and the religious" in which the former emerges through the exception of the latter. The "specificity" of "the juridico-political" as a *kind* of "phenomenon," then, rests on an open-ended process of exclusion itself cast as self-evident, as an obvious difference between "fields" rather than an act based on the kind of sovereign violence Agamben critiques.

The fact that the "ethnographic concept" of "taboo" is taken to mark the (failure to note the) discrepancy between political and other phenomena is of particular significance in light of the above analysis of the metapolitical invention of statuses for Indigenous peoples. Taken from Polynesian societies, with which European explorers came into contact in the late eighteenth century, the term *taboo*, or *kapu*, refers to a power of prohibition managed by rulers on the basis of spiritual ideals.[50] A complex phenomenon to which I here cannot devote the consideration it is due, it certainly challenges the notion that in those systems of governance "the political and the religious" were readily differentiable "fields." In other words, Agamben produces a pure vision of politics by disowning the introduction of concepts from other modes of governance as a category mistake, as an intrusion into or deformation of that which is authentically "political." From that perspective, any practice or principle can be dismissed or displaced as an "ethnographic" error, as the inappropriate transposition of one kind of thing into the domain properly occupied by another. In this way, one can see how "the cultural" categorically may be contradistinguished from "the political," producing a threshold of differentiation that the state can deploy in ways that both subordinate the former to the latter and preserve the exclusive power of the state to determine what constitutes the "field" of politics.

The threshold between culture and politics, then, reactivates the same logic of exception through which Native peoples are incorporated into the geopolitical imaginary of the settler state. This dynamic can be seen in James Tully's influential effort to rethink sovereignty. In *Strange Multiplicity: Constitutionalism in an Age of Diversity*, he describes the "struggles of Aboriginal peoples" as "demands for cultural recognition" that "are aspirations for appropriate forms of self government," and he further notes that "forms of self rule appropriate to the recognition of any culture vary" and that "the language employed in assessing claims to recognition continues to stifle cultural differences and impose a dominant culture, while masquerading as culturally neutral, comprehensive or unavoidably ethnocentric."[51] In Tully's account, "culture" provides an idiom through which to index the ways Native forms of governance may not conform to those "dominant" within the settler state while also highlighting how the adjudication of Native claims by the state relies on an unnecessarily homogenizing vision of national culture that forecloses "recognition" of the multiplicity of political formations existing within national space. As Elizabeth Povinelli has illustrated, though, the *recognition* of Indigenous cultural difference within liberal multiculturalist governance tends to reaffirm the coherence of the nation-state, fetishize an anachronizing vision of Native identity, and exonerate continuing forms of imperial superintendence. Focusing on Australia, she argues that "national pageants of shameful repentance and celebrations of a new recognition of subaltern worth remain inflected by the conditional (as long as they are not repugnant; that is, as long as they are not, at heart, not-us and as long as real economic resources are not at stake)."[52] The state's performance of its redemption from a violent colonial past depends on the embrace, or more accurately the invention, of a version of aboriginality that is consistent with the moral norms of settler-state law yet still strange enough to generate the frisson of diversity/discrepancy, creating the thrill of Indigenous authenticity while not validating acts or ideas "repugnant" to the sensibilities of non-Native citizens. The effort to locate and outline Native cultures occurs against the background of unquestioned settler-state jurisdiction, continuing to code Native populations as both exceptional and as collections of individual domestic subjects. Tully himself repeatedly makes such a move.

Characterizing the state's "accommodation" of Indigenous peoples' struggle for self-determination as "an intercultural dialogue in which culturally diverse sovereign citizens of contemporary societies negotiate agreements," he further indicates that "each citizen is a member of more than one culture," taking the nation-state as axiomatic, understanding that belonging to it as the precondition for such dialogue, and thus predicating conversation on the subordination of "culture" to "citizen"-ship in the state.[53]

As I have been suggesting, then, the topos of sovereignty designates less a content that can be replaced (a racist vision of Indian savagery, a Eurocentric resistance to Native customs) than a process of compulsory relation, one predicated on the supposedly unquestionable fact of national territorial boundaries. While contesting the various discourses that reaffirm the validity of assorted elements of settler-state jurisdiction certainly can do powerful work in challenging and changing particular policies, creating greater tactical room for maneuver in a range of struggles, such an approach cannot fully address the structuring force of sovereignty, the ways the exceptionalization of Native peoples works to legitimize the unconstrained metapolitical power of the United States to invent, enforce, and alter the statuses/categories/concepts in which Native peoples are made to signify.

The Question of (or Quest for) Legitimacy

If U.S.-Indian policy in its circulation of the figure of sovereignty has the potential to displace Native polities entirely, why not do so? Why not simply erase this ongoing threat to the jurisdictional imaginary of the nation?[54] To do so would foreground the very unilateral will—the theoretically limitless imperial violence—on which U.S. territoriality rests, exacerbating the very structural crisis of legitimacy the topos of sovereignty works to dissimulate. In other words, the claim of sovereignty appears at moments in which a gap has opened in the operative logics of U.S. law, offering a way of resolving legal and political questions that threaten to undo the geopolitics of the settler state. If Native peoples are the subjects of treaties, how are they not foreign? Why can the United States pass laws applicable to people on Native lands?

On what basis can the federal government claim the right to regulate political entities that predate the existence of the United States? The official answer provided for all of these questions is that Native populations and lands are within the domain over which the U.S. is sovereign. While tautological, self-serving, and resting on nothing more than outright assertion, this response is an attempt to provide a foundation for the exercise of U.S. authority, seeking to validate the domestication of Native peoples by generating terminologies and doctrines that appear to offer a logical/legal explanation.[55]

Simply to present U.S. superintendence as a function of brute force would undercut the very legitimizing aim of the arguments in which sovereignty is employed, thwarting their effort to cover the inability of U.S. law philosophically to ground itself in the ground of the nation. The citation of sovereignty, therefore, is less a confident and self-assured indication of untroubled control than a restless performance in which the failure to find a normative foundation on which to rest the legitimacy of national jurisdiction remains a nagging source of anxiety. Justice Clarence Thomas addresses this dynamic in his concurrence to the decision in *U.S. v. Lara* (2004).[56] Thomas observes that there is a contradiction at the heart of U.S.-Indian policy. "In my view, the tribes either are or are not separate sovereigns, and our federal Indian law cases untenably hold both positions simultaneously," and he later adds, "The Federal Government cannot simultaneously claim power to regulate virtually every aspect of the tribes through ordinary domestic legislation and also maintain that the tribes possess anything resembling 'sovereignty.'"[57] Despite the fact that the majority opinion describes tribes' "inherent sovereignty" as the source of their still circumscribed criminal jurisdiction, it also indicates that such "sovereignty" can be abridged, restored, and reconfigured at will by Congress, suggesting that the powers reaffirmed by the court under the rubric of tribal sovereignty actually are not predicated on the existence of Native peoples as autochthonous ("separate") entities but instead on the authority arrogated by the U.S. government to redefine the status of Native collectivities according to any principle it wishes. Still substantively conditioned by Congressional sanction, the legalism of "inherent sovereignty," not unlike "domestic dependent nation," draws attention away from the untenability of the United States' overriding claim to sovereignty itself, or rather the absence of a legitimate legal claim (or basis for making one) that is registered by the citation of the figure of sovereignty.

That process of invention signals an effort to cloak U.S. imperial modes of exception as something other than, in Agamben's terms, "sovereign violence," to cover the degree to which Native peoples are left "exposed and threatened on the threshold" of national territoriality.[58] The attempt to locate legitimacy for U.S. jurisdiction in something other than its own imposed, circular obviousness can be found even in the most strident declarations of sovereignty. In *Oliphant*, for example, the majority opinion suggests that "Indian tribes do retain elements of 'quasi-sovereign' authority after ceding their lands to the United States" and that they "give up their power to try non-Indian citizens" after "submitting to the overriding sovereignty of the United States."[59] Such moments suggest a point at which Native peoples voluntarily surrender certain forms of political authority. While quite doubtful as a way of characterizing the actual workings of the treaty system or the ways it was understood by Native signatories (assuming that sale or lease of particular plots of land is tantamount to a wholesale acceptance of unconstrained regulation by the United States over every aspect of Native life), this description does predicate federal power on consent ("ceding," "submitting"), seeking to cast U.S. sovereignty as encompassing yet fundamentally noncoercive.

This effort to find a way to ameliorate the force of settler-state jurisdiction suggests that part of the metapolitical generation of categories, concepts, and statuses is the attempted simulation of legitimacy as well. If the notion of "inherent sovereignty" as employed in U.S.-Indian policy is somewhat of a placeholder given its continued subjection to potential congressional reworking (the supposed "overriding sovereignty" of the federal government), it still provides a discursive entry point that can be occupied by Native peoples in ways that expose the domination at play in the deployment of the topos of sovereignty by the settler state. In other words, exploiting the kind of logical incoherence and underlying normative crisis toward which Thomas points, the discourse of sovereignty can be mobilized to deconstruct U.S. rule by illustrating how the settler state exerts a monopoly on the production of legitimacy—the ways statuses are imposed on Native peoples in the context of their axiomatic yet constitutionally indefensible subjection to U.S. authority. The countercitation of sovereignty can reveal and contest the operation of such a monopoly by drawing attention to the organizing indistinction between force and law in Indian policy—the operation of a geopolitical state of exception.

This position, though, runs against the grain of two understandings of Native articulations of "sovereignty" prominent in Indigenous political theory: as the adoption of a specific set of principles of governance imposed by settler states, or as a pragmatic attempt to make Indigenous concepts intelligible within state terminologies and to state institutions.[60] The first, presented perhaps most forcefully by Taiaiake Alfred in his essay "Sovereignty," envisions sovereignty as a particular form of government, one derived from alien conventions. The problem for Native peoples in utilizing the discourse of sovereignty is that doing so reifies a "European notion of power and governance" that is fundamentally at odds with Native beliefs and practices: "Sovereignty itself implies a set of values and objectives that put it in direct opposition to the values and objectives found in most traditional indigenous philosophies."[61] Alfred suggests that "the process of de-colonization" has focused on "the mechanics of escaping from direct state control and . . . gain[ing] recognition of an indigenous governing authority" while losing track "of the end values of the struggle."[62] More than distinguishing between a politics focused on outside "recognition" and one concerned with the needs, desires, and self-understandings of Indigenous peoples, Alfred insists that "Indigenous leaders engaging themselves and their communities in arguments framed within a liberal paradigm have not been able to protect the integrity of their nations"; instead, "the benefits accrued" by such a strategy requires a de facto "agree[ment] to abandon autonomy."[63] The issue, then, is not only what Native communities want for themselves but what ultimately will "protect" their "autonomy" from state intervention and management. In describing "sovereignty" as a set of "values" at odds with "indigenous philosophies," Alfred presents "retraditionalization," eschewing settler-state terminologies and ideologies in favor of the "wisdom coded in the languages and cultures of all indigenous peoples," as the vehicle for "achiev[ing] sovereignty-free regimes of conscience and justice."[64] However, what I have been arguing is that "sovereignty itself" is empty, a topological placeholder through which to displace, or contain, the paradox of asserting "domestic" authority over populations whose existence as peoples precedes the existence of the state. Thus, adopting a different set of principles—an Indigenous rather than European "notion . . . of governance"—does not secure "autonomy" from settler-state superintendence, from being coded as an "anomaly" axiomatically subject to the metapolitical authority of the settler state.

While Alfred raises the immensely important questions of whether Indigenous peoples desire a form of government that is structured around the principles of liberalism and whether the acceptance of such a structure does irrevocable damage to traditions that historically have been crucial to such communities, these issues are askew with respect to contesting "sovereignty itself" or mapping, in Agamben's terms, "the very threshold of the political order" of settler-state imperialism. Alfred's argument relies on the juxtaposition of Indigenous political models with European ones without addressing how the settler state narrates its jurisdiction over national space and justifies its extension of regulatory control over Native peoples. He suggests that "sovereignty" designates "a conceptual and definitional problem centered on the accommodation of indigenous peoples within a 'legitimate' framework of settler state governance," adding that they "must conform to state-derived criteria and represent ascribed or negotiated identities," but he stops short of investigating the ways the topos of sovereignty works to validate a range of discrepant (kinds of) "identities" that Native peoples at various times have been and are called on to inhabit.[65] By giving sovereignty a determinate content, then, Alfred runs into similar problems to those raised by the invocation of "culture." An insistence on difference cannot unsettle the state's assertion of the authority to adjudicate the status of Indigenous polities, because "sovereignty" is the vehicle not of implementing a stable set of "values and objectives" but of repudiating any challenge to the territorial imaginary of the nation. Moreover, articulations of difference can be refracted back through the prism of Native "peculiar"-ity, possibly reinforcing the process of exceptionalization. Put another way, Alfred draws attention to a particular type of identity (liberal bureaucracy) imposed by the state rather than the state's fraught and uneven effort to generate legitimacy for its management of Native identities.

As against Alfred's call for eschewing the framework of "sovereignty," Dale Turner insists that the protection of Native peoples involves making their concerns and representations intelligible within the legal and political structures of the settler state. In *This Is Not a Peace Pipe*, Turner argues that the political terrain on which Native peoples must move has been mapped by the settler state and that if they are to gain greater traction for their land claims and assertions of governmental autonomy, they will need to express them in ways that non-Native people and institutions can understand: "*As a matter of survival,* Aboriginal intellectuals must engage the non-Aboriginal intellectual landscapes from which their political rights and sovereignty are articulated and put to use in Aboriginal communities."[66] Given that non-Native political processes already are active in shaping the terms of Indigenous governance and social life, Native peoples cannot afford simply to ignore them or to insist on the significance of "traditional" knowledge in ways that speak past non-Native modes of articulation. Turner suggests that such translation is the work of "the word warrior," whose "most difficult task will be to reconcile indigenous ways of knowing with the forms of knowledge that define European intellectual traditions."[67] "Survival" for Native polities, from this perspective, is predicated on a kind of communication in which discrepant "ways of knowing" can be bridged. However, to what extent does Turner's notion of "reconcil[ing]" knowledges also present the struggle over sovereignty as a function of cultural dissonance between Indigenous peoples and the settler state? The central question he poses is, "How do we explain our differences and in the process empower ourselves to actually change the state's legal and political practices?"[68] But does transposing Indigenous concepts into non-Native terminologies intervene in the logic structuring "the state's legal and political practices"? Does such a conversion challenge the jurisdictional imperative and imaginary driving the settler-state assertion of authority over Native peoples?

The idea of "explain[ing]" Indigenous "differences" acknowledges the imperial force exerted under the sign of sovereignty, but it does not contest the state's monopoly over the legitimate exercise of legitimacy, nor does it prevent those "differences" from being reified, regulated, and subordinated as "culture" in the ways discussed earlier. Alongside the discussion of the necessity for translation by "word warriors," Turner also calls for a thorough accounting of the violences of settler-state imperialism: "The project of unpacking and laying bare the meaning and effects of colonialism will open up the physical and intellectual space for Aboriginal voice to participate in the legal and political practices of the state."[69] Later, he suggests that Indigenous intellectuals should pursue three goals: "(a) they must take up, deconstruct, and continue to resist colonialism and its effects on indigenous peoples; (b) they must protect and defend indigeneity; and (c) they must engage the legal and political discourses of the state in an effective way."[70] What kind of "participat[ion]" and "engage[ment]" do such strategies yield?

Although Turner tends to answer this question by focusing on the possibility of explaining Indigenous intellectual traditions, making them comprehensible to non-Natives, the above comments offer another option, namely, deconstructing the dynamics of settler-state power—problematizing the ways it seeks to generate legitimacy for itself. He describes such intervention as "understanding . . . how colonialism has been woven into the normative political language that guides contemporary Canadian legal and political practices," and folding deconstruction back into the elaboration of "differences" between Natives and non-Natives, he argues, "indigenous peoples must use the normative language of the dominant culture to ultimately defend world views that are embedded in completely different normative frameworks."[71] Highlighting the horizon of "difference" positions deconstruction as a tool for elaborating the distinction between "normative" systems, but what falls away in this formulation is the violence of demanding that Native polities, regardless of the content or contours of their political systems, be subjected to the superintendence of settler-state regimes due to the brute, unfounded assertion of the former's domesticity with respect to the latter. In other words, the kinds of "normative" claims made by the settler state are not simply distinct from Indigenous ones but are aporetic, themselves predicated on the (thread)bare insistence that the state maintains an "overriding sovereignty." Instead, by "unpacking and laying bare" the logical and legal emptiness of sovereignty, the "space" opened is precisely that which has been placed in the state of exception, illustrating how Native "peculiar"-ity—and the various statuses derived from it—is less a function of a mistranslation of Indigenous difference than the marker of an enforced structural relation.

As Agamben suggests in *Means Without End*, sovereignty "is the guardian who prevents the undecidable threshold between violence and right ... from coming to light."[72] Emphasizing the normative crisis over which the topos of sovereignty is stretched does not so much make room for Indigenous principles within Euro-American terminologies and institutions as refuse in toto the right claimed by the state to assess and adjudicate Native governance, drawing attention to the state's inability to ground Indian policy in anything but the forced incorporation of Native persons and lands into the nation. Might this deconstructive approach not be open to the same pragmatic critique Turner makes of Alfred, that it fails to appreciate the exigencies faced by Native communities and the consequent need to find a more "effective way" of engaging with settler-state policy? Reacting to a similar question with respect to his discussion of the need to challenge the racist stereotypes embedded in the precedents cited by the U.S. Supreme Court, Robert Williams observes, "the legal history of racism in America teaches us that the most successful minority rights advocates of the twentieth century recognized that the real waste of time was trying to get a nineteenth-century racist legal doctrine to do a better job of protecting minority rights."[73] While his emphasis on the "metaprinciple of Indian racial inferiority" cannot fully address the geopolitics of settler-state jurisdiction, as discussed earlier, his caution here seems quite relevant in considering the value of directly challenging the process by which the United States legitimizes its management of Indigenous peoples. In the three cases on which I have focused, the assertion of Native autonomy threatens to disrupt the U.S. territorial/jurisdictional imaginary, and that potential rupture is contained by the citation of "sovereignty"—a concept whose substance keeps shifting and out of which emerge statuses and classificatory schemes that determine the institutional intelligibility of Native identities and claims. That process of exceptionalization has no check—the "plenary power" or "overriding sovereignty" of the United States is taken to license complete control over Native collectivities, including in what ways and to what extent, if any, they in fact will be recognized as collectivities (never mind as self-determining polities). To leave uncontested the topology of settler-state sovereignty, then, is to allow for Native peoples to remain abandoned to, in Agamben's terms, a "zone of indistinction between ... outside and inside, violence and law."[74]

Moreover, that "zone" is less a function of a self-confident exercise of power than a sign of the normative tenuousness of U.S. authority. As Clarence Thomas's comments suggest, the creation of a concept such as "inherent sovereignty" works to cover without unsettling the "overriding" and potentially limitless authority exerted by the U.S. government, specifically Congress, in Indian affairs, providing the impression of a legal logic that can guide or legitimize U.S. actions. I am suggesting, however, that it might be possible to occupy the contradiction embedded in a formulation like "inherent sovereignty" in ways that do not endorse the category as (continually re)formulated within U.S.-Indian policy, disown it as the imposition of an alien norm, or translate Indigenous traditions into its terms. Instead, the status can be used as a discursive entry point through which to highlight the groundlessness of U.S. claims to Native land and the impossibility of reconciling Indian policy with the principles of constitutionalism, drawing attention to the difficulty of validating the incorporation of Native peoples into the mapping of the jurisdictional geography of the state except through recourse to violence. Such a strategy emphasizes the coercive imposition of domesticity on Native peoples who neither sought nor desired it, foregrounding the ways the narration of Indigenous polities as subjects of domestic law depends on a process of exceptionalization in which they axiomatically are consigned to a "peculiar," and thus regulatable, internality that forcibly disavows their autonomy and self-representations.[75]

If such a deconstructive argument were successful—in Turner's terms "open[ing] up the physical and intellectual space for Aboriginal voice"—what might the resulting relationship look like? I have been arguing that the United States exerts metapolitical authority over Indigenous peoples, setting the terms of what will constitute politics and inventing statuses through which to interpellate Native polities, but I also have suggested that process is animated by a persistent anxiety about the validity of U.S. rule, the invented categories of Indian law marking an effort to generate legitimacy for national jurisdictional mappings. The disjunction between the supposed fact of Indians' domesticity and their existence as independent political collectivities before the formation of the United States appears perhaps most visibly in the negotiation of treaties, and that tension supposedly is allayed by the assent of Native peoples to these documents. Yet as suggested earlier, the discourse of consent at play in the treaty system is not simply an expression of the free will of Native peoples, instead serving as a way of validating the process of land acquisition those agreements enabled.

Moreover, while certainly less unilateral than the declaration of authority over Native populations contained in *Kagama* and *Oliphant*, treaties were not free from U.S. efforts to regulate what would constitute viable forms of political subjectivity, representing Native governance and land tenure in ways that facilitated the project of white expansion. That being said, as the process within U.S. constitutionalism most suited to the recognition of extraconstitutional entities, treaty making seems the most viable vehicle for a "sovereignty-free" politics. Rather than trying to contain the geopolitical difficulties that Indigenous occupancy generates for the imaginary of the settler state, treaties can serve as sites of negotiation, not simply over particular concrete issues but over the terms of engagement themselves.[76] When no longer subordinated to the assertion of an overriding, underlying, preemptive, or plenary authority, such dialogue could perform the kind of translation Turner describes between different traditions or frameworks of governance, displacing sovereignty in favor of politics. In *Means Without End*, Agamben suggests, "*Politics is the exhibition of a mediality: it is the act of making a means visible as such*. Politics is the sphere neither of an end in itself nor of a means subordinated to an end,"[77] and in this vein, treaties freed from the end of securing the obviousness of national territoriality become a "mediality" of negotiation. The forms of recognition emerging from that process would not function as part of a mode of regulation and would not be predicated on casting Native peoples as an exception *within* the sphere of U.S. politics and law.

What I have sought to do, then, is to use Agamben's analysis of the violence of sovereignty in its reliance on the production of a state of exception to suggest the absence of a normative framework for U.S.-Indian policy and more broadly for the geopolitics of the settler state. The coding of Native peoples as "peculiar" within U.S. governance depends on the assertion of a territorially based jurisdiction over them that further licenses the regulation of their entry into the shifting field of national politics, generating various (kinds of) categories that they are called on to occupy. While offering rigorous critique of such statuses, including their racializing premises and inability to engage with traditional philosophies and practices, Indigenous political theory largely has not contested the broader ways violence is transposed into legitimacy through the circulation of the enveloping yet empty sign of "sovereignty." Exposing that transposition, potentially through the countercitation of Native sovereignty (giving deconstructive force to what largely operates as a placeholder within settler-state governance), can work to disrupt the attendant metapolitical matrix through which Native identities are produced and managed. As Justice Thomas suggests, "The Court should admit that it has failed in its quest to find a source of congressional power to adjust tribal sovereignty."[78] Emphasizing that failure and thus the location of Native peoples at the threshold between law and violence, between "ordinary domestic legislation" and imperialism, opens the state of exception to the possibility of self-determination, in which Indigenous polities cease to be axiomatically enfolded within the ideological and institutional structures of the settler state.

Notes

1. *Cherokee Nation v. Georgia*, 30 U.S. 1 (1831), 16–18; *U.S. v. Kagama*, 118 U.S. 375 (1886), 381–82; *Oliphant v. Suquamish Indian Tribe*, 435 U.S. 191 (1978), 208–10. These three cases are central precedents for federal Indian law that continue to be cited within contemporary decisions. In *Cherokee Nation v. Georgia*, the plaintiffs were suing to get an injunction against the operation of a series of laws passed by Georgia annexing Cherokee territory to state counties. The court found that "Indian tribes" are not "foreign nations" but instead "domestic dependent nations," so they are not one of the entities that can bring a suit to the Supreme Court under its constitutionally regulated original jurisdiction. The case, therefore, was dismissed for want of jurisdiction. *U.S. v. Kagama* concerned the murder of one Indian by two others on the Hoopa Valley Reservation, and the issue at stake was the constitutionality of the Major Crimes Act (1885), which made murder on reservation—as well as several other acts—a federal crime regardless of the race of the perpetrators or victims. The court found that Congress had the authority to limit the jurisdiction of Native governments on Native lands due to the presence of the latter within the boundaries of the United States. In *Oliphant v. Suquamish*, the issue was whether

an Indian tribe, specifically the government of the Port Madison Reservation, had the authority to try non-Indian residents, and the court found that tribes do not because of the limits, both explicit and implied, placed on tribal jurisdiction by Congress as well as the general loss of "inherent jurisdiction" over certain matters of governance due to tribes' supposed "status." For discussion of these cases, see Sidney L. Harring, *Crow Dog's Case: American Indian Sovereignty, Tribal Law, and United States Law in the Nineteenth Century* (New York: Cambridge University Press, 1994); Jill Norgren, *The Cherokee Cases: The Confrontation of Law and Politics* (New York: McGraw Hill, 1996); David E. Wilkins, *American Indian Sovereignty and the United States Supreme Court* (Austin: University of Texas Press, 1997); and Robert A. Williams Jr., *Like a Loaded Weapon: The Rehnquist Court, Indian Rights, and the Legal History of Racism in America* (Minneapolis: University of Minnesota Press, 2005).

2. Giorgio Agamben, *Homo Sacer: Sovereign Power and Bare Life*, trans. Daniel Heller Roazen (Stanford, CA: Stanford University Press, 1998). For commentary on Agamben and examples of the circulation of his work, particularly *Homo Sacer*, see Judith Butler, "Indefinite Detention," in *Precarious Life: The Powers of Mourning and Violence* (New York: Verso, 2004), 50–100; Matthew Calarco and Steven DeCaroli, eds., *Giorgio Agamben: Sovereignty and Life* (Stanford, CA: Stanford University Press, 2007); Diane Enns, "Bare Life and the Occupied Body," *Theory and Event* 7, no. 3 (2004); Lilian Friedberg, "Dare to Compare: Americanizing the Holocaust," *American Indian Quarterly* 24, no. 3 (2000): 353–80; Andrew Norris, ed., *Politics, Metaphysics, and Death: Essays on Giorgio Agamben's* Homo Sacer (Durham, NC: Duke University Press, 2005); Jacques Rancière, "Who Is the Subject of the Rights of Man?" *South Atlantic Quarterly* 103, no. 2 (2004): 297–310; William Rasch, "Human Rights as Geopolitics: Carl Schmitt and the Legal Form of American Supremacy," *Cultural Critique* 54 (Spring 2003): 120–47; and Donald E. Pease, "The Global Homeland State: Bush's Biopolitical Settlement," *Boundary 2* 30, no. 3 (2003): 1–18.

3. Agamben, *Homo Sacer*, 19, 26.

4. Agamben, *Homo Sacer*, 64. In distinguishing Indian policy from the constitutional principles structuring U.S. law, I am neither suggesting that the latter provides a normative framework toward which Indian policy should aspire nor that dissolving Indian policy into the rest of U.S. law would erase or ease the violence I describe. Rather I am arguing that the production of a national

territoriality for "domestic" law depends on the abandonment of Native polities to a state of exception. Conversely, while many scholars have suggested that violence is endemic to the operation of law, a position theorized perhaps most eloquently in the work of Robert Cover, I am suggesting that such violence is different from the imperial force at play in the domestication of Native peoples in that the latter brackets the Constitution in seeking to produce the supposedly self-evident space of U.S. jurisdiction. In this vein, marking the difference between the state of exception and the ubiquitous gap between legal norm and application, Agamben suggests that in the exception, "the lacuna does not concern a deficiency in the text of the legislation that must be completed by the judge; it concerns, rather, a *suspension* of the order that is in force in order to guarantee its existence" (Agamben, *State of Exception*, 31). For critiques of Agamben that present what he refers to as "exception" as actually framed by law, see Peter Fitzpatrick, "Bare Sovereignty: *Homo Sacer* and the Insistence of Law," in *Politics, Metaphysics, and Death: Essays on Giorgio Agamben's* Homo Sacer, ed. Andrew Norris (Durham, NC: Duke University Press, 2005), 49–73; Rainer Maria Kiesow, "Law and Life," in Norris, *Politics, Metaphysics, and Death*, 248–61; and Ernesto Laclau, "Bare Life or Social Indeterminacy," in Calarco and DeCaroli, *Giorgio Agamben*, 11–22.

5. Joanne Barker suggests that "there is no fixed meaning for what *sovereignty* is," that it "is embedded within the specific social relations in which it is invoked and given meaning"; see Joanne Barker, "For Whom Sovereignty Matters," in *Sovereignty Matters: Locations of Contestation and Possibility in Indigenous Strategies for Self-Determination*, ed. Joanne Barker (Lincoln: University of Nebraska Press, 2005), 21. While acknowledging the multiplicity of the term's uses, I want to suggest, via Agamben, that there is a regularity to its citation in settler-state governance, particularly U.S.-Indian policy, and that the variability of its apparent meanings is part of the topological work it performs.

6. In shifting from discussion of particular U.S. legal decisions to "the settler state," I am not suggesting that U.S. policy can serve as a stand-in for *all* settler-state regimes, especially given their numerous variations. Rather, I suggest that placing Agamben's argument in dialogue with U.S.-Indian policy can generate analysis of how the topos of "sovereignty" works to support a particular settler-state regime and therefore might be useful as a way of approaching other settler states as well.

7. David Wilkins (*American Indian Sovereignty*, 2) observes, "We see ... that 'federal Indian law' as a discipline having coherent and interconnected premises is wholly a myth."
8. Agamben, *Homo Sacer*, 1.
9. Ibid., 4.
10. Ibid., 6. Some scholars, when writing about Agamben, though, seem to confuse his notion of "bare life" with an actual prepolitical natural state rather than seeing it as a way of designating the biopolitical process by which states employ discourses of nature and the body to various ends. See William E. Connolly, "The Complexities of Sovereignty," in Calarco and DeCaroli, *Giorgio Agamben*, 23–42; Fitzpatrick, "Bare Sovereignty"; and Laclau, "Bare Life or Social Indeterminacy."
11. Agamben, *Homo Sacer*, 6.
12. Ibid., 28–29.
13. Ibid., 166.
14. Ibid., 174–76.
15. Ibid., 177.
16. Ibid., 12.
17. Ibid., 169–70.
18. I should clarify that I am not trying to compare the Nazi Final Solution to U.S. Indian policy, but I am gesturing toward the ways taking the camp as paradigmatic of modern statehood can efface the geopolitics of statehood and thus the dynamics of settler-state imperialism. For such a comparison, which utilizes Agamben, see Friedberg, "Dare to Compare." On the problems that attend trying to put different genocides into dialogue, see Jodi A. Byrd, "'Living My Native Life Deadly': Red Lake, Ward Churchill, and the Discourses of Competing Genocides," *American Indian Quarterly* 31, no. 2 (2007): 310–32. In discussing the Nazi concentration camp, Agamben (*Homo Sacer*, 166–67) acknowledges that it can be traced to earlier Spanish and British tactics in which "a state of emergency linked to a colonial war is extended to an entire civil population," yet he does not explore how the German program of extermination might arise out of imperial ambitions/projects. For discussion of the ways European nationalities (in terms of space and citizenship) were carved out of broader imperial fields through the employment of shifting discourses of race, see Ann Laura Stoler, *Race and the Education of Desire: Foucault's* History

of Sexuality *and the Colonial Order of Things* (Durham, NC: Duke University Press, 1995).

19. On Agamben's tendency to fetishize the relation between individuals and the state and to overlook challenges to the latter by collectives/communities, see Laclau, "Bare Life or Social Indeterminacy," and Rancière, "Who Is the Subject of the Rights of Man?"

20. For prominent examples of these dynamics, see Arjun Appadurai, *Modernity at Large: Cultural Dimensions of Globalization* (Minneapolis: University of Minnesota Press, 1996); Butler, "Indefinite Detention"; Paul Gilroy, *The Black Atlantic: Modernity and Double Consciousness* (Cambridge, MA: Harvard University Press, 1993); Michael Hardt and Antonio Negri, *Empire* (Cambridge: Harvard University Press, 2000); and Amy Kaplan, "Where Is Guantánamo?," *American Quarterly* 57, no. 3 (2005): 831–58. For discussion of the problem of space in contemporary theory, see Matthew Sparke, *In the Space of Theory: Postfoundational Geographies of the Nation-State* (Minneapolis: University of Minnesota Press, 2005). The process I am describing can be illustrated by the tendency, in *Homo Sacer* and the work of many other contemporary scholars, to make the refugee/migrant paradigmatic in critiquing the state form. Agamben (*Homo Sacer*, 126) argues that the figure of the refugee, the stateless person, "who should have embodied the rights of man par excellence . . . signals instead the concept's radical crisis" since the rights that ostensibly derive from being human "show themselves to lack every protection and reality at the moment in which they can no longer take the form of rights belonging to citizens of a state." Humanitarian efforts predicated on the prepolitical status of the human "can only grasp human life in the figure of bare or sacred life and therefore, despite themselves, maintain a secret solidarity with the very powers they ought to fight" (Agamben, *Homo Sacer*, 133), reinforcing the very logic of biopolitical exception through which sovereignty is exercised. Supposedly "breaking the continuity between man and citizen, *nativity* and *nationality*," the figure of the refugee serves for Agamben as "a limit concept that radically calls into question the fundamental categories of the nation-state" (Agamben, *Homo Sacer*, 131, 134), but can that example of the proliferation of "bare life," of persons denied access to the rights of citizenship and thus made vulnerable to unrestrained state violence, speak to collectivities who have "had their nationality

forcibly changed in their own homeland" (Haunani-Kay Trask, *From a Native Daughter: Colonialism and Sovereignty in Hawai'i* [Honolulu: University of Hawai'i Press, 1999], 30), who have seen themselves and their lands subsumed by the state?

21. *Cherokee Nation v. Georgia*, 16.
22. Ibid., 17.
23. *U.S. v. Kagama*, 381.
24. *Oliphant v. Suquamish*, 108–9.
25. Congress did so through an amendment to an appropriations bill in 1871, although treaty-like "agreements" continued to be negotiated with Native peoples, but they did not have the same constitutional status as treaties. On the history of U.S. treaty making, see Francis Paul Prucha, *American Indian Treaties: The History of a Political Anomaly* (Berkeley: University of California Press, 1994); Robert A. Williams Jr., *Linking Arms Together: American Indian Treaty Visions of Law and Peace, 1600–1800* (New York: Oxford University Press, 1997).
26. Assumptions central to the treaty system include the existence of a centralized government with the power to enforce its decisions on the population and a clearly delimited land base separate from that of other peoples, parts of which can be sold as property. For discussion of this process of translation, see Taiaiake Alfred, *Peace, Power, Righteousness: An Indigenous Manifesto* (New York: Oxford University Press, 1999); Eric Cheyfitz, "The Navajo-Hopi Land Dispute: A Brief History," *Interventions* 2, no. 2 (2000): 248–75; Mark Rifkin, "Documenting Tradition: Territoriality and Textuality in Black Hawk's Narrative," *American Literature* 80, no. 4 (2008): 677–705; and Claudio Saunt, *A New Order of Things: Property, Power, and the Transformation of the Creek Indians, 1733–1816* (New York: Cambridge University Press, 2003). For accounts that emphasize treaties' recognition of Native populations as polities while underplaying the ways the treaty system seeks to script the meaning/contours of political identity, see Chadwick Allen, "Postcolonial Theory and the Discourse of Treaties," *American Quarterly* 52, no. 1 (2000): 59–89; Maureen Konkle, *Writing Indian Nations: Native Intellectuals and the Politics of Historiography, 1827–1863* (Chapel Hill: University of North Carolina Press, 2004); and Craig S. Womack, *Red on Red: Native American Literary Separatism* (Minneapolis: University of Minnesota Press, 1999). I should be clear that I am in no way

suggesting that existing treaties simply can be dispensed with as charades. Treaties under the Constitution are the "supreme law of the land," and when the government seeks to ignore them by presenting them as merely an historical expediency, it vitiates its own claims to be governed by the rule of law.

27. As Joanne Barker ("For Whom Sovereignty Matters," 4) notes, the nation defined by the Constitution "was contingent upon it being recognized as legitimate by other already recognized nations," and Indian treaties emerged as "a mechanism for both the exercise of nationhood and the recognition of national sovereignty," showing other countries that the United States could function as a state. Although beyond the limits of this essay, then, the assertion of settler-state jurisdiction also needs to be situated within international formations that, while in many ways still reaffirming the absolute territoriality of states against Indigenous claims, also suggest another scale at which sovereignty is cited, circulated, and can be contested. On the production and circulation of notions of "sovereignty" within suprastate formations, see Thomas J. Biersteker and Cynthia Weber, eds., *State Sovereignty as Social Construct* (Cambridge: Cambridge University Press, 1996).

28. *Cherokee Nation v. Georgia*, 18.

29. Butler, "Indefinite Detention," 82. In the phrase elided by my use of ellipses, she also suggests that "sovereignty" is not "a domain that the US is said 'to occupy,'" but I am suggesting that sovereignty appears in the service of constituting just such a "domain": national space itself.

30. *U.S. v. Kagama*, 381–82.

31. Ibid., 19.

32. Ibid.

33. Ibid., 28.

34. As Steven DeCaroli argues, "when the edges of the sovereign field are made to appear arbitrary, the challenge is directed at the heart of sovereignty itself, and . . . those actions that warrant banishment share the characteristic of having called into question the legitimacy of this boundary"; Steven DeCaroli, "Boundary Stones: Giorgio Agamben and the Field of Sovereignty," in Calarco and DeCaroli, *Giorgio Agamben: Sovereignty and Life*, 51. Yet he, like Agamben, treats the "boundary" as a figure for the organizing logic of law rather than as designating its literal spatial field of exercise.

35. For discussion of the various statuses created and managed by U.S.-Indian policy, especially the judiciary, see Wilkins, *American Indian Sovereignty*, and David Wilkins and K. Tsianina Lomawaima, *Uneven Ground: American Indian Sovereignty and Federal Law* (Norman: University of Oklahoma Press, 2001).
36. The importance of this distinction is suggested by the ongoing struggle of global Indigenous movements to have the phrase "Indigenous peoples" rather than "Indigenous people" included in international covenants as well as the continuing effort by settler states (especially Anglophone) to block that usage. See S. James Anaya, *Indigenous Peoples in International Law* (New York: Oxford University Press, 1996); Maivân Clech Lâm, *At the Edge of the State: Indigenous Peoples and Self-Determination* (Ardsley, NY: Transnational, 2000); and Ronald Niezen, *The Origins of Indigenism: Human Rights and the Politics of Identity* (Berkeley: University of California Press, 2003).
37. *Cherokee Nation v. Georgia*, 17.
38. Ibid.
39. *U.S. v. Kagama*, 383–84.
40. Ibid., 384–85.
41. As Agamben (*Homo Sacer*, 105) argues in his discussion of the dynamics of banishment/abandonment through which bare life is constituted as such, "the state of nature is not a real epoch chronologically prior to the foundation of the City but a principle internal to the City."
42. Williams, *Like a Loaded Weapon*, xxviii, 21.
43. Ibid., 127. The reference here is to *Brown v. the Board of Education* (1954), which struck down the principle of "separate but equal" that had legalized segregation for nearly fifty years since the phrase first was propagated by *Plessy v. Ferguson* (1896).
44. Williams, *Like a Loaded Weapon*, xxv.
45. It is worth noting that race is not the only biopolitical tactic/mode through which U.S. sovereignty operates. Ideologies of gender also have been and are crucial to the organization and validation of settler-state dominance. For examples of Native feminist work that explores this relation, see Joanne Barker, *Native Acts: Law, Recognition, and Cultural Authenticity* (Durham, NC: Duke University Press, 2011); Mishuana Goeman, *Mark My Words: Native Women Mapping Our Nations* (Minneapolis: University of Minnesota Press, 2013); Dian Million, *Therapeutic Nations: Healing in an Age of Indigenous Human Rights*

(Tucson: University of Arizona Press, 2014); Renya K. Ramirez, *Native Hubs: Culture, Community, and Belonging in Silicon Valley and Beyond* (Durham, NC: Duke University Press, 2007).

46. *Oliphant v. Suquamish*, 209.
47. Agamben, *Homo Sacer*, 72–73, 83.
48. Ibid., 74.
49. Ibid., 80.
50. My understanding of *kapu* primarily comes from discussions of Hawaiian history and culture. For examples, see Lilikalā Kameʻeleihiwa, *Native Land and Foreign Desires: How Shall We Live in Harmony?* (Honolulu: Bishop Museum Press, 1992); Jocelyn Linnekin, *Sacred Queens and Women of Consequence: Rank, Gender, and Colonialism in the Hawaiian Islands* (Ann Arbor: University of Michigan Press, 1990); and Marshall Sahlins with Dorothy B. Barrére, *Anahulu: The Anthropology of History in the Kingdom of Hawaii*, vol. 1, *Historical Ethnography* (Chicago: University of Chicago Press, 1992).
51. James Tully, *Strange Multiplicity: Constitutionalism in an Age of Diversity* (Cambridge: Cambridge University Press, 1995), 4, 35.
52. Elizabeth A. Povinelli, *The Cunning of Recognition: Indigenous Alterities and the Making of Australian Multiculturalism* (Durham, NC: Duke University Press, 2002), 17. The dynamic Povinelli describes is perhaps most visibly at play in U.S.-Indian policy within the process of attaining federal recognition. See Renée Ann Cramer, *Cash, Color, and Colonialism: The Politics of Tribal Acknowledgment* (Norman: University of Oklahoma Press, 2005); Les W. Field with the Muwekema Ohlone Tribe, "Unacknowledged Tribes, Dangerous Knowledge: The Muwekema Ohlone and How Indian Identities are 'Known,'" *Wicazo Sa Review* 18, no. 2 (2003): 79–94; Eva Marie Garroutte, *Real Indians: Identity and the Survival of Native America* (Berkeley: University of California Press, 2003); Dan Gunter, "The Technology of Tribalism: The Lemhi Indians, Federal Recognition, and the Creation of Tribal Identity," *Idaho Law Review* 35 (1998): 85–123; and Anne Merline McCulloch and David E. Wilkins, "'Constructing' Nations Within States: The Quest for Federal Recognition by the Catawba and Lumbee Tribes," *American Indian Quarterly* 19, no. 3 (1995): 361–88.
53. Tully, *Strange Multiplicity*, 184, 207.
54. The United States has at times adopted policy designed to eliminate the existence of tribes as legally recognized entities, but the government subsequently

has changed course as a result of challenges to the legitimacy of such actions by other U.S. officials, Native leaders and intellectuals, and concerned non-Native organizations. For an overview of the history of U.S.-Indian policy, see Vine Deloria Jr. and Clifford M. Lytle, *The Nations Within: The Past and Future of American Indian Sovereignty* (Austin: University of Texas Press, 1998).

55. In this vein, Agamben (*State of Exception*, 1) observes that "exceptional measures" are "juridical measures that cannot be understood in legal terms" such that "the state of exception appears as the legal form of what cannot have legal form."

56. Finding that tribes have the power to prosecute nonmember Indians, the case turned on whether such authority is one that tribes hold by themselves or one delegated to them by the federal government.

57. *U.S. v. Lara*, 215, 225. While Thomas ultimately is trying to argue that Native peoples are merely subjects of U.S. law and not distinct sovereigns, the trajectory of his logic heads in the opposite direction. He observes that "tribes ... are not part of this constitutional order, and their sovereignty is not guaranteed by it," and if Native polities are extraconstitutional entities, their authority over themselves and their lands cannot be defined or circumscribed by reference to constitutionally licensed principles and institutions. Extraconstitutional entities cannot simply become objects of regular constitutional power ("ordinary domestic legislation") by congressional will; otherwise, the Constitution is reduced to the unrestricted/unrestrictable operation of governmental fiat. On the "extraconstitutional status of tribal nations," see Wilkins, *American Indian Sovereignty*.

58. Agamben, *Homo Sacer*, 64, 28.

59. *Oliphant v. Suquamish*, 208, 210.

60. Both of the scholars cited, Taiaiake Alfred and Dale Turner, are addressing Native relations with the Canadian state rather than the United States. However, they offer versions of arguments also made by those focused on U.S. policy, many referencing Alfred in particular, and engaging with their work helps frame the issues I consider as relevant beyond the U.S. context while also contextualizing the United States as a settler state.

61. Taiaiake Alfred, "Sovereignty," in *Sovereignty Matters: Locations of Contestation and Possibility in Indigenous Strategies for Self-Determination*, ed. Joanne Barker (Lincoln: University of Nebraska Press, 2005), 43. For a more extensive

elaboration of Alfred's critique of the concept of "sovereignty," see Alfred, *Peace, Power, Righteousness*.

62. Alfred, "Sovereignty," 41.
63. Ibid., 39. My argument focuses on the confrontation/negotiation between Native polities and the settler state rather than on the processes of self-definition and self-determination within the former, and it is from this perspective that I approach Alfred's work. On the everyday negotiation of Native political identities, particularly nationalism, see Audra Simpson, *Mohawk Interruptus: Political Life Across the Borders of Settler States* (Durham, NC: Duke University Press, 2014). On the ways the relationship between U.S. and Native governments is gendered, see note 45 above.
64. Alfred, "Sovereignty," 40, 49.
65. Ibid., 34–35, 43. See Field, "Unacknowledged Tribes"; Garroutte, *Real Indians*; Gunter, "Technology of Tribalism"; Niezen, *Origins of Indigenism*; Povinelli, *Cunning of Recognition*; and Paige Sylvia Raibmon, *Authentic Indians: Episodes of Encounter from the Late-Nineteenth-Century Northwest Coast* (Durham, NC: Duke University Press, 2005).
66. Dale Turner, *This Is Not a Peace Pipe: Towards a Critical Indigenous Philosophy* (Toronto: University of Toronto Press, 2006), 90.
67. Ibid., 93.
68. Ibid., 101.
69. Ibid., 30–31.
70. Ibid., 96.
71. Ibid., 30, 81.
72. Giorgio Agamben, *Means Without End: Notes on Politics*, trans. Vincenzo Binetti and Cesare Casarino (Minneapolis: University of Minnesota Press, 2000), 113.
73. Williams, *Like a Loaded Weapon*, xxxii.
74. Agamben, *Means Without End*, 64.
75. In many ways, such a strategy already is at play in Indigenous internationalism. See Anaya, *Indigenous Peoples*; Clech Lâm, *At the Edge of the State*; Niezen, *Origins of Indigenism*; Trask, *From a Native Daughter*; and Williams, *Like a Loaded Weapon*, 170–95.
76. David Wilkins (*American Indian Sovereignty*, 309) offers a similar formulation, calling for the repudiation of the "plenary power" doctrine and the reaffirmation

of a policy predicated on Native consent. His argument, though, underplays the metapolitical power exerted over the terms of "consent" through the citation of "sovereignty," whether expressed specifically as plenary power or not.

77. Agamben, *Means Without End*, 116–17.
78. *U.S. v. Lara*, 225.

12
King of the Line

The Sovereign Acts of Jean-Michel Basquiat

Frances Negrón-Muntaner with Yasmin Ramirez

For the subway crown motif—
"king of the line"—is always there.
ROBERT FARRIS THOMPSON[1]

Every line means something.
JEAN-MICHEL BASQUIAT[2]

When evoking artist Jean-Michel Basquiat, it is difficult not to think of kings. Born to a Haitian father and a Brooklyn-born Puerto Rican mother in 1960, since the beginning of his career as part of the wall-writing team SAMO© in the late 1970s, Basquiat consistently probed the limits and possibilities of sovereign symbols, particularly crowns.[3] A globally recognizable emblem of monarchical and divine power, royal status, and glory, Basquiat's incorporation of the crown is evident in multiple ways: from his signature sign—a pared-down, three-peaked crown that he deployed in thousands of paintings, drawings, and objects—to his own hair, which he at times styled into crown-like spines to claim his status as king of the art world.[4] In the words of historian Robert Farris Thompson, Basquiat "continually crowned himself king of painters, calling on fortune to extend his status."[5] Yet what exactly did being "king" mean for, and in, Basquiat?

For Basquiat and others of his generation, to be art royalty was to be recognized as a major artist, among or above towering (white) figures such as

Figure 12.1. Jean-Michel Basquiat, *Untitled (Crown)*, 1988.

Leonardo da Vinci and Pablo Picasso and famous contemporaries such as Andy Warhol, Robert Rauschenberg, and Cy Twombly.[6] It additionally meant to conquer all media, that is, to have your work featured in every important gallery, museum, biennial, and art magazine in the world as well as to have legions of prestigious patrons and corporate heads buying (and bowing to) your talent. Moreover, within the context of the 1980s—when art acquired the liquidity of money and artists were treated as celebrities—royal rank included having an entourage who catered to your every wish, parting the crowds when you pulled up to nightclubs, and having access to expensive goods, including designer clothes and drugs.[7] In sum, being king meant undisputed stardom, a status unavailable to the vast majority of artists.

Yet while Basquiat's graffiti sought to occupy specific art "territory" in downtown Manhattan, and he more than once expressed a real or figurative desire to "fight" other artists like Julian Schnabel or Andy Warhol,[8] his attention to crowns went beyond a desire to be famous or assert control over others. It also went further than what critics Jordana Moore Saggese and Richard Marshall have described as Basquiat's "obsession"[9] "or "interest"[10] in commerce, although this is not irrelevant. Instead, we would argue that Basquiat was less fixated on trade than invested in visualizing the relationship between capitalism, modernity, colonialism, racism, and Western sovereignty. Basquiat was similarly consumed by the challenge of disrupting Eurocentric knowledge and institutions that delegitimize and marginalize African, Afro-diasporic, and indigenous epistemologies and imagination.

In this regard, Basquiat's use of crowns and related symbols constitute a critical vocabulary of contestation that resignifies the concept of sovereignty in at least three distinct, if at times overlapping, ways. At one level, as Basquiat mined black stereotypes and inquired into the production of racist/colonial orders, his texts recall scholar Scott Richard Lyons's notion of "rhetorical sovereignty" in the context of Native American studies. According to Lyons, the goal of most Native American writing is to achieve sovereignty through the eradication of "stereotypes, cultural appropriation, exclusion, ignorance, irrelevance," and the "rhetorical imperialism" embedded in U.S. (and European) law and discourse.[11] At another level, Basquiat's pursuit of a (royal) place in Western art history led to a persistent inquiry into the relationship between subjectivity, lineage, and authority for Afro-diasporic artists. In this, Basquiat dialogues with Barbadian writer George Lamming's term *sovereignty of the imagination*, defined as "an unending process of thinking of how one has always to rework the ways in which one claims and exercises the power and the authority of an individual."[12] Finally, Basquiat's frequent deployment of crowns to honor black men is akin to Frantz Fanon's characterization of postcolonial "true sovereignty" as the affirmation of black dignity and self-worth.[13] Overall, Basquiat's ontological and critical view of sovereignty sought to leverage the might of black (art) kings toward a different mode of knowing, relating, and being. Or as Basquiat once put it in a poem: "You can't sell a human / You've done this scratching / This was not blank."[14]

By reading Basquiat in this way, we are not implying that he is "theorizing" in conventional or disciplinary terms. We are instead arguing that Basquiat produced critical, complex, and "implicated"[15] thought regarding the nature of royal status, sovereign power, and the political and symbolic order that came about with the conquest and settlement of the Americas and the extension of the imperial project to Africa. Specifically, by representing "bodily, emotional, and psychological sensation,"[16] through various aesthetic means, including collage, repetition, improvisation, copying, scaling, designing, and color, Basquiat generated a dense sensorial archive that revised, related, and recontextualized black, Caribbean, indigenous, and other knowledges, affects, and memories. Inviting an active engagement, Basquiat's signifying practices resemble a "decolonial" hypertext where viewers/readers can "delink" from "the colonial matrix of power,"[17] in Walter Mignolo's phrase, through multiple "networks of nodes which readers are free to navigate in a non-linear fashion."[18]

Revealingly, although Basquiat's iconic vocabulary of sovereignty appears more centrally in the 1980–1983 period, it continues to be present in his work until 1986, nearly the end of his career. Equally significant, the waning of these images and words and their displacement by Afro-diasporic spiritual figures, animals, and images of flight can be understood in part as a reckoning with the complexities and limitations of sovereign discourse as a black praxis of liberation. Within, across, and in between texts, Basquiat demonstrates an awareness of the importance of representation to legitimizing royal and sovereign claims and raises two core questions that have haunted not only Basquiat but many other black artists and political thinkers throughout the twentieth century: Is black sovereignty, even of or in the imagination, viable or desirable? Can sovereignty ultimately offer a path to freedom?

Enter the King

Given the ubiquity of the crown in Basquiat's work and public persona, family and peers have offered various accounts regarding its source and meaning. According to Basquiat's father, Gerard, "the crown meant that he was from royalty."[19] Suzanne Mallouk, Basquiat's companion in the early 1980s, claims that the crown originated in *The Little Rascals* show, a favorite of the artist: "there is a crown—sketched on the screen—and a title: King World

Productions."[20] For fellow artist Francesco Clemente, "Jean-Michel's crown has three peaks, for his three royal lineages: the poet, the musician, and the great boxing champion."[21] Scholars have similarly weighed in. While for critic bell hooks the crowns symbolize fame and were "offered as the only possible path to subjectivity for the black male artist,"[22] for Moore Saggese they refer to the "assertion of the artist's power."[23] Yet though all these versions may be part of the story, Basquiat's crowns are less a stable sign or symbol than an evolving method of producing and authorizing decolonial knowledge.

In its initial iteration, the crown inscribes and enacts the power of a black artist to recognize and render visible what he considers honorable and prized. This is evident in one of Basquiat's first paintings to include a crown, *Untitled* (1981), where he draws a blue cityscape populated by buildings, street signs, and a plane flying overhead. These images are in turn related to other keywords and symbols: a crown in the middle of the composition, a crowned male head to the left, and a notary seal to the right of the crown. In the bottom right of the canvas, Basquiat writes *RESPO*—possibly a truncated form of the Spanish term *respeto* (respect)—and places it at the top of one of the buildings. In this context, Basquiat appears to simultaneously authorize himself as an artist, confer value on specific objects and figures, and demand respect from the city. The crown acts, in Marshall's words, as "Basquiat's own trademark as well as a symbol of respect and admiration that he bestows."[24]

The ways that crowns authorize and perform recognition of royal status—and the stakes of such acts—are even more evident in numerous works on canvas and paper from 1981 to 1983. In these, Basquiat "proliferated sovereignties"[25] by placing crowns or crown-like haloes on top of the heads or names of both famous and "ordinary" black men to note achievements obtained against great odds, honor the dignity denied by racism, and signal Basquiat's own identification and kinship. With equal force, Basquiat acknowledged boxing legends Jack Johnson and Sugar Ray Robinson, jazz great Charlie Parker, an unknown man arrested by unscrupulous cops (*Untitled*, 1981), and a sweeper in a prisoner-style uniform holding a broom in the manner of "an African warrior posing with his spear" (*Untitled*, 1981).[26] Through the aesthetic act of crowning, Basquiat redefines what royalty is and how (by whom and why) this status is conferred, recasting nobility as a "figure of speech" that can be granted by the black artistic imagination.

Likewise, Basquiat's crowning of both the famous (if suffering) and the socially invisible visualizes a politics that recalls literary theorist Mikhail Bakhtin's notion of the "carnivalesque." As Bakhtin suggested, in European carnival, not only do people in the lower social rungs represent themselves as royalty, and "real" royalty is made fun of, but also social and political life itself is represented as "a perpetual 'crowning and uncrowning,' " asserting the possibility of social change and transformation.[27] Moreover, Basquiat's recognition of black royalty recalls the syncretic carnival traditions of the Caribbean in which participants "named their own leaders, expressing hierarchy in their own community that built on memories of different types of African social organization."[28] In this regard, the crown operates as a metaphor, in literary scholar Mark Rifkin's sense of "redescribing reality, disorienting current modes of description and classification in order to reference 'the polysemy of being.' "[29]

Even further, the act of crowning not only may confer worth, recognize value, or reclassify categories of knowledge; it also literally directs the viewer's gaze to the subjects' upper bodies, particularly their heads. While Basquiat has called his portrayal of faces "instinctual" and journalists such as Cathleen McGuigan have linked them to the early influence of Picasso,[30] his attention to heads is neither arbitrary nor does it conceptually resemble Picasso's. Following scholar Simon Gikandi, Picasso viewed African art objects (including sculpted heads and masks) as means or raw material to modernize European painting rather than as a form of engagement with black bodies, histories, or aesthetics.[31]

In contrast, Basquiat's emphasis on and placement of heads positions black subjects on higher ground, moving them away from visual representations that locate them in subordinate or subservient positions in relation to other figures, objects, or aesthetic traditions. By emphasizing heads—or as Basquiat sometimes wrote in Spanish on his canvases, "cabezas"—Basquiat unsettles the Eurocentric assumption that black or African-descended peoples are closer to nature through the sensuality of their bodies and insists on their creative capacities. In curator Kellie Jones's succinct words, "the intellect is emphasized, lifted up to notice, privileged over the body and the physicality that these figures—black men—commonly represent in the world."[32] Or in other terms, to the extent that in the Americas, the possessor of knowledge became naturalized since the sixteenth century as a "western Christian man,"[33] Basquiat's crowned heads overtly refute the idea that blacks (and other nonwhite groups) could be conceived as matter/nature/object rather than mind/human/subject.[34]

Moreover, the focus on heads explicitly references African knowledge, cultural, and religious systems such as sub-Saharan sculpture, in which the head is represented as exceptionally large and often highlighted by wearing elaborate hairstyles and headdresses, among other items.[35] In Yoruban visual and philosophical thought, one of the most influential in the Americas, the head is also "a metaphor for supremacy and chieftainship"[36] and the place of *ashé* (power) as well as a person's *ìwà* (character).[37] The importance of the head is similarly present in Afro-diasporic arts and religious practices with which Basquiat was probably familiar. This includes the Haitian vodou concept of *mèt tèt*, or the "master of the head," the spirit that is particular to each individual. The head is likewise the "seat of vodun power where a vodun [spirit] rests when it enters the body during possession," as Suzanne Preston Blier has noted.[38]

Equally relevant, crowns are important elements to signify artistic distinction and create "brand" recognition in black and Latino popular cultures. In the 1970s graffiti scene, Basquiat's first artistic setting, crowns were drawn to connote rank and identity as wall writers competed for the title of "king" of specific subway lines and other public spaces that they claimed.[39] The one that had the most visible tags or was "up" the longest at any given moment was recognized as "king of the line" until inevitably he or she would be "knocked off" by another more prolific or visible writer.[40] In addition, when a graffiti writer became famous either for the quality of their work or its ubiquity and others acknowledged the feat, a crown could appear next to the writer's tag to mark this status. Similarly, sports figures, singers, and other artists often claim royal titles both to indicate their exceptional abilities as well as to defy race, gender, and other hierarchies.[41] Among the many examples in the jazz world alone, which was widely referred to in Basquiat's work, are Count Basie (William James Basie), Lady Day (Billie Holiday), and Duke Ellington (Edward Kennedy Ellington).

Given these multiple associations, it is not surprising that Basquiat deployed crowns to visualize his own worth in the art world. Royal symbols were a way to establish genealogies that secured his place as a legitimate successor in a line of (Western) art kings and to enjoy immortality. A key example is *Red Kings* (1981), a painting that comprises two crowned and simply drawn skull-like faces against a red background. Within the eyes and nose of the face to the left, Basquiat places the letters *Q*, *B*, and *S*, suggesting that the image may refer to Basquiat himself and perhaps allude to his New York origins: all three letters correspond to city subway lines, including one that connects east and west, and two Brooklyn routes. On the right, there is a second crowned face, which has been read by some critics as reimagining Picasso's *Self-Portrait Mougins* (1972).[42] If this second figure can be viewed as referencing Picasso, the text implies that Basquiat is as great a king of the art world as the Spanish master. The succession motif similarly appears in other works such as *Dos Cabezas* (1982), a playful portrait reportedly produced in a few hours after Basquiat visited Andy Warhol in his studio. Here, Basquiat depicts himself to the left of Warhol, his own crown-like hair standing on end and reaching slightly higher above Warhol, whose face is, however, larger in the frame.

The ways that crowns can denote exceptional artistic talent also make them accessible and economic symbols to represent the battle over who can compete for, and be excluded from, royal status in art history. By seizing the signs of sovereign power, Basquiat aimed to symbolically take on the racism of the art world itself, an industry that writer Greg Tate described during the 1980s as "a bastion of white supremacy, a sconce of the wealthy whose high-walled barricades are matched only by Wall Street and the White House and whose exclusionary practices are enforced 24-7-365."[43] One of his most well-known treatments is the overt *Obnoxious Liberals* (1982). In this painting, three men appear under a crown to resist the force of the "obnoxious liberals": a chained black figure named "Samson" who stands in between the word *ASBESTOS* repeated three times and the word *GOLD*; a black and red figure in a top hat resembling the vodou *lwa* of the dead Baron Samedi holding five arrows and wearing a sign on his chest that reads "NOT FOR SALE"; and a third male figure in his underwear featuring a cowboy hat whose face is framed by dollar signs. In this instance, via crowns and other signs,

Basquiat contested the subordination of artists to both white and moneyed interests to raise one of the ultimate questions of Western art: who are the true sovereigns of the modern art world, artists or (white) patrons?

Furthermore, Basquiat's insistence on the sovereignty of the artist recalls the Spanish painter Diego Velázquez's move in *Las Meninas* (1656). In this canonical painting, the artist dared to imagine himself as sovereign of the canvas, equal to the king who was his patron. While historian Michel Foucault arguably misreads *Las Meninas* as emblematic of a "classic" rather than "modern" episteme, he nevertheless contends that one of the reasons that *Las Meninas* gestures toward modernity is because for the first time in Western art, "That space where the king and his wife hold sway belongs equally well to the artist and to the spectator."[44] Before this point, the European artist's role was to create images for, and of, royalty, to praise and sustain dynasties. Velázquez, however, not only turned a royal portrait into a self-portrait, he depicted himself among the royal entourage and visualizes himself as part of the royal family. By placing the painter as part of sovereign power, Velázquez portrays the royal family as his subjects as well.

Basquiat extended Velázquez's critique as he sought to erode Western conceptions of royalty as inherently white, European, and of noble (or upper) class. Yet both artists suggest that the exercise of institutional sovereignty requires aesthetic acts and that artistic production is not only essential to maintaining sovereign power but also to undermining specific political orders. This may explain why Basquiat rarely visualizes "real" kings, rulers, or military leaders such as Napoleon, Benito Mussolini (aka Il Duce), or even the Haitian revolutionary hero Toussaint L'Ouverture wearing crowns. Overall, although Basquiat's sovereign acts are political in the sense that he questions how and by whom power is exercised, he never makes them on behalf of states or nations, and the crown rarely represents actual sovereigns (mere heads of state). Instead, the crowns tend to recognize those who are black kings of imagination and connote the transformative act of regarding and imagining oneself and others as royal (having a "big head").

Significantly, from 1982 to 1985, Basquiat expands his study of Western sovereignty as a form of state and discursive power that seeks control over territories, resources, and populations while he experiments with multipanel paintings, canvases with exposed stretcher bars, and increasingly dense writing, collage, and new imagery. Through more elaborate means, Basquiat expands his critique of the long-term devastation brought on by the European settler colonial and capitalist project, which in the name of God and the king subjugated and enslaved Africans and indigenous people. In these works, Basquiat focuses not on the power of black sovereigns but on how European (and American) sovereignty and its symbols are implicated in the process of colonial dispossession. At this juncture, Basquiat's working premise is akin to that of Maori scholar Nin Tomas: "the concept of 'sovereignty' justified brutal force and legalized the taking of lands and territory from people who would not otherwise have willingly given them up. Notions of 'the Crown' as the central, ultimate, sovereign source of all political and legal power, clinched the deal."45

The toxic power of European imperial sovereignty is manifest in several of Basquiat's best-known works, including the aptly titled *Native Carrying Some Guns, Bibles, Amorites on Safari* (1982). At the top of the canvas, Basquiat provides an ironic touch by writing "COLONIZATION: PART TWO IN A SERIES, VOL. VI," possibly referring to the European colonization of Africa and the first wave of European imperialism exemplified by Spain and Portugal in the sixteenth century (followed by the Netherlands and Britain), the expansion of "crown rule" into parts of Asia in the nineteenth century, and the rise of the United States in the twentieth. On the left of the canvas, Basquiat paints a black male with eyes wide open, carrying a crate that reads "ROYAL SALT INC©"; overhead is a crown next to various phrases and words linking sovereign power, capital, religion, and colonialism. In this case, capital is connoted by the reference to "INC" (incorporated) and to salt, one of the earliest human currencies and forms of taxation. On the right, Basquiat sketches a simply drawn and expressionless safari-clad male figure with a rifle by his side. Above him is a series of capitalized terms that suggest what is required to make "JOLLY GOOD MONEY IN SAVAGES": "NOBLE," "PROVISIONS," "POACHERS," "GOD," "MISSIONARIES," "TUSK$," "$Kin$." The fact that between the men is an arrow originating from the black man's eye to the second's face implies that the black figure is both "eyeing" the latter and aware of the greed that drives the colonial venture.

In the lower right corner, Basquiat mines the connection between European sovereignty and capital further, by ironically writing "I WON'T EVEN MENTION GOLD (ORO)."46 The reference to gold is a reminder of the implicit part 1—the colonization of the Americas—and how this imperial history informs and anticipates colonial occupation in Africa. One way that Basquiat links these junctures is through drawing an arrow upward from ORO to a series of terms. First he points to the words "CORTE," "CORTE" (crossed out), and "CORTE Z" or "CORTE" "Z"; then he writes BISHOP (comma) and LANDAU, both crossed out.

The mention of "LANDAU, BISHOP" is possibly a reference to the Spanish missionary and Franciscan friar Diego de Landa, who in 1562 led an inquisition against the Maya in Yucatán, which included torture, killings, and the burning of numerous Maya codices and thousands of religious objects. Here, Basquiat seems to refer to the role of God, church, and state in the colonial enterprise, and the injustice of imperial law. Although de Landa appeared before the Council of the Indies with the charge of launching an illegal inquisition that killed Mayans and aimed to erase the group's religious, cultural, and historical memory, the court took no official action on the case. Eventually, de Landa's order exonerated him and later named him the second bishop of Yucatán.[47]

The relationship between gold and the variations of the word *corte* can likewise be understood as referencing Hernán Cortés, the Spanish "conqueror" who also stopped at Yucatán before sailing to the Aztec capital of Tenochtitlán. The "z" in "CORTE Z" may allude to both Cortés's last name, sometimes spelled "Cortez" with a "z" in English, and to the Aztec empire. The single "corte" (which means "court" in Spanish) possibly relates to the sovereign power of the king, while the crossed-out "corte" suggests how Cortés, with the support of the Spanish royal court, produced a historically devastating *corte*, or "cut," in the indigenous world. This slash came after the Aztec ruler Moctezuma II gave the Spaniard gifts of gold and the latter held Moctezuma hostage, demanding even more gold in ransom. Eventually, the European hunger for gold killed Moctezuma and destroyed the Aztec empire.

Moreover, the inclusion of the word *savages* is significant. The term underscores the importance of categories of knowledge and language to European and U.S. imperialisms and is in itself a core category of colonial domination that determines who is and is not considered a human. As scholar Jodi A. Byrd has noted, "Savage, animal, and female were differentiated in order to cohere civilized, human, and male."[48] It likewise refers to the ways that blackness has been historically associated to savagery in the Eurocentric imagination. In Fanon's concise terms, "Black Africa is looked on as a region that is inert, brutal, uncivilized—in a word, savage."[49] Not surprisingly, it was also a category familiar to Basquiat. From the start of his career, art critics insisted on labeling him a "black primitive,"[50] despite his evident knowledge of Euro-American art history and awareness of his relationship to it. Basquiat himself once commented that most reviewers "have this image of me... [as a] wild man, monkey man."[51]

Basquiat's emphasis on "savage" is then not merely descriptive. Its prominence can be grasped as a call for a different epistemology, one that insists on and has faith in the unsettling effect of words on the world. In Rifkin's terms, "the ostensibly animistic belief in the ability of language to effect alterations in the material world has been repeatedly castigated in Euro-American intellectual work as 'savage philosophy.' ... Thus, the 'error' labeled 'savage' lies in understanding language as exceeding representation, as not simply reflecting but helping constitute material phenomena."[52] Fittingly, toward the end of his life, and after many conflicts with the white-dominated art establishment led him to declare that "nothing [was] to be gained" in the art world, Basquiat expressed a desire to leave painting behind and become a writer.[53] Writing, however, had been a key part of Basquiat's sovereign signifying acts from the start.

Say the Word

While crowns constituted Basquiat's most iconic sign, language was no less central to his critique of Eurocentric knowledge and assertion of sovereignty over the Euro-American art tradition, or "the royal house of western painting,"[54] in critic Dick Hebdige's terms. Since his days as SAMO© with Al Diaz, Basquiat's "literary graffiti" sought to gain recognition while challenging the privatization of public space and the racism of the art world.[55] Over time, language increasingly figures as source material and includes quotes originating in books, poems, aphorisms, and songs. As Basquiat put it, "I get my facts from books, stuff on atomisers, the blues, ethyl alcohol, geese in the Egyptian style."[56] In retrospect, the extent and depth of Basquiat's incorporation of language is such that artist/scholar Fahamu Pecou has recently observed that his work should not even be described as "paintings" at all but as writings. In Pecou's words, "writing was his medium."[57]

Contrary to some early reviewers and critics who have written that there is no "logic" to Basquiat's words or more current approaches that view his writing as mostly an artistic innovation "amalgamating" language and image,[58] we argue that his words neither constitute "nonsense writing"[59] nor that their importance is purely formal. Rather, through relating text and image, Basquiat repeatedly probed both the signs of sovereignty and the sovereignty of signs, that is, the seemingly arbitrary and miraculous process through which words acquire and sustain authority and power. Noted by Luca Marenzi and others, this is evident in his great attention to terms that refer to legal processes, such as *copyright*, which protects certain intellectual property, and *notary*, a seal that makes specific words lawful "literally as magic,"[60] or, as Basquiat once stated, "alchemy."[61] Basquiat likewise evoked not only writing in his texts but also the erasure and repression of stories, knowledge, and histories by way of "scratching on these things": crossing out, smudging, and painting over letters.[62] Expectedly, Basquiat's first dealer advised him to avoid text in his paintings even though this had become common in contemporary art because, according to critic Rene Ricard, "the words bothered the collectors . . . [and] the words tended more and more frequently to raise unpleasant issues."[63]

Deploying collage and cut-up techniques that were partly inspired by writer William Burroughs, Basquiat employed words in a similar manner as he did crowns: to move and direct the reader's eye to consider alternative associations that disrupt knowledge that has become so naturalized that it appears as "empirical truths."[64] In Ricard's terms, "Using one or two words he reveals a political acuity, gets the viewer going in the direction he wants."[65] Basquiat's drawing/together, writing/apart, and re/positioning linguistic signs and symbols, including lines and arrows that point the way, recalls both the "cannibalizing" tendencies of Caribbean culture[66] and the Martinican writer Édouard Glissant's notion of "poetics of relation," both of which reject binary thinking and articulate a "creolization" of thought. Or in art historian Henry F. Skerritt's words, "In the concept of Relation, Glissant offers a framework to move beyond these polarities. . . . Instead of fixed places of origin, he offers sites of connectivity, where multiple histories and ways of being can coexist. Instead of roots, he offers the dynamic process of creolization, a poetics defined by its openness to transformation."[67]

In Basquiat, a turn to "creoleness," as he himself once called it, is not surprising and emerges from several contexts. For one, Basquiat had Puerto Rican and Haitian family roots and lived experience in the Caribbean, a region in which the clashes between Native, African, Asian, and European peoples and knowledge systems have produced not only syncretic cultures but also ways of thinking about culture as syncretic. Moreover, Basquiat came of age at a time and in a place—New York City, 1960–1980—where numerous creolizations involving different ethnic and racial groups were prominently in motion.[68]

Basquiat's generation was among the first to dance to James Brown's "Say It Loud—I'm Black and I'm Proud" (1968), Joe Cuba's boogaloo fusion, as well as disco and funk. This generation was also the first to read black and Puerto Rican history comic books and other "alternative" popular reading materials. In addition, they actively participated in the creation of Nuyorican poetry, Afro-diasporic spoken word, and hip-hop, cultural forms that critiqued racism and coloniality and were themselves grounded in notions of empowerment via "the word."[69] Not coincidentally, in the early 1980s the idiom "word" carried similar connotations as the Yoruban concept of "ashé," which refers to the power of language to make things happen, enable change, and bring balance to the world: "When one agreed with someone or when another did something 'supreme,' you praised them by saying 'word.'"[70]

During this period, a collective faith in language was validated in both the cultural realm and the larger political context as new forms of speech and discourses were part of broader political movements available via the mass media. Growing up, Basquiat probably watched figures such as Malcolm X and Martin Luther King Jr. speak on television and listened to the demands of Black, Puerto Rican, and Native American civil rights movements that would identify cultural production and symbolic disruption as fundamental to liberation. Equally important, the struggles of these years—as exemplified by groups like the Young Lords, the Black Panthers, and Real Great Society—were organized as much around basic survival issues, such as affordable housing and access to employment, as around new ways to understand, represent, and narrate the self and collective history outside colonial frameworks (see chap. 9).

In keeping with the valorization of writing in Haitian vodou, Basquiat repeated words, numbers, and symbols to interrupt settled meanings and bring different realities into being.[71] Basquiat's repetitions recall Rachel Beauvoir Dominique's fruitful observation: "[O]f special importance is the spellbinding mastery of sequence and number: counting, literally translated as *kontwol* (control) in Creole. . . . Line, stroke, numerology, alphabet, gibberish . . . aesthetics of sign and symbol. . . . '*Circle, square, alphabet and* *number, elements of order . . . the fact of writing more significant than what is actually written. "E.T.C.**.I.BA.L.SA.F.S.NJ. E.Z."* "[72] Repetition, as well as other hip-hop practices familiar to Basquiat such as assonance, alliteration, and rhyme is also related to a broader black poetics in which, as Hebdige has written, "duplicity, doubleness, and undecidedness are divested of the negative connotations generally attached to them in Western culture."[73]

In addition, Basquiat often refused spelling conventions, a practice that can be read as a rejection of the process of language standardization that favors the institutions, groups, and interests of the powerful. This is evident in the ink drawing *Flats Fix* (1981), which pays tribute to working-class Brooklyn.[74] A bare black-and-white drawing, it features a thin irregular tire above capital letters that read "FLATS FiX" rather than the grammatically "correct" "flats fixed." This gesture reminds us of curator Donald J. Cosentino's generative question in relation to the lack of standardization of Haitian Kreyol: "In the rendering of a given word, which history is empowered, and which obscured? Whose pronunciation is privileged? What are the politics of naturalization?"[75]

Less discussed, Basquiat frequently invoked U.S. minoritized languages and cultural codes to dispute the Eurocentric project of epistemological homogenizing.[76] In art critic Robert Farris Thompson's words, "Jean-Michel gracefully embodied the power to deal with history and facts in several languages."[77] Equally relevant, though Basquiat adopted various languages, he did not translate to the U.S. cultural center—that is, privilege the English monolingual observer—thus requiring a multilingual literacy to fully engage with his texts. This is consistent with SAMO© cocreator Al Diaz's comment concerning the importance of linguistic plurality to their wall writing: "some things can't get translated. Bilingualism was a way to 'see' that opened up artistic possibilities and new meanings."[78]

One of many examples of this method is *Anybody Speaking Words* (1982), a text portraying a black figure with a cracked-open head against a yellow background in which the word "OPERA" is reiterated three times. Whereas English speakers may read the idiom *opera* in the context of Italian musical traditions and Italian speakers may also interpret it as "work of art," Spanish-speaking people will further recognize the word as related to the verb *operar* (to operate). True to form, in *Anybody Speaking Words*, Basquiat appears to be referring to "OPERA" in all of these senses: from a neck cavity, music seems to pour out while the body is made of multiple lines implying stitches, veins, and DNA strands, suggesting either that an operation took place or it is required. The text itself is "art."

Although Basquiat knew some French; referenced Haitian religion, history, and culture; and at times saw in kreyol a powerful trope for his own artistic practice, he mostly employed Spanish, a language that he associated with Puerto Rican history and experience to demonstrate mastery over the high-art tradition, insert Latin America and its diaspora into global history, and inscribe specific Puerto Rican structures of feeling that are rendered invisible by U.S. sovereignty. Having lived in both Puerto Rico and New York, Basquiat was probably exposed to not only the stigmatization of Spanish-speaking groups in the United States and the pressure for Latino immigrant children to lose their native tongue but also American efforts to impose English in the Puerto Rican school system. To insist on Spanish was then a knowing defiance toward colonial control and submission to American national culture on the island and diaspora.[79] In choosing Spanish, Basquiat affiliated with a broader Puerto Rican linguistic politics that for nearly a century at that point viewed the retention of "la lengua materna," or Spanish mother tongue, as a mode of resistance and contestation.

Significantly, Basquiat enacted this critique in personal, performative, and textual ways, underscoring its political importance. Personally, as Farris Thompson observed, Basquiat "switched to Spanish when he wanted to make a covert point or camouflage a question"[80] and to establish the terms of financial negotiations. According to Farris Thompson, "One day, in the summer of 1986, a friend (who spoke Spanish) appeared at his door in the company of a rich and famous woman. I was there, and watched them walk around. Suddenly, the woman asked, point-blank, 'How much is that painting over there?' Jean-Michel (in a whisper) to his friend: ¿para tí o para ella? (For you or for her?) Meaning: high price for a stranger, low price or even no price for a friend."[81]

Textually, Spanish words abound in Basquiat's work, within and in titles such as *Crowns (Peso Neto)* (1981), *El gran espectaculo—The History of Black People in 3 Parts* (1983), and *J's Milagro* (1985). Basquiat also introduces Puerto Rican (and other Latin American) vernacular terms such as *gringo*, which explicitly imply distance from American (white) identity and U.S. actions on the global stage. An example is the early painting *Gringo Pilot (Anola Gay)* (1981); in this work, Basquiat references the devastating act of Paul Tibbets, pilot of the Enola Gay, the plane that carried the first of the two atomic bombs dropped on Japan during World War II. Basquiat likewise frequently juxtaposed Spanish and English to produce new meanings and associations that refuse translation. A largely overlooked example is the poetic *Fuego Flores* (1983), which includes a black figure who appears to be declaiming in the midright of the canvas against a multicolored background, and to the top left, a sequence of words in English and Spanish. The first two rows read as a standard translation: "FLOWER—FLOWERS, FLORES" and "FIRE—FIRE(S). FUEGO." Below them, however, Basquiat twice encloses "FIRE" and "FUEGO" in an elliptical shape to radically redefine what the words will now mean: "FIRE—FLORES."

Additionally, the association of English and Spanish serves to highlight commonalities and differences in the black experience of the Americas and pressures English to convey Afro-Latino perspectives. The word *cabeza* (head), found in the titles of and within various works, is significant, as it inscribes specific Afro-Latino worth in contrast to European and American artists such as Warhol and Picasso, both of whom originate in nations that have been (and in many ways continue to be) colonial powers in Puerto Rico. Basquiat similarly named Afro-diasporic figures such as griots in Spanish, as it is evident in the multipaneled *Grillo* (1984), which includes references to African and Afro-Caribbean religious practices. Basquiat's extensive usage of the term *Negro* can likewise be understood to simultaneously refer to a pre–civil rights era, when the devaluation of enslaved Africans and their descendants was certified by law, but also in the ambivalent way—as a term of endearment and depreciation—that it is employed among Puerto Ricans.

Moreover, in the bilingual *Cassius Clay* (1982), Basquiat's ambiguous tribute to boxer Muhammad Ali, he ironically integrates several of these modalities. Here, Ali appears as a masklike head with a "big red mouth" against an envy-green background speckled with various, mostly Spanish, words. Written on Clay's hair, is the common (and racist) Hispanic Caribbean phrase *pelo malo* (bad hair) to describe Afro-textured hair, which is, however, knocked out by the fact that the boxer is a "ROMPE CABEZA" (literally, "head breaker," but also puzzle) and a "CAMPEON DE BOXEO" (boxing champ). Intriguingly, while Basquiat places a crown on the "reality" that Clay is a champ, he only dignifies the challenger Floyd Patterson's name with a crown even if Patterson (like Basquiat) does not refer to Clay by his chosen name and despite the fact that Patterson lost on two occasions to Ali, signified by writing and crossing out the name "FLOYD PATTERSON" twice.[82] At the end, Cassius Clay/Muhammad Ali is subtly rendered as "malo," certainly a famous champion but perhaps not "the greatest" king.

In this regard, curator Kellie Jones's assessment that Basquiat relied on Spanish to primarily refer to the intimate and the feminine, including "family, food, and community . . . the Spanish-speaking world, and the realm of the mother," is not altogether accurate.[83] Whereas Basquiat did draw on Spanish to reference a range of intimate practices and memories (cooking in *Arroz con pollo*, 1981) and family figures (*Abuelita*, 1983) he most often referred to political figures (conquistadors like Hernán Cortés, Puerto Rican politician Luis Muñoz Rivera) as well as terms associated with capitalism (*peso neto*), slavery, racism, and colonialism as they were specifically experienced in Latin America and the Caribbean (*gringo, negro, pelo malo*).

Ultimately, Basquiat's multilingual textuality has much in common with Nuyorican poetics and poets like Abraham Jesús "Tato" Laviera who use Spanish to disrupt the hegemony of English and Anglophone culture and destabilize dominant meanings. Or in Laviera's voice, "pues estoy creando Spanglish / bi-cultural systems . . . two dominant languages / continentally abrazándose / en colloquial combate."[84] He is also part of a longer Afro-Latino genealogy, emblematized by figures such as the public intellectual and historian Arturo Alfonso Schomburg (1874–1938). Like Schomburg, Basquiat referenced Afro-Latino history to complicate Anglocentric narratives on blackness and viewed what he would call "Spanish American" black history as a central part of global history. Basquiat's work thus recalls Henry Louis Gates Jr.'s well-known argument of "signifyin'" as a method "to critique the nature of (white) meaning itself, to challenge through a literal critique of the sign meaning of meaning"[85]—except that white/black is not the only axis of power at play.

Figure 12.2. Jean-Michel Basquiat, *Cassius Clay*, 1982.

Sovereign Impossible?

Through the acts of writing and crowning, Basquiat repeatedly demonstrated that the affirmation of black sovereignty and royal status can produce a forceful critique of capitalist and colonial structures. Yet as multiple critics have argued, there is a caveat. Even when Basquiat recognizes black achievement or condemns European and U.S. colonialisms, he does not fail to note that whereas the rhetoric of sovereignty can be transformed into a compelling idiom of contestation, becoming sovereign in Western terms within the current symbolic, economic, and political order may be inherently violent and expose the black subject to various and continuous forms of violence.

One of the most telling signs of this violence is in how Basquiat often visualized the faces of those he recognized as kings, particularly the famous: with hallowed eyes, frozen features, and/or bloody mouths. An understudied example is *Lye* (1983). In this text, Basquiat paints a black male face with empty eye sockets and a red mouth on the top left of the canvas and a Mona Lisa figure wearing black on the bottom-right side. In between these images, he places a yellow crown over the names "NAT" "KING" "COLE©." Above the crown, he writes "PROCESSED HAIR." "KONKED" "GASSED" "#@!?)" and draws a line linking the words to the head. Through doubling the sign of "King" with a crown, Basquiat acknowledges that imagining the self as royalty is an impressive creative act and notes all the transformative work that it entails, from the singer's adoption of the name "King" (which was not his surname) to his "konked" hair and his breakout Academy Award–winning song referencing the most iconic work of Western art, Leonardo da Vinci's *Mona Lisa* (c. 1503). At the same time, the text appears to ask, "What was the price of becoming King?" And one plausible answer is "Lye"—referencing both the act of accommodating white expectations and the corrosive chemical found in hair relaxer products.

In this way, Basquiat's work demonstrates how even a black critique of Western sovereignty may be couched in terms intelligible to the powerful and primarily make sense in that context. Although Basquiat's work appears to fully validate philosopher Charles Taylor's dictum that "nonrecognition or misrecognition can inflict harm,"[86] it also goes further in proposing that Eurocentric recognition is a form of "imprisoning" that locks colonized peoples in the other's conception of self and recruits them into the reproduction of existing power relations, what bell hooks named "the tragedy of black complicity."[87] This is partly the case because, as political theorist Glen Coulthard (chap. 2) has argued, the recognition offered by dominant institutions is "*asymmetrical and nonreciprocal*" (his emphasis). To the extent that recognition is always "granted" to colonized or racialized peoples without eradicating the colonizers' authority and legitimacy, sovereignty enacts a "failure to significantly modify, let alone transcend, the breadth of power at play in colonial relationships" (Coulthard, chap. 2).

Moreover, Basquiat suggests that the desire for sovereignty distorts what the black subject wants, producing self-alienation. There is perhaps no better example in Basquiat's corpus than the heartbreaking *Irony of Negro Policeman* (1981). In this text, he portrays a black officer wearing a badge shaped like a crown on the right side of his chest. To the left of the officer, Basquiat writes the words "IRONY," "IRONY OF NEGRO PLCEMN," and "PAW," a word that resembles *pawn* and implies that the officer may also have a "beastly" side. The officer's hollowed features and severed arm and leg further conjures that he has been dismembered by his desire. The importance of Basquiat's insight cannot be underestimated and elaborates on Fanon's trope of "black skin, white masks"[88]: if the black subject draws from the (white) sovereign an image of the self, the result will likely be "sovereign" desire, both in the sense of "colonial" and "overbearing."

In addition to the quandary of recognition, Basquiat considered the difficulties of nation-state sovereignty projects for Afro-diasporic polities and politics. This is not surprising given the three national contexts that shaped his own family's history. Haiti, where Basquiat's father reportedly escaped political persecution, is the site of the first successful slave revolution in the world (1804) and is an independent nation-state that continues to be militarily intervened and economically exploited by global powers. Puerto Rico, from where his maternal grandparents migrated, has been a colonial possession for its entire modern history, since 1493, and is currently on the verge of financial collapse even if it has been a colony of the self-described wealthiest democracy in the world for 119 years. Finally, Basquiat grew up in the United States, a nation-state whose prosperity and influence has been greatly produced by the removal of already-constituted indigenous political entities, the enslavement of Africans, and the imposition of U.S. state sovereignty on other nations.

A demanding text that examines the pitfalls and paradoxes of sovereignty in the Caribbean is the densely drawn *50 Cent Piece* (1983). Here, he evokes three Caribbean contexts—Haiti, Puerto Rico, and Jamaica. Each national space is inscribed in part by alluding to the names of leading political icons. These include "DR. FRANCIOS DUVALLIER" (François Duvalier) and "L'OVERTUR" (Toussaint L'Ouverture) from Haiti, "L S M N O R E R" (Luis Muñoz Rivera) from Puerto Rico, and "MARCUS GARVEY" from Jamaica. While the text mentions various figures, the title of *50 Cent Piece* most likely refers to the "Elizabeth II" version of the Marcus Garvey coin issued in 1975, which was worth 50 cents. Consistently, above Garvey's portrait, Basquiat writes "RT EXCLLNE," which approximates what appears on the actual coin, "The RT. [right] EXCELLENT," an honorary mode of address in Jamaica that is used for members of the Order of National Hero; below the image Basquiat writes "BANK OF JAMAICA TM."

The focus on Garvey and the form of visualization as currency critically evokes tensions between national sovereignty, race, fame, and capitalism. At one level, issuing currency is one of the most important national sovereign powers even if the very small denomination of the coin suggests a limited or low value, and American economic hegemony. At another level, the coin underscores Garvey's importance to state discourse as the country's first declared national hero even if he had a strained relationship with Jamaica, a nation he once described as "the place next to hell" due, not coincidentally, to poverty and lacking a "system of economics."[89] Fittingly, Garvey often described himself in cosmopolitan not national terms. As he commented in 1935, "My garb is Scotch, my name is Irish, my blood is African, and my training is half American and half English, and I think that with that tradition I can take care of myself."[90]

Garvey is then a transnational subject defined by continuous movements and crossings of national lines: at various points, he immigrated to Central America, the United States, and the United Kingdom; politically, he led a so-called messianic back-to-Africa movement headquartered in Harlem that sought land in Liberia in response to the relentless racism and violence against blacks in the United States. Toward the end of his life, he became an exile in his own homeland, deported from the United States to Jamaica only to leave again for London, where he died "alone . . . broke and unpopular" according to a premature obituary.[91] In this regard, Basquiat's memorialization of Garvey's as a "big head" on a coin underscores the limits of black intellect, creativity, and fame to affirming sovereignty over the self or a black national polity.

At the same time, *50 Cent Piece* overtly contextualizes many of the challenges of contemporary Caribbean sovereignty on the "collective memory of an ongoing history of violence" that points to a specific sovereign power: the United States.[92] Deploying words and symbols, Basquiat references the brutal U.S. occupation of Haiti, to which he assigns two endings—1921 and 1936—rather than the standard 1915-1934. The alternative periodization may be aimed at highlighting the 1921 U.S. investigation of abuse claims in Haiti in which the marine commander declared that over two thousand Haitians had been killed resisting the occupation; it could similarly refer to the forced migration of Haitians to Cuba and the Dominican Republic during this period. Moreover, while the 1936 year does not appear to refer to any specific event, in offering different end dates that do not match the "official" dates, these numbers suggest that the occupation continued beyond 1934 and that it is ongoing.

50 Cent Piece likewise considers the central place of movement to Caribbean national politics. In addition to different spellings and repetitions of "back to Africa," which call attention to the desire to migrate in order to escape the American state violence toward blacks, *50 Cent Piece* also contains the phrase "Operation Bootstrap," the name given to Puerto Rico's U.S.-led economic modernization plan that stimulated the mass migration of hundreds of thousands of Puerto Ricans to cities such as New York starting in the 1940s to serve as cheap labor. Significantly, Basquiat writes "OPERATION BOOTST/RAP" at the same level and in proximity to "US OCCUPATION OF HAITI ENDS 1921," linking different migratory flows originating in U.S. invasion and economic dispossession. Perhaps to underscore that the Puerto Rican exodus is a result of the invasion and not simply an immigrant phenomenon, Basquiat does not mention Luis Muñoz Marín, the Puerto Rican coarchitect of the migration policy, but his father, Luis Muñoz Rivera, who was acting as secretary of state and chief of the cabinet for the autonomist government of Puerto Rico when the United States invaded the island on July 25, 1898.

50 Cent Piece, however, is relatively rare in Basquiat's corpus in that he envisions that the Caribbean will, regardless, stay afloat by making use of its own, spiritual, devices. This view is connoted through the reiteration of the phrases "300 CUBITS LONG" and "THE ARK," which alludes to the dimensions of Noah's biblical ark but similarly contains at least two other referents: the slave ship and the vodou spirit of water, Agwe, who possesses a boat and receives offerings in small vessels made of bark and other materials. The evocation of Agwe is present in both the portraying of the ark against which the word "WOOD" is written on the side of the ship and in the crossing out of the phrase "THE ARK" to say "T E A K," a type of wood found in Asia and Latin America. In relating all three referents, the ark signifies the various means that blacks in the Americas have imagined to protect what is valuable in Caribbean life and escape the many "floods" that accompany it, including slave ships, invasions, dictators, and destructive policies imposed from inside and outside.

At the same time, though Caribbean survival is imagined, sovereignty ultimately appears as impossible. This is despite, or perhaps because, as Basquiat writes, the islands possess coveted wealth via excellent "BLUE RIBBON" commodities—"SALT," "SUGAR," "RUM WHITE," "BANANAS," "BAUXITE," and, more importantly, "BRAIN" (like Garvey)—whose worth make them subject to external market and political forces. Sovereignty is then elusive regardless of whether the islands are nation-states, like Jamaica and Haiti, or are territories, like Puerto Rico, that belong to wealthy nations like the United States, as they remain measured by value systems that classify them as useful or useless according to the interests of current and former colonial powers. If as Bataille suggests, "life beyond utility is the realm of sovereignty," to be sovereign would require that "one must step out of the relations which condition him or her for being useful . . . [and] break up the temporal sequence in which the past, present and future are so arranged as to make expectation possible."[93]

Significantly, the figuration of capital as an impediment to sovereignty is not limited to Caribbean history and space. A work that can be read as a metatext of how capitalist greed throws black political and spiritual sovereignty out of balance is *K* (1982). Here, Basquiat draws two symbols of sovereignty under the phrase "SEPARATION OF THE 'K.'" On the left side, Basquiat writes the name of an imagined Egyptian king "AOPKHES." Below this name he paints a nonhuman figure, a heart, and a set of scales. Basquiat seems to be referring to the female Egyptian demon Ammit—who was

Figure 12.3. Jean-Michel Basquiat, *El gran espectaculo—The History of Black People in 3 parts*, 1983.

known as "Devourer of the Dead," "Greatness of Death," and closer to this analysis, "Eater of Hearts"—and Anubis, the god of the afterlife. According to Egyptian mythology, Ammit sits under the scales of justice of Ma'at, the goddess of truth, where Anubis weighs the hearts of the dead against an ostrich feather. If the heart is heavier than the feather due to the gravity of past deeds, it is judged to be impure. Ammit will then devour it, and the soul will die a second death and not continue the voyage toward immortality.

On the right side, Basquiat paints a crown with the word "ORO" (gold) topped by dollar signs. Below it, the name AOPKHES is written four times, one of them as a question. In the bottom right of the canvas, a human face appears trapped. The left side thus alludes to an African society's construction of its own systems of engagement in the human and supernatural world in contrast to the colonial equation of royal power with gold. Significantly, the text evokes ambivalence to the question of whether African sovereigns are an alternative to capital by writing at the bottom of the left panel, "¿Disease culture?" Yet in answering assertively in the panel on the right—"<u>Disease</u> Culture"—Basquiat seems to propose that the African pharaoh and his gods, powerful as they may be, are no match for King Gold.

By stressing that the opposite of the desired black sovereignty (defacement) is produced both when capital superexploits labor (slavery) and when it handsomely pays off (stardom), Basquiat suggests that sovereignty via capital is an illusion that ends up isolating and consuming you. This insight continues to resonate and influence younger artists who have witnessed the marketing of black bodies in ways that Basquiat himself may not have even imagined possible. In his *Branded Head* (2003), which features an African American man with a raised scar in the shape of the Nike logo,[94] visual artist Hank Willis Thomas makes a similar observation as Basquiat albeit in starker terms: that sovereignty imagined through capitalist recognition as a brand is not freedom from, but submission to, capital—even if people may often enjoy branding themselves.[95]

This leads to an unavoidable conclusion: it is capital that "rules" art, politics, and life, rather than famous artists. Even when the artist or black king appears to be the sovereign of the artwork—crowning and uncrowning, writing and crossing out at will—the victory is pyrrhic. To the extent that capital's logic is sovereign in the conventional sense of supreme or absolute control, all peoples, men included, are subject to the market.⁹⁶ This reminds us of political theorist Wendy Brown's assessment of Marx's critique of sovereignty: "Man is proclaimed king but limited by his powerlessness and alienation; his crown ultimately serves to bewilder, isolate, and humiliate him."⁹⁷ If capital rules and racialized/colonized lives are instrumentalized as labor or as consumers, neither nation-state status nor commodified stardom can produce a sovereign black man or polity.

Moreover, Basquiat's gendering of sovereignty as male and his coupling of black sovereignty to white male recognition calls attention to another limitation. Like other black intellectuals such as Marcus Garvey, who, in Agustin Lao-Montes's words, "conceived . . . a trans-nationalist project in search of sovereignty and peoplehood, and therefore partly as a battle between Afrodiasporic and western masculinities,"⁹⁸ Basquiat was unable to free himself from this deadly pairing. Tellingly, while he frequently placed crowns on top of celebrated black musicians and athletes, visualized African and diasporic cultural practices, and by claiming the crown located himself in a pantheon of black kings,⁹⁹ Basquiat rarely, if ever, alludes to black visual artists with whom he had commonalities, such as Wifredo Lam, Jacob Lawrence, and Romare Bearden, suggesting that he alone was in line to succeed the greatest white male artists.

In this sense, although a handful of scholars (including Negrón-Muntaner) have argued elsewhere that Basquiat linked creativity to his mother('s) tongue and recognized women as bearers of the gift of communication in rare images such as *Abuelita* (1983), a portrait of his maternal grandmother seemingly coming from the market,¹⁰⁰ it is clear that for Basquiat the struggle over art history, public space, and sovereignty was a male affair.¹⁰¹ As Greg Tate has observed, "to Basquiat 'making it' . . . meant going down in history, ranked beside the Great White Fathers of Western painting in the eyes of the major critics, museum curators, and art historians who ultimately determine such things."¹⁰² Which is why crowns are for kings, not queens, and why it is only kings, as evident in paintings such as *Charles the First* (1982), who "GET THEIR HEADS CUT OFF."

Yet whereas Basquiat equated black sovereignty with masculinity and mostly focused on the challenges of black recognition by white institutions, he was no less aware that even if understood as relating to the self and not to territories or polities, any project founded on a desire for control faces a most unyielding obstacle: the physical body itself. His many representations of human bodies (black or white) as fragile, vulnerable to physical trauma and emotional breakdown, attest to everyone's inability to be fully sovereign over ourselves in the most basic of ways.

This is present in *Untitled (Head)* (1981), where Basquiat investigates how the head—the epicenter of Western rationality and African intelligence and rank—has both inside and outside dimensions and is a precarious construction put together by uncertain physical and emotional circuitry. In the print *Back of the Neck* (1983), Basquiat draws anatomical and X-ray-like images of various body parts. At the center is an X-ray of a spinal column, the term *SPINE* followed by a copyright symbol and an opaque crown resting above as if to affirm that we do not even own our bones, however grand our ambitions. More explicitly, in the three-panel installation titled *Gravestone* (1987) in memory of artist Andy Warhol, the central panel repeats the word *PERISHABLE* twice, while the left features the images of a black rose and cross, and the right a white and red mask-like face. Moreover, the style in which the surface is painted—smudged, crossed over, barely readable—reinforces the human destiny of eventual decay and death.

Exit the King

Not surprisingly, toward the end of his life, Basquiat painted fewer crowns and related terms, choosing to largely abdicate the Western language of sovereignty. In Basquiat's last years, his emphasis was increasingly on the human body and its frailties—dangling feet, severed hands, bleeding hearts, damaged kidneys—and his surfaces were wood and found materials. There are also less human heads and many more depictions of animals, particularly the previously dreaded monkeys or "monos" as well as Afro-Caribbean spiritual beings such as African griots. European law was giving way to African and Afro-diasporic *lwas*, a plural, reciprocal, and complex manner to conceive of power and take care of the self.

The timing of this shift may not have been accidental or purely intellectual. In addition to Basquiat receiving criticism regarding the repetition of his imagery, this was also the year in which he faced one of the most painful moments of his career. Whereas *New York Times* critic Vivian Raynor wrote in 1984 that Basquiat had "a chance of becoming a very good one [painter], as long as he can withstand the forces that would make of him an art-world mascot," in 1985 she concluded that Basquiat had already become "a mascot." Basquiat had famously responded that "I wanted to be a star, not a gallery mascot,"[103] but perhaps the damage was done. Three years later, Basquiat died of an overdose, seemingly unable to cope with the loss of friends and negative reviews.

Retrospectively, it is undeniable that Basquiat's career illustrated the power of sovereign acts to challenge symbolic structures, including on his own turf of art history, the street, and museum walls. A testament to this is that Basquiat is persistently remembered as he initially wished he would be: as one of the great and therefore, immortal, kings of art history. Basquiat's success in being viewed in this way is such that a simple outline of his signature crown is enough to connote him. For instance, after Basquiat's death, artist Keith Haring memorialized him with a painted triangle full of crowns titled, *A Pile of Crowns, for Jean-Michel Basquiat* (1988). Almost a decade later, in the opening scene of Julian Schnabel's film *Basquiat* (1996), the artist appears as a young boy being crowned the heir of modern art after looking at Picasso's *Guernica*. Most recently, a range of commodities, including sneakers, mugs, and the Urban Outfitter "Junk Food Basquiat Crown Tee," hauntingly conjure Basquiat through his crown.

Yet similar to Caribbean diaspora intellectuals Claude McKay and C. L. R. James before him, the arc of Basquiat's work tends toward the conclusion that being king over institutions, discourses, or even the self is not the same as freedom; that in this sense, the vocabulary of sovereignty may still be too tied up with unitary notions of power, utility, and control. It is perhaps in this context that one of Basquiat's last paintings, *Riding with Death* (1988) can be considered as a particularly compelling visualization of another direction. If in most other works the black figure has his arms up, as if he was being arrested by sovereign desire and frightened by white recognition, the arms of the rider are lower, without a halo or crown, down to the bone, refusing the gaze, soaring to the unknown. Prefigured through his own works such as *Gold Griot* (1984) and Da Vinci's *Allegorical Composition* (c. 1472–1519) and deploying an "ashé" gesture—"right hand up, left hand down, calls on God and the horizon"[104]—he references a different source of power in the religious practices of the African diaspora, in which death "is a new beginning . . . a passage into the spirit realm."[105] Basquiat himself never made it to this new place where freedom may have dethroned sovereignty; but here, still as king of the line, he is drawing from it.

Notes

1. Robert Farris Thompson, "Royalty, Heroism, and the Streets: The Art of Jean-Michel Basquiat," in *The Hearing Eye: Jazz and Blues Influences in African American Visual Art*, ed. Graham Lock and David Murray (New York: Oxford University Press, 2009), 254.
2. Cathleen McGuigan, "New Art, New Money" *New York Times Magazine* (online), February 10, 1985, https://www.nytimes.com/books/98/08/09/specials/basquiat-mag.html.
3. Greg Tate, "Nobody Loves a Genius Child: Jean-Michel Basquiat, Flyboy in the Buttermilk," in *Flyboy in the Buttermilk: Essays on Contemporary America* (New York: Simon and Schuster, 1992), 62.
4. Jordana Moore Saggese, *Reading Basquiat: Exploring Ambivalence in American Art* (Berkeley: University of California Press, 2014), 103. According to Moore Saggese, in 1982 alone, Basquiat drew halos and crowns in at least sixteen works.
5. Thompson, "Royalty, Heroism, and the Streets," 267.
6. Tate, "Nobody Loves a Genius Child."
7. Moore Saggese, *Reading Basquiat*, 2.
8. Henry Geldzahler, "New Again: Jean-Michel Basquiat," *Interview*, April 18, 2012, http://www.interviewmagazine.com/art/new-again-jean-michel-basquiat-/#_. Originally published January 1983. See also Anthony Haden-Guest, "Burning Out," *Vanity Fair*, April 2, 2014, http://www.vanityfair.com/news/1988/11/jean-michel-basquiat.
9. Moore Sagesse, *Reading Basquiat*, 122.

10. Richard Marshall, "Repelling Ghosts," in *Jean-Michel Basquiat*, ed. Richard Marshall (New York: Whitney Museum of American Art, 1992), 16.
11. Scott Richard Lyons, "Rhetorical Sovereignty: What Do American Indians Want from Writing?," *College Composition and Communication* 51, no. 3 (February 2000): 462.
12. David Scott, "The Sovereignty of the Imagination: An Interview with George Lamming," *Small Axe* 12 (September 2002): 123.
13. Alexander Hirsch, "Sovereignty Surreal: Bataille and Fanon Beyond the State of Exception," *Contemporary Political Theory* 13, no. 3 (August 2014): 288.
14. Larry Warsh, ed., *Jean-Michel Basquiat: The Notebooks* (Princeton, NJ: Princeton University Press, 2015). See also Dieter Buchhart, "Basquiat's Notebooks: Words and Knowledge, Scratched and Sample," *Cleveland Art* (online magazine), January/February 2017, https://www.clevelandart.org/magazine/cleveland-art-januaryfebruary-2017/basquiats-notebooks.
15. Dick Hebdige, "Welcome to the Terrordome: Jean-Michel Basquiat and the 'Dark' Side of Hybridity," in Marshall, *Jean-Michel Basquiat*, 65.
16. Mark Rifkin, *The Erotics of Sovereignty: Queer Native Writing in the Era of Self-Determination* (Minneapolis: University of Minnesota Press, 2011), 2.
17. Walter Mignolo, *The Darker Side of Western Modernity: Global Futures, Decolonial Options* (Durham: Duke University Press, 2011), xxvii.
18. Christopher Keep, Tim McLaughlin, and Robin Parmar, "Hypertext," The Electronic Labyrinth (1993–2000), http://www2.iath.virginia.edu/elab/hfl0037.html.
19. Quoted in Moore Saggese, *Reading Basquiat*, 6.
20. Quoted in Moore Saggese, *Reading Basquiat*, 55.
21. Francesco Clemente, "For Diego," in *Basquiat* (Milan: Charta, 1999), L. Exhibition catalog.
22. bell hooks, "Altars of Sacrifice: Re-membering Basquiat," in *Art on My Mind: Visual Politics* (New York: New Press, 1995), 43.
23. Moore Sagesse, *Reading Basquiat*, 54.
24. Marshall, "Repelling Ghosts," 16.
25. Brent Hayes Edwards interview.
26. Eric Fretz, *Jean-Michel Basquiat* (Santa Barbara, CA: Greenwood Biographies, 2010), 86.
27. Ella Shohat and Robert Stam, *Unthinking Eurocentrism: Multiculturalism and the Media* (New York: Routledge, 1994), 306.

28. "Carnival in Brazil and the Caribbean" (2006), Encyclopedia.com, http://www.encyclopedia.com/history/encyclopedias-almanacs-transcripts-and-maps/carnival-brazil-and-caribbean.
29. Rifkin, "Introduction," in Rifkin, *Erotics of Sovereignty*, 16.
30. McGuigan, "New Art, New Money," 10.
31. Simon Gikandi, "Picasso, Africa, and the Schemata of Difference," *Modernism/modernity* 10, no. 3 (September 2003), 468.
32. Kellie Jones, "Lost in Translation: Jean-Michel in the [Re]Mix," in *Basquiat*, ed. Marc Mayer (Brooklyn: Brooklyn Museum, 2005; repr., London: Merrel, 2010), 171.
33. Walter D. Mignolo, "Delinking: The Rhetoric of Modernity, the Logic of Coloniality and the Grammar of Decoloniality," in *Globalization and the Decolonial Option*, ed. Walter Mignolo and Arturo Escobar (New York: Routledge, 2013), 312.
34. Gikandi, "Picasso, Africa, and the Schemata of Difference," 456.
35. I thank Elizabeth West Hutchinson for pointing me in this direction.
36. George Brandon, "Orisha," in *Encyclopaedia Britannica*, https://www.britannica.com/topic/orisha.
37. Margarite Fernández Olmos and Lizabeth Paravisini-Gebert, eds. *Sacred Possessions: Vodou, Santería, Obeah, and the Caribbean* (New Brunswick, NJ: Rutgers University Press, 1997), 131.
38. Suzanne Preston Blier, "Vodun: West African Roots of Vodou," in *Sacred Arts of Haitian Vodou*, ed. Donald J. Cosentino (Los Angeles: UCLA Fowler Museum of Cultural History, 1995), 67.
39. There are a number of resonances between Basquiat's use of crowns to signify power and higher purpose and the Latin Kings gang founded in Chicago. Yet given that the organization did not have a distinct branch in New York, the Almighty Latin Kings and Queens, until 1986, it is unclear if Basquiat was familiar with their iconography. According to multimedia artist and Basquiat colleague Michael Holman, "I didn't really hear about the Latin Kings until the 1990s. [Basquiat] never mentioned them"; e-mail message to author, March 19, 2017.
40. Richard Lachmann, "Graffiti as Career and Ideology," *American Journal of Sociology* 94, no. 2 (1988): 237.
41. Moore Saggese, *Reading Basquiat*, 55.

42. Simon Abrahams, "Basquiat's Crowns (1981–82)," EPPH (website), November 20, 2010, http://www.everypainterpaintshimself.com/article/basquiats_crowns.
43. Tate, "Nobody Loves a Genius Child," 234.
44. Michel Foucault, *The Order of Things: An Archaeology of Human Sciences* (New York: Vintage, 1994), 15.
45. Nin Tomas, "Maori Concepts and Practices of Rangatiratanga, Kaitiakitanga, the Environment, and Property Rights," in *Property Rights and Sustainability*, vol. 11, *Legal Aspects of Sustainable Development*, ed. David Grinlinton and Prue Taylor (Leiden, The Netherlands: Nijhoff, 2011), 220.
46. hooks, "Altars of Sacrifice," 71.
47. David E. Timmer, "Providence and Perdition: Fray Diego de Landa Justifies His Inquisition Against the Yucatecan Maya," *Church History* 66, no. 3 (September 1997): 477–88.
48. Jodi A. Byrd, "Mind the Gap: Indigenous Sovereignty and the Antinomies of Empire," in *The Anomie of the Earth: Philosophy, Politics, and Autonomy in Europe and the Americas*, ed. Frederico Luisetti, John Pickles, and Wilson Kaiser (Durham, NC: Duke University Press, 2015), 120–121, 122.
49. Frantz Fanon, "The Pitfalls of National Consciousness," in *The Wretched of the Earth* (New York: Grove 1961), 10.
50. For a broader discussion on the representation of Basquiat as a "primitive" artist, see Moore Saggese, *Reading Basquiat*, 4–5.
51. Jean-Michel Basquiat in *Jean-Michel Basquiat: The Radiant Child*, directed by Tamra Davis, 2010.
52. Rifkin, "Introduction," 15.
53. Klaus Kertess, "Brushes with Beatitude," in *Jean Michel Basquiat*, ed. Richard Marshall (New York: Whitney Museum of American Art, 1992), 50–55.
54. Hebdige, "Welcome to the Terrordome," 60.
55. Cited in Fretz, *Jean-Michel Basquiat*, 44.
56. Quoted in Louis Armand, "Jean-Michel Basquiat and the Art of (Dis)Empowerment," reproduced in https://culturenightlosangeles.wordpress.com/tag/african-symbol-system-in-basquiats-paintings/.
57. Fahamu Pecou, remarks at Jean-Michel Basquiat conference, Brooklyn Museum, March 26, 2016.
58. This last reading is becoming more visible in recent exhibits such as "Words Are All We Have: Paintings by Jean-Michel Basquiat," curated by Dieter Buch-

hart at the Nahmad Contemporary Gallery, New York, and on exhibit from May 2 to June 18, 2016.

59. Fretz, *Jean-Michel Basquiat*, 70.
60. Luca Marenzi, "Pay for Soup / Build a Fort / Set That on Fire," in *Basquiat*, catalog of an exhibition held in Museo Revoltella, Trieste, May 15–September 15, 1999 (Milan: Charta, 1999), xxxiv.
61. Geldzahler, "New Again."
62. Buchhart, "Basquiat's Notebooks."
63. Rene Ricard, "World Crown: Bodhisattva with Clenched Mudra," in Marshall, *Jean-Michel Basquiat*, 48.
64. Robert Farris Thompson, "Activating Heaven: The Art of Jean-Michel Basquiat," in *Aesthetic of the Cool: Afro-Atlantic Art and Music* (Pittsburgh, PA: Periscope, 2011), 38–43; Warsh, *Jean-Michel Basquiat: The Notebooks*; Rifkin, *Erotics of Sovereignty*, 14.
65. Cited in Fretz, *Jean-Michel Basquiat*, 87.
66. Joan Dayan, "Vodoun, or the Voice of the Gods," in *Sacred Possessions: Vodou, Snatería, Obeah, and the Caribbean*, ed. Margarite Fernández Olmos and Lizabeth Paravisini-Gebert (New Brunswick, NJ: Rutgers University Press, 1997), 27.
67. Henry F. Skerritt, "Book Review: Édouard Glissant, *Poetics of Relation*," Henry F. Skerritt (blog), August 16, 2012, https://henryfskerritt.com/2012/08/16/book-review-edouard-glissant-poetics-of-relation/. See also Édouard Glissant, *Poetics of Relation* (Ann Arbor: University of Michigan Press, 1997).
68. See Juan Flores, "The Diaspora Strikes Back," in *None of the Above: Puerto Ricans in the Global Era*, ed. Frances Negrón-Muntaner (New York: Palgrave, 2007), 211–16, and Frances Negrón-Muntaner, *Boricua Pop: Puerto Ricans and the Latinization of American Culture* (New York: New York University Press, 2004), 145–76.
69. Franklin Sirmans, "In the Cipher: Basquiat and Hip-Hop Culture," in Mayer, *Basquiat*, 94.
70. Yasmin Ramirez (unpublished essay, May 2014).
71. Sidney Mintz and Michel-Rolph Trouillot, "The Social History of Haitian Vodou," in Donald J. Cosentino, ed., *Sacred Arts of Haitian Vodou* (Los Angeles: UCLA Fowler Museum of Cultural History, 1995), 129.
72. Rachel Beauvoir-Dominique, "Underground Realms of Being: Vodoun Magic," in Consentino, *Sacred Arts of Haitian Vodou*, 169, 170, 172–73.

73. Hebdige, "Welcome to the Terrordome," 64.
74. Fretz, *Jean-Michel Basquiat*, 63.
75. Consentino, *Sacred Arts of Haitian Vodou*, xiii.
76. For discussions of the relationship between Basquiat and language, see Frances Negrón-Muntaner, "The Writing on the Wall: The Life and Passion of Jean-Michel Basquiat," in Negrón-Muntaner, *Boricua Pop*, and Thompson, "Royalty, Heroism, and the Streets."
77. Thompson, "Royalty, Heroism, and the Streets," 257.
78. Al Diaz, remarks at Jean-Michel Basquiat conference, Brooklyn Museum, March 26, 2016.
79. Frances Negrón-Muntaner, "Sin pelos en la lengua: Last Interview with Rosario Ferré," *CENTRO: Journal of the Center for Puerto Rican Studies* (2012): 154–71.
80. Thompson, "Royalty, Heroism, and the Streets," 257.
81. Ibid., 30.
82. Matt Christie, "On This Day: Muhammad Ali Toys with Poor Floyd Patterson," *Boxing News*, November 22, 2016, http://www.boxingnewsonline.net/on-this-day-muhammad-ali-toys-with-poor-floyd-patterson/.
83. Jones, "Lost in Translation," 170.
84. Tato Laviera (Abraham Jesús "Tato" Laviera), "Spanglish," *Poetry Foundation*, https://www.poetryfoundation.org/poems-and-poets/poems/detail/58198.
85. Cited in Moore Saggese, *Reading Basquiat*, 99.
86. Charles Taylor, "The Politics of Recognition," in *Multiculturalism*, ed. Amy Gutmann (Princeton, NJ: Princeton University Press, 1994), 25–73.
87. hooks, "Altars of Sacrifice," 30.
88. Frantz Fanon, *Black Skin, White Masks* (New York: Grove, 2008).
89. Carolyn Cooper, "Why Is Marcus Garvey a National Hero?," *Gleaner*, August 19, 2012, http://jamaica-gleaner.com/gleaner/20120819/cleisure/cleisure3.html.
90. *Daily Gleaner*, January 19, 1935.
91. George Padmore, "Marcus Garvey Dies In London: Lost Wealth and Prestige Before Death," *Chicago Defender*, May 18, 1940, 1.
92. Rifkin, *Erotics of Sovereignty*, 3.
93. Mete Ulaş Aksoy, "Hegel and Georges Bataille's Conceptualization of Sovereignty," *Ege Academic Review* 11, no. 2 (April 2011), 219.

94. Sonia K. Katyal, "BRANDED: On the Semiotic Disobedience of Hank Willis Thomas," *Brooklyn Rail*, March 4, 2016, http://brooklynrail.org/2016/03/critics page/branded-on-the-semiotic-disobedience-of-hank-willis-thomas.
95. For further discussion on Basquiat's relationship to capitalism, see Frances Negrón-Muntaner, "The Writing on the Wall: The Life and Passion of Jean-Michel Basquiat," in Negrón-Muntaner, *Boricua Pop*, 115–44.
96. Gail Turley Houston, *Royalties: The Queen and Victorian Writers* (Charlottesville: University Press of Virginia, 1999), 63.
97. Wendy Brown, *States of Injury: Power and Freedom in Late Modernity* (Princeton, NJ: Princeton University Press, 1995), 107–8.
98. Agustin Lao-Montes, "Decolonial Moves: Translocating African Diaspora Spaces," *Cultural Studies* 21, no. 2 (2007): 314.
99. Brent Hayes Edwards, e-mail message to author May 15, 2017.
100. Negrón-Muntaner, *Boricua Pop*, 2004.
101. Ibid.
102. Tate, "Nobody Loves a Genius Child," 237.
103. *Basquiat*, catalog of an exhibition held in Museo Revoltella, Trieste, May 15–September 15, 1999 (Milano: Edizione Charta, 1999), 136.
104. Thompson, "Activating Heaven."
105. Elizabeth McAlister, "A Sorcerer's Bottle: The Visual Art of Magic in Haiti," in Consentino, *Sacred Arts of Haitian Vodou*, 309.

Contributors

Michael Lujan Bevacqua is assistant professor at the University of Guam. He received an MA in ethnic studies from the University of California, San Diego, in 2007 and was conferred a PhD in 2010. Since 2006, Bevacqua has worked as the assistant managing editor for two academic journals: *Social Identities* and *African Identities*. He was also coeditor of *Chamoru Childhood*, an anthology of Chamoru stories published by Achiote Press in 2009. Furthermore, Bevacqua served as the editor for the online Chamorro zine *Minagahet*, which is dedicated to the revitalization of Chamorro language and culture, the decolonization of Guam, and the dissemination of information regarding current events in Guam. In addition, he maintains a number of other websites, including Chamorro.com, Decolonize Guam, and his personal blog No Rest for the Awake—Minagahet Chamorro.

Glen Coulthard is a member of the Yellowknives Dene First Nation and an associate professor in the First Nations and indigenous studies program and the Department of Political Science at the University of British Columbia. Coulthard has written and published numerous articles and chapters in the areas of indigenous thought and politics, contemporary political theory, and radical social and political thought. He lives in Vancouver, Coast Salish

Territories. His book *Red Skin, White Masks: Rejecting the Colonial Politics of Recognition* (University of Minnesota Press) was released in August 2014 to critical acclaim. His coedited book *Recognition Versus Self-Determination: Dilemmas of Emancipatory Politics* was released in spring 2014 by University of British Columbia Press. Coulthard was also a featured contributor to the groundbreaking anthology *The Winter We Danced: Voices from the Past, the Future, and the Idle No More Movement* (ARP Books), which was released in March 2014.

Jennifer Nez Denetdale is a citizen of the Diné/Navajo Nation. Denetdale is currently associate professor of American studies at the University of New Mexico. She is the author of *Reclaiming Diné History: The Legacies of Navajo Chief Manuelito and Juanita* (2007) and has published numerous articles on Native and Diné history.

Adriana María Garriga-López is associate professor of anthropology at Kalamazoo College in Michigan. Born and raised in San Juan, Puerto Rico, she holds PhD (2010), MPhil (2006), and MA (2003) degrees in cultural anthropology from Columbia University and a BA (2001) in anthropology and comparative literature from Rutgers, the State University of New Jersey. In addition to her academic research, she writes poetry and fiction in English and Spanish. She is also a performance artist, muralist, and soprano.

Jessica A. F. Harkins is a doctoral candidate in the American studies department at the University of New Mexico, completing a certificate in women's studies as well. Her dissertation is focused on the role of heteronormativity as a tool of U.S. colonialism, looking specifically at the 2006 same-sex marriage ban in the Cherokee Nation.

Brian Klopotek is an associate professor of ethnic studies and director of the Native American studies minor at the University of Oregon. His first book, *Recognition Odysseys: Indigeneity, Race, and Federal Tribal Recognition Policy in Three Louisiana Indian Communities* (Duke University Press, 2011), examines the ways Louisiana Indians have responded to and been affected by federal recognition policy, the politics of indigeneity, and racial thinking. With

Brenda Child, he coedited *Indian Subjects: Hemispheric Perspectives on the History of Indigenous Education* (SAR Press, 2014). The book explores educational histories across the Americas and the Pacific, moving toward more hemispheric and global understandings of indigenous experiences and politics. He is currently completing a collaborative project with the Tunica-Biloxi Tribe of Louisiana, a revised and updated second edition of *The Tunica-Biloxi Tribe: Its Culture and People* (Tunica-Biloxi Tribe, 2017).

Davianna Pōmaikaʻi McGregor, professor and founding member of ethnic studies at the University of Hawaiʻi, Manoa, is a historian of Hawaiʻi and the Pacific. Her ongoing research endeavors to document the persistence of traditional Hawaiian cultural customs, beliefs, and practices in rural Hawaiian communities, including the island of Molokaʻi; the districts of Puna and Kaʻu on Hawaiʻi; Keʻanae-Wailuanui on Maui; and Waiahole-Waikane on Oʻahu. This work is featured in her 2007 University of Hawaiʻi Press book *Kuaʻaina: Living Hawaiian Culture*, which won the Kenneth W. Balridge Prize for best book in any field of history written by a resident of Hawaiʻi from 2005 to 2007. She lives in Kaiwiʻula, Oʻahu, and Hoʻolehua, Molokaʻi, and is a member of Protect Kahoʻolawe.

Frances Negrón-Muntaner is a filmmaker, writer, curator, scholar, and professor at Columbia University, where she is founding director of the Media and Idea Lab. Among her books and publications are *Puerto Rican Jam: Rethinking Colonialism and Nationalism* (University of Minnesota Press, 1997, coedited with Ramón Grosfoguel), *Boricua Pop: Puerto Ricans and the Latinization of American Culture* (New York University Press, *Choice* award, 2004), and *The Latino Media Gap: A Report on the State of Latinos in US Media* (2014). Her most recent films include *Small City, Big Change* (2013), *War for Guam* (2015), and *Regarding Vieques* (2017). For her work, Negrón-Muntaner has received Ford, Truman, Scripps Howard, Rockefeller, Pew, and Chang-Chavkin fellowships and support from the Social Science Research Council, Andy Warhol Foundation, and Independent Television Service. In 2008, the United Nations' Rapid Response Media Mechanism recognized her as a global expert in the areas of mass media and Latin/o American studies; in 2012, she received the Lenfest Award, one of Columbia University's most prestigious recognitions for excellence in teaching and scholarship. Negrón-Muntaner is also founding curator of the Latino Arts and Activism Archive at Columbia's Rare Books & Manuscripts Library and former director of the Center for the Study of Ethnicity and Race.

Yasmin Ramirez holds a PhD in art history from the Graduate Center of the City of New York. Currently an independent curator, Ramirez's institutional affiliations include El Museo Del Barrio, Taller Boricua, The Caribbean Culture Center, The Center for Puerto Rican Studies, and Hunter College. She has published numerous essays and reviews, notably "The Creative Class of Color in New York" (*Grantmakers in the Arts Reader*, 2009); "The Activist Legacy of Puerto Rican Artists in New York and the Art Heritage of Puerto Rico" (International Center for the Arts of the Americas, Documents of 20th-Century Latin American and Latino Art, 2007); and "Parallel Lives, Striking Differences: Notes on Chicano and Puerto Rican Graphic Arts of the 1970s" (*CENTRO: Journal of the Center for Puerto Rican Studies*, 1999).

Mark Rifkin is director of the Women's and Gender Studies Program and professor of English at the University of North Carolina at Greensboro. He received his PhD in 2003 from the English department at the University of Pennsylvania. He is the author of five books: *Manifesting America: The Imperial Construction of U.S. National Space* (Oxford University Press, 2009); *When Did Indians Become Straight? Kinship, the History of Sexuality, and Native Sovereignty* (Oxford University Press, 2011, winner of the 2012 John Hope Franklin prize for best book in American studies); *The Erotics of Sovereignty: Queer Native Writing in the Era of Self-Determination* (University of Minnesota Press, 2012); *Settler Common Sense: Queerness and Everyday Colonialism in the American Renaissance* (University of Minnesota Press, 2014); and *Beyond Settler Time: Temporal Sovereignty and Indigenous Self-Determination* (Duke University Press, 2017). Along with Daniel Heath Justice and Bethany Schneider, he coedited *Sexuality, Nationality, Indigeneity*, a special double issue of *GLQ* (2010 winner of the award for best special issue from the Council of Editors of Learned Journals). He also has published over two dozen essays in scholarly journals and collections and has served as the president of the Native American and Indigenous Studies Association.

Madeline Román is professor of sociology at the University of Puerto Rico–Rio Piedras. She is the author of several books on crime and violence in Puerto Rico, including, *Estado y criminalidad en Puerto Rico: Un abordaje criminológico alternativo* (Publicaciones Puertorriqueñas, 1993), *Lo criminal y otros relatos de ingobernabilidad* (Publicaciones Puertorriqueñas, 1998), and *Estallidos: polisemia y polimorfia del derecho y la violencia* (Publicaciones Puertorriqueñas, 2006). She is also Director of the Research Institute on Violence and Complexity (http://violenciacomplejidad.blogspot.com/) and the Mobile Observatory for the Study of Violence (http://www.observatoriomo vil.com).

Stephanie Nohelani Teves is an assistant professor of ethnic studies and women's and gender studies at the University of Oregon, where she teaches courses on indigenous feminism, Pacific Island studies, and Native studies. She is coeditor of *Native Studies Keywords* (University of Arizona Press, 2015) and has published articles on Hawaiian hip-hop, film, and sexuality in the Pacific. Her articles have appeared in *American Indian Quarterly*, the *American Indian Cultural and Research Journal*, and the *International Journal of Critical Indigenous Studies*. Her book *Defiant Indigeneity: The Politics of Hawaiian Performance* is forthcoming from the University of North Carolina Press in the Critical Indigeneities Series (spring 2018). She received her PhD from the University of Michigan, was a recipient of the Ford Foundation Postdoctoral and Dissertation Fellowship, and is a founding member of Hinemoana of Turtle Island, a collective of Pacific Islander feminists residing in California and Oregon.

Fa'anofo Lisaclaire Uperesa is a senior lecturer in Pacific Studies at University of Auckland. She holds a PhD in anthropology from Columbia University and has taught at the University of Hawai'i-Manoa and Hofstra University. In 2014 she coedited a special issue of *The Contemporary Pacific* on "Global Sport in the Pacific" and was a contributor to the acclaimed anthology *Formations of U.S. Colonialism*, which was released by Duke University Press later that year. She is working on a book manuscript titled *Fabled Futures and Gridiron Dreams: Migration, Mobilities, and Football in American Samoa*.

Index

acts, 26. *See also* sovereign acts
African-American Civil Rights Movement (1954–1968), 264
African Americans: in relation to Puerto Ricans, 260, 268; Young Lords and, 259–61. *See also* black-Indian relations; Black Panthers; blacks; Cody, Radmilla; Krystilez
African ancestry, 236–41; Basquiat and, 341; Cherokees and, 164; Clifton-Choctaws and, 233–36, 241, 243–44, 246–47; Indian identity and, 164, 230, 232, 234; of Marcus Garvey, 357; Navajo and, 163–64; Puerto Ricans and, 67. *See also* Basquiat, Jean-Michel; "mulattos"
African diaspora, 362, 363, 365. *See also* Basquiat, Jean-Michel
Africans: enslavement of, 345, 352, 356. *See also* blackness; blacks

Agamben, Giorgio, 300–302, 306, 311–12, 318, 328n20; on bare life, 290, 298, 300–301, 311, 327n10, 328nn19–20; biopolitics and, 290, 298, 300–303; on the citizen-subject, 287; on exceptions, 298, 300–301, 326n4; *Homo Sacer: Sovereign Power and Bare Life*, 298, 300, 328n20, 331n41; *Means Without End*, 321, 323; on Nazi concentration camps, 301, 327n18; on politics, 312, 323; on the sovereign, 286; on sovereign power, 290; on sovereign violence, 298, 312, 316; on sovereignty, 298, 302, 321; on state of exception, 298, 302–3, 326n4, 333n55; *State of Exception*, 326n4, 333n55; on *zoē* vs. *bios*, 300–301
'aha ali'i (council of chiefs), 129
'āina (land-based organizations), 136
Akaka, Daniel, 138–39

Akaka Bill (Native Hawaiian Government Reorganization Act of 2009), 139, 206
Aksoy, Mete Ulaş, 24
Alfred, Taiaiake, 21, 33n45, 90–91, 95, 333–34nn60–63
Ali, Muhammad (Cassius Clay), 352–53, 354f
ali'i nui (high chief), 129
Ali'i trusts, 145n4
Aloha 4 All, 139
American Indian Religious Freedom Act of 1978, 138
American Samoa, 68–69; attitudes toward U.S. corporation, 19; as authentically ambivalent, 50–54; capitalist relations and communal ownership, 18–19; citizenship and, 19; history, 15, 42; land, political status, and the law, 54–59; negotiating the unincorporated category, 60–63; political imaginaries, indigeneity, and sovereignty, 64–65; politics, 19; sovereign (political) discourse in, 18, 41; status and categorization, 18–19, 43, 46, 50 (see also unorganized territory)
American Samoa, Constitution of, 19, 51, 54–55
American Samoa Future Political Status Study Commission (ASFPSSC), 51, 58
anticolonialism, 15–16, 64, 101n7, 101n9, 182; defined, 101n9
Apology Resolution, 126–27, 139, 205, 225n25
Appadurai, Arjun, 287–88
Arakaki v. Lingle, 139–40

Arendt, Hannah, 24, 287
art. See Basquiat, Jean-Michel
Arvin, Maile, 211
Assembly of First Nations (AFN), 82–83
"Associated Free State" designation, 45–46. See also Estado Libre Asociado de Puerto Rico
Atalig, Commonwealth of the Northern Mariana Islands v., 55
attenuated sovereignty: forms of, 41, 44; zones of, 40, 69, 71n8, 81n112
Aupuni Hawai'i (multiethnic Hawai'i nation-state), 127–34, 147n23; challenges in achieving independence, 142; Lāhui 'Ōiwi and, 127–30, 132, 133, 135, 147n23; Lāhui 'Ōiwi compared with, 143t; organizations seeking the independence of, 136–37; strategies for independence, 141–42; two entities, two kinds of status, and two movements, 127–28
autochthonous, self-governing Native polities, 307
autochthonous ("separate") entities, native peoples as, 315
autochthonous Native collectivities, 304
autochthonous political imaginaries, 40
autochthonous rights, 310
autochthony, debates over, 40
autonomous practice, spaces of, 64
autonomous unit, the subject as an, 291
autonomy, 303, 305, 308, 310, 311, 317–19, 321, 322; cultural, 14, 86, 203; desire for, 16; Glenn Petersen on, 61; of Hawai'i, 14; Indian policy and, 307;

individual, 90; limits of nation-state, 20; of Puerto Rico, 47, 64, 68, 358; rights of, 289; of Samoa, 64–65; self-determination and, 90, 289; sovereignty and, 286; unincorporation and, 60–61; of women, 172n42, 265; zones of, 64–65; zones of political ambiguity and, 39

Bacchilega, Cristina, 212
Badillo, Herman, 269
Bakhtin, Mikhail, 341
Balke, Friedrich, 24, 25
Barbry, Earl, Sr., 247
bare habitance, 299, 302, 303
bare life: as the basis of the exception, 298; Giorgio Agamben on, 290, 298, 300–301, 311, 327n10, 328nn19–20 (*see also Homo Sacer: Sovereign Power and Bare Life*)
Barker, Joanne, 180, 326n5, 330n27
Basquiat, Gerard, 339
Basquiat, Jean-Michel, 336; artwork, 337f; early work, 339–47; emphasis on and placement of heads, 341–42 (*see also* crowns); languages used by, 350–52; later life, 363–65; sovereign acts of, 23, 336–65; use of crowns, 336–44, 337f, 345, 351, 353–55, 361–64, 367n37
Bataille, Georges, 23, 24, 26, 292–93, 359
Bayonet Constitution, 131, 132
Bennett, Kay Curley, 171n33
berdache, 182. *See also* Two-Spirit
Berlin, Treaty of (1889), 42, 54, 59
Berman Santana, Déborah, 66–67
bilingualism, 350, 352–53
Bill of Rights, 297

biopolitical body: conceptualizing the nation as a whole, 302; Giorgio Agamben on, 300–302; production/creation of a, 300, 301
biopolitics: geopolitics and, 298, 301–3, 307, 309; Giorgio Agamben and, 290, 298, 300–303; nation/sovereignty/global, 286–91
biopower, 290
black artists, 361–62. *See also specific artists*
black complicity, tragedy of, 355
black-identified culture, 200
black-Indian relations: alternative futures, alternative sovereignties, 245–48; regulating racial categories, 237–45; research in Louisiana Indian communities, 233–37
black intellect, 357–58, 362
Black Panthers, 259–61, 263–65
Black Skin, White Masks (BSWM) (Fanon), 87–89, 101n9; Charles Taylor and, 89; Hegel's *Phenomenology*, master-slave relation, and, 93–94, 97, 99; liberation, freedom, and, 87–88, 99; recognition and, 84, 87–88, 92–94, 98. *See also* Fanon, Frantz
"black skin, white masks" (Fanon), 356
black sovereignty, 354–56, 359, 361, 362; masculinity and, 362
blackness: associated with savagery, 346; Puerto Ricans and, 67. *See also* African ancestry; "mulattos"; racism
blacks: Frantz Fanon and, 338, 346. *See also* African Americans; Africans

"Bloodline" song (Krystilez), 203, 208–14, 219
"Bloodline" video (Krystilez), 211–13, 216, 217, 219, 228n50
Blount, James, 131, 133
"blowing up," 216
Bonilla, Yarimar, 17, 20
Bosque Redondo, 155–56, 158
Braidotti, Rosi, 291
Brooks, Daphne A., 258
Brown, Sharon, 242
Brown, Wendy, 24, 285, 362
Bureau of Indian Affairs (BIA), 241, 246
Byrd, Jodi A., 346

Cabranes, José A., 46–47, 64
Calvo, Eddie Baza, 16
Camp X-Ray (Guantanamo), 5
Canada: self-determination and, 82, 83, 87; sovereignty and, 11–13
Cane River Creoles of Color, 236–37, 240
capitalism, 18–19, 89, 90
Caribbean Decolonization seminar, 62
Carleton, James, 155, 156
carnivalesque, 341
Carranza, Humberto, 271
Carson, Kit, 155
Chamorro Land Trust Act, 115, 116
Chamorro Land Trust Commission, 116
Chamorros, 24, 107–18
Chamoru, Nasion, 115–18
Changing Woman, 162–63
Charles I of England. *See* Charles the First
Charles the First (Basquiat), 362
Chato, Genevieve, 157

Chatterjee, Partha, 81n108
Cherokee Nation, same-sex marriage in, 175–78, 181; discourse of native "regression," 190–92. *See also* Reynolds and McKinley case
Cherokee Nation v. Georgia, 10–11, 296, 303, 307, 311, 324n1
Cheyfitz, Eric, 10
Chicago, Young Lords Organization of, 254–56, 261, 276
Choctaws, 239–40, 245; Mississippi, 232. *See also* Clifton-Choctaws
choice, 64
citizenship, 292, 302; U.S., 49
Civil Rights Act of 1964, 205
Civil Rights Movement, 264
Clay, Cassius (Muhammad Ali), 352–53, 354f
Clemente, Francesco, 340
Cleveland, Grover, 14, 133
Clifton-Choctaws, 233–44, 246; African ancestry and, 233–36, 241, 243–44, 246–47
Clinton, William "Bill", 14
clothes, change of, 257–59
Cody, Radmilla, 163–65
coerced consensus, 59–60
Collins, Patricia Hill, 250n16
colonial desire, 111–12
colonial relationship, 83, 87, 94, 95, 101n7, 356. *See also* colonialism; *specific topics*
colonialism: meaning and nature of, 101n7; terminology, 81, 101n7
"commonwealth," 17, 18
"Commonwealth of Puerto Rico," 43

Conte, Christine, 157
concentration camps, 301, 302, 327n18. *See also* inclusive exclusion
connective marginality, 200
consent, 64, 69, 258, 316, 325n76; vs. coercion, 41; vs. conquest, 63; discourse of, 323; mutual, 16, 45, 64
Constitution, U.S. *See* United States Constitution
Constitution Act, 1982 (Canada), 12
Constitution of American Samoa, 19, 51, 54–55
Constitution of Puerto Rico. *See* Puerto Rican Constitution
constitutional law, emphasis on the individual vs. tribe/nation in, 10
constitutional reform, 64
constitutionalism, 69, 322, 323, 333n57
constrained agency, 64, 79n96
Cortés, Hernán, 346
Cosentino, Donald J., 350
costume, 258. *See also* clothes
Coulthard, Glen, 27
Cover, Robert, 309
Craddick v. Territorial Registrar, 56
creative states, 20–25
Creoles of Color, 236–37, 240
"creolization" of thought, 348
Crown, 12, 83, 345
Crown sovereignty, 94
crowning: aesthetic act of, 340–41, 354; and uncrowning, 341, 361
crowns: Basquiat's use of, 336–44, 337f, 345, 351, 353–55, 361–64, 367n37; blacks and, 362; gender and, 362
Cuban July 26 Movement, 263
cultural change and cultural decline, 245

cultural recognition, 90. *See also* recognition
culture, 311, 313; dependence, race, and the tabooing of, 306–14

Dakota Access Pipeline protests, 4
Dawes Act of 1887, 11
Day, Richard, 90
Day v. Apoliona, 211
death, 114
DeCaroli, Steven, 330n34
Declaration on the Rights of Indigenous Peoples, 67, 206
declension model, 245
decolonial deadlock, 110; in Guam, 109–12
decolonial movements, 25, 27, 53. *See also specific movements*
decolonization, 29, 107, 111, 216; acts of, 28, 114–20; colonial desire and, 111–12; the colonized initiating the process of, 97; Frantz Fanon on, 93, 112–13 (*see also Wretched of the Earth*); heteropatriarchy and, 218; history of, 3, 16; nature of, 111–14; political recognition and, 27–28; problems with and criticisms of, 109–12; process of, 317; resistance to (*see* decolonial deadlock); sexism, gender violence, and, 180; violence and, 98, 112–13. *See also specific topics*
dedicated sovereignty, 8
Defense of Marriage Act of 1996 (DOMA), 176
defiant indigeneity, 209–14
Deleuze, Gilles, 28

Delgamuukw v. British Columbia, 94
Dene Nation, 82
Denetdale, Jennifer Nez, 180, 224n14
Department of the Interior (DOI), 58, 140, 206, 207
dependence, race, and the tabooing of culture, 306–14
Derrida, Jacques, 24, 25
desire, killing, 111–14
Diné, 166n2. *See also* Navajo Nation
Diné Marriage Act of 2005, 194
dissensus, 24
divine right, 10
divisible sovereignty, 8
Dole, Sanford B., 13
domestic dependent nations, 10–11, 14, 28, 206, 296, 307, 315, 324n1
double colonization of a Hawaiian hip-hop feminist, 217–22
Downes v. Bidwell, 48
dramatic persona, 23
Driskill, Qwo-Li, 177

Ea, 14, 207–208
elimination, logic of, 178
eminent domain, right of, 115
Equal Protection Amendment, 57. *See also* Fourteenth Amendment to the U.S. Constitution
Equal Protection Clause, 55, 56, 78n73, 138. *See also* Fourteenth Amendment to the U.S. Constitution
eroticism, 292–93. *See also* sexuality
Estado Libre Asociado de Puerto Rico (ELA), 17, 43, 44, 63, 262
Estado Libre Asociado Soberano (Sovereign Free Associated State), 17

ethnographic entrapment, forms of, 65
European imperial sovereignty, toxic power of, 345–46
exceptional measures, 333n55
exceptionalization, 305, 311, 314; process of, 318, 321, 322
exception(s), 287, 306, 307, 309, 312, 313; bare life as the basis of, 298; Giorgio Agamben on, 298, 300–301, 326n4; and the process of distinction, 301; U.S. imperial modes of, 316. *See also* state of exception
exclusion. *See* inclusive exclusion
extraconstitutional entities, 323, 333n57

fa'amatai (chiefly system), 19, 50–53, 55, 58–60, 63, 74n40
fa'asāmoa (Samoan way/Samoan culture), 19, 50–52, 56, 59, 65, 74n40, 78n73
Faleomavaega, Eni Fa'aua'a Hunkin, Jr., 50, 57, 62
Fanon, Frantz, 84, 113, 114; on Africa, 346; on anticolonial violence, 98; anticolonialism and, 101n1; *Black Skin, White Masks (BSWM)*, 84, 87–89, 92–94, 97–99, 101n9; "black skin, white masks," 356; blacks and, 338, 346; Charles Taylor and, 87, 89, 90, 92, 96; on decolonization, 93, 112–13 (*see also Wretched of the Earth*); dialectic of recognition, 103n37; on equality, 87–88; on freedom, 87–88, 113; Hegel and, 84, 93, 96–99, 103n37; on inferiority complex of colonized subjects, 91–92; Marxism and,

89–90; misrecognition and, 87, 89, 91–92; and the problem of recognition in colonial contexts, 87–96; sovereignty and, 338; *The Wretched of the Earth*, 87, 98, 112
Farris Thompson, Robert, 350, 351
Federal Acknowledgment, Office of, 27
federal recognition process, 237
feminism, 172n42; double colonization of a Hawaiian hip-hop feminist, 217–22; Native, 218
Fifteenth Amendment of the U.S. Constitution, 137, 205
50 Cent Piece, 356–58
Financial Oversight and Management Board of Puerto Rico ("la Junta de Control Fiscal"), 4–5, 45
First Nations, Assembly of, 82–83
Five Civilized Tribes of Oklahoma, 232
flag(s): "follow that flag," 46, 47; Hawaiian, 205; Puerto Rican, 261–63, 269; U.S., 46, 47, 51, 54
Foley, Neil, 250n17
Foraker Act of 1900, 43
Foucault, Michel, 24, 25, 256, 293; on aesthetics and sovereignty, 23, 256; on biopolitics, 291; on ethics, 293–94; on governability, 290; on *Las Meninas*, 344; power and, 26, 290
Fourteenth Amendment to the U.S. Constitution, 56, 138, 139. *See also* Equal Protection Amendment; Equal Protection Clause
Free Associated State. *See* "Associated Free State" designation; Estado Libre Asociado de Puerto Rico

freedom, 113; decolonization and, 113; Frantz Fanon on, 87–88, 113; intersubjective conditions required for the realization of, 85
fugitive indigeneity, 67
"full blood," 242, 252n27. *See also* African ancestry; "mulattos"; racial purity laws
Fuller, Melville, 48
Fulton, LeNora, 153, 159

Garbage Offensive, 269–71
García Canclini, Néstor, 287
Garvey, Marcus, 357, 362; coin showing the face of, 357–58
Gates, Henry Louis Jr., 353
Gelpí, Gustavo A., 72n18
gender: and nation, 158–66. *See also* feminism; women
gender roles, 153–54
General Allotment Act of 1887, 11
geographies of sovereignty, 6–15
geopolitics, 299, 305, 306; biopolitics and, 298, 301–3, 307, 309; of the settler state, 313, 314, 321, 323
geopoltical imaginary, 306, 313, 323
geopoltical state of exception, 317. *See also* state of exception
Gikandi, Simon, 341
Gilley, Brian, 177, 183
Glissant, Édouard, 348
globalization, 3, 8–9, 19, 26; paradox of nationhood and, 287
Gonzalez, Gloria, 273–74
González, Juan, 274, 276
Goodman, Amy, 190–91
Gordon, Deborah, 172n40

governmentality, 290
great migration, 45
Guam, 107–9, 119; anticolonial political discourse in, 15–16; decolonial deadlock, 109–12; history, 108–9
Guzmán, Pablo "Yoruba," 254, 255, 261, 267, 269, 271, 272, 276

Haiti, 356, 357; U.S. occupation of, 358
Haitian vodou, 342, 349. See also vodou
Hale, Albert, 163–64
"half-breeds." See African ancestry; "mulattos"; racial purity laws
Hantel, Max, 20
Hawai'i: U.S. government and, 127, 132–34. See also Aupuni Hawai'i; Kingdom of Hawai'i
Hawai'i Apology Resolution, 225n25
Hawai'i for the Hawaiians, 130
Hawai'i 'Ōiwi, 144n2. See also Native Hawaiians
Hawai'i state, multiethnic. See Aupuni Hawai'i
"Hawaiian," meanings and uses of the term, 222n4
Hawaiian Affairs, Office of. See Office of Hawaiian Affairs
Hawaiian flag, 205
Hawaiian Homes Commission Act of 1920 (HHCA), 115, 209, 224n16, 226n36
Hawaiian Kingdom. See Kingdom of Hawai'i
Hawaiian League, 131
Hawaiian nationalist movement, 130, 132–34, 218
Hawaiian Political Association (Hui Kālai'āina), 132

Hawaiian sovereignty, 13–14, 205–8
Hawaiians, Native. See Lāhui 'Ōiwi
Hebdige, Dick, 347, 350
Hegel, Georg Wilhelm Friedrich, 84; Charles Taylor and, 85, 86, 93, 96; colonialism and, 99; Frantz Fanon and, 84, 93, 96–99, 103n37; freedom and, 85; identity formation and, 84–86; master-slave narrative, 84–86, 92–94, 99; recognition and, 84–85, 93, 94, 96, 103n37
Herz, Ansel, 272
heteronormative values, 177, 186. See also Reynolds and McKinley case
heteronormativity, 191, 192, 210, 214, 218, 220; and tradition within U.S. settler colonialism, 178–81
heteropatriarchy, 189, 200–201, 211, 218–20
hip-hop, Hawaiian, 199–201; definitions, 222n4; keeping it Maoli, 214–17. See also Krystilez
Hobsbawm, Eric J., 292
Hodel, Presiding Bishop v., 56
Hokowhitu, Brendan, 216–17
Holocaust, 327n18
homo sacer, 311, 312
Homo Sacer: Sovereign Power and Bare Life (Agamben), 298, 300, 328n20, 331n41
homonationalism, 187, 192, 193; defined, 187
homophobia, 183–84, 188, 190, 192; as colonial tool, 177; of Krystilez, 219, 220; Native "regression" to, 188, 190, 191; tradition and, 180–81
hooks, bell, 99, 340, 345–46, 355

Hoopa Valley Reservation. See *Kagama, U.S. v.*
Howland, Douglas, 8
Hui Aloha ʻĀina (Hawaiian Patriotic League), 132–34
Hui Kālaiʻāina (Hawaiian Political Association), 132, 134
Human Rights Campaign (HRC), 186
human rights discourse, 8, 40
Hupa. See *Kagama, U.S. v.*

Identity formation, Hegel's theory of, 84–86
imaginary: geopolitical, 306, 313; jurisdictional, 297, 304, 306, 314, 321; of sovereignty, 289, 290; territorial, 297, 318, 321. *See also* political imaginaries
imagination, sovereignty of the:defined, 338. *See also* political imagination
imperial formations, 81n112, 88; unincorporation of, 71n8
imperialism, 99; colonialism and, 101n7; meaning and nature of, 101n7; "rhetorical," 338; settler-state, 318–20, 327n8; terminology, 81, 101n7; U.S., 178–79
impractical and anomalous test, 55, 78n73
inclusive exclusion, the domain of: the camp and the reservation, 300–306
incorporation doctrine. *See* Territorial Incorporation Doctrine
Indian Act of 1876, 12, 100n1
Indian Affairs, Bureau of. *See* Bureau of Indian Affairs
Indian Appropriations Act of 1871, 11

Indian Reorganization Act of 1934 (IRA), 157, 193
Indian reservations. *See* reservations
Indian termination policy, 11
"Indians," definition of what constitutes "real," 242
indigeneity, 60; as a political category, 67
indigenous peoples, 246; efforts to make them "straight," 178–79; terminology, 331n36
inferiority complex of colonized subjects, 91
inherent sovereignty, 10, 14, 126, 315–16, 322
Inouye, Daniel, 138
insular areas/insular territories, 43, 49–50. *See also* Insular Cases
Insular Cases, 15, 41–50, 56–57, 72n16, 73n27
intellectual sovereignty, 22
internalization, 179

Jackson, Jerry, 242
Jena Band of Choctaw Indians (Jena Choctaw), 241, 242
Jiménez, José "Cha Cha," 254–55
Jones, Kellie, 341–42, 353
Jones, Mary Jackson, 242
Jones-Shafroth Act of 1917, 43
Joseph, Nathan, 260–61
jurispathic form of racism, 309–10

Kagama, U.S. v., 11, 303, 308, 311, 323, 324n1
Kalākaua, 131
Kalmo, Hent, 20
Kamehameha I, 126, 129

Kamehameha III, 129–30
"Kanaka Maoli" ("true people"/"real people"), 144n2, 222n4. *See also* Native Hawaiians
Kanaka ʻŌiwi, 144n2. *See also* Native Hawaiians
kapu, 312. *See also* taboo
Katz, Robert A., 55, 58
King v. Morton, 55
Kingdom of Hawaiʻi: 1840 Constitution of the, 130; 1887 Constitution of the, 13, 131, 132; overthrow of, 13–15, 127, 131, 133
Klor de Alva, Jorge, 65
Kozol, Wendy, 173
Krystilez, 201–5; defiant indigeneity, 209–14; Hawaiian sovereignty and, 205–8; keeping it Maoli, 214–17; The "O," 202–5, 213, 216; videos, 202, 203f, 204, 205, 218 (*see also* "Bloodline" video). *See also* "Bloodline" song
kuleana consciousness, 208

Lacan, Jacques, 26
LaForme, Harry S., 13
Lāhui ʻŌiwi, 144n2. *See also* Native Hawaiians
Lait, Jack, 269
Lambert, Valerie, 245
land, political status, and the law, 54–59
land-based organizations (*ʻāina*), 136
land tenure, 11, 54–56, 76n55, 76n59, 303, 323
Lao-Montes, Agustin, 362
Lara, U.S. v., 315, 333n57
Las Meninas (Velázquez), 344

Laughlin, Stanley, 60
Laviera, Abraham Jesús "Tato," 353
Lawrence and Garner v. Texas, 185, 189
legitimacy, the question of (or quest for), 314–24
lesbian, gay, bisexual, and transgender (LGBT) persons, 182, 185, 259. *See also* homophobia; Reynolds and McKinley case
liberal pluralism, 84
liberalism, 90, 318, 343; Charles Taylor on, 85–86, 90; role in Reynolds and McKinley case, 184–87
Liberation Day (Guam), 115
Liliʻuokalani, Queen, 125, 132–34
"look of sovereignty," 23, 256, 276; defined, 23, 256. *See also* Young Lords Organization
Louisiana Indian communities, 241, 243; research in, 232–37
Loving v. Virginia, 232
Lowell, Abbott Lawrence, 46–48
Luciano, Felipe, 257, 265, 266, 276
Luhmann, Niklas, 289, 294
Lumbees, 232
Lyons, Scott Richard, 9–10, 20, 215, 338, 339

MacDonald, Peter, 170n30
machismo, 266–67
Major Crimes Act of 1885, 324n1
Mallouk, Suzanne, 339–40
Maracle, Brian, 13
Markell, Patchen, 85
Marshall, John, 10–11, 336, 340
Marx, Karl: critique of sovereignty, 362
Marxists, 89–90

masculinity: black sovereignty and, 362.
  See also machismo
master-slave narrative, Hegel's, 84–86,
  92–94, 99
McClintock, Anne, 165–66
McKinley, Dawn. *See* Reynolds and
  McKinley case
Meléndez, Miguel "Mickey," 255, 258,
  263, 264, 269
memory, symbolic, 59–60
Mendez, Mervin, 256
Meninas, Las (Velázquez), 344
Merrell, James, 232
metapolitical authority, 25, 299, 310,
  314, 318, 322. *See also* dependence;
  legitimacy
Miles, Tiya, 244
Miner, Dylan, 20
misrecognition, 92; Charles Taylor on,
  86, 87, 89, 355; Frantz Fanon on, 87,
  89, 91–92; Fraser on, 91
Miss Navajo Nation, 153, 161–65
Miss Navajo Nation, Office of, 162
Mississippi Band of Choctaw Indians
  (Mississippi Choctaw), 232
Mitchell, Frank, 157
mixed-blood. *See* African ancestry;
  "full blood"; "mulattos"; racial purity laws; "Redbones"
Moctezuma II, 346
modernity, 300
Modernity, 289, 290, 293, 294
"modernity of Modernity," 289
Mohanty, Chandra, 165
Mohawks, 13
Mona Lisa (da Vinci), 355
Moore Saggese, Jordana, 340

Morales, Iris, 275
Morgensen, Scott, 178
Morrison, Sean, 77nn66–67, 78n73
Morrison, Toni, 244, 250n17
Mortimer, Lee, 269
"mulattos," 232, 234, 235, 239–41. *See
  also* African ancestry
Mulford Act of 1967, 264
Mulroney, Brian, 13
Muñoz Rivera, Luis, 358

naachid (regional gathering), 154
Nasion Chamoru, 115–19
nation, concept of, 153–54
nation-state and sovereignty, 286–89.
  See also under sovereignty
"national being," 292
nationalism: Anne McClintock on,
  165–66; gender and, 161, 162, 165,
  166; Hawaiian, 130, 132–34, 218;
  Navajo, 154, 161, 162, 180
Native American Graves Protection
  and Repatriation Act of 1990
  (NAGPRA), 139
Native Hawaiian Government Reorganization Act of 2009 (Akaka Bill),
  139, 206
Native Hawaiian women, power of,
  229n61
Native Hawaiians (Lāhui ʻŌiwi/Kanaka
  Maoli), 125–26, 128–29; as an indigenous minority, 134–37; branching out
  in different directions, 129–32; compared with Aupuni Hawaiʻi, 142, 143t;
  demographics, 134–35; as indigenous
  people vs. racial group, 137–40; a new
  pathway for, 140–41;

Native Hawaiians (*continued*)
  self-determination, 14, 125, 127–28, 138, 141, 142, 205, 206, 221; sovereignty and governance, 126–27; terminology, 144n2, 222n4; two entities, two kinds of status, two movements, 127–28
NativeOUT, 182
natural communities, 154, 155
Navajo Nation, 153–54; nation and gender, 158–66 (*see also* Navajo women); terminology, 166n2; from traditional government to, 154–58
Navajo nationalism, 154, 161, 162, 180
Navajo treaty of, 1868, 156, 158
Navajo women, 153–54, 157, 160, 165–66, 168n10, 172nn40–42; Miss Navajo Nation, 153, 161–65. *See also* Navajo Nation: nation and gender
Nazi concentration camps, 301, 302, 327n18. *See also* inclusive exclusion
Nazi Germany, 327n18
Negrón-Muntaner, Frances, 362
nested sovereignty, 4
New York Young Lords, 255–57, 259, 261, 263, 267, 269–70, 273, 274, 276
Newlands Joint Resolution of Annexation (Newlands Resolution), 134
nobility, 341. *See also* crowns
noble savagery, 69, 216
Nonintercourse Act (1790), 10
nonrecognition, 86, 87, 91, 94
Norris, Christine, 241

"O," The (Krystilez), 203–5, 215, 219
Obnoxious Liberals (Basquiat), 343

Office of Federal Acknowledgment, 27
Office of Hawaiian Affairs (OHA), 138–41, 206, 207, 211; creation of, 226n35; responsibility for homestead lands transferred to, 209; *Rice v. Cayetano* and, 137, 205, 225n26
Oka Crisis, 13
Oklahoma, 197n39. *See also* Navajo
Oklahoma, Five Civilized Tribes of, 232
Oliphant v. Suquamish Indian Tribe, 296–97, 303–4, 310–11, 316, 323, z324n1
Oliver, Denise, 266–67
Omi, Michael, 253n36
one-drop rule, 210, 239
overriding authority, 322
overriding sovereignty, 297, 299, 304, 311, 315–16, 320, 321

Pabón, Carlos, 68
Padilla, Felix, 259
Paris, Treaty of (1898), 42
Parkins, Wendy, 258
Peace of Westphalia, 8
Pearl Harbor (Puʻuloa), 131
Pecou, Fahamu, 347
peoples, "the people," and "the People," 303
Perez, Cecilia T., 118–19
Perez, Richie, 265
persona, dramatic, 23
Petersen, Glenn, 61–62
Picasso, Pablo, 341
Pierite, Herman, 247
Pierite, Joe, Sr., 246

plenary power, 10, 15, 42–45, 57, 299, 321
plenary power doctrine, 69, 334n76
pluralism, liberal, 84
pluralist ethic, 40
political imaginaries, 65, 69, 70, 285, 286, 289. *See also* imaginary
political imagination, 68, 272, 273. *See also* imagination
political imaginings, 22
political status. *See* land, political status, and the law
politics: Giorgio Agamben on, 323. *See also* biopolitics
politics of recognition, defined, 83
"Politics of Recognition, The" (Taylor), 83, 85–87, 93
Ponce Massacre of 1937, 274
Ponsa, Christina Duffy, 8
possessory right, 305
Povinelli, Elizabeth, 313
primitives, 94, 200, 346
proliferated sovereignties, 340
PROMESA (Puerto Rico Oversight, Management, and Economic Stability Act of 2016), 4–5, 18, 45
Property Clause. *See* Territorial Clause of U.S. Constitution
psychologizing, 91
Public Enemy, 199
Puerto Rican Constitution, 45, 46
Puerto Rican constitutional referendum, 1952, 17, 43, 44, 63–64
Puerto Rican Day Parade, 272
Puerto Rican flag, 261–63, 269
Puerto Rican Nationalist Party, 262, 269

Puerto Rican Revolutionary Workers Organization (PRRWO), 275, 276
Puerto Rico: autonomy, 47, 64, 68, 358; bodies for new organs, 42–45; decolonization, 64, 68; disembodied, 45–50; emigration, 45; negotiating the unincorporated category, 60–64; political imaginaries, indigeneity, and sovereignty, 64–68; self-determination, 17, 42, 43, 46, 49, 64–65, 69, 273. *See also* Young Lords Organization
Puerto Rico Federal Relations Act of 1950, 43
Puerto Rico Oversight, Management, and Economic Stability Act of 2016 (PROMESA), 4–5, 18, 45
Puʻuloa (Pearl Harbor), 131

Quebecois nationalist movement, 13

race, dependence, and the tabooing of culture, 306–14
racial categories, regulating, 237–45
racial classification, 56, 205
racial formations, 250n17; defined, 253n36; indigeneity and, 27, 231; white supremacist, 245
racial projects: defined, 253n36; white supremacist, 247
racial purity. *See* African ancestry; "full blood"; "mulattos"
racial purity laws, 232. *See also* one-drop rule
racial rights/racially-based rights, 230–31
racial theory, 230

racism: antiblack, 67, 230, 232, 234, 237, 238, 245–48; jurispathic form of, 309–10. *See also* white supremacy
Radewagen, Aumua Amata, 57
Raheja, Michelle H., 20, 34n65
Rancière, Jacques, 24
Real Great Society (RGS), 257, 270
reciprocal recognition, 87, 93. *See also* reciprocity: recognition and
reciprocity, 83, 93, 96; recognition and, 83–84, 87, 92–94
Reciprocity Treaty of 1875, 130, 131, 133, 134
recognition, 82; asymmetrical and nonreciprocal forms of, 84, 355; dialectic of, 84, 103n37; federal recognition process, 237; Frantz Fanon and the problem of recognition in colonial contexts, 87–96; Hegel and, 84–85, 93, 94, 96, 103n37; need for relations of recognition to be mutual, 85; reciprocity and, 83–84, 87, 92–94; self-recognition and anticolonial empowerment, 96–98; weaknesses in Taylor's theory of (*see* Taylor: shortcomings in the work of)
recognition-redistribution debate, 90
Red Kings (Basquiat), 343
"Redbones," 234, 240
reservation period, early, 156, 157
reservations, 11, 157, 240, 302–3. *See also* inclusive exclusion
reserves, defined, 12
Resta, Eligio, 286
retraditionalization, 33n45, 317
Reynolds, Kathy. *See* Reynolds and McKinley case

Reynolds and McKinley case, 175–78, 192–93; role of U.S. liberalism in, 184–87; tradition and Two-Spirit, 181–84; U.S. sexual exceptionalism, settler colonialism, and, 187–90
rhetorical imperialism, 338
rhetorical sovereignty, 338; defined, 20
Ricard, Rene, 348
Rice v. Cayetano, 137, 149n39, 205, 225n26
Rifkin, Mark, 178–79, 341; on heteronormativity, 178–79; on language, 346–47; on metapolitical authority, 25; on sovereignty, 9, 25
Rivera Ramos, Efrén, 49
Roessel, Ruth, 155, 156, 160–61
Roldán, Julio, 254, 263, 272
Román, Madeline, 26
Rountree, Helen, 232
royalty, 340–41. *See also* crowns

same-sex marriage, 190–91; terminology, 194n3; use of the term, 194n3
Samoa. *See* American Samoa
"Samoa for Samoans" policy, 56
Sampson, Marshall, 247
Sánchez, José Ramón, 270, 272
Sanchez Valle, Puerto Rico v., 18, 47
Santos, Angel Leon Guerrero, 23–24, 116–19
Sarpy, Theresa Clifton, 233–36, 243
Sassen, Saskia, 4
Saunt, Claudio, 237
"savages" and "savagery," 49, 314, 345–47; blacks and, 346; Indians and, 237, 299, 309, 310, 314; Native Hawaiians

and, 215, 216; Samoans and, 69. *See also* noble savagery
Savater, Fernando, 292
Schmitt, Carl, 7
Schomburg, Arturo Alfonso, 353
segregation, 238–39
self-affirmation, 97, 99, 101n9
self-determination, 54, 57, 85, 87, 92, 214, 289, 324; autonomy and, 90, 289; black, 260; Canada and, 82, 83, 87; Chamorro, 118; dominance of the legal approach to, 95–96; eroticism and, 293; Frantz Fanon on, 95–97; Hegel and, 85, 94; incorporation doctrine and, 60; Native Hawaiian, 14, 125, 127–28, 138, 141, 142, 205, 206, 221; Puerto Rican, 17, 42, 43, 46, 49, 64–65, 69, 273; right to, 82–83, 118, 127, 138, 142, 205, 206, 289; Samoan, 42, 54, 57, 60, 61; self-affirmation and, 97; sovereignty and, 9, 60, 82; struggles for, 82, 90, 125, 127–28, 289, 314; Taiaiake Alfred on, 90, 95–96
self-governance, 52, 58, 132; Puerto Rico and, 44, 71nn12–13. *See also specific topics*
self-government, 13, 16, 60, 313; First Nations' inherent right to, 83
self-recognition and anticolonial empowerment, 96–98
Sen, Amartya, 288
sexism, 166, 177, 180–81, 218, 265–66
sexual autonomy, 265. *See also* autonomy: of women
sexual exceptionalism, U.S., 187–92
sexuality: colonial biopolitics of modern, 178. *See also* eroticism

shadow stereotype, 238, 250n16
Shepherdson, Mary, 160, 172n40
Simpson, Audra, 4, 20–21, 65, 207
singularity thesis, 310
sinthome, 121n11
Skerritt, Henry F., 348
Skinner, Quentin, 20
slavery, 244, 345, 352, 356. *See also* master-slave narrative
Smith, Andrea, 65, 178–80
Smith, Cheryl, 241–42
social status, 91
sovereign action, 28, 42, 264; colonial stereotype of Puerto Ricans as incapable of, 258
sovereign acts, 6, 23–26, 28, 70; of Basquiat, 23, 344 (*see also* Basquiat, Jean-Michel); defined, 25; power to challenge symbolic structures, 364; of Young Lords, 259, 264 (*see also* Young Lords Organization)
sovereign subjects, 291–94
sovereignty: alternative sovereignties, 245–48; appearing impossible, 354–59, 361–63; attributes associated with, 286; concept of, as discursive placeholder with no determinate content, 8, 299, 316–18, 324; definitions and conceptions of the term, 7–8, 20, 21, 24, 28, 114, 214, 292, 317, 318; desire for, 356; epistemological bases of the concept of, 40; intensification of its relevance as a political signifier, 12; life with/out, 29; Michel Foucault and, 23, 24, 256, 293–94; nation and, 285–87; national, 285–86, 290; nature of, 5–6, 9–10, 302, 305, 321, 359; praxis, 3, 25; and

sovereignty (*continued*)
  related terms and concepts, 25–26; types of, 20, 317 (*see also specific types of sovereignty*); use of the term, 29; U.S's performative citation of, 305. *See also specific topics*
Spanish-American War, 15, 42, 46, 109
Sparks, Carol Douglas, 168
Spivak, Gayatri, 191
Stade, Roland, 118
Standing Rock protests, 4
state of exception, 299, 301, 317, 324; Giorgio Agamben on, 298, 302–3, 326n4, 333n55. *See also* exception(s)
status, 68. *See also specific topics*
stereotypes, shadow, 238
Stewart, Irene, 159–60
Stoler, Ann Laura, 71n8
Sunia, Tauese P. F., 62
Supreme Court, U.S., 138, 309, 321. *See also specific cases*
Supreme Court of Canada, 94
symbolic separation, 117

taboo, 312; ethnographic concept of, 311–12
Taíno, 65–67
Tate, Greg, 343, 363
Taylor, Charles, 83; capitalism and, 89, 90; Frantz Fanon and, 87, 89, 90, 92, 96; Hegel and, 85, 86, 93, 96; on liberalism, 85–86, 90; on misrecognition, 86, 87, 89, 355; on nonrecognition, 86–87, 355; "The Politics of Recognition," 83, 85–87, 93; on reciprocal recognition among equals, 93; shortcomings in the work of, 90–92

Territorial Clause of U.S. Constitution, 17, 71n13
Territorial Incorporation Doctrine, 41, 42, 46, 48, 60. *See also* unincorporation, doctrine of
territorial unincorporation. *See* unincorporation
Texas annexation, 148n34
theatrics, state, 24
Thomas, Clarence, 315, 322, 333n57
Thomas, Hank Willis, 361
Thurston, Lorrin A., 13
Tilley, Benjamin Franklin, 51
Tohe, Laura, 172n42
Tom, Orlando, 164
Tomas, Nin, 345
transformative praxis, 92, 99
transnational capital, 288
Trask, Haunani-Kay, 21, 217–18
treaty making, 304, 323, 329n25
Treaty of Friendship and Cooperation between Puerto Rico and the United States, 53
treaty system, 304, 305, 316, 323, 329n26
Trias, Jasmine, 219
tribal sovereignty, 27, 166, 180, 244, 245; affirming, 166; Clarence Thomas and, 315, 324; federal recognition of, 230, 245–46; race and the legal notion of, 27; Supreme Court cases and, 180, 315, 324
Tripartite Convention of 1899, 15
Trump, Donald J., 3, 4
Tuaua v. United States, 19, 56, 58
Tully, James, 313–14
Turner, Dale, 319–20, 323
26th of July Movement, 263

Two-Spirit, 177, 182–83, 188–90, 192, 193, 194n3; Brian Gilley and, 177, 183; defined, 182; meanings and use of the term, 182, 188; Qwo-Li Driskill on, 177, 182, 183; Reynolds and McKinley case and, 182–84, 188, 189; tradition and, 182–83

Two-Spirit movement, 182–83

Two-Spirit organizations, 194

Underwood, Robert, 107, 115

unincorporated "America," critical sovereignties in, 15–20

unincorporated category, negotiating the, 60–64

unincorporated territories, defined, 15

unincorporation, doctrine of, 40–44, 46, 49, 69, 71n8. *See also* Territorial Incorporation Doctrine

United Nations (UN): Declaration on the Rights of Indigenous Peoples, 67, 206; list of non-self-governing territories, 44, 71n12, 142

United States Constitution, 46–51, 54–58, 138, 297; Puerto Rico and, 41–42. *See also specific amendments*

United States Department of the Interior (DOI), 58, 140, 206, 207

United States flag, 51, 54; "follow that flag," 46, 47

United States Supreme Court, 138, 309, 321. *See also specific cases*

unorganized territory, American Samoa as, 18–19, 40, 50, 52–53, 74n41

V for Vendetta (film), 290–91

Varese, Stefano, 19

Velázquez, Diego, 344

Vietnam War, 262

violence, 113, 180; decolonization and, 98, 112–13; illusion and, 288; sovereign, 286–88, 298, 312, 316, 345

visual sovereignty, 20, 22; defined, 20

vodou, 342, 343, 349, 359

voting: by Puerto Ricans, 269; in U.S. elections, rights to, 17, 43, 50, 107, 130, 137, 205, 288

war, law of, 142

"ward"-ship, 308

Warhol, Andy, 337, 343

Warrior, Robert Allen, 22, 244

Wauneka, Annie Dodge, 159

Westphalia, Peace of, 8

Weyermann, Debra, 163–64

White, Luise, 8

white supremacy, 94, 211, 230, 237, 238, 245, 247, 343; meanings and uses of the term, 250n13

Williams, Robert A., 309–11, 321

Winant, Howard, 253n36

Wolfe, Tom, 260, 267

women: autonomy, 172n42, 265; Black Panther, 260; Kanaka Maoli and, 217, 219, 229n61 (*see also* feminism); Krystilez and, 218, 220; Navajo, 153–54, 157, 160, 165–66, 168n10, 172nn40–42 (*see also* Miss Navajo Nation; Navajo Nation: nation and gender); power and, 153–55, 160, 229n61 (*see also* Navajo Nation); Puerto Rican, 79n96; Young Lords,

women: autonomy (*continued*)
265–66. *See also* Reynolds and McKinley case
Wretched of the Earth, The (Fanon), 87, 98, 112. *See also* Fanon, Frantz

Yglesias, José, 265
Young, Robert, 97
Young Lords Organization (YLO), 254–57; change of clothes, 257–59; as lords of style, 259–67; in the media, 267–72; New York Lords, 255–57, 259, 261, 263, 267, 269–70, 273, 274, 276; Puerto Rico and the implosion of, 272–77
Young Lords Party, 255, 271, 275, 276

Žižek, Slavoj, 114, 117, 121n11
zone of indistinction, 298–99, 321–22